NEW DIRECTIONS IN NEURAL NETWORKS

Frontiers in Artificial Intelligence and Applications

Volume 193

Published in the subseries

Knowledge-Based Intelligent Engineering Systems

Editors: L.C. Jain and R.J. Howlett

Recently published in KBIES:

Vol. 186. G. Lambert-Torres, J.M. Abe, J.I. da Silva Filho and H.G. Martins (Eds.), Advances in Technological Applications of Logical and Intelligent Systems – Selected Papers from the Sixth Congress on Logic Applied to Technology

Vol. 180. M. Virvou and T. Nakamura (Eds.), Knowledge-Based Software Engineering – Proceedings of the Eighth Joint Conference on Knowledge-Based Software Engineering

Vol. 170. J.D. Velásquez and V. Palade, Adaptive Web Sites – A Knowledge Extraction from Web Data Approach

Vol. 149. X.F. Zha and R.J. Howlett (Eds.), Integrated Intelligent Systems for Engineering Design

Vol. 132. K. Nakamatsu and J.M. Abe (Eds.), Advances in Logic Based Intelligent Systems – Selected Papers of LAPTEC 2005

Recently published in FAIA:

Vol. 192. M. Van Otterlo (Ed.), Uncertainty in First-Order and Relational Domains

Vol. 191. J. Piskorski, B. Watson and A. Yli-Jyrä (Eds.), Finite-State Methods and Natural Language Processing – Post-proceedings of the 7th International Workshop FSMNLP 2008

Vol. 190. Y. Kiyoki et al. (Eds.), Information Modelling and Knowledge Bases XX

Vol. 189. E. Francesconi et al. (Eds.), Legal Knowledge and Information Systems – JURIX 2008: The Twenty-First Annual Conference

Vol. 188. J. Breuker et al. (Eds.), Law, Ontologies and the Semantic Web – Channelling the Legal Information Flood

Vol. 187. H.-M. Haav and A. Kalja (Eds.), Databases and Information Systems V – Selected Papers from the Eighth International Baltic Conference, DB&IS 2008

Vol. 186. G. Lambert-Torres et al. (Eds.), Advances in Technological Applications of Logical and Intelligent Systems – Selected Papers from the Sixth Congress on Logic Applied to Technology

Vol. 185. A. Biere et al. (Eds.), Handbook of Satisfiability

ISSN 0922-6389

New Directions in Neural Networks

18th Italian Workshop on Neural Networks: WIRN 2008

Edited by

Bruno Apolloni

Università degli Studi di Milano,
Dipartimento di Scienze dell'Informazione, Milano, Italy

Simone Bassis

Università degli Studi di Milano,
Dipartimento di Scienze dell'Informazione, Milano, Italy

and

Maria Marinaro

International Institute for Advanced Scientific Studies,
Vietri sul Mare (Salerno), Italy

IOS Press

Amsterdam • Berlin • Tokyo • Washington, DC

ISBN 978-1-58603-984-4
Library of Congress Control Number: 2009921089

Publisher
IOS Press BV
Nieuwe Hemweg 6B
1013 BG Amsterdam
Netherlands
fax: +31 20 687 0019
e-mail: order@iospress.nl

Distributor in the UK and Ireland
Gazelle Books Services Ltd.
White Cross Mills
Hightown
Lancaster LA1 4XS
United Kingdom
fax: +44 1524 63232
e-mail: sales@gazellebooks.co.uk

Distributor in the USA and Canada
IOS Press, Inc.
4502 Rachael Manor Drive
Fairfax, VA 22032
USA
fax: +1 703 323 3668
e-mail: iosbooks@iospress.com

PRINTED IN THE NETHERLANDS

New Directions in Neural Networks
B. Apolloni et al. (Eds.)
IOS Press, 2009

Preface

The book is a collection of selected papers from the 18th WIRN workshop, the annual meeting of the Italian Neural Networks Society (SIREN). As 18 marks the year young people come of age in Italy, the Society invited two generations of researchers to participate in a common discussion: those new to the field and those with extensive familiarity with the neural paradigm. The challenge lay in understanding what remains of the revolutionary ideas from which neural networks stemmed in the eighties, how these networks have evolved and influenced other research fields, and ultimately what are the new conceptual/methodological frontiers to trespass for a better exploitation of the information carried by data.

From this discussion we selected 27 papers which have been gathered under two general headings, "Models" and "Applications," plus two specific ones, "Economy and Complexity" and "Remote Sensing Image Processing." The editors would like to thank the invited speakers as well as all those who contributed to the success of the workshops with papers of outstanding quality. Finally, special thanks go to the referees for their valuable input.

We are also pleased that non-SIREN member researchers joined us both at the meeting and in this editorial venture, bearing witness to a wide sphere of interest in the debate. We hope, moreover, that the book will serve in making a scientific contribution to the discovery of new forms of cooperative work – so necessary today for the invention of efficient computational systems and new social paradigms too.

November 2008

Bruno Apolloni
Simone Bassis
Maria Marinaro

Organizing-Scientific Commitee

B. Apolloni (Univ. Milano), A. Bertoni (Univ. Milano), N.A. Borghese (Univ. Milano), D.D. Caviglia (Univ. Genova), P. Campadelli (Univ. Milano), F. Celada (Univ. Genova), J. Chanussot (Univ. Grenoble, France), A. Chella (Univ. Palermo), A. M. Colla (ELSAG Genova), M. Corazza (Univ. Venezia), A. Esposito (Univ. Napoli II), G. Facchinetti (Univ. Modena e Reggio Emilia), F.M. Frattale Mascioli (Univ. Roma "La Sapienza"), C. Furlanello (ITC-IRST Trento), S. Giove (Univ. Venezia), M. Gori (Univ. Siena), T. Kavzoğlu (Univ. Gebze, Turkey), M. Marinaro (Univ. Salerno), F. Masulli (Univ. Pisa), C. Morabito (Univ. Reggio Calabria), P. Morasso (Univ. Genova), G. Orlandi (Univ. Roma "La Sapienza"), F. Palmieri (Univ. Napoli), T. Parisini (Univ. Trieste), E. Pasero (Politecnico Torino), A. Petrosino (Univ. Napoli "Parthenope"), V. Piuri (Univ. Milano), P. Richmond (Trinity College, Ireland), R. Serra (Univ. di Modena e Reggio Emilia), F. Sorbello (Univ. Palermo), A. Sperduti (Univ. Padova), R. Tagliaferri (Univ. Salerno), J. Taylor (King's College London), A. Uncini (Univ. Roma)

Referees

Apolloni Bruno, Bassis Simone, Bertoni Alberto, Borghese Alberto, Corazza Marco, Di Gregorio Salvatore, Esposito Anna, Faggini Marisa, Fuller Robert, Gaito Sabrina, Giove Silvio, Gori Marco, Goffredo Haus, LaForesta Fabio, Lombardi Gabriele, Malchiodi Dario, Marinaro Maria, Martone Raffaele, Frattale Mascioli Fabio Massimo, Masulli Francesco, Morabito Carlo, Nicosia Giuseppe, Palmieri Francesco, Pasero Eros, Pasi Gabriella, Rovetta Stefano, Scarpetta Silvia, Serra Roberto, Sorbello Filippo, Sperduti Alessandro, Tagliaferri Roberto, Uncini Aurelio, Valentini Giorgio, Valerio Lorenzo, Vitabile Salvatore, Zippo Antonio, Zoppis Italo

Contents

Preface v
Bruno Apolloni, Simone Bassis and Maria Marinaro

Chapter 1. Application

A Neural Based WSN Mote Trajectory Reconstruction for Mining Periodic Patterns 3
Alfredo Petrosino and Antonino Staiano

Sugeno Model Based Control for Semi Active Vehicle Suspension 12
Francesco Voci and Fabio Massimo Frattale Mascioli

Automatic Classification of Defects in an Industrial Environment 22
N. Alberto Borghese

STLmax Joint Mutual Information for Quantifying Independence in the Epileptic Brain 30
Nadia Mammone, Fabio La Foresta, Francesco C. Morabito and Mario Versaci

Neural Networks for the Parameters Characterization of ECG Dynamical Model 40
Matteo Cacciola, Fabio La Foresta, Francesco C. Morabito and Mario Versaci

Multiresolution Minimization of Renyi's Mutual Information for Fetal-ECG Extraction 50
Fabio La Foresta, Nadia Mammone, Giuseppina Inuso, Francesco C. Morabito and Andrea Azzerboni

Classification of DNA Microarray Data with Random Projection Ensembles of Polynomial SVMs 60
Alberto Bertoni, Raffaella Folgieri and Giorgio Valentini

An Embedded Fingerprints Classification System Based on Weightless Neural Networks 67
Vincenzo Conti, Carmelo Militello, Filippo Sorbello and Salvatore Vitabile

Discovering Regression Data Quality Through Clustering Methods 76
Dario Malchiodi, Simone Bassis and Lorenzo Valerio

Chapter 2. Models

A Flexible Natural Gradient Approach to Blind Separation of Complex Signals 89
Michele Scarpiniti, Daniele Vigliano, Raffaele Parisi and Aurelio Uncini

Single Channel Polyphonic Music Transcription 99
Angelo Ciaramella

Genetic Regulatory Networks and Neural Networks 109
Roberto Serra, Alex Graudenzi and Marco Villani

An Experimental Comparison of Kernel Clustering Methods 118
Maurizio Filippone, Francesco Masulli and Stefano Rovetta

Diffusion Learning and Regularization 127
Marco Gori

Sources of Asymmetric Randomness 138
Bruno Apolloni and Simone Bassis

Random Projections Preserving the Hamming Distance Between Words 148
Stefano Arca, Alberto Bertoni and Giuseppe Lipori

Notes on Factor Graphs 154
Francesco Palmieri

Chapter 3. Economy and Complexity Workshop

Safety Loading in the Annuity Pension Fund Dynamics 165
Marilena Sibillo, Mariarosaria Coppola, Valeria D'Amato and Emilia Di Lorenzo

Early Warning Systems: An Approach via Self Organizing Maps with Applications to Emergent Markets 176
Marina Resta

Optimal Partial Questioning in Large Dimensional AHP 185
Michele Fedrizzi and Silvio Giove

Evaluation of Fuzzy Quantities by Means of a Weighting Function 194
Gisella Facchinetti and Nicoletta Pacchiarotti

Neural Network Sieve Bootstrap Prediction Intervals: Some Real Data Evidence 205
Francesco Giordano, Michele La Rocca and Cira Perna

Fuzzy Interval Net Present Value 214
Marco Corazza and Silvio Giove

Interactive Visualization Tools for Meta-Clustering 223
Ida Bifulco, Francesco Iorio, Francesco Napolitano, Giancarlo Raiconi and Roberto Tagliaferri

Chapter 4. Remote Sensing Images Processing

Remote Sensing Imagery for Soil Characterization: A Wavelet Neural Data Fusion Approach 235
Matteo Cacciola, Francesco Carlo Morabito and Vincenzo Barrile

Application of Self Organizing Maps to Multi-Resolution and Multi-Spectral Remote Sensed Images 245
Ferdinando Giacco, Silvia Scarpetta, Luca Pugliese, Maria Marinaro and Christian Thiel

Comparison of Neural Classification Algorithms Applied to Land Cover Mapping 254
Christian Thiel, Ferdinando Giacco, Friedhelm Schwenker and Günther Palm

Author Index 265

Chapter 1

Application

New Directions in Neural Networks
B. Apolloni et al. (Eds.)
IOS Press, 2009

doi:10.3233/978-1-58603-984-4-3

A Neural Based WSN Mote Trajectory Reconstruction for Mining Periodic Patterns

Alfredo PETROSINO [a] and Antonino STAIANO [a,1]
[a] *Dipartimento di Scienze Applicate, Università di Napoli "Parthenope" Centro Direzionale - Isola C4, I-80143 Napoli, Italy*

Abstract. The problem of reconstruction and mining object trajectories is of interest in the applications of mining transport enterprise data concerning with the route followed by its delivery vans in order to optimize time and space deliveries. The paper investigates the case of Wireless Sensor Network (WSN) technology, not primarily designed for localization, and reports a technique based on recurrent neural networks to reconstruct the trajectory shape of a moving object (a sensor on a Lego train) from the sensor accelerometer data and to recover its localization. The obtained patterns are thus mined to detecting periodic or frequent patterns, exploiting a recently proposed technique based on clustering algorithms and associative rules to assert the ability of the proposed approach to track WSN mote localizations.

Keywords. Wireless Sensor Networks, Spatio-Temporal Data mining, Recurrent Neural Networks

Introduction

The efficient management of spatio-temporal data has gained much interest during the past few years [7,2], mainly due to the rapid advancement in telecommunications which facilitate the collection of large data set of such information. Management and analysis of moving object trajectories are challenging due to the vast amount of collected data and novel types of spatio-temporal queries [5]. In many applications, the movements obey periodic patterns, i.e., the objects follow the same routes (approximately) over regular time intervals. Objects that follow approximate periodic patterns include transportation vehicles (buses, boats, airplanes, trains, etc.), animals, mobile phone users, etc. The problem of discovering periodic patterns from historical object movements is very challenging. Usually, the patterns are not explicitly specified, but have to be discovered from the data. The approximate nature of patterns in the spatio-temporal domain increases the complexity of the mining tasks.

One of the most challenging problems is how discovering periodic patterns from historical object movements, in an independent manner from the adopted technology

[1]Corresponding Author: Antonino Staiano, Dipartimento di Scienze Applicate, Università di Napoli "Parthenope", Centro Direzionale - Isola C4, I-80143 Napoli, Italy; E-mail: antonino.staiano@uniparthenope.it.

that not always may assure the complete covering of the object localizations. As known, a possible solution is to let mobile nodes deploy expensive global positioning systems (GPS) to get their locations. However, many applications require sensor network mobility in the environments where GPS signals may not be available, therefore a GPS solution is not feasible. In recent years Wireless Sensor Networks (WSNs) have emerged as one of the key enablers for a variety of applications such as environment monitoring, vehicle tracking and mapping, and emergency response [8]. The network of such devices, called sensor network, forms a distributed and adaptive platform for data gathering, fusion and aggregation of the observed process.

In this paper we focus our attention on two important and related issues concerning with the tracking of a moving object by adopting WSNs. The aim is to develop and study a small scale system from which to derive, although with some assumptions and constraints, the trajectory of a WSN single moving sensor placed on a Lego train and to mine the periodic patterns from the reconstructed trajectory.

The first issue is how to locate a node's (a moving sensor) position. Although many localization algorithms have been proposed for wireless sensor networks, they assume that the nodes inside the networks are static. Little research has been presented on considering localization in cases where the network cannot be assumed static (see [9] and references therein). Here we describe a procedure to gain some insights to determine the trajectory out of acceleration reading from a moving mote located on the object. Extrapolating a trajectory out of acceleration is very difficult, since the accumulative error of the accelerometer equipping the motes gets too large. If one gets a model of the train tracks, then it might be possible to use the accelerometer information to detect the various turns and use that to keep track of the train's position. To highlight the proposed model property, we made experiments by using a little Lego [10] train that follows different controlled tracks.

The second addressed issue is to proper analyze the spatiotemporal data acquired. Although several algorithms for mining frequent patterns in large databases have been proved very effective for a variety of static data, no one is well suited for spatio-temporal sequences. An interesting and effective approach is described in [2], where an algorithm based on the well known DBScan [4] clustering method and a variant of the algorithm Apriori-TID [1] for the analysis of associative rules is proposed.

The paper is organized as follows: in Section 1 we describe the problem of determining the trajectory out of accelerometer data and the proposed approach based on a recurrent neural network. In Section 2, the problem of mining periodic patterns is introduced and the adopted algorithms are described. Experimental results, showing how to compute the trajectory shape and the coordinates of a Lego train equipped with a Tmote Invent and how discover periodic patterns from the data are described in Section 3. Finally, in Section 4, some concluding remarks and the description of possible applicative scenarios close the paper.

1. Computing trajectory coordinates

Motes are equipped with an accelerometer which provides the base station with the acceleration measures on the $x--y$ axes. One possible solution to derive location information from acceleration is to double integrate acceleration over time to derive the sensor resulting movement. However, the motes have an operating frequency at 50Hz making them very sensitive to any vibration. Furthermore, the battery life cycle is very short so that the accelerometer readings might differ largely even for the same piece of trajectory in different timestamps. This introduces an overall very high noise over the signal so that the integration leads to a very poor representation of the actual trajectory even for very simple piece of route such as a straight line. This led us to consider the trajectory shape reconstruction and then to derive the mote positions by adding some constraints on the train movements on the tracks.

1.1. Trajectory reconstruction

The idea is to recognize pieces of the circuit followed by the train considering that when the train is on a back straight the corresponding acceleration values are near zero, if the train is turning left the acceleration values are negatives, while if the train is turning right the corresponding acceleration values are positives. Therefore, after a preprocessing step to reduce noise over the acceleration signal acquired by the sensor through a FIR filter, an Elman neural network [3,6] is used to recognize pieces of the circuit followed by the train.

1.1.1. Elman network

The Elman network is a recurrent feed-forward neural network. Recurrent neural networks allows to model dynamic mappings according to which the input and output variables change over time and time is not represented explicitly but by the effect it has on processing and not as an additional dimension of the input. This class of neural networks are well suited, among all, for times series prediction [6]. The Elman network differs from a classical feed-forward neural network structure for a further layer placed at the same level of the input layer, called *context unit layer* (for which the weights are fixed to 1), whose task is to hold memory of the hidden layer output at the previous time instant. Therefore, when the input is fed to te network at time t, its output is computed also on the base of the hidden layer neuron activations at time $t-1$, i.e.

$$u_k = g(W_1' I_k + W_1'' y_{k-1}^h + b_1) \qquad y_k = f(W_2 u_k + b_2) \tag{1}$$

where g and f are respectively the hyperbolic tangent and logistic sigmoid functions, W_1' the weight matrix from input to hidden layers, W_1'' the weight matrix from hidden to context layers and W_2 the weight matrix from hidden to output layers. The Elman network is trained with the backpropagation to adjust the hidden-to-output weights and the input-to-hidden weights, while the recurrent connections are fixed at 1 and are not subject to adjustment. Our Elman network takes, each time, an acceleration value as input, from a training set, and tries to recognize if that value correspond to a back straight, a left turn or a right turn on the base of the previous time instants. Each segment is coded by a 1-of-c coding, so three output values are used to code a segment shape class (100 for back straights, 010 for left turns and 001 for right turns). The network is trained over a data set of segments of curve of each direction taken over different real mote trajectories and labelled by hand. Since the network gives evidence of the segment turn but not localizations in the the corresponding $x-y$ coordinates, we need to properly assemble each recognized segment to obtain the shape and the coordinates of the entire circuit.

1.1.2. Circuit segments assembling

First of all, the train speed is assumed to be constant over the entire route making it possible to calculate the coordinates of each recognized circuit segment. In fact, with a constant speed, and knowing that the accelerometer sampling rate is 0.1 seconds, it is possible to compute the coordinates for the back straights through a simple procedure. For left and right turns, it is necessary to establish the train time to go through a left or right curve. Here a further assumption comes, i.e., we consider that each turn is at least a 90° curve (corresponding to 4 pieces of Lego tracks) and all its multiples $(180°, 270°)$. Therefore, knowing that the circumference length assembled by the Lego curve tracks (64 cm), it is possible to compute the coordinates of the 90° curve.

The procedure determines the positions of the first segment, then it recognizes the next segment on the base of the Elman network output, and finally calculates the positions of the recognized segment updating the route orientation. These steps are iterated for the entire circuit. The starting point is assumed to be the $(0, 0)$ coordinate, updated by the last location obtained for each computed segment. The orientation is updated by considering three conditions, namely, the orientation of the previous segment, the turn (left or right) and the dimension $(90°, 180°, 270°)$. As an example, let us consider a simple elliptic circuit assuming that the train started its path on a back straight. At first step, the algorithm computes the locations of the first circuit segment, next it recognizes that the train turns on the left by 180° and calculates its coordinates by combining two 90° curves. These curves are properly translated to overlap the origin of the curve with the last location of the previous segment; the orientation is next updated. These steps are iterated for the entire circuit. The step-wise results are shown in Figure 1.

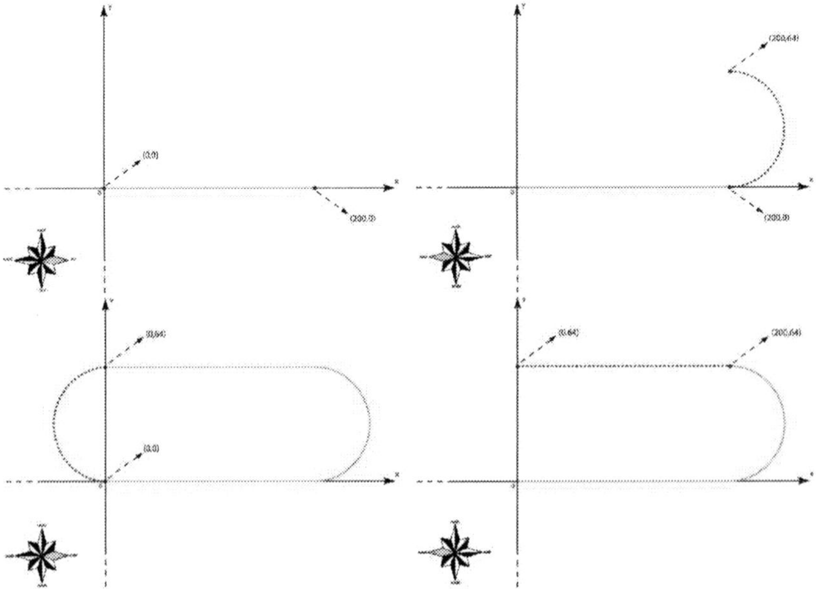

Figure 1. Steps of the reconstruction procedure.

2. Periodic routes detection

The problem may be defined as follows. An object movement is defined as a n-length sequence S of spatial locations, one for each time point (l_i, t_i), $i = 0, \ldots n-1$, where l is the object location at time t. Each location l_i, is a spatial location (x_i, y_i). Given a minimum support min_sup $(0 < min\_sup \leq 1)$ and an integer T (the period), the goal is to discover movement patterns that repeat themselves every T time points. The pattern is defined as a T-length sequence of the form $P = r_0, r_1, \ldots, r_{T-1}$, where r_i is a spatial region or a wild-card character $*$ indicating any region of the whole spatial universe. As an example, the pattern $ABC**$ denotes that the object is in region A at the starting point, and in the next two time intervals it is in region B and C, respectively, while in the last two time intervals it moved irregularly (at every time point it is in a different region), until a new cycle begins. The patterns are required to be followed by the object in at least α ($\alpha = min\_sup \cdot \lfloor \frac{n}{T} \rfloor$) periodic intervals in S. Since it is unlikely that an object repeats an identical sequence of (x, y) locations precisely, the exact locations are replaced by the regions which contain them.

STPMine1 (SpatioTemporal periodic Pattern Min(E)ing1) is the first algorithm for mining periodic patterns proposed in [2] and is the one we used. In the following we discuss it informally, the interested reader may refer to [2] for a complete description. The algorithm is structured in two parts:

1. First, the algorithm uses DBScan clustering approach to discover 1-length patterns. So doing each spatial location is assigned, in automatic way, a spatial region which is a valid cluster found to which the spatial location belongs. A valid cluster is a cluster containing at least MinPoint elements (MinPoint is a user defined parameter of the algorithm). For each cluster found a 1-length pattern is generated.
2. Starting from the 1-length patterns of the previous step, STPMine1 implements a variant of the Apriori-TID algorithm to find, iteratively, patterns of length greater than 1. For this aim, it generates candidate patterns joining pairs of patterns. Here, eventually invalid candidate pattern are pruned (patterns whose subpatterns are not frequent patterns). Once a valid candidate pattern is generated it is checked whether its regions are still clusters. This is a validation procedure: points at non-* candidate pattern positions could not be a valid cluster. The procedure is iterated until no candidate patterns can formed anymore. The last valid pattern formed will be the discovered frequent pattern.

3. Experimental results

The trajectory reconstruction approach and STPMine1 algorithm for mining periodic patterns have been tested on several circuit shapes. In the following only the obtained results on a Z-shaped circuit (two joining ellipses, see Figure 2, corresponding to 92 spatial locations) are described.

3.1. Trajectory reconstruction

To properly comment the trajectory reconstruction results, some details on parameter setting should be introduced.

Table 1. Circuit segment reconstruction errors. Each column is a circuit segment, i.e., Back straight, Right and Left curves. The length are in cm.

	90°R	B1	90°L	B2	180°R	B3	90°R	B4	90°L	B5	180°R	B6
Track	-	6	-	8	-	8	-	6	-	8	-	9
Length	-	75	-	100	-	100	-	75	-	100	-	112.5
Ref length	-	72	-	97	-	102	-	70	-	98	-	120
Error	-	-3	-	-3	-	+2	-	-5	-	-2	-	+7.5

- Train speed. As stressed in Section 1, one assumption is the constant speed of our train. The actual speed has been measured by an external chronometer by considering the time necessary to go through a one meter length back straight. Several measurements, under the same conditions, have been made. The constant train speed was chosen as the mean speed of $1.14\frac{m}{s}$, over all the measurements.
- Elman network. The training sets have been obtained by acquiring the accelerometer data over two laps of each considered circuit in both directions (east-west and west-east) in order to provide the network with similar circuits with all possible segment directions. The employed network is a one input - three output (1 of c coding) network, with 15 hidden neurons (therefore 15 context unit neurons), 500 learning epochs and a threshold error set to 0.01.

After the training phase, the Elman network has been evaluated on a test set and procedures as descibed above were applied to derive the shape and locations of the entire circuit. Figure 2 illustrates the original and the reconstructed circuit. As shown, the shape of the reconstructed circuit is very close to the original. Table 1 shows the the reconstruction error on each segment, corresponding to an overall error on the entire circuits of 22.5 cm (4% of the total length).

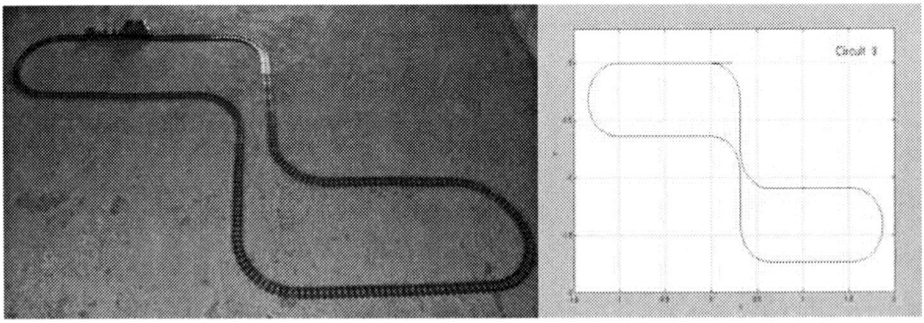

Figure 2. The original Z-shaped circuit (left) and the reconstructed circuit (right).

3.2. Mining frequent patterns

Starting from the circuit spatial location computed as described in Section 1, several variants of the same circuit are ncessary to find periodic patterns. Therefore, we generated, from the circuit spatial locations, n similar pseudo-random circuits with different coordinates. The STPMine1 algorithm was applied to the Z-shaped circuit and its generated variants (see Figure 3). In the following we see two different experiments where some

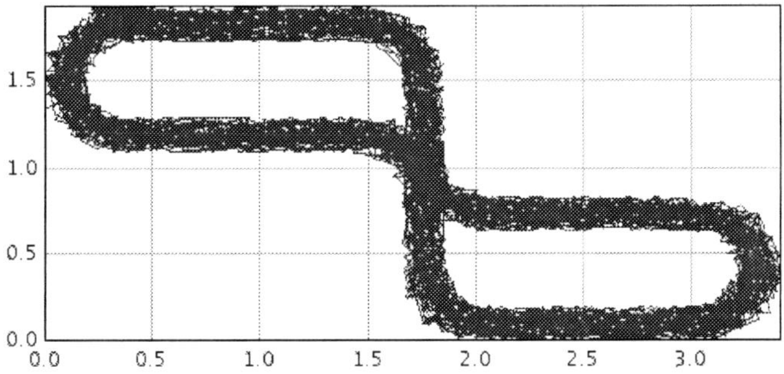

Figure 3. The Z-shaped circuits generated.

STPMine1 critical parameters are changed. In particular, the parameter Eps (points minimum distance to find clusters) of DBScan is changed ($Eps = 0.05$ and $Eps = 0.09$) in order to observe its impact on the discovered patterns. Indeed, an Eps low value causes DBScan to find just few clusters, while, on the other side, a very high value causes DBScan to detect all $1-$length pattern as one cluster. Obviously, this latter case implies high time costs. In Table 2, the results for $Esp = 0.05$ are reported. It is interesting to note the computing time and a frequent pattern of reduced size with respect to the length of the timestamps (92) of the circuit. In Table 3, instead, DBScan carries out a more accurate cluster detection, so the algorithm is able to detect the entire 92 timestamps of the circuit as periodic pattern.

Table 2. Discovered pattern for the first experiment.

Settings: period=92, Eps=0.05, MinPts=4, Min_sup=0.01	
Discovered pattern:	$* * * * 4 * 6 * 8 *$ $* * * 13\ 14\ 15 * * * 19$ $* * * * * 25 * 27 * 29$ $* * 32 * * 35 * * 38\ 39$ $* * * * * * 46\ 47\ 48\ 49$ $* * * * 54 * * * * 59$ $60 * * 63\ 64 * 66 * * *$ $* * 72\ 73 * 75 * * 78 *$ $* * * * 84\ 85 * * * *$ $* *$
Execution Time:	1405 ms
Size:	30

Table 3. Discovered pattern for the second experiment.

Settings: period=92, Eps=0.09 MinPts=4, Min_sup=0.01	
Discovered pattern:	1 2 3 4 5 6 7 8 9 10 11 12 13 14 15 16 17 18 19 20 21 22 23 24 25 26 27 28 29 30 31 32 33 34 35 36 37 38 39 40 41 42 43 44 45 46 47 48 49 50 51 52 53 54 55 56 57 58 59 60 61 62 63 64 65 66 67 68 69 70 71 72 73 74 75 76 67 78 79 80 81 82 83 84 85 86 77 88 89 90 91 92
Execution Time:	61324 ms
Size:	92

4. Conclusions

Mining of spatio-temporal sequences in transport applications is very important for commercial and governmental enterprise which try to optimize routes and times of their means of transporting. We investigated the chance to mine spatio-temporal patterns coming from standard commercial motes not equipped with GPS or gyroscope. The reported procedures over simulated circuits followed by a single mote on a Lego train appear to give appreciable results. This allows to adopt well assested mining procedures for the problem at hand. Specifically, STPMine1, is able to detect the periodic pattern as described in [2], even though, the computation costs increase with some critical algorithm parameter. The reported study is of specific applicability, but it addresses important issues concerning with WSNs and could help to gain some knowledge about this topic. The method could be applied to model individual behavior, investigating data coming from mobile phone, as an example, or animal movements if equipped with a proper sensor.

Acknowledgments

The authors would like to thank Luca Biscardi and Luigi Mozzillo for their hard work in the Java implementation of the software, Huiping Cao for providing us the C code of STPMine1 and her technical support and Giovanni Schmid for his valuable suggestions.

References

[1] R. Agrawal, R. Srikant, Fast Algorithms for Mining Association Rules. *Proceedings Very Large Data Bases Conference*, (1994), 487–499.

[2] H. Cao, N. Mamoulis, D.W. Cheing, Discovery of Periodic Patterns in Spatiotemporal Sequences. *IEEE Transactions on Knowledge and Data Engineering*, **19**, 4 (2007), 453–467.

[3] J.L. Elman, Finding Structure in Time. *Cognitive Science*, **14**, (1990), 179–211.

[4] M. Ester, H.P. Kriegel, J. Sander, X. Xu, A density-based algorithm for discovering clusters in large spatial databases with noise. *Proceedings of 2nd International Conference on KDD*, 1996.

[5] J. Han, G. Dong, Y. Yin, Efficient Mining of Partial Periodic Patterns in Time Series Databases. *Proceedings of Int'l. Conf. on Data Eng.*, (1999), 106–115.

[6] S. Haykin, *Neural Networks-A comprehensive Foundation*, 2nd Ed. P. Hall, 1999.

[7] D. Pfoser, C.S. Jensen, Y. Theodoridis, Novel Approaches in Query Processing for Moving Objects Trajectories. *The VLDB Journal*, (2000), 395–406.

[8] K. Sohraby, D. Minoli, T. Znati, *Wireless Sensor Networks*. Wiley and Sons, 2007.

[9] Y. Xu, Y. Ouyang, Z. Le, J. Ford, F. Makedon, Mobile Anchor-free Localization for Wireless Sensor Networks. *Dist. Comp. in SNs*, LNCS **4549**, (2007), 96–109.

[10] *http://shop.lego.com/ByTheme/Product.aspx?p=B7898&cn=96*

New Directions in Neural Networks
B. Apolloni et al. (Eds.)
IOS Press, 2009

doi:10.3233/978-1-58603-984-4-12

Sugeno Model Based Control for Semi active Vehicle Suspension

Francesco Voci[1] , Fabio Massimo Frattale Mascioli[1]

[1] InfoCom Dept., Faculty of Engineering, "La Sapienza" University of Rome,
Via Eudossiana, 18 – 00184 Rome Italy
{voci, mascioli } @infocom.ing.uniroma1.it

Abstract. In this paper a fuzzy Sugeno rule based controller is used to manage a semi-active suspension of ¼ vehicle model. Our semi-active suspensions have the characteristic to change the damping constant in order to reduce vertical oscillation of the vehicle, to restrain the shell vehicle acceleration and consequently to be more comfortable for passengers. On the other hand, if no control is present, the suspension works in passive mode, i.e. without damping parameters changing. The inputs of our fuzzy controller, three in total, are the dynamic wheel load described by five membership functions, its derivative and the vertical acceleration both described by three membership functions. By comparing the performances of the suspension with and without control, the Sugeno based model controller results in a more comfortable and safe system.

Keywords: Fuzzy, Sugeno, Least Recursive Square, Simulink.

1 Introduction

Suspension control system design is usually characterized by several parameters, conflicting objectives and stochastic disturbances which requires a synthesis of a mathematical model, necessary for the control method design. With the term "Semi-active" we mean a adjustable suspension system which combines the passive spring element found in a passive suspension, with a damper element whose mechanical characteristics can be adjusted by a controller. Such a type of suspension system has been under consideration for vehicle applications, to reduce the spring mass transmissibility improving the passengers comfort, and reducing the spring oscillation resulting to a better road holding ability and improved vehicle stability.

Many strategies control has been proposed aiming to improve stability and comfort. In [2] the authors propose a control for semi-active suspensions based on model-predictive control (MPC) techniques. The proposed control optimizes the suspension performances by minimizing a quadratic error function ensuring that the controlled forces satisfy the physical constraints of passive damping. In [3] an observer based controller for commercial vehicle using a quarter car suspension model is proposed. A quarter car model is used also in [4] where the control algorithms are limited to feedback schemes based on absolute and relative velocity measurements. Ride comfort, road holding, and suspension travel are investigated with random input velocity to simulate road roughness. In [5] a fuzzy rule based control, based on the Mandami model, is proposed. The input linguistic variables chosen for the fuzzy controller are sprung mass velocity and the suspension velocity. The method described is [6] is based on fuzzy controllers steered by genetic algorithm (GA). The genetic based operations give an estimation of the parameters in fuzzy controllers, that is the input variables, membership functions and fuzzy control rules which are all encoded into the chromosomes.

In this paper we present a Fuzzy Rule Based Sugeno Model for solenoids actuated suspension. This type of semi-active suspension consists in a solenoid valve, inside the damper, that drives the flow of the hydraulic fluid changing the dampening characteristics of the suspension system. The solenoid drive circuit is connected to the output of the fuzzy controller whose inputs are: the vertical acceleration, the dynamic wheel load and its derivative. Gaussian shaped functions, used to describe the inputs, return a smooth decision surface.

2 System Description

Since only the vertical acceleration of the suspension supported mass and the vertical dynamic load is considered, omitting roll and pitch related motion, we consider a ¼ vehicle model. Therefore, our model consists in one quarter shell body mass, $\boldsymbol{m_s}$, one dumper, one linear spring with stiffness coefficient ***Ks***, and a mass $\boldsymbol{m_w}$, connected with a spring with stiffness ***Kw*** which represent the wheel model.

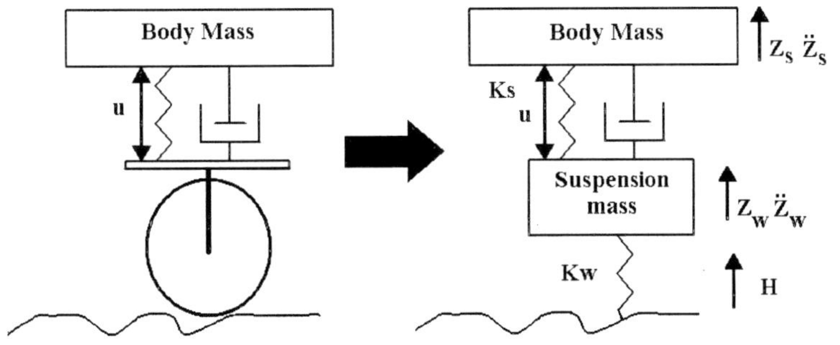

Fig. 1. Vertical dynamic of ¼ Vehicle

Defining the displacement shell-wheel as ***Zw-Zs***, the displacement wheel-road H-***Zw*** and $\boldsymbol{F_D}$ the applied dumper suspension force, the state-space model of the above system can be described as:

$$m_S\ddot{z}_S = K_S(z_W - z_S) + F_D \quad (1)$$

$$m_w\ddot{z}_W = -K_S(z_W - z_S) - F_D + K_W(H - z_W) \quad (2)$$

The force F_D, which can not be described by a linear model, can be consider as sum of three terms:

$F_D = F_V + F_L + F_R$, where $F_V = d_{Anl}(\dot{z}_W - \dot{z}_S)^{\frac{2}{1+2n}}$, is the force connected with the unidirectional dumper piston valve, $F_L = d_{Al}(\dot{z}_W - \dot{z}_S)$ is the force originated by the laminar flux and $F_R = F_0 sign(\dot{z}_W - \dot{z}_S)$ is the Coloumb friction. Because typical value of the n coefficient is 1.5, the expression of F_D becomes:

$$F_D = d_{Anl}\sqrt{|\dot{z}_W - \dot{z}_S|}(1 + sign(\dot{z}_W - \dot{z}_S))/2 + d_{Al}(\dot{z}_W - \dot{z}_S) +$$
$$+ F_0 sign(\dot{z}_W - \dot{z}_S)$$

By substituting the expression of F_D in equation 1 and equation2 the model of ¼ vehicle is given by:

$$m_S\ddot{z}_S = K_S(z_W - z_S) + d_{Anl}\sqrt{|\dot{z}_W - \dot{z}_S|}\frac{1 + sign(\dot{z}_W - \dot{z}_S)}{2}$$
$$+ d_{Al}(\dot{z}_W - \dot{z}_S) + F_0 sign(\dot{z}_W - \dot{z}_S) \quad \textbf{(3)}$$

$$m_w\ddot{z}_W = -K_S(z_W - z_S) + K_W(H - z_W)$$
$$- d_{Anl}\sqrt{|\dot{z}_W - \dot{z}_S|}\frac{1 + sign(\dot{z}_W - \dot{z}_S)}{2} - d_{Al}(\dot{z}_W - \dot{z}_S) + F_0 sign(\dot{z}_W - \dot{z}_S) \quad \textbf{(4)}$$

In our experiment, the displacement wheel-road H is modelled by a square wave pseudo-casual and the controller hands the shell acceleration by modifying the values of parameters d_{Al} and d_{Anl}.

Thus, indicating the control signal as ***sc(t)***, the force F_D should be described as follows:

$$F_D = (1 + sc(t))d_{Anl}\sqrt{|\dot{z}_W - \dot{z}_S|}(1 + sign(\dot{z}_W - \dot{z}_S))/2$$
$$(1 + sc(t))d_{Al}(\dot{z}_W - \dot{z}_S) + F_0 sign(\dot{z}_W - \dot{z}_A))/2$$

As said before, we have chosen to estimate the four variable parameters, m_s, k_v, d_{Al} and d_{Anl} with the recursive least square estimator. Note that also ***ms*** is variable since variable is the number of passenger on the vehicle. We have fixed the nominal values of the parameters a follows:

m_s = 300 Kg; k_v =2.5·105 N/m; d_{Al} =700 Ns/m and d_{Anl} = 800 Ns/m

Before to proceed in the description of the fuzzy control strategy, we spend few words about the semi-active hydraulic system working. Low damping rate is achieved by compressing a large volume of gas (or fluid) and therefore by opening the valve. For high damping the valve is closed and the hydraulic fluid is forced inside a smaller volume resulting in a higher damping force. The hydraulic circuit for the damper is shown schematically in figure 2a. A high speed valve Pv1 controls the pressure regulating the damping coefficient. A reservoir accommodates the oil displaced by the volume of the piston rod in the high pressure circuit and is pressurized with nitrogen gas to prevent *cavitation* phenomenon. A PID controller drives the valve in order to have a fast response without high overshoot. As shown in figure 2b, the inner loop has a linear PID controller, which acts to control the spool position and the valve orifice area. The linear PID controller in the outer loop achieves control of the force generated by the damper. A linear gain K_f is used to estimate a compensation solenoid current *Ic*, that is $Ic=Kf|\dot{v}|$ where $\dot{v}$ is the damper speed. A solenoid converts the supply current from the power amplifier into axial force acting on the valve spool.

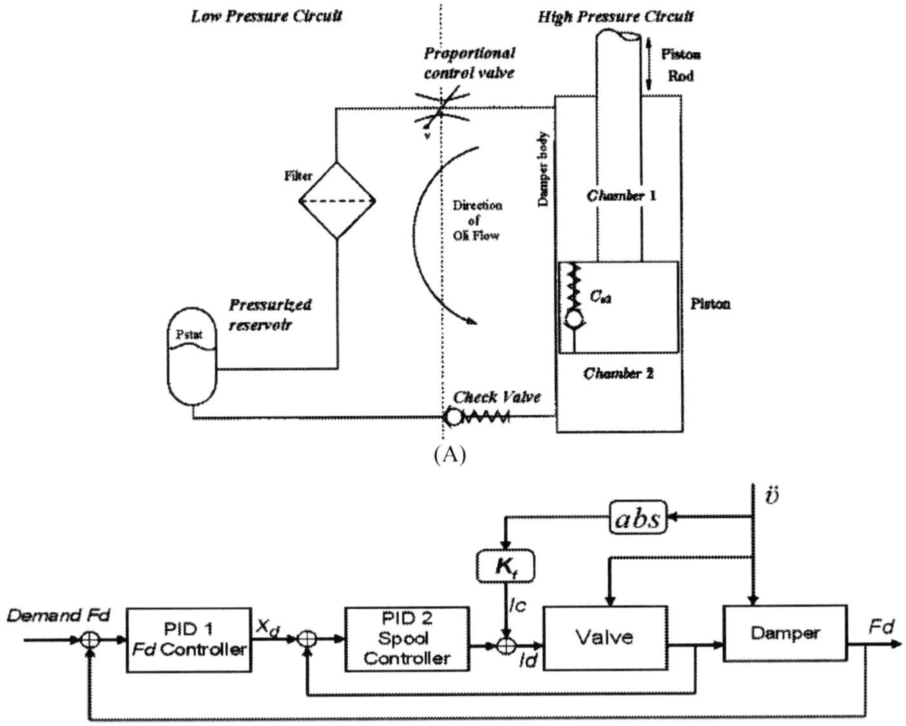

(B)

Fig. 2. A semi active suspension circuit with solenoid valve (A) and a schematic control system for valve spool

3 Parameter Estimation via Least Recursive Square

Let's briefly review the least recursive square algorithm. We start by considering a linear system described by the following equation: $\varphi_1(t)\,\theta_1 + \varphi_2(t)\,\theta_2 + \ldots\, \varphi_n(t)\,\theta_n = y(t)$, where $\varphi j(t)$ (j = 1, 2, ..,n) and $y(t)$ are known quantities and measurements respectively while θj (j = 1, 2, ..,n) are parameters to be determined. In matrix-vector form, we get the following set of over-determined linear algebraic equations, $\Phi^T(t)\Theta(t) = Y(t)$.

In least square estimation unknown parameters of a linear model are chosen in such a way that the sum of the squares of the difference between the actually observed and the computed values, is a minimum. For a linear system this translates into finding the parameters that minimizes the following "error-function",

$$E(\theta,n)=\sum_{i=1}^{n}\left(y(i)-\Phi^{T}(i)\hat{\theta}\right)^{2}$$

It can be shown that the least square recursive solution [11] is given by

$$\Theta(t+1)=\Theta(t)+P(t+1)\Phi(t+1)^{T}\left[Y(t+1)-\Phi(t+1)\Theta(t)\right]$$

$$P(t)=\left(\Phi(t)^{T}\Phi(t)\right)^{-1};$$

$$P(t+1)=P(t)-\frac{P(t)\Phi(t)^{T}\Phi(t)P(t)}{1+\Phi(t)P(t)\Phi(t)^{T}}=P(t)\left[I-\frac{\Phi(t)^{T}\Phi(t)P(t)}{1+\Phi(t)P(t)\Phi(t)^{T}}\right];$$

Let's consider our suspension analytical system by setting the Coloumb friction to zero, we have for equation 3:

$$-K_{S}\left(z_{W}-z_{S}\right)=-m_{S}\ddot{z}_{S}+$$
$$+d_{Anl}\sqrt{\left|\dot{z}_{W}-\dot{z}_{S}\right|}\left(1+sign(\dot{z}_{W}-\dot{z}_{S})\right)/2+d_{Al}\left(\dot{z}_{W}-\dot{z}_{S}\right)$$

Since the left side of equation represents the known measures that we indicate with the vector $Y=[y_1;y_2]$, we can write: $-K_{S}\left(z_{W}-z_{S}\right)=y_{1}$ and the right side can be written in the form:

$$\left[-\ddot{z}_{S},\sqrt{\left|\dot{z}_{W}-\dot{z}_{S}\right|}\left(1+sign(\dot{z}_{W}-\dot{z}_{S})\right)/2,\left(\dot{z}_{W}-\dot{z}_{S}\right)\right]\cdot\begin{bmatrix}m_{S}\\ d_{Anl}\\ d_{Al}\end{bmatrix}=\Phi^{T}\Theta$$

In the same way for equation 4 we can write:

$$m_{w}\ddot{z}_{W}+K_{S}\left(z_{W}-z_{S}\right)=y_{2};$$

$$\left[\left(H-z_{W}\right),-\sqrt{\left|\dot{z}_{W}-\dot{z}_{S}\right|}\left(1+sign(\dot{z}_{W}-\dot{z}_{S})\right)/2,-\left(\dot{z}_{W}-\dot{z}_{S}\right)\right]\cdot\begin{bmatrix}K_{W}\\ d_{Anl}\\ d_{Al}\end{bmatrix}=\Phi^{T}\Theta$$

To correctly estimate the varying model parameters it is suitable the assumption that their rate of change is substantially slower than the sampling time. An exponential forgetting scalar factor λ, a decay weight such that $0<\lambda<1$, is multiplied to the recursive LMS in order to assign heavier weighting to the most recent data, and lower weights to older measurement. In particular the expression of $P(t+1)$ becomes:

$$P(t+1)=\frac{1}{\lambda}P(t)\left[I-\frac{\Phi(t)^{T}\Phi(t)P(t)}{\lambda+\Phi(t)P(t)\Phi(t)^{T}}\right];$$

Initial values of LMS algorithm may be set [3] in the following way: $P(0)=\delta I$ where I is the identity matrix and δ is a positive real number while the vector of unknown parameters $\Theta(0)$ may be arbitrarily fixed.

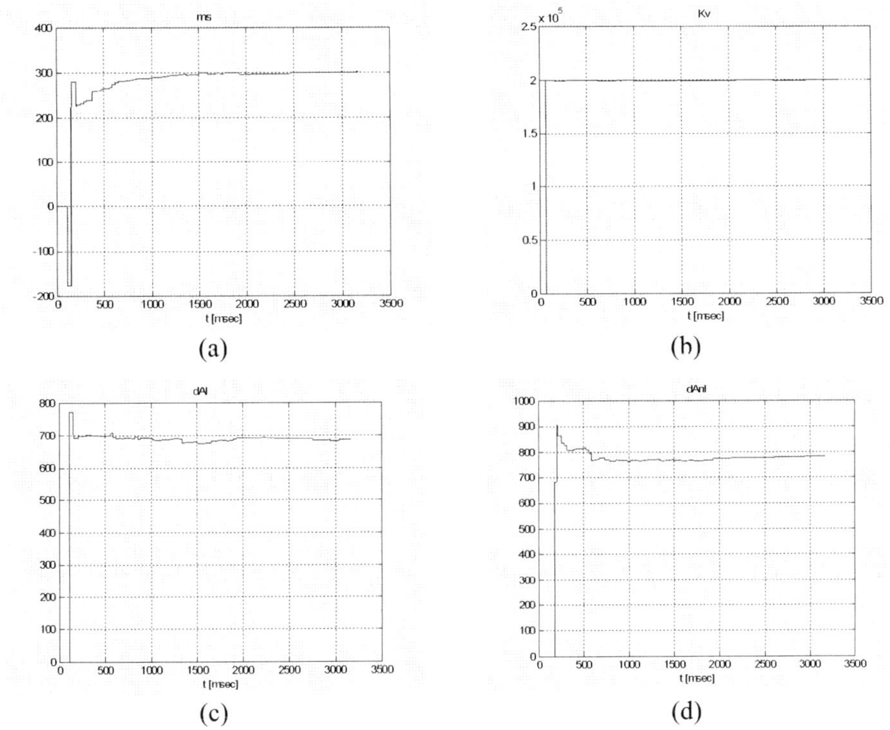

Fig. 3. Estimation by the Least Mean Square method of the parameters *ms, Kw, dAl,dAnl*

The above algorithm for the estimation of parameters *Kw, ms, dAnl, dAl*, has been implemented with un S-Function in Simulink® environment. An S-Function can describe a continuous, discrete, and hybrid systems as well. After few seconds from simulation starting time, (about 2~3) the parameter are estimated reaching the nominal values as showed in figure 3.

4 Fuzzy Controller

In our proposed method, the control signal is applied to the dynamical wheel load $Fz=Kw(H-Zw)$, and to the shell acceleration d^2z/dt^2. The strategy of Fuzzy Control is based on getting low the suspension dumping after the ground wheel impact in order to restrain the shell vehicle acceleration and consequently to be more comfortable for passengers. When the acceleration comes back to zero the dumping must be higher to decrease oscillation. It is necessary to distinguish the cases $Fz = 0$ when the wheel is oscillating and the cases $Fz = 0$ when impact is being dumped. This requirement leads to the use of dFz/dt.

For this reason the fuzzy controller has three inputs: d^2z/dt^2, Fz and dFz/dt where Fz is described by five membership functions while the other two inputs are described by three membership functions.

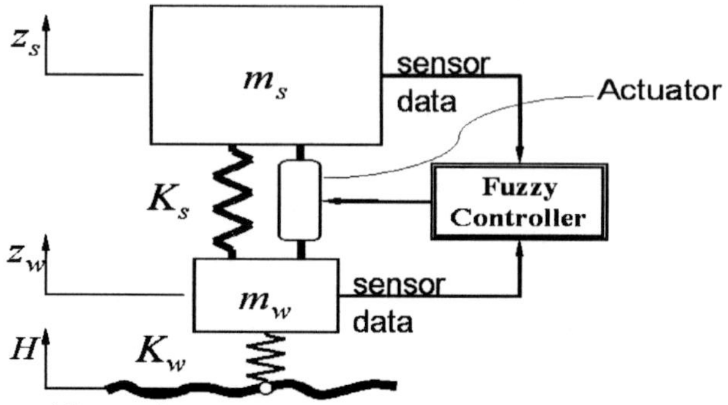

Fig. 4. Control System Layout

Below the body acceleration d^2z/dt^2 is indicated with the variable *az* and is labeled ad “highneg” if it is high toward the bottom, “highpos” if it is high toward the up and “low” when it has a small amplitude. In any case when *az* is high the control must be “soft”, i.e. the suspension damping coefficient must be low, then the rules have the following expression:

```
If (az is highneg) or (az is highpos) then (CS is soft)
```

The reduction of oscilation after the bump is done by the rules as follows:

```
If (az is low) and (Fz is highpos) and (dFz/dt is neg)
then (CS is hard)

If (az is low) and (Fz is low) and (dFz/dt is zero)
then (CS is soft)
```

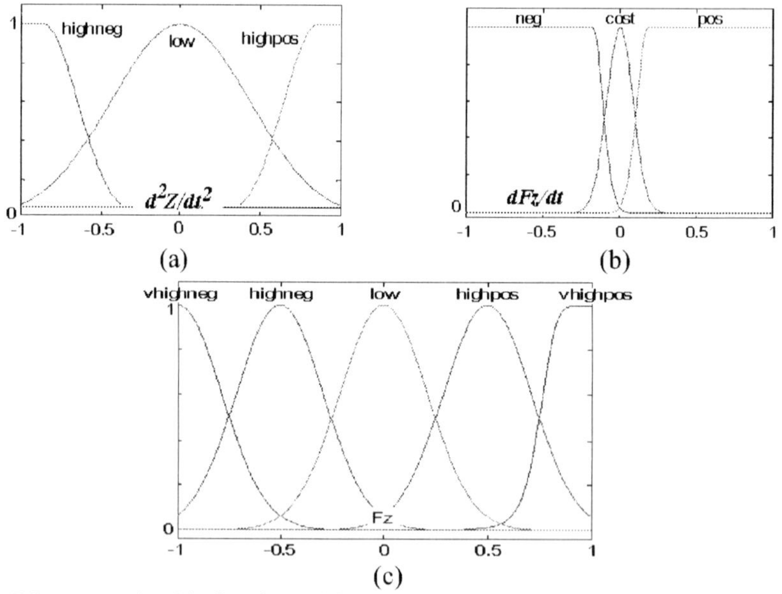

Fig. 5. Input membership functions of fuzzy controller

The model is based on Sugeno method, which implies impulsive type output membership functions. These output function have -1, 0 and 1 values, indicating a soft control, a zero control and an hard control respectively. Fuzzy surface decision is showed in figure 6. The smoothed character guarantees of a good quality control of the actuator.

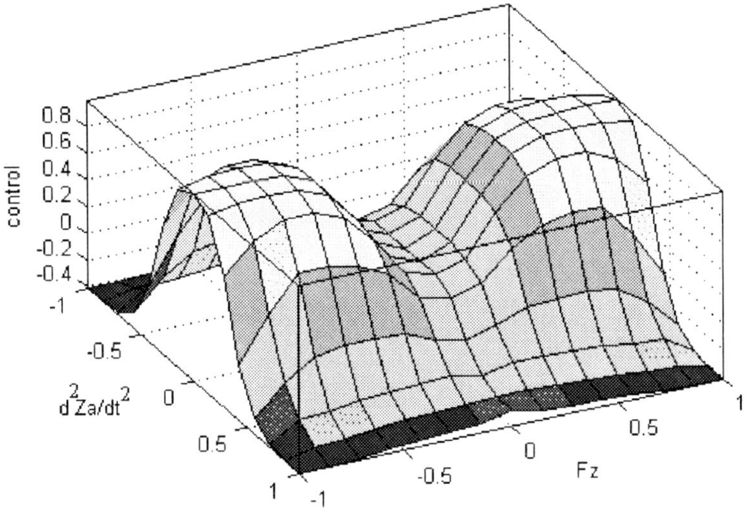

Fig. 6. Decision Surface of fuzzy controller

In figure 7 the suspension displacement and body acceleration without control (passive suspension) and controlled by the fuzzy inference (semi-active) are compared. With the fuzzy controller both displacement and acceleration are substantially reduced.

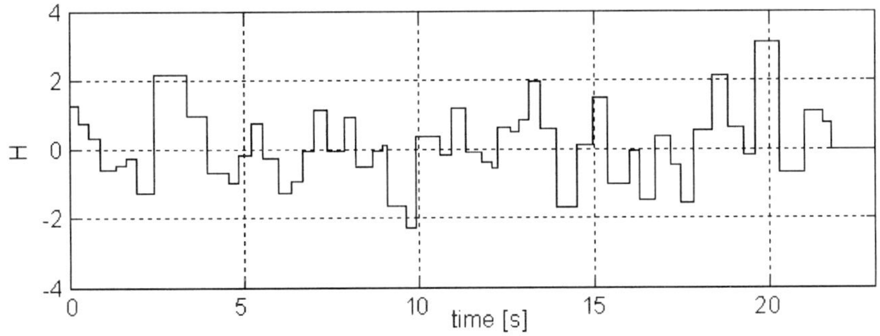

(a)

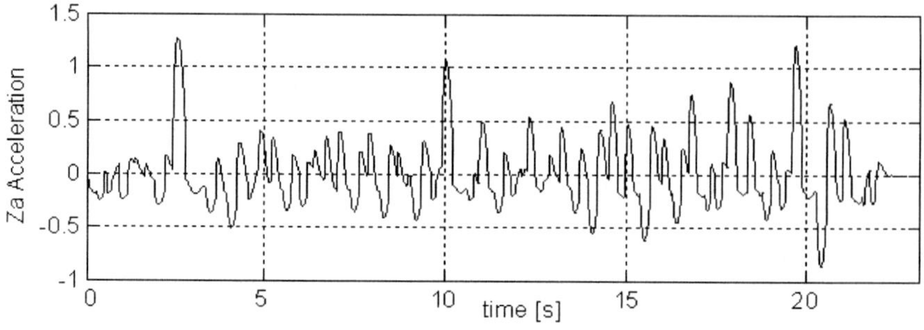

(b)

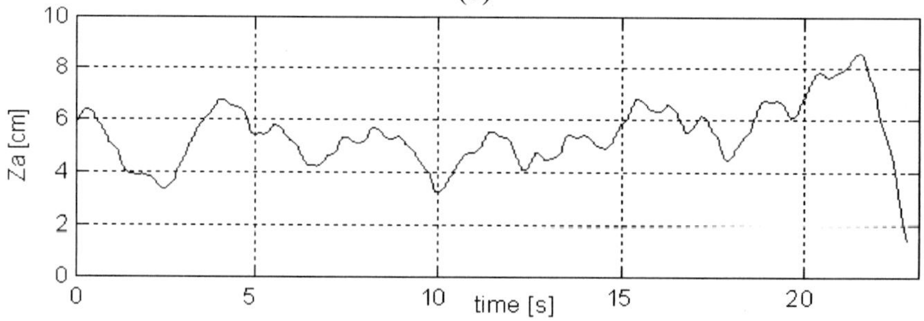

(c)

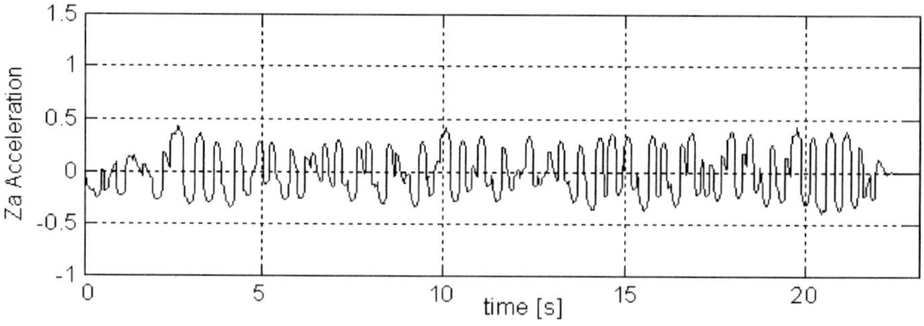

(d)

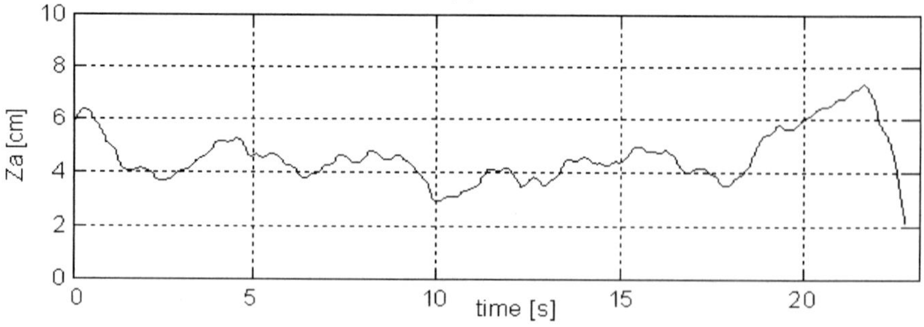

(e)

Fig. 7. The ground displacement H in (a) causes the Body acceleration (b) without control and with fuzzy control (c). The body displacement without control (passive mode) in (d) is higher then the displacement with the presence of fuzzy control in (e)

5 Conclusions

Comparing the characteristic of the suspensions without control (passive mode), with the controlled suspension it has been experimented that the proposed fuzzy controller steering the solenoid valve, used to generate the variable damping coefficient, decreases the sprung mass displacement and improve ride comfort of the automobile. The choice of gauss type membership functions results in a very smooth decision surface that is always preferable for a whichever actuator. Further work will be the control of semi-active suspension based on magnets-rheological fluid. In a magneto-rheological fluid, soft particles (micro-spheres) are magnetically suspended in a synthetic hydrocarbon fluid. When a current is applied to an electromagnetic coil inside the damper's piston, the resulting magnetic field changes the rheology of the fluid. The particles react to the field by forming a dense lattice of chains, changing the fluid from a liquid to a near solid and back to a liquid in milliseconds.

References

1. Kitching K.J., Cole D.J. and Cebon D. In: "Performance Of A Semi-Active Damper For Heavy Vehicles" ASME Journal of Dynamic Systems, Measurement, and Control, 122, pp. 498-506, 2000
2. Canale, M. Milanese, M. Novara, C. In: "Semi-Active Suspension Control Using 'Fast' Model-Predictive Techniques". In: IEEE Transactions on Control Systems Technology. Vol. 14, issue:6, pp. 1034-1046. November 2006.
3. Sankaranarayanan, V. et all, In: "Observer based semi-active suspension control applied to a light commercial vehicle". In: International Conference on Advanced Intelligent Mechatronics, pp. 1-7 4-7 Sept. 2007.
4. Miller, L. R.,: In "Tuning Passive, Semi-Active, and Fully Active Suspension Systems," Proceedings of the IEEE Conference on Decision and Control. Vol. 3, pp. 2047-2053.
5. Mehrdad N. Khajavi, and Vahid Abdollahi In: "Comparison between Optimized Passive Vehicle Suspension System and Semi Active Fuzzy Logic Controlled Suspension System Regarding Ride and Handling". Proceedings of World Academy Of Science, Engineering And Technology. Vol. 21 pp. 57-61. January 2007.
6. Hashiyama, T., Behrendt, S., Furuhashi, T., Uchikawa, Y., In: "Fuzzy controllers for semi-active suspension system generatedthrough genetic algorithms". IEEE International Conference on Systems, Man and Cybernetics. Vol. 5, pp: 4361-4366. October 22-25 1995
7. Ahmadian, M., In: "Ride Evaluation of a Class 8 Truck with Semiactive Suspensions," Dynamic Systems and Control, Vol. 52, ASME, 1993, pp. 21-26.
8. Ivers, D. E. and Miller, L. R., In: "Experimental Comparison of Passive, Semi-Active On/Off, and Semi-Active Continuous Suspensions," SAE Technical Paper Series No. 892484.
9. Karnopp, D., Crosby, M. J., and Harwood, R. A., In: "Vibration Control Using Semi-Active Force Generators," Journal of Engineering for Industry, 96, ASME, 1974, pp. 619-626.
10. Ross, T. J., "Fuzzy Logic with Engineering Applications", McGraw-Hill, Inc., NewYork, 1995.
11. Monson H. Hayes, In "Statistical Digital Signal Processing and Modeling", John Wiley & Sons. Inc., New York, pp. 541-551. 1996.

New Directions in Neural Networks
B. Apolloni et al. (Eds.)
IOS Press, 2009

doi:10.3233/978-1-58603-984-4-22

Automatic classification of defects in an industrial environment

N. Alberto BORGHESE
Applied Intelligent Systems Laboratory (AIS-Lab)
Department of Computer Science,
University of Milano
Via Comelico 39, 20135 Milano - I
borghese@dsi.unimi.it

Abstract. We describe here a system, based on boosting, for the classification of defects on material running on a production line. It is constituted of a two-stages architecture: in the first stage a set of features are extracted from the images surveyed by a linear camera located above the material. The second stage is devoted to the classification of the defects from the features. The novelty of the system resides in the ability to rank the defects with respect to a set of classes, achieving a rate of identification of dangerous defects very close to 100%.

Keywords: Boosting. Automatic Classification. Features. Production line. Defects. Image processing. Ranking.

Introduction

Defects in the material are one of the major threats that the companies who produce tissue are trying to limit: a multi-million dollar suit has been raised by a woman who found an insects inside the plastic sheet of the diaper of her baby. To avoid this, investments in quality control have greatly raised in the last few years, and in particular systems for Automatic Defect Classification (ADC) have been introduced.

Most of these systems share the same architecture, where a first layer analyzes the data picked up in real-time from the industrial plant (e.g. images) and outputs a set of features aimed to characterizing the defects. In the second layer, these features are analyzed and classified according to pre-defined classes [1, 2, 3].

Classification algorithms can be grouped into three broad categories: clustering based [2, 4], support vector machines [3, 5] and boosting [6, 7].

Clustering is based on finding sub-regions in the features space, characteristic of each class. However, the high space dimensionality and the sparseness of the representation of each class, makes this solution difficult to be used, and different approaches have been explored. Support vector machines transform the defect images into a vector space where the different classes can be separated through hyperplanes. This transformation is non-linear and it is achieved through a mapping function, which has to be designed ad-hoc, which can become a difficult task. Boosting appears the most natural approach to defect classification as it is based on combining a set classifiers, each working on a single feature.

We present here a system based on a multi-class version of Adaboost [14]. The system is able to correctly classify most of the defect images; in particular it reaches almost zero false negative for the critical classes.

1. Method

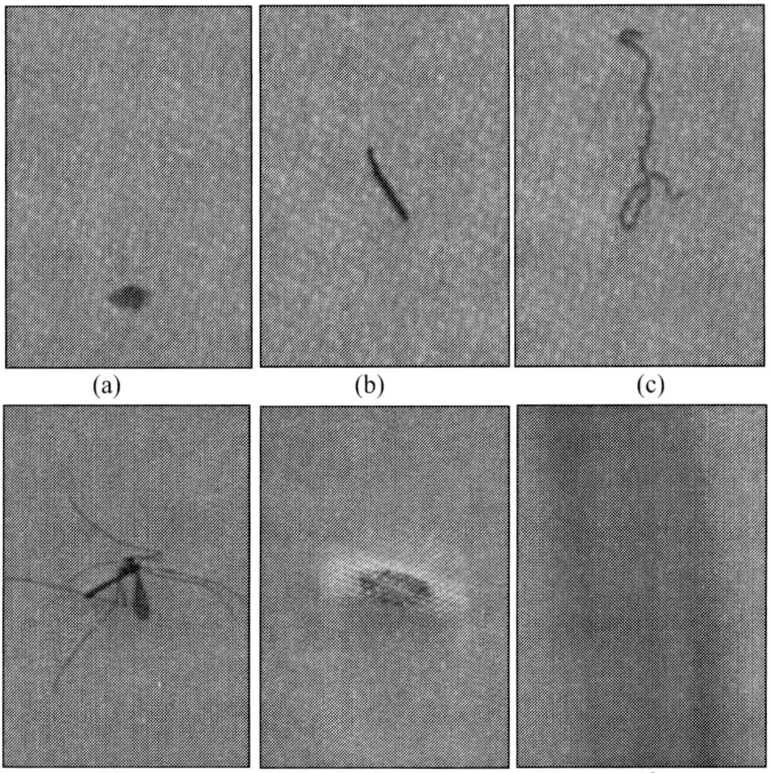

(a) (b) (c) (d) (e) (f)

Figure 1 An example of defect image for each of the seven classes identified by the domain expert: a) regular contaminations, b) elongated defects, c) threads (cotton thread), d) insects, e) dense spots, f) tissue folds. Irregular defects, are those which do not fit into one of these classes.

For the present work, defects have been classified into seven different classes by a domain expert: 1) regular contaminations, 2) irregular contaminations, 3) elongated defects, 4) threads (e.g. metallic staples or cotton threads), 5) insects, 6) dense spots, 7) tissue folds (cf. Fig. 1). Threads and insects are defects which have to be always correctly spotted as the system must have no false negatives on these two classes.

The system receives in real-time the image of the defect, acquired by an inspection module while the material is running on the assembly line. For the present work the Flexin^{TM} inspection system [8] has been adopted to collect the defect images. The system first extracts a set of features through dedicated image processing and the uses these features to classify the image. Its output is a rank of the image with respect to each of the seven classes.

1.1 Preprocessing

The images acquired by FlexIn, I^0, have dimension of 140 x 200 pixels on 8bpp and are assembled from a pair of linear cameras sampling the scene at a high frequency, 4Khz, required by the very high motion speed of the material on the assembly line. Lighting is calibrated such that defects appear as dark shadows on a lighter background and that no defect goes undetected.

As the two cameras may easily have slightly different parameters, the images have to be equalized and normalized before processing. First the mean gray level of the odd columns is set equal to the mean value of the even columns. To this aim, the ratio between the mean luminance of odd and even columns is computed and the luminance of the even columns multiplied by such factor (gain equalization). Afterwards, the gray levels of each image are stretched to cover the entire gray level range (usually 256 values) to get normalized images.

Lastly, image I^0 is binarized into I^B, using adaptive global thresholding [9]; holes are then filled through standard Region Growing [10]. To factor out the orientation, the principal directions of the defect are computed through the singular value decomposition of the dispertion matrix computed on the binarized image [11].

1.2 Extracted features

A set of features have been extracted following the suggestion of the domain expert.

The first set of features considered for the regular defects are related to the degree of homogeneity. To this aim I^B is clustered into three or two classes using [15] and the statistics of the difference between the gray level associated to each cluster and that of its pixel is measured. An additional feature is is the number of distinct blobs obtained after clustering. A second set of features related to regular defects is obtained from the horizontal and vertical histogram profile (Fig. 2a): their peaks are searched and are characterized in terms of width and steepness. The standard deviation of the pixels inside and outside each peak is computed and used as a measure of homogeneity.

Elongated defects suggest using the normalized principal components to evaluate the elongation. Threads tend to have a constant local thickness. This can be evaluated determining for each defect pixel, P_d, the minimum length segment through P_d, contained entirely inside the defect. The mean and standard deviation of the length of these segments, measured along eight equally spaced directions, constitute the features inspired by threads.

Insects are characterized mainly by a body, which can be assimilated to a regular defect, and a set of legs and wings. In particular, legs can be defined as thin segments departing from the insect body. Because of background inhomogeneity and texture, legs can go easily un-detected and a specific processing has been developed aimed to tuning of the binarization threshold. To the scope, we have filtered I by a set of matched filters with different orientations and widths (1.5 pixels wide by 5 pixels long and 2 pixels wide by 6 pixels long, equally spaced by $\pi / 6$) and built the image containing, for each pixel, the maximum value output by the filters is created. The co-occurrence matrix is created for this image, by analyzing a 3x3 sliding window according to [12]. Values larger than zero are concentrated close to the diagonal and as appreciated in Fig. 2b assume a Gaussian-like shape. The standard deviation of this Gaussian can be used to set a tighter binarization threshold on I. In Figs. 2c and 2d the binarized image before and after the addition of the legs components is reported.

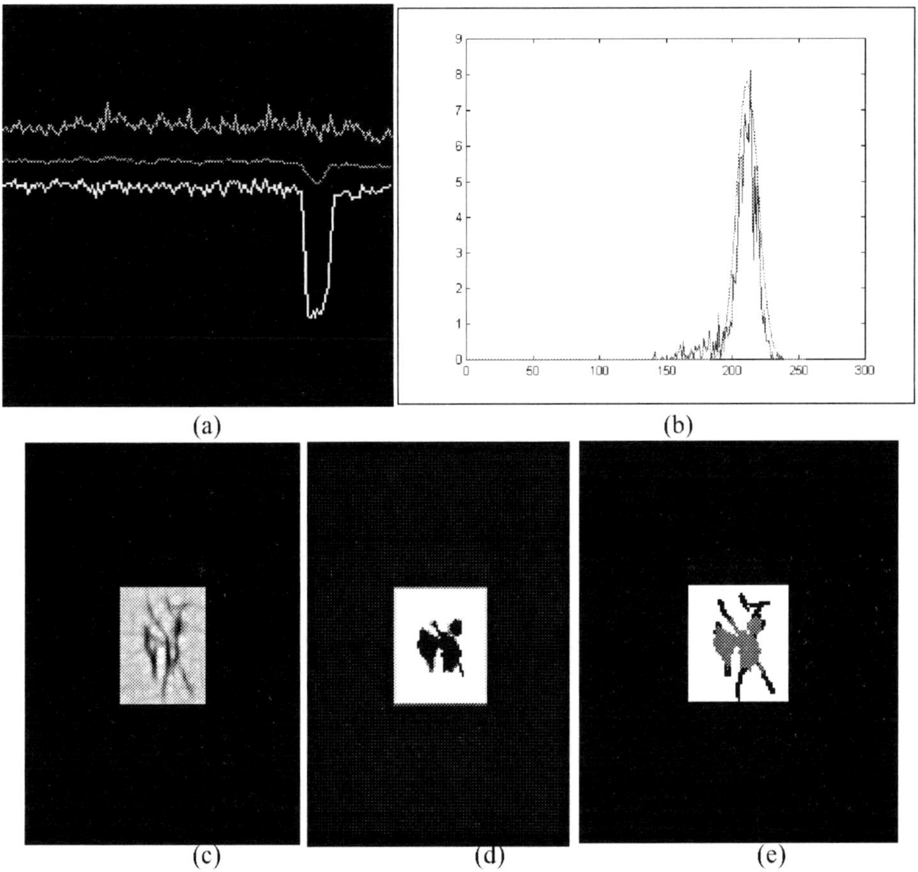

Figure 2. The horizontal profile (minimum, mean and maximum), is shown in panel (a); in panel (b) the profile extracted from the co-occurrence matrix is displayed. In panels (c) the original defect image, in panel (d) the image binarized and in (e) the image binarized through the adaptive threshold defined through the co-occurrence matrix.

Dense spots occur when fibers are stretched locally, which produces areas more transparent to the camera light and therefore lighter. The presence of areas above threshold is therefore a characteristic of these defects. Folds occur along the entire width of the tissue and therefore occupy the entire defect image. The mean and standard deviation of the first and last few lines of the image is computed and compared to that of the background to produce a feature inspired by this class.

1.3 Classification Engine

Classification engine is based on Ada-boosting [13, 14]. In its basic approach, the classifier is built iteratively: at each iteration a new elementary classifier is added to the global classifier in three steps: choice of the classifier, computation of its associated coefficient, updating of the images weight obtaining the final following shape:

$$H_{single\_class}\left(I_i^{\,0}\right) = sign\sum_{t=1}^{T}\alpha_t h_{f(t),\vartheta(t),t}\left(I_i^{\,0}\right) \tag{1}$$

where each elementary classifier, $h_{f,\vartheta}(I^0)$ maps a defect image, I^0, into a binary value, ±1, depending on the comparison of the value of the feature, *f*, extracted from I^0 with a threshold θ. Eq. (1) is usually called a committee of weak classifiers.

This approach has been extended to a multi-class setting [7], where the classifier output produces a ranking of the image with respect to the *M* different classes. In this setting, the classifier output assumes the following form:

$$H\left(I_i^{\,0}, m_k\right) = \sum_{t=1}^{T}\alpha_t h_{f(t),\vartheta(t),t}\left(I_i^{\,0}, m_k\right) = C_k \in R \tag{2}$$

and outputs a real value, C_k, such that $C_j > C_i$ if the image I^0 is more likely to belong to class *j* than to class *i*.

Each elementary classifier, *h(.)*, outputs a different value for the different classes (labels, m_k). *H(.)* is evaluated by measuring the number of *crucial* misorders, that is the number images for which, $H(I^0, m_i) < H(I^0, m_j)$ when I^0 is more likely to belong to m_i instead that to m_j. This measure is called *ranking loss*.

In our case, a ranking of all the classes is not given and the multi-class approach described in [14] has been adapted to the video inspection framework as described in [15], where the only crucial misorderings considered are those which do not rank the correct classification first. Nothing is said about other possible classifications. Nevertheless, the system second choice is very reasonable as it will be shown in the next section.

2. Results

A data set, I_D, constituted of 215 images well balanced over the different classes: 40 images of regular defects, 40 of irregular defects, 40 of elongated defects, 50 of threads, 45 of insects, extracted randomly. A larger number of threads and insects were inserted because of the intrinsic difficulties and criticity of these two classes. The classification accuracy was assessed through five-fold cross-validation. To the scope, the images in I_D are distributed randomly into two sets: a training set, I_{DS}, constituted of 172 images (equal to 80% of the images) and a test set, I_{TS}, of 43 images. Results are obtained averaging 10 experiments in each of which the images were shuffled 5 times randomly. Boosting was iterated 100 times.

Error on the training and test data sets is reported in Fig. 3. As it can be seen the average error approaches 94%. For a very few combinations of data and test sets this error can be larger, but this can be explained by the lack of good examples in the training sets for these very few cases

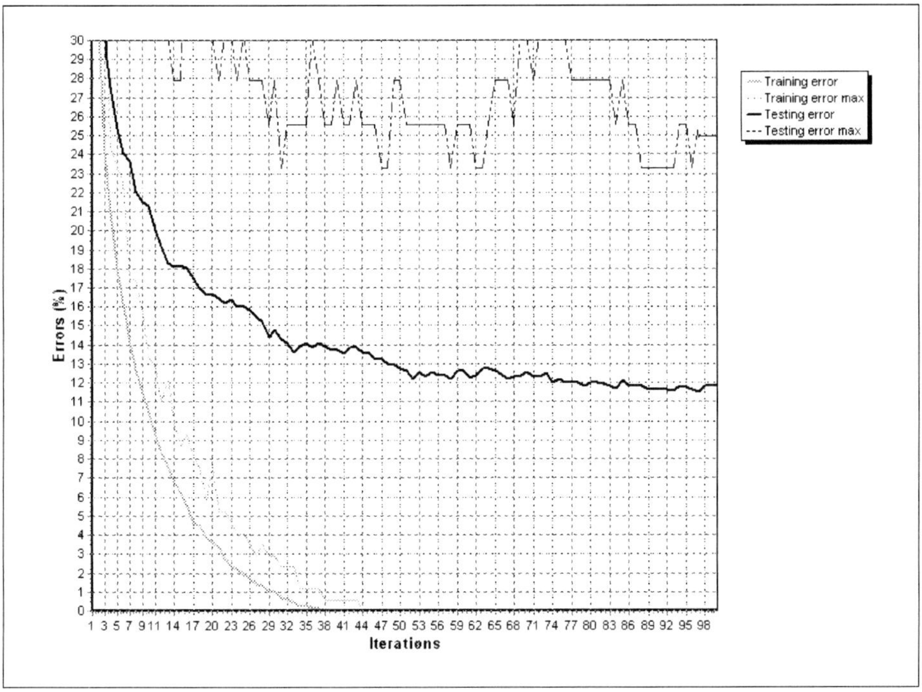

Figure 3 – Classification error (--) and training error (-) are reported for a typical set of experiments in which enhanced features are considered. Notice that the error is reduced down to 12% on the average, considering both false positive and false negative. The number of classification error is therefore around 6%.

	Class #1		Class #2		Class #3		Class #4		Class #5	
	#	%	#	%	#	%	#	%	#	%
Conf. with #1	0,0	0,0	0,52	1,21	0,0	0,0	0,0	0,0	0,32	0,74
Conf. with #2	0,36	0,84	0,0	0,0	0,24	0,56	0,52	1,21	0,32	0,74
Conf. with #3	0,0	0,0	0,16	0,37	0,0	0,0	0,36	0,84	0,0	0,0
Conf. with #4	0,04	0,09	0,60	1,39	0,52	1,21	0,0	0,0	0,20	0,46
Conf. with #5	0,04	0,09	0,68	1,58	0,76	1,77	0,20	0,46	0,0	0,0
Total	0,44	1,02	1,96	4,56	1,52	3,53	1,08	2,51	0,84	1,95

Table I. The number of errors committed by the global classifier for all the classes. Please notice that both false negative and positive are considered.

A closer analysis is shown in Table I, in which both false positive and negative are considered as errors. We did not report results for Classes 6 and 7 as the classification error is zero for these classes. The only errors larger than 1% are in the elongated class, for which images can be erroneously classified as threads or insects. All the other classes show errors less than 1%.

Moreover, in most of the cases, the output produced by the classifier for the true class, is very close (and ranked second), with respect to the class ranked first. Therefore, taking the first two classes the error goes to zero for elongated defects, and almost to zero for all the other classes. The system therefore is able to correctly identify the risky defects and prompt the operator for examining them.

2 choices	Class #1		Class #2		Class #3		Class #4		Class #5	
	#	%	#	%	#	%	#	%	#	%
Conf. with #1	0,0	0,0	0,04	0,09	0,0	0,0	0,0	0,0	0,0	0,0
Conf. with #2	0,0	0,0	0,0	0,0	0,0	0,0	0,08	0,19	0,04	0,09
Conf. with #3	0,0	0,0	0,0	0,0	0,0	0,0	0,0	0,0	0,0	0,0
Conf. with #4	0,04	0,09	0,20	0,46	0,0	0,0	0,0	0,0	0,16	0,37
Conf. with #5	0,0	0,0	0,16	0,37	0,0	0,0	0,08	0,19	0,0	0,0
Total	0,04	0,09	0,40	0,93	0,0	0,0	0,16	0,37	0,20	0,46

Table II. The number of errors committed by the global classifier for all the classes when the first two choices are considered. Please notice that both false negative and positive are considered.

3. Conclusion

We have presented here a novel methodology to design an intelligent inspection system. Its key elements are a video inspection model, a robust feature extraction design and a flexible and adaptive classifier.

The boosting machinery allows identifying the features and the range of each feature which are suitable to identify that class. For this reason only a subset of features is considered for each class inside Eq. (1).

In this respect this system can be considered an evolution of the expert systems popular in the seventies, based on explicit reasoning or fuzzy systems.

References

[1] X. Yang, J. Gao, G. Pang, and N. Yung. "Textile Defect Classification Using Discriminative Wavelet Frames". *Proc. IEEE Int. Conf. Inform. Acquisition*, (2005), pp. 54-58.

[2] A. Malhi, and R.X. Gao, PCA-Based Feature Selection Scheme for Machine Defect Classification, *IEEE Trans. on Instr. & Measur.*, **53(6)**, (2004), 1513-1525.

[3] V. Murino, M. Bicego, I.A. Rossi, Statistical Classification of Raw Textile Defects, *Proc. the 7th Int. Conf. on Pattern Recognition* (ICPR'04), **2**, (2004), 311-314.

[4] J. Iivarinen, and A. Visa, "An Adaptive Texture and Shape Based Defect Classification", *Proc. Int. Conf. on Pattern Recognition, ICPR*, **1**, (1998), 117-123.

[5] P. Chen, C. Lin, and B. Schölkopf. "A Tutorial on ν-Support Vector Machines". *Tech. Report. Max Planck Institute for Biological Cybernetics*, Tübingen, Germany, 2001.

[6] S. Hwa Lee, H. Kim, N. Cho, Y. Jeong, K. Chung, and C. Jun.. "Automatic Defect Classification Using Boosting". *Proc. Fourth Int. Conf. on Machine Learning and Applications* (ICMLA'05), (2005), 45-52.

[7] Y. Freund. R. Iyer, R.E. Schapire, and Y. Singer, "An efficient boosting algorithm for combining preferences in Machine Learning": *Proc. Fifteenth Int. Conf. Machine Learning, ICML-98*, (1998), 176-184.

[8] Electronic Systems, FlexIn home page:http://www.eletronicsystems.it/application_en.html.

[9] N. Otsu, A threshold selection method from gray level histograms, *IEEE Trans. Systems, Man and Cybernetics*, **9**, (1979), 62-66.

[10] R.C. Gonzalez, and R.E. Woods. "*Digital image processing*", third edition. Prentice Hall, 2008.

[11] W.H. Press, S.A. Teukolsky, W.T. Vetterling, and B.P. Flannery. "*Numerical Recipies in C: the Art of Scientific Computation*", third edition. Cambridge University Press, 2000.

[12] G. Pok, J. Liu, and A. Nair, Selective Removal of Impulse Noise Based on Homogeneity Level Information, *IEEE Trans. on Image Processing*, **12(1)**, (2003), 85-92.

[13] R. E. Schapire, "A Brief Introduction to Boosting". AT&T Labs, Shannon Laboratory, 1999.

[14] R. E. Schapire, Y. Singer. "Improved Boosting Algorithms Using Confidence-rated Predictions". Machine Learning, **37(3)**, (1999), 297-336.

[15] T. Uchiyama, and M.A. Arbib, Color image segmentation using competitive learning, *IEEE Trans. PAMI*, **16(12)**, 1994, 1197-1206.

New Directions in Neural Networks
B. Apolloni et al. (Eds.)
IOS Press, 2009

doi:10.3233/978-1-58603-984-4-30

STLmax joint Mutual Information for quantifying independence in the epileptic brain

Nadia MAMMONE [1], Fabio LA FORESTA, Francesco C. MORABITO, and Mario VERSACI

DIMET - "Mediterranea" University of Reggio Calabria
via Graziella Feo di Vito, I-89122 Reggio Calabria, ITALY

Abstract. Results in literature show that the convergence of the Short-Term Maximum Lyapunov Exponent (STLmax) time series, extracted from intracranial EEG recorded from patients affected by intractable temporal lobe epilepsy, is linked to the seizure onset. When the STLmax profiles of different electrode sites converge (high entrainment) a seizure is likely to occur. In this paper Renyi's Mutual information (MI) is introduced in order to investigate the independence between pairs of electrodes involved in the epileptogenesis. A scalp EEG recording and an intracranial EEG recording, including two seizures each, were analysed. STLmax was estimated for each critical electrode and then MI between couples of STLmax profiles was measured. MI showed sudden spikes that occurred 8 to 15 min before the seizure onset. Thus seizure onset appears related to a burst in MI: this suggests that seizure development might restore the independence between STLmax of critical electrode sites.

Keywords. Chaos Theory, Short-Term Maximum Lyapunov Exponent, Mutual Information, Electroencephalography.

Introduction

The Scientific Community began being interested in epileptic seizure prediction during '70s: some results in literature showed that seizures were likely to be stage of an epileptogenic process rather than an unpredictable and sudden event. Therefore a new hypothesis was proposed: the evolution of brain dynamics towards seizures was assumed to follow this transition: interictal- preictal-ictal-postictal. The ictal stage starts at the seizure's onset and ends at the seizure's end, the preictal stage is the period preceding the seizure onset, the postictal stage is the period following the seizure end. The period between the postictal stage of one seizure and the preictal stage of the next seizure is called interictal stage.

Iasemidis' research group firstly applied non linear techniques to epilepsy [1]: EEG recordings of patients affected by temporal lobe epilepsy were studied during pre-ictal,

[1] Corresponding Author: Nadia Mammone, DIMET - *Mediterranea* University of Reggio Calabria, Via Graziella Feo di Vito, I-89122 Reggio Calabria, ITALY; E-mail: nadia.mammone@unirc.it.

ictal and post-ictal stages, fitting chaos theory to EEG analysis. This group introduced an efficient version of the Largest Lyapunov Exponent (Lmax) named *Short Term Maximum Lyapunov Exponent* (STLmax), and proved the relationship between the temporal evolution of Lmax and the development of epileptic seizures [2]. During those years also Lopes da Silva applied non linear techniques to EEG quantifying bifurcations by correlation measures [3]-[4]. Hively used chaos theory to predict epileptic seizures [5], Lerner exploited correlation integral to detect EEG changes [6], whereas some non linear measurements like entropy were introduced by Pezard et al. [7]. Paul et al. proposed wavelet-based residual entropy [8].

Iasemidis et al. presented a STLmax-based real time algorithm to predict seizures [9]. Further results achieved by the same group endorsed the hypothesis that a kind of resetting involves the brain during the seizure [10].

In the subsequent years, the major idea was to try to precisely discriminate between the pre-ictal and the ictal stage, this is why Le Van Quyen et al. [11] estimated phase measures to measure the synchronisation of the activity of different electrode sites. In the same period, cross correlation and phase synchronization in analyzing intracranial EEG (IEEG) were studied by Jerger [12]; Jouny et al. [13] used two methods, one of which, Gabor atom density, estimates intracranial EEGs in terms of synchrony and complexity. The parameter proposed by Esteller [14] was the mobile average energy of EEG signal, Harrison et al. [15] measured the amount of energy in EEG signal and its power averaged within moving windows. Genetic algorithms to select features from EEG signals were exploited by D'Alessandro as an input of a classifier [16].

STLmax is also the heart of a novel brain mapping that was recently proposed and could become a tool for the spatio-temporal analysis of the chaotic behaviour of the epileptic brain [17]. The convergence of STLmax profiles of critical electrode sites, extracted from intracranial EEG recorded from patients affected by intractable temporal lobe epilepsy, seems to be linked to the seizure onset and it can be measured by *Tindex* [9], what we would like to study in this paper is the independence between STLmax profiles of critical electrode sites, in order to investigate if there is any relationship between independence and seizure development. To this purpose Mutual Information (MI), in particular the Renyi's definition of MI [18], was introduced.

The paper is organized as follows: Section 1 will introduce STLmax for epileptic EEG analysis, Section 1.2.1 and Section 1.2.2 will introduce Tindex and MI respectively, Section 2 will illustrate the results and Section 3 will report the conclusions.

1. Analysis of pre-ictal EEG segments

The neurons communicate by means of electrical impulses and generate a bioelectromagnetic field that propagates through the brain tissues, the skull and the scalp. By means of some electrodes placed over multiple areas of the brain, we can detect and record the electric field that, even though attenuated, reflects the underlying brain activity: the resulting traces are called electroencephalogram (EEG). Electroencephalography, in fact, is the neurophysiologic measurement of the electrical activity of the brain and can be recorded through electrodes placed on the scalp (EEG) or directly in the brain tissues (IEEG), through surgically implanted electrodes. Figure 1 and Figure 2 show the scalp montage and the intracranial montage used in this paper.

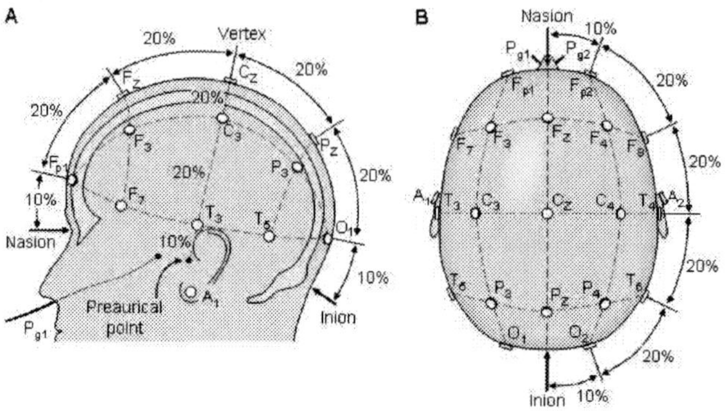

Figure 1. The international 10-20 system seen from (A) left and (B) above the head. A = Ear lobe, C = central, Pg = nasopharyngeal, P = parietal, F = frontal, Fp = frontal polar, O = occipital.

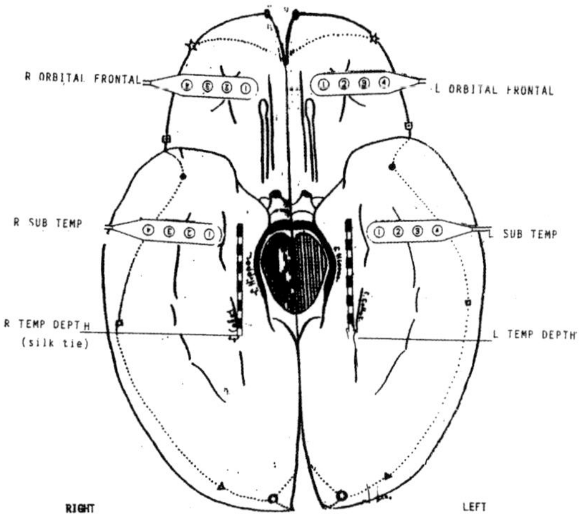

Figure 2. The intracranial electrode montage.

EEG can be conceptualized as a time series of numerical values (voltages) over time. Being a multichannel recording, the EEG can be seen as the output of a multidimensional system, thus it has statistical properties that depend on both time and space [19]: this makes the EEG a multivariable time series.

A technique for visualizing the dynamical behaviour of a multidimensional (multivariable) system is to generate a phase space portrait of the system. A phase space, introduced by Willard Gibbs in 1901, is a space in which all possible states of a system are represented, with each possible state of the system corresponding to one unique point in the phase space. A phase space portrait is created by treating each time-dependent variable of the system as a component of a vector in a multidimensional space, usually called state or *phase space* of the system.

If the portrait in the phase space creates an object confined over time to a sub-region, these sub-regions are called *attractors*. The global state of the system is strictly related to the geometrical properties of the attractor. The geometrical properties of the portrait can be measured through parameters linked to the dynamics of the system.

Time delay embedding, or establishing a phase space representation of a system using current and delayed values from a sampled time series, is a useful technique for characterising nonlinear behaviour of a system [20]. Takens showed that an embedding of dimension larger than twice the dimension of a smooth manifold containing an attractor is a true embedding, in other words, the phase space is topologically equivalent to the state space of the attractor [21].

To determine whether an attractor is behaving chaotically, without knowing the exact equations of the system under consideration, one can compute the value of the largest Lyapunov exponent [22]. The Lyapunov exponents measure the average rate of expansion and folding that occurs along the local eigen-directions within an attractor in phase space.

The estimation of the largest Lyapunov exponent (Lmax) in a chaotic system has been shown to be more reliable and reproducible than the estimation of the remaining exponents, especially when D changes over time as it does with nonstationary data. We will now summarize the algorithm to estimate STLmax from nonstationary data.

1.1. Short Term Maximum Lyapunov Exponent

A relevant time scale should always be used in order to quantify the physiological changes occurring in the brain. Furthermore, the brain being a nonstationary system, algorithms used to estimate measures of the brain dynamics should be capable of automatically identifying and appropriately weighing existing transients in the data. The method developed for estimation of STLmax, an estimate of Lmax for nonstationary data, extract the exponents from 10.24sec non-overlapping windows and is explained in detail in [2].

Construction of the embedding phase space from a data segment $x(t)$ of duration T can be carried out with the method of delays. The vectors X_i in the phase space are constructed as:

$$X_i = [x(t_i), x(t_i + \tau), ..., x(t_i + (p-1)\tau)]^T \tag{1}$$

where T denotes the transpose, τ is the selected time lag between the components of each vector in the phase space, p is the selected dimension of the embedding phase space, and $t_i \in [1, T-(p-1)\tau]$. If we denote by L the estimate of the short term largest Lyapunov exponent STLmax then:

$$L = \frac{1}{N_a \Delta t} \Sigma_{i=1}^{M} \log_2 \frac{|\delta X_{ij}(\Delta t)|}{|\delta X_{ij}(0)|} \tag{2}$$

with:

$$\delta X_{ij}(\Delta t) = X(t_i + \Delta t) - X(t_j + \Delta t) \tag{3}$$

and

$$\delta X_{ij}(0) = X(t_i) - X(t_j) \quad (4)$$

where:

- $X(t_i)$ is the point of the fiducial trajectory $\Phi(X(t_0))$ with $t = t_i$, $X(t_0) = [x(t_0), x(t_0 + \tau), ..., x(t_0 + (p-1)\tau)]^T$, and $X(t_j)$ is a properly chosen vector adjacent to $X(t_i)$ in the phase space (see below).
- $\delta X_{ij}(0) = X(t_i) - X(t_j)$, is the displacement vector at t_i, that is, a perturbation of the fiducial orbit at t_i, and $\delta X_{ij}(\Delta t) = X(t_i + \Delta t) - X(t_j + \Delta t)$ is the evolution of this perturbation after time Δt.
- $t_i = t_0 + (i-1)\Delta t$ and $t_j = t_0 + (j-1)\Delta t$, where: $i \in [1, N_a]$ with $i \neq j$.
- Δt is the evolution time for δX_{ij}, that is the time one allows δX_{ij} to evolve in the phase space. If the evolution time Δt is given in sec, then *L* is in bit/sec.
- t_0 is the initial time point of the fiducial trajectory and coincides with the time point of the first data in the data segment of analysis. In the estimation of L, for a complete scan of the attractor, t_0 should move within $[0, \Delta t]$.
- N_a is the number of local Lmax's that will be estimated within a duration T data segment. Therefore, if Dt is the sampling period of the time domain data, $(N-1)\Delta t = N_a \Delta t + (p-1)\tau$.

Results from simulation data of known attractors have shown the improvement in the estimates of L achieved by using of these modifications [23]. Details of STLmax estimation can be found in [24].

1.2. Measuring the entrainment

1.2.1. Tindex

If a similar transition occurs at different cortical sites, the STLmax of the involved sites are expected to converge to similar values ("locking") prior to this transition. Iasemidis et al. have called such participating sites "critical sites", and such a convergence "dynamical entrainment" [9].

The tool exploited to quantify the entrainment is *T-index* (based on second order statistics, from the well-known t-test for comparisons of means of paired-dependent observations) it is a measure of the distance between the mean values of pairs of STLmax profiles over time and it is inversely proportional to the entrainment.

T-index $T_{i,j}$ measures the average distance between the STLmax profiles of two channels *i* and *j* (Eq. 5), estimating the mean of the difference between the two STLmax profiles over 10 min overlapping windows (with a 10.24sec overlap), and dividing by the variance $\sigma_{i,j}$. It is worth pointing out that Tindex is computed backwards, including past 10min with respect to time point *t*.

$$T_{i,j}(t) = \frac{|E\{STLmax_i(t) - STLmax_j(t)\}|}{\frac{\sigma_{i,j}(t)}{\sqrt{w}}} \quad (5)$$

In Eq. 5, *t* is the initial time point of the current $10min$ window and *w* is the number of STLmax samples to be considered ($w = 60$ because there are 60 STLmax samples in 10 min, since we have a STLmax sample every 10.24 sec). The global entrainment is computed estimating the mean of the partial T-indexes of the couples of critical electrode sites.

1.2.2. Renyi's Mutual Information

Mutual information of two random variables X and Y is a quantity that measures the mutual dependence of the two variables. Mutual information quantifies the distance between the joint distribution of X and Y and what the joint distribution would be if X and Y were independent. We propose the use of Renyi's definition of mutual information as the criterion for estimating the entrainment between pairs of STLmax profiles in order to investigate whether higher order statistic can provide additional information about the entrainment with respect to Tindex.

Renyi's mutual information of order α between n random variables with the joint pdf $f_Y(y)$ is given by:

$$I_{R_\alpha(y)} = \frac{1}{\alpha - 1} log \int_{-\infty}^{+\infty} \cdots \int_{-\infty}^{+\infty} \frac{f_Y^\alpha(y_1, ..., y_n)}{\prod_{i=1}^{n} f_{Y_i}(y_i)^{\alpha-1}} dy_1, ..., dy_n \tag{6}$$

Thanks to the expected value definition:

$$I_{R_\alpha(y)} = \frac{1}{\alpha - 1} logE \left[\frac{f_Y(y_1, ..., y_n)}{\prod_{i=1}^{n} f_{Y_i}(y_i)} \right]^{\alpha-1} \tag{7}$$

The pdf's are estimated by the Parzen windowing method [25]:

$$f_{Y_i}(y_i) = \frac{1}{N} \sum_{i=1}^{n} k_\sigma(y - y_i) \tag{8}$$

where k_σ is the kernel function, N is the number of samples. We chose a Gaussian kernel with zero mean and variance σ^2, with $\sigma = 0.25$, according to [25], and we set $\alpha = 2$ (Renyi's quadratic MI). When we substitute the estimated pdf (8) in (6):

$$I_{R_\alpha(y)} = \frac{1}{\alpha - 1} log \frac{1}{N} \sum_{j=1}^{N} \left[\frac{\frac{1}{N} \sum_{i=1}^{N} \left[\prod_{o=1}^{n} k_{\sigma_o}(x_j^o - x_i^o) \right]}{\prod_{o=1}^{n} \left[\frac{1}{N} \sum_{i=1}^{N} k_{\sigma_o}(x_j^o - x_i^o) \right]} \right]^{\alpha-1} \tag{9}$$

Renyi's MI at time t was estimated backwards, as well as Tindex, including past 10min with respect to time point t.

2. Results

2.1. EEG data description

The analyzed intracranial EEG were acquired by means of a Nicolet BMSI 4000 recording system, the amplifiers were set in the input range of $\pm 0.6mV$ and the frequency range of the filters was set at $0.5 - 70Hz$. The signals were sampled at 200Hz and they were finally stored. The analyzed segment consists in about 800min and includes 2 seizures, the first one occurred at minute 426 and the second one at minute 763. Electrographically, every event came from right mesial temporal lobe (RD2) and also from the mesial aspect of left sub-temporal strip (LT2). Intracranial channel location is shown in Figure 2. Either Intracranial and scalp EEG were not preprocessed for artifact removal.

The analyzed scalp data consist in a 19-channels EEG from a patient affected by frontal lobe epilepsy. The time duration is 34.63min, the EEG was high pass filtered at 0.5Hz and the sampling rate was set at 128Hz. The EEG tracing includes two seizures: the first one occurred at minute 16 and the second one occurred at minute 31. Scalp channel location is shown in Figure 1. The critical electrodes are Fp1, Fp2, F7, F8 and T3.

2.2. Measuring the entrainment

We first processed intracranial EEG. STLmax was estimated for the two critical electrodes, RD2 and LT2, as described in Section 1.1. The Tindex between the two STLmax profiles was then computed according to Section 1.2.1, whereas Mutual Information was estimated as described in Section 1.2.2.

Tindex profile (Figure 3, bottom) is consistent with the state of the brain, in fact, it shows a decreasing shape (increasing entrainment) until the first seizure onset, then it suddenly increased (decreasing entrainment) and began decreasing again soon, until the onset of the second seizure. The critical transition for Tindex is the first drop below the threshold 2.662 [9] and this event occurred at minute 315 (about 110min before the first seizure) and at minute 530 (233 min before the second seizure).

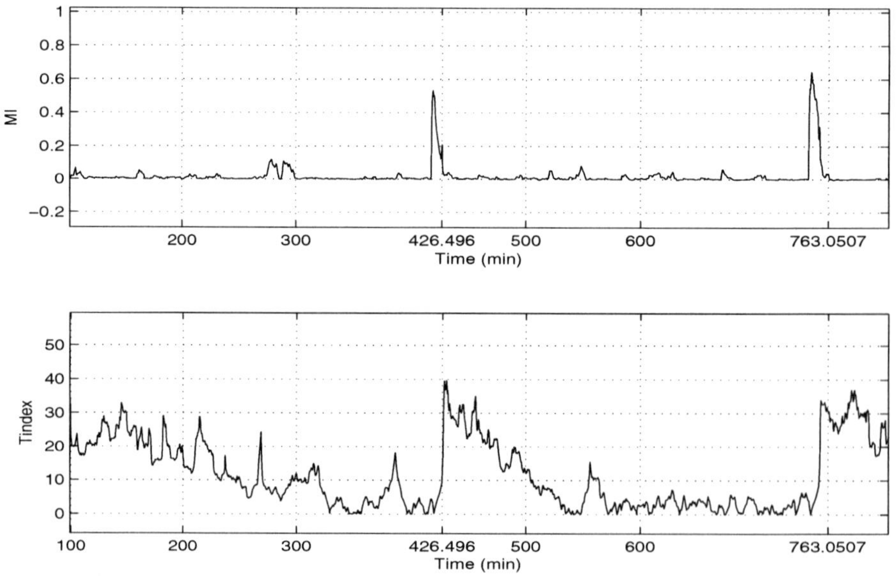

Figure 3. Mutual Information between the two critical electrodes vs Tindex between the same electrodes for IEEG. Seizures were marked by vertical hatched lines. MI has a quite stable behaviour (MI approximately null) until a sudden spike occurred at min 530 (15 min before the second seizure).

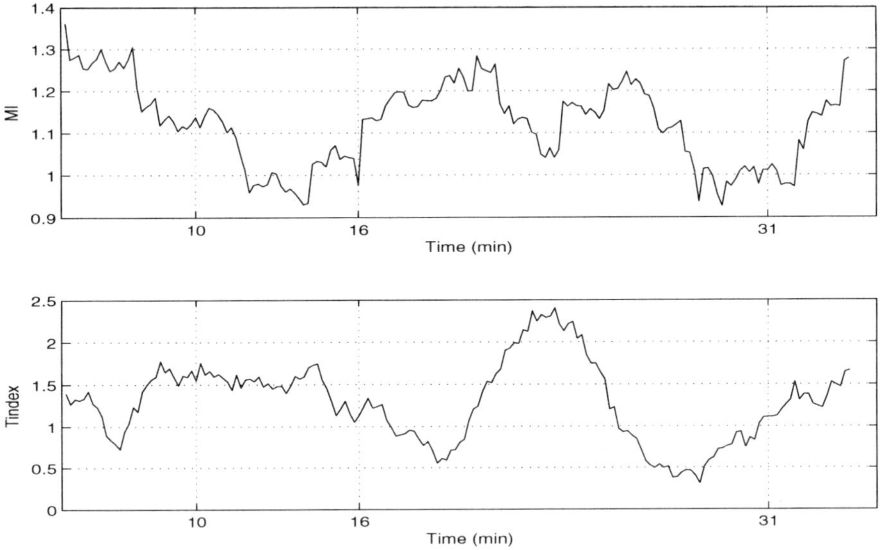

Figure 4. Mutual Information of the group of critical electrodes vs Tindex of the same group for scalp EEG. Seizures were marked by vertical hatched lines.

If we look at the shape of MI, we can point out a quite stable behaviour (MI approximately null) until a sudden spike occurred at min 418 (8min before the first seizure, see Figure 3, top) and at min 530 (15 min before the second seizure). Once MI had reached the top it began decreasing and the seizure occurred when MI was low again. Thus seizure onset appears preceded by a burst in MI: this suggests that seizure development might consist in resetting MI, therefore the dependence, between STLmax of critical electrode sites, this way restoring independence.

The procedure yielded similar results for scalp EEG, even tough the short duration did not allow us to fully appreciate the difference between inter-ictal and pre-ictal behaviour of MI. STLmax was estimated for the five critical electrodes, then Tindex and MI were computed.

Tindex showed a decreasing behaviour during the first seizure and before the second seizure (Figure 4, bottom). MI was high at first and decreased until the first seizure onset, then it began increasing again until min 26 when it began decreasing until the second seizure onset (Figure 4, top).

Looking in particular at results from IEEG, MI seems to provide additional information about interictal to preictal transition: Tindex crossed the critical threshold many minutes before the onset (110 to 233 minutes before), whereas MI showed a bursting behaviour 8 to 15 minutes before the onset. The hypothesis that seizure development might be associated to restoring independence should be investigated measuring MI over many interictal-preictal-ictal-postictal transitions, processing either scalp and intracranial EEG.

3. Conclusions

In this paper the issue of epileptic seizure prediction was addressed. A technique for measuring the entrainment, based on STLmax and Tindex, was described and Renyi's Mutual information (MI) was introduced in order to investigate the independence between pairs of electrodes involved in the epileptogenesis. A scalp EEG recording, from a patient affected by frontal lobe epilepsy, and an intracranial EEG recording, from a patient whose seizures arose from the right mesial temporal lobe and from the mesial aspect of left sub-temporal strip were analysed. Each recording included two seizures. STLmax was estimated for each critical electrode, then MI between couples of STLmax profiles was measured. Looking at the shape of MI, we can point out a quite stable behaviour (MI approximately null) during the inter-ictal stages, until sudden spikes occurred 8 to 15 min before the seizure onset. Once MI had reached the top it began decreasing and the seizure occurred when MI was low again. Thus epileptogenesis seems to be linked to a burst in MI: this suggests that seizure development might reset MI between STLmax of critical electrode sites, restoring independence. STLmax MI should be validated on several either pathological normal datasets before thinking about it as a prediction parameter. Further investigation will be pursued in the future in order to endorse or reject this hypothesis.

Acknowledgements

The authors would like to thank the *Brain Dynamics Bioengineering Research Partnership* (University of Florida, Gainesville, Florida, USA) for providing the intracranial EEG.

References

[1] Iasemidis L.D., Zaveri H.P., Sackellares J.C., and Williams W.J. Linear and nonlinear modeling of ecog in temporal lobe epilepsy. In *25th Annual Rocky Mountains Bioengineering Symposium*, pages 187–193, 1988.

[2] Iasemidis L. D. and Sackellares J. C. The temporal evolution of the largest lyapunov exponent on the human epileptic cortex. In Duke D. W. and Pritchard W.S., editors, *Measuring chaos in the human brain*. World Scientific, Singapore, 1991.

[3] Lopes da Silva F. H., Pijn J. P., and Wadman W. J. Dynamics of local neuronal networks: Control parameters and state bifurcations in epileptogenesis. *Prog. Brain Res.*, 102:359–370, 1994.

[4] Pijn J. P. M., Velis D. N., Van der Heyden M. J., DeGoede J., Van Veelen C. W. M., and Lopes da Silva F. H. Nonlinear dynamics of epileptic seizures on basis of intracranial eeg recordings. *Brain Topogr.*, 9:249–270, 1997.

[5] Hively L. M., Clapp N. E., Daw C. S., and Lawkins W. F. Nonlinear analysis of eeg for epileptic events. *Oak Ridge National Laboratory, Oak Ridge*, 9, 1995.

[6] Lerner D. E. Monitoring changing dynamics with correlation integrals: a case study of an epileptic seizure. *Physica D*, 97:563–576, 1996.

[7] Pezard L., Martinerie J., Breton F., Bourzeix J. C., and Renault B. Nonlinear forecasting measurements of multichannel eeg dynamics. *Electroencephalogr. Clin. Neurophysiol.*, 91:383–391, 1994.

[8] Paul J.S. andPatel C.B., Al-Nashash H., Zhang N., Ziai W.C., Mirski M.A., and Sherman D.L. Prediction of ptz-induced seizures using wavelet-based residual entropy of cortical and subcortical field potentials. *IEEE Trans Biomed Eng.*, 50(5):640–648, 2003.

[9] L.D. Iasemidis, Deng-Shan Shiau, W. Chaovalitwongse, J.C. Sackellares, and P.M. Pardalos. Adaptive epileptic seizure prediction system. *IEEE Transactions On Biomedical Engineering*, 50(5):616–627, 2003.

[10] Iasemidis L. D., Shiau D-S., Pardalos P. M., Chaovalitwongse W., Narayanan K., Prasad A., Tsakalis K., Carney P. R., and Sackellares J. C. Long-term prospective on-line real-time seizure prediction. *Clin Neurophysiol.*, 116:532–544, 2005.

[11] Le Van Quyen M., Soss J., Navarro V., Robertson R., Chavez M., Baulac M., and Martinerie J. Preictal state identification by synchronization changes in long-term intracranial eeg recordings. *Clin Neurophysiol.*, 116:559–568, 2005.

[12] Jerger K. K., Weinstein S. L., Sauer T., and Schiff S. J. Multivariate linear discrimination of seizures. *Clin Neurophysiol.*, 116:545–551, 2005.

[13] Jouny C. C., Franaszczuk P. J., and Bergey G. K. Signal complexity and synchrony of epileptic seizures: is there an identifiable preictal period. *Clin Neurophysiol.*, 116:552–558, 2005.

[14] Esteller R., Echauz J., D'Alessandro M., Worrell G., Cranstoun S., Vachtsevanos G., and Litt B. Continuous energy variation during the seizure cycle: towards an on-line accumulated energy. *Clin Neurophysiol.*, 116:517–526, 2005.

[15] Harrison M. A. F., Freiy M. G., and Osorio I. Accumulated energy revisited. *Clin Neurophysiol.*, 116:527–531, 2005.

[16] D'Alessandro M., Vachtsevanos G., Esteller R., Echauz J., Cranston S., Worrell G., Parish L., and Litt B. A multi-feature and multi-channel univariate selection process for seizure prediction. *Clin Neurophysiol.*, 116:506–516, 2005.

[17] Mammone N., Principe J. C., and Morabito F. C. Visualization of the short term maximum lyapunov exponent topography in the epileptic brain. In *28th IEEE EMBS Annual International Conference*, pages 4257–4260, New York City, USA, Aug 30-Sept 3, 2006.

[18] Hild K. E. II, Erdogmus D., and Principe J. C. Blind source separation using renyi's mutual information. *IEEE Signal Proc. Letters*, 8(6):174–176, 2001.

[19] Lopes da Silva F. Eeg analysis: theory and practice; computer-assisted eeg diagnosis: pattern recognition techniques. In E. Niedermeyer, F. Lopes da Silva F, Urban, and Schwarzenburg, editors, *Electroencephalography; basic principles, clinical applications and related fields*. Baltimore, 1987.

[20] Abarbanel H.D.I. *Analysis of observed chaotic data*. Springer-Verlag, New York, 1996.

[21] Takens F. Detecting strange attractors in turbulence. In D.A. Rand and L.S. Young, editors, *Dynamical systems and turbulence: Lecture notes in mathematics*. Springer-Verlag, Heidelburg, 1981.

[22] Wolf A., Swift J.B., Swinney H.L., and Vastano J.A. Determining lyapunov exponents from a time series. *Physica D*, 16:285–317, 1985.

[23] L.D. Iasemidis. *On the dynamics of the human brain in temporal lobe epilepsy, PhD Dissertation*. University of Michigan, Ann Arbor, 1991.

[24] Iasemidis L.D., Sackellares, J.C., Zaveri H.P., and W.J. Williams. Phase space topography and the lyapunov exponent of the electrocorticograms in partial seizures. *Brain Topogr.*, 2:187–201, 1990.

[25] Erdogmus D., Hild K. E. II, and Principe J. C. Blind source separation using renyiŠs marginal entropies. *Neurocomputing*, 49:25–38, 2002.

New Directions in Neural Networks
B. Apolloni et al. (Eds.)
IOS Press, 2009

doi:10.3233/978-1-58603-984-4-40

Neural Networks for the Parameters Characterization of ECG Dynamical Model

Matteo CACCIOLA [a,1], Fabio LA FORESTA [a], Francesco Carlo MORABITO [a] and Mario VERSACI [a]

[a] *University "Mediterranea" of Reggio Calabria, DIMET*
Via Graziella Feo di Vito, 89100 Reggio Calabria, Italy

Abstract. The Electrocardiogram (ECG) is the recording of the effects produced from the bioelectric field generated by the cardiac muscle during its activity. Specific changes in ECG signals can reveal pathologic heart activity. For this reason, a dynamic model - that accurately describes the heart bioelectric behavior and that can be mathematically analyzed - could be a practical way to investigate heart diseases. The aim of this paper is to introduce a dynamic model to simulate pathological ECG as well as to evaluate an Artificial Neural Network able to distinguish the impact of some modeling parameters on specific and peculiar features of EGC's trend.

Keywords. Electrocardiogram, heart disease, Neural Network regression

Introduction

Since its discovery by Waller and Einthoven, the electrocardiogram (ECG) has been widely used in cardiological diagnosis, like arrhythmia, atrial-ventricular (A-V) fibrillation, A-V block, myocardial ischemia and other disorders in the heart activation. The ECG is a registration of the heart electrical activity and its relationship with the body surface potentials. It is originated from the bioelectric field produced by the cardiac muscle during its contractions. In fact during atrial and ventricular contractions, the sodium and potassium ions concentration is not balanced and the heart is not electrically neutral. In other words, the heart can be considered equivalent to an electric dipole and it can be described by a vector that changes its amplitude and its orientation during the depolarization and repolarization processes of the heart muscle cell: this is the theoretic basis of the modern ECG [1,2,3]. Therefore, the ECG is the major diagnostic instrument of cardiac electrophysiology and its extensive use occurs for two simple reasons: first because it is not invasive and secondly because the ECG recordings are distorted also from a little abnormalities of the cardiac cycle, i.e. an accurate information about the heart functionality can be obtained by the ECG inspection. In the last years, several algo-

[1]Corresponding Author: Matteo Cacciola, University Mediterranea of Reggio Calabria, DIMET - Via Graziella Feo di Vito, 89100 Reggio Calabria, Italy; Email: matteo.cacciola@unirc.it.

rithms are developed for the ECG analysis and interpretation [4]. The researchers have directed their studies towards two aspects: one concerns the morphology of waves and complexes which make up a complete cardiac cycle; the other is concerned to timing of events and variations in patterns observed over many beats. The availability of ECG databases and the implementation of heart models are the foundation of the discoveries and the improvements in the cardiac diseases diagnosis. In particular computer modeling of the heart is a useful theoretical tool for the investigation and the interpretation of cardiac physiology and pathology [5,6]. The main reason that drives the researches to implement cardiac models is essentially the impossibility to distort the heart activity in order to study the related effect on the ECG. Evidently this problem can be partially bypassed trough the analysis of ECG database recordings [7]. On the other hand, the creation of heart models has the undeniable advantage to allow a mathematical characterization of the complete cardiac cycle and to simulate fatal cardiac diseases. In addition, the generation of synthetic ECG facilitates the testing of signal processing algorithms. The aim of this paper is to introduce a parametric dynamic model able to simulate ECG signals. The proposed model is based on the generalization of the well known model, developed from McSharry et al. [5], for synthesizing single-channel ECG signals. The model parameters are characterized by a neural network based on Radial Basis Function (RBFANN), in order to evaluate the impact of the model's parameters on the trend of ECG. This kind of network has been chosen since it is highly recommended for pattern estimation problems [8]. In particular, we firstly evaluated the performances of RBFANN by varying its spread factor (please, see 2 for details) for each one of the considered significant features extracted by the ECG. Subsequently, we selected the useful spread factor by considering a trade-off between performances and complexity of the neural network. Finally, we trained the suitable RBFANN and tested its performances. Therefore, in the next Section, we discuss the parametric model for ECG signal reproducing. Section 2 presents the RBF's theory and its application to the case-of-study. Finally, a discussion about results and our conclusions are drawn in Section 3.

1. Parametric Dynamic EGC model

Each heart beat can be observed as a series of deflections away from the baseline on the ECG. These deflections reflect the time evolution of electrical activity in the heart which initiates muscle contraction. A single normal cycle of the ECG, corresponding to a heartbeat, is traditionally labeled with the letters P, Q, R, S, and T on each of its turning points, as shown in Fig. 1. The normal ECG signal includes various deflections: P-wave represents atrial depolarization, the ventricular depolarization causes the QRS complex, and repolarization is responsible for the T-wave (for more details see [5]). It is well known that heart diseases distort the PQRST complexes; vice versa specific changes in ECG signals reveal a pathological activity of the cardiac muscle. In other words, the morphology analysis of ECG is the simplest way to investigate the majority of cardiac disorders. The single-channel ECG modeling is based on the idea that the PQRST complex can be obtained as a succession of Gaussians having different characteristics. McSharry et al. [5] showed that ECG signal can be simulated by solving three coupled ordinary differential equations [5]. If we indicate with $s(t)$ the ECG signal, it can be synthesized by:

Table 1. Parameters of the model.

	P	**Q**	**R**	**S**	**T**
time (s)	-0.250	-0.025	0	0.025	0.250
θ_i (rad)	- $\pi/3$	-$\pi/12$	0	$pi/12$	$pi/2$
a_i	1.25	-5.00	30.00	-8.00	1.00
b_i	0.25	0.1	0.1	0.1	0.5

$$\dot{s}(t) = \sum_{i \in \{P,Q,R,S,T\}} a_i |\theta - \theta_i|_{2\pi} \exp\left[-\frac{\Delta\theta_i^2}{2b_i^2}\right] - s(t) \tag{1}$$

where $|\ |_{2\pi}$ denotes the "module 2π" operation $(a_i,\ b_i,\ \theta_i)$ are empirical parameters, whose values are summarized in Table 1, and θ is an angular dynamic parameter that influences the ECG deflections. McSharry et al. [5] have proposed to calculate the parameter by coupling (1) with:

$$\begin{cases} \dot{\chi} = \alpha\chi - \omega\gamma \\ \dot{\gamma} = \alpha\chi + \omega\gamma \end{cases} \tag{2}$$

where $\alpha = 1 - \sqrt{\chi^2 + \gamma^2}$ and ω is related to the heart rate. The θ parameter is obtained from (2) as $\theta = \arctan 2(\gamma, \chi)$. In other words, θ can be dynamically estimate by moving around the χ-γ limit trajectory (i.e. the unit radius cycle) with angular velocity ω. The model (1) could be also used to simulate heart diseases by changing a_i, b_i and θ_i; thus the model would become more complicated and less flexible. The proposed model is based on the parametrization of the χ-γ limit trajectory by modifying (2). So doing, the limit trajectory can be dynamically adapted and the PQRST complex can be controlled *beat by beat*. Thus, we propose to generalize the limit cycle with an elliptic trajectory, as shown in Fig. 2, by introducing a linear transformation and a rotation:

$$\begin{bmatrix} \hat{\chi} \\ \hat{\gamma} \end{bmatrix} = \begin{bmatrix} \cos\phi & \sin\phi \\ -\sin\phi & \cos\phi \end{bmatrix} \cdot \begin{bmatrix} k_1 & 0 \\ 0 & k_2 \end{bmatrix} \cdot \begin{bmatrix} \chi \\ \gamma \end{bmatrix} \tag{3}$$

the θ parameter is now obtained as $\arctan 2(\hat{\gamma}, \hat{\chi})$; note that for $k_1 = k_2 = 1$ and $\phi = 0$ (3) is equivalent to (2). This choice has two advantage: first the computation complexity of the model is almost unvaried and secondly we can characterize the distortion of the PQRST complex by the parameters k_1, k_2 and ϕ. In Fig. 3, we show an example of the ECG morphology alteration: continuous line is related to normal ECG and it is simulated by $k_1 = k_2 = 1$ and $\phi = 0$; while dotted and dashed lines (related to pathologic ECG signals) are obtained respectively by $k_1 = 1$, $k_2 = 0.7$, $\phi = 0$ and $k_1 = 1$, $k_2 = 0.7$, $\phi = \pi/2$ (or $k_1 = 0.7$, $k_2 = 1$, $\phi = 0$). Note that changes in QRS-complex length are typical of bradycardia and tachycardia; whereas the prolongation of PR-interval is typical of A-V block (for more details about ECG diagnosis see [1] pp. 320-335).

1.1. The exploited data

In order to use a "learning by sample" model, it is necessary to collect a suitable database able to be exploited during the so called training procedure of the heuristic system. Therefore, we produced a synthetic ECG database by means of the previously described model. It has been solved by a 4th order Runge-Kutta method [9] with a fixed time step

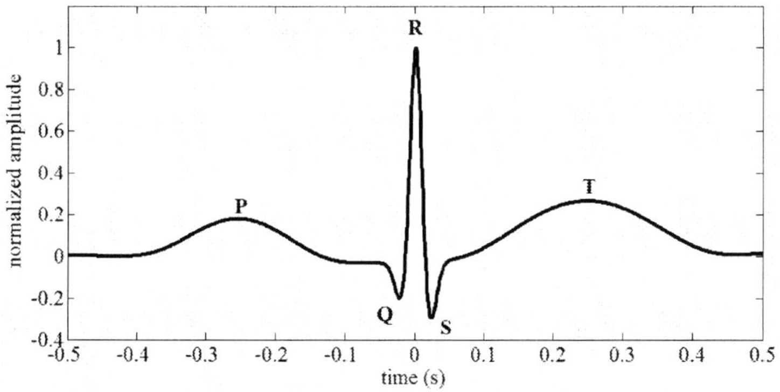

Figure 1. The normal ECG signal: morphology of PQRST-complex.

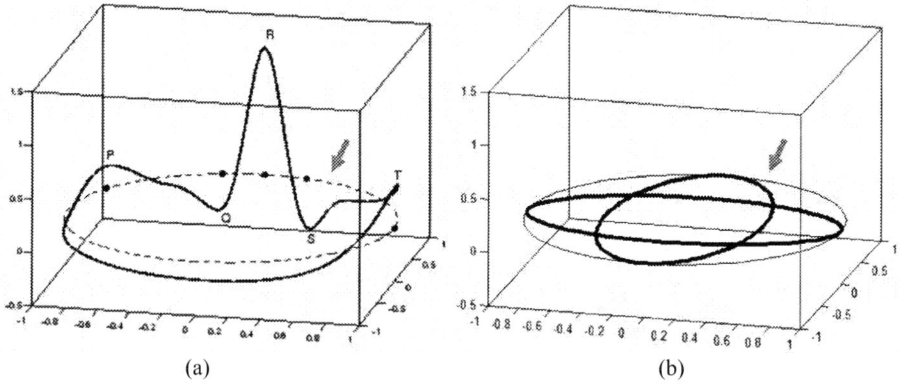

Figure 2. Typical trajectory generated by the dynamical model [3], the dashed line reflects the limit cycle while the small circles show the positions of the P, Q, R, S, and T events. (b) Generalization of the χ-γ limit trajectory.

$\Delta t = 1/f_s$, where f_s is the sampling frequency. According to the proposals of McSharry et al. [5], we calculated the time intervals between two consecutive heart beats (i.e., the RR-intervals), the amplitude, in terms of Volts, between the R- and S-peak within each heart beat (i.e., the RS-amplitudes), and the time interval, within each heart beat, between Q- and T-peak (i.e., the QT-intervals). All these features have been evaluated within an ECG synthetic recording, made of various heart beats, by varying the deformation parameters , i.e. $0.5 \leq k_1, k_2 \leq 1$ and the rotating angle, i.e. $\frac{-\pi}{2} \leq \phi \leq \frac{\pi}{2}$. Other parameters used within the model (1)-(3) are resumed by Table 2. The ranges used for k_1 and k_2 have been selected in order to avoid the generation of inconsistent ECGs. The collected database, composed by 750 patterns, has been used for the simulations described in the next section. It has been randomly split into two subsets, the training and testing subsets. The former is composed by the 80% of the synthesized patterns, whereas the latter is made by the remaining patterns. Therefore, the number of inputs (k_1, k_2 and ϕ) as well as of outputs (RR-intervals, RS-amplitudes, QT-intervals) of the learning machine are equal to 3. Concluding this section, let us explain the importance of the features taken into account.

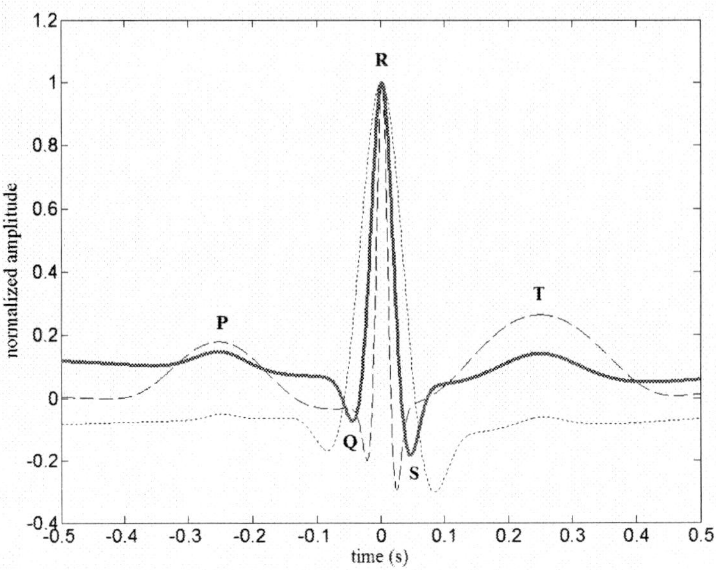

Figure 3. The synthesized ECG signals: continuous line is related to normal ECG ($k_1 = k_2 = 1, \phi = 0$), dotted ($k_1 = 1, k_2 = 0.7, \phi = 0$) and dashed ($k_1 = 1, k_2 = 0.7, \phi = \pi/2$ or $k_1 = 0.7, k_2 = 1, \phi = 0$) lines are related to pathological ECG.

Table 2. ECG parameters used for implementing and solving the ECG proposed model.

Parameter	Value
ECG sampling frequency	256
Approximate number of heart beats	256
Additive uniformly distributed measurement noise	0
Mean heart rate	80
Standard deviation of heart rate	1 beat per minute
Low frequency/High frequency (LF/HF) ratio	0.5
Internal sampling frequency	512 Hertz

RR-intervals. RR-intervals reveals important information about the physiological state of the subject. In fact, they characterize some particular heart disease, such as bradycardia or tachycardia. Within an ECG recording, the two main frequency bands of interest are referred to as the LF band [0.04, 0.15] Hz and the HF band [0.15, 0.4] Hz [5]. Sympathetic tone is believed to influence the LF component whereas both sympathetic and parasympathetic activity have an effect on the HF component [10]. The ratio of the power contained in the LF and HF components has been used as a measure of the sympathovagal balance [10]. In our paper, the LF/HF ratio is defined as the ratio of power between [0.015, 0.15] Hz and [0.15, 0.4] Hz in the RR tachogram [10].

RS-amplitudes. The largest-amplitude portion of the ECG, caused by currents generated when the ventricles depolarize prior to their contraction, is known as QRS-complex. The RS-amplitude measures the distance, in terms of voltages, of the second part of this complex, i.e., the end of ventricular depolarization. An increase in the RR-interval implies that the trajectory has more time to get pushed into the peak and trough

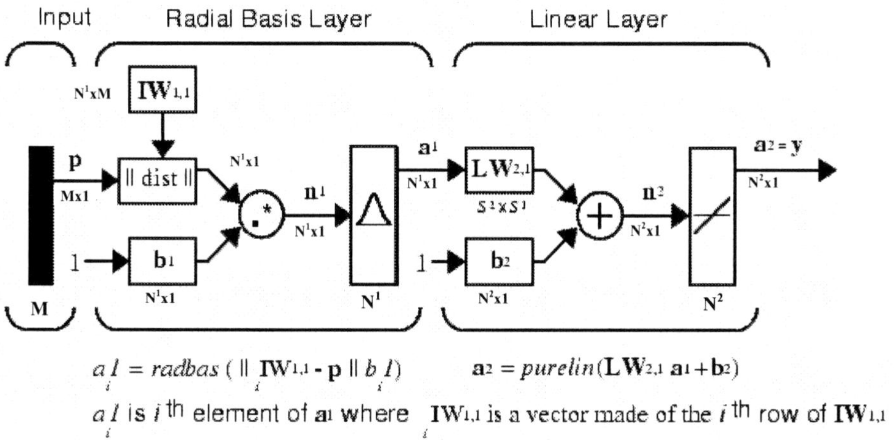

Figure 4. Schematic representation of a RBFANN.

given by the R and S events. This is reflected by a strong correlation between the RR-intervals and the RS-amplitude (please, see [5] for more details).

QT-intervals. It is the time between the onset of ventricular depolarization and the end of ventricular repolarization. Prolonged QT-interval may be associated with delayed ventricular repolarization which may cause ventricular tachyarrhythmias leading to sudden cardiac death [11].

2. RBFANN: theory and application in the case of study

Artificial Neural Networks are systems that "learn" something to carry out correctly, e.g., complicated, non-linear and multi-variable relations. Particularly, RBFANNs are able to solve function approximation problems. A RBFANN consists of 3 layers of nodes: besides input and output layers, RBFANN has a hidden layer, where Radial Basis Functions are applied on the input data [8]. A schematic representation of RBFANN is described by Fig. 4, where M represents the number of elements in input vector, N^1 and N^2 the number of neurons in layer 1 and 2, respectively. The activation function of N^1 neurons is a Radial Basis Function, whilst N^2 neurons has a linear activation function (namely, "radbas" and "purelin" in Fig. 4, respectively). The $\|dist\|$ box in Fig. 4 accepts the input vector $\mathbf{p}$ and input weight matrix $\mathbf{IW}_{1,1}$, and produces a vector having N^1 elements. The elements are the distances between the input vector and vectors ${}_i\mathbf{IW}_{1,1}$ formed from the rows of the input weight matrix. The net input to the "radbas" transfer function is the vector distance calculated by the $\|dist\|$ box, multiplied element-by-element by the bias b_1. Let us remark how the transfer function for a "radbas" neuron is $radbas(n) = e^{-n^2}$. The Radial Basis Function has a maximum of 1 when its input is 0. As the $\|dist\|$ result decreases, the output increases. Thus, a "radbas" neuron acts as a detector that produces 1 whenever the input $\mathbf{p}$ is identical to its weight vector. The bias b_1 allows the sensitivity of the "radbas" neuron to be adjusted. For example, if a neuron had a bias of 0.1 it would output 0.5 for any input vector $\mathbf{p}$ at vector distance of 8.326 $(0.8326/b)$ from its weight vector ${}_i\mathbf{IW}_{1,1}$. Therefore, each neuron's output is its net input passed through "radbas".

If a neuron's weight vector is equal to the input vector (transposed), its weighted input is 0, its net input is 0, and its output is 1. If a neuron's weight vector is a distance of spread from the input vector, its weighted input is spread, its net input is $\sqrt{-\log 0.5}$ (or 0.8326), therefore its output is 0.5. Thus, performance of RBFANN has to be evaluated by varying the spread factor Sp, representing a measure of the function smoothing: the larger the spread, the smoother the function approximation. But a too large spread can cause numerical problems. Thus, Sp should be large enough that the active input regions of the "radbas" neurons overlap enough, so that several "radbas" neurons always have fairly large outputs at any given moment. This makes the network function smoother and results in better generalization for new input vectors occurring between input vectors used in the design. However, Sp should not be so large that each neuron is effectively responding in the same large area of the input space. In our work, the algorithm sets the first-layer weights equal to the transpose of input matrix, and the first-layer biases are all set to $0.8326/Sp$, resulting in Radial Basis Functions that cross 0.5 at weighted inputs of $\pm Sp$. The second-layer weights $\mathbf{LW_{2,1}}$ and biases $\mathbf{b_2}$ are found by simulating the first-layer outputs $\mathbf{A_1}$ and then solving the following linear expression:

$$\left[\mathbf{LW_{2,1}}\ \mathbf{b_2}\right]\begin{bmatrix}\mathbf{A_1}\\ \mathbf{I}\end{bmatrix} = \mathbf{T} \tag{4}$$

where $\mathbf{I}$ and $\mathbf{T}$ are the identity and the output matrix, respectively. RBFANN performances, i.e. the closeness of the estimated features to the observed ones, have been evaluated by varying the spread value, in terms of the Root Mean Squared Error (RMSE):

$$RMSE = \sqrt{\frac{1}{l}\sum_{i=1}^{l}\left(x_i - \tilde{x}_i\right)^2} \tag{5}$$

where $\tilde{x}$ represents the predicted feature, and l is equal to the number of testing patterns. The trend of RMSEs as functions of Sp were considered by varying Sp between 0.25 and 20, with a 0.25 numerical step. Obviously, as Fig. 5 depicts, we obtained a RMSE trend for each one of the considered features. In order to select a value for Sp which can be useful for all the features, we had to carry out a trade-off between the complexity of the network and the same performances. Therefore, the selected value for Sp is 0.75. The time elapsed for this kind of evaluation was 52min 43sec on an AMD Athlon XP 3000+ with 2 GB of RAM (OS: Windows XP, Matlab R2007b). In this way, a 30-hidden-neurons RBFANN has been trained by using the training subset, with a training elapsed time equal to 1.353sec. Besides RMSE, performances have been quantitatively evaluated even considering the Willmott's Index of Agreement (WIA), the Root Relative Squared Error (RRSE), the Mean Absolute Error (MAE) and the Relative Absolute Error (RAE):

$$WIA = 1 - \frac{\sum_{i=1}^{l}\left(x_i - \tilde{x}_i\right)^2}{\sum_{i=1}^{l}\left(|x_i - \bar{x}| + |\tilde{x}_i - \bar{x}|\right)^2} \quad RRSE = \sqrt{\frac{\sum_{i=1}^{l}\left(\tilde{x}_i - x_i\right)^2}{\sum_{i=1}^{l}\left(x_i - \bar{x}\right)^2}} \tag{6}$$

$$MAE = \frac{\sum_{i=1}^{l}|\tilde{x}_i - x_i|}{l}; \quad RAE = \frac{\sum_{i=1}^{l}|\tilde{x}_i - x_i|}{\sum_{i=1}^{l}|x_i - \bar{x}|}$$

where $\bar{x}$ is the average value of observed sequence. WIA values are included between 0 and 1: the closer to 1 the WIA, the closer the predicted sequence is to actual values, and

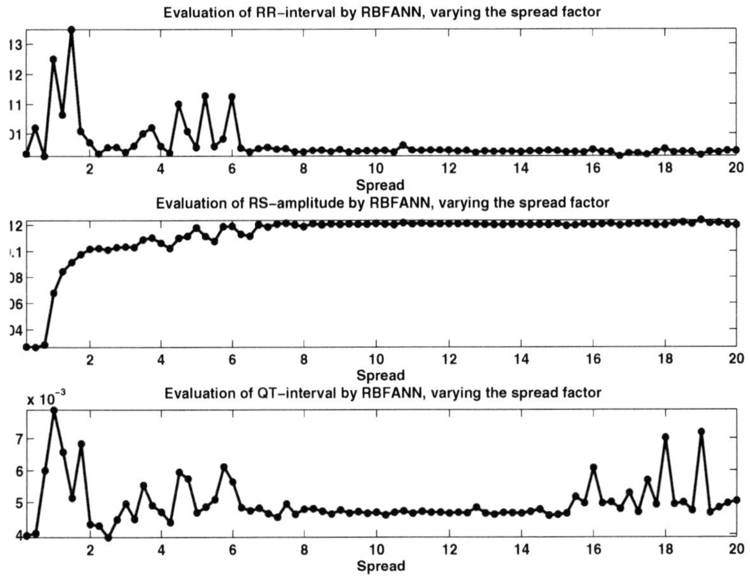

Figure 5. Evaluation of RBFANN RMSE as a function of the spread factor in estimating RR- and QT-intervals, and RS-amplitudes.

Table 3. Evaluation of RBFANN performances by using statistical quantifiers.

	RMSE	RRSE	MAE	RAE	WIA
RR-intervals	0.003	0.32	0.003	0.36	0.977
RS-amplitudes	0.035	0.217	0.022	0.184	0.987
QT-intervals	0.006	0.319	0.004	0.314	0.974

then the greater the robustness of the estimator. Moreover, let us denote how the other quality indicators range from 0 to infinity, with 0 corresponding to the perfect fit. The obtained performances are resumed by Table 3 and Fig. 6.

3. Discussion about results and conclusions

Since their introduction into the scientific environment, RBFANNs have been largely used as a Computational Intelligence technique able to solve complex regression problems. Nowadays, the extensive usage of this kinds of techniques allows to solve complex estimation problems, such as those involving the solution of differential equation systems. In this paper, the RBFANNs' performances have been evaluated within the context of a biomedical problem, i.e. the estimation of particular features characterizing ECG recordings. They can be medically related to heart diseases, and therefore their estimation could be very useful in order to synthesize pathological ECGs, starting from a self-modified dynamic model. Synthetic EGCs can, in their turn, be employed to assess biomedical signal processing techniques which are used to compute clinical statistics from the ECG itself. Obtained results demonstrated that the proposed heuristic technique

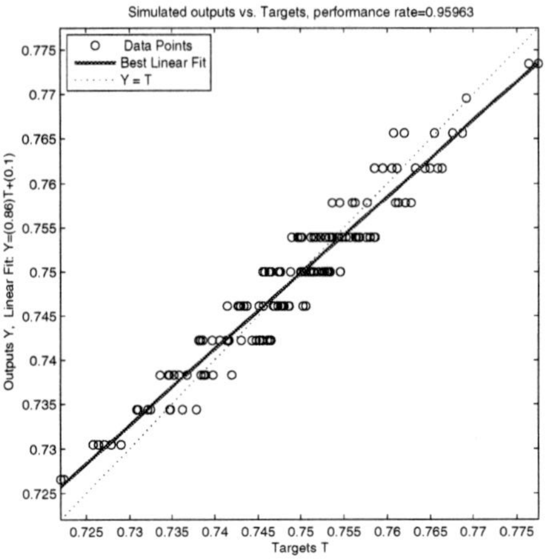

(a) RR-intervals

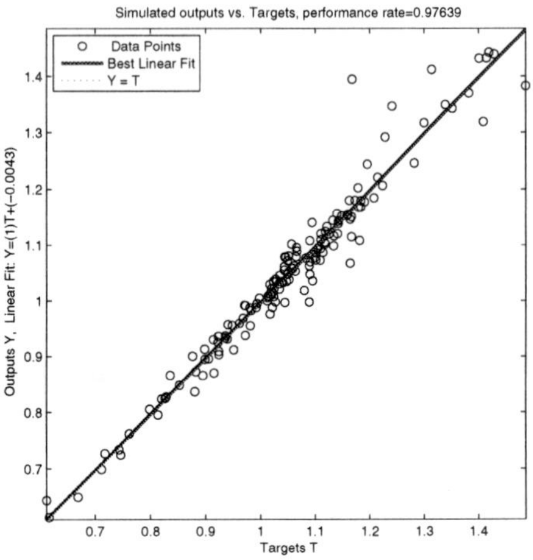

(b) RS-amplitudes

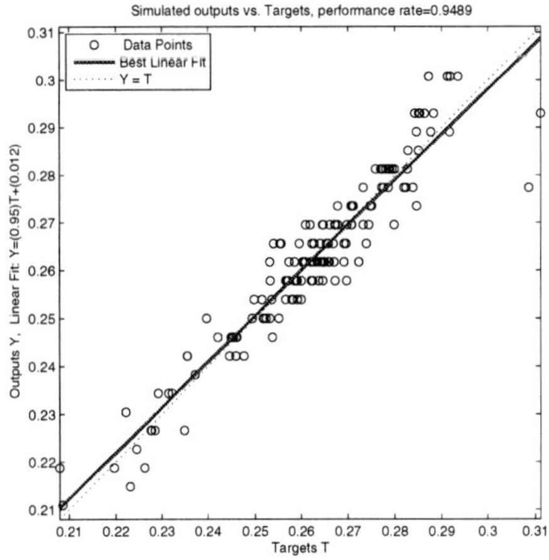

(c) QT-intervals

Figure 6. Post-processing regression for the considered ECG features, in order to graphically evaluate the RBFANN performances.

for estimating ECG's feature was really reliable. It can be used in order to retain useful k_1, k_2 and ϕ values, according to the in-study disease, able to modify the dynamic model composed by Equations (1)-(2) in order to obtain pathological ECG acting in the state domain.

References

[1] J.A. Malmivuo and R. Plonsey (Eds.), Bioelectromagnetism, Principles and Applications of Bioelectric and Biomagnetic Fields, Oxford University Press, New York, pp. 119–146, 277–289, 320–335, 1995.

[2] O. Dössel, Inverse problem of electro- and magnetocardiography: review and recent progress, *International Journal of Bioelectromagnetism* **2**(2) (2000).

[3] A. van Oosterom, Beyond the dipole; modeling the genesis of the electrocardiogram, *100 Years Einthoven* (2002), 7–15.

[4] G.D. Clifford, F. Azuaje, P. McSharry, *Advanced Methods and Tools for ECG Data Analysis*, Artech House Publishers, London, UK, 2006.

[5] P.E. McSharry, G.D. Clifford, L. Tarassenko, L.A. Smith, A dynamical model for generating synthetic electrocardiogram signals, *IEEE Transactions on Biomedical Engineering* **50**(3) (2003), 289–294.

[6] R. Sameni, G.D. Clifford, C. Jutten, M.B. Shamsollahi, Multichannel ECG and Noise Modeling: Application to Maternal and Fetal ECG Signals, *EURASIP Journal on Advances in Signal Processing*, article ID 43407 (2007), 14 pages.

[7] The PTB Diagnostic ECG Database, `http://www.physionet.org/physiobank/database/ptbdb/`.

[8] S. Chen, C.F.N. Cowan, P.M. Grant, Ortogonal Least Squares Learning Algorithm for Radial Basis Function Network, *IEEE Transaction on Neural Networks* **2**(2) (1991), 302–309.

[9] J. Lambert, *Numerical Methods for Ordinary Differential Systems*, John Wiley and Sons, Chichester, NY, 1991.

[10] M. Malik, A.J. Camm, *Heart Rate Variability*, Futura, Armonk, NY, 1995.

[11] P.J. Schwartz, S. Wolf, Q-T interval as predictor of sudden death in patients with myocardial infarction, *Circulation* **57** (1978), 1074–1077.

New Directions in Neural Networks
B. Apolloni et al. (Eds.)
IOS Press, 2009

doi:10.3233/978-1-58603-984-4-50

Multiresolution Minimization of Renyi's Mutual Information for fetal-ECG Extraction

Fabio LA FORESTA [a,1], Nadia MAMMONE, [a] Giuseppina INUSO, [a] Francesco C. MORABITO, [a] and Andrea AZZERBONI [b]

[a] *DIMET - "Mediterranea" University of Reggio Calabria, ITALY*

[b] *Department of Gynecological, Obstetrics Sciences, and Reproductive Medicine, University of Messina, ITALY*

Abstract. Fetal electrocardiogram (fECG) monitoring yields important information about the fetus condition during pregnancy and it consists in collecting electrical signals by some sensors on the body of the mother. In literature, Independent Component Analysis (ICA) has been exploited to extract fECG. Wavelet-ICA (WICA), a technique that merges Wavelet decomposition and INFOMAX algorithm for Independent Component Analysis, was recently proposed to enhance fetal ECG extraction. In this paper, we propose to enhance WICA introducing MERMAID as the algorithm to perform independent component analysis because it has shown to outperform INFOMAX and the other standard ICA algorithms.

Keywords. Fetal electrocardiogram, Independent Component Analysis, Wavelet Transform.

Introduction

The fetus heart can be monitored by invasive and non-invasive techniques: hopefully, non-invasive monitoring techniques will become more and more reliable for prenatal diagnosis. Fetal ECG monitoring consists in collecting electrical signals, generated by the fetal heart, by some sensors properly held on the body of the mother. Despite its limitations, the fetal heart rate (FHR) tracing analysis is the best monitor of the fetal wellbeing during labour and fECG shape monitoring could show cardiac pathologies. Unfortunately, the exact shape of fECG is not detectable and the fetal heartbeat signal yielded by this recording technique is quite weaker than the mother's heartbeat signal, also due to the attenuation during the propagation through tissues; moreover, many other signals overlap to the two heartbeats: artifacts such as breathing, uterine contractions, diaphragm, electrical line noise, etc. Because of the low amplitude and the poor SNR, the fECG is hopelessly contaminated by the artifacts, therefore it is quite difficult to extract its shape.

[1]Corresponding Author: Fabio La Foresta, DIMET - *Mediterranea* University of Reggio Calabria, Via Graziella Feo di Vito, I-89122 Reggio Calabria, ITALY; E-mail: fabio.laforesta@unirc.it.

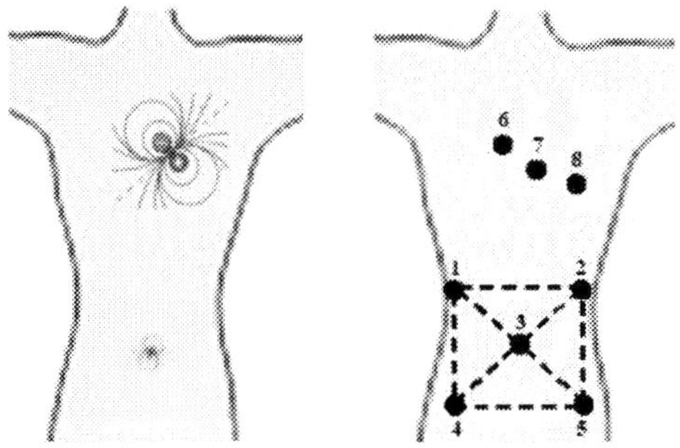

Figure 1. The heart is equivalent to a electric dipole and it can be described by a vector whose parameters change during the cardiac activation. A simple model results from assuming that the cardiac source is represented by a dipole located at the center of a sphere representing the torso, hence at the center of the equilateral triangle (the Einthoven triangle). In case of pregnant woman, two dipoles can be hypothesized.

Fetal ECG extraction is a typical blind source separation (BSS) problem and the first application of BSS techniques to fECG extraction was done by De Lathauwer et al. [6]. It is well accepted that Independent Component Analysis (ICA) is a suitable tool for separating the fECG "source" from the rest; some different ICA based procedures has been exploited so far: ICA estimated by INFOMAX algorithm [3], ICA by JADE algorithm and a Wavelet-postprocessing consisting in baseline removal and denoising [8], Singular Value Decomposition (SVD) and ICA by FastICA algorithm [9] (applied to a single channel recording), ICA by MERMAID algorithm [11], a sensor array and electrode selection algorithm for fECG extraction by ICA proposed by F. Vrins et al. [10]. Here we propose to optimize the Wavelet-Independent Component Analysis (WICA) method [7] through MERMAID algorithm, in order to improve the reliability of fECG extraction.

The paper is organized as follows: Section 1 will address Wavelet-Independent Component Analysis and in particular MERMAID algorithm, Section 2 will introduce the application to fetal-Electrocardiogram (fECG) and Section 3 will report the conclusions.

1. Wavelet-ICA for fECG extraction

1.1. Limitations of ICA in fECG extraction

It is widely accepted that fetal ECG signal is statistically independent from the rest of the signals involved in ECG recording (mother ECG, breathing, contractions, etc.): this is why ICA has been proposed in literature for fECG extraction.

ICA is usually able to concentrate fECG information in a single component, however, this component carries non-fetal information as well, thus fECG shape could be overwhelmed by other signals in a large extent.

Moreover, ICA performance depends on the size of the dataset (number of samples): the larger the processed dataset, the higher the probability that the effective number of sources will overcome the number of channels (*overcomplete ICA*), because the number of channels is fixed over time, but the number of contributions from different non-fetal sources is likely to increase with the length of the recording. In this case redundancy is not sufficient to estimate the sources and an independent component might account for

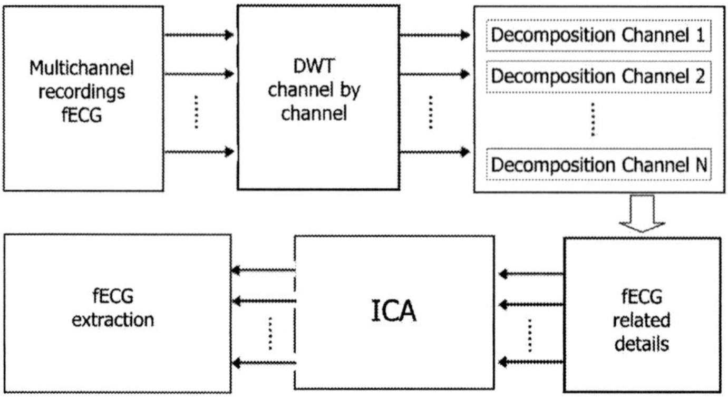

Figure 2. WICA block scheme.

more than one contribution, in other words, the algorithm might not be able to separate fECG signal from the rest. On the contrary, the smaller the number of samples, the more difficult the estimation of the parameters, and thus the performance of ICA suffers. The best choice is a trade-off between a small dataset and a high performance. In order to overcome this limitation, the proposed methodology includes a step prior to ICA that increases the redundancy of the dataset, thanks to wavelet decomposition, bypassing the possible problem of overcomplete ICA.

1.2. WICA methodology

Suppose to detect fECG in one channel and to decompose the channel into a certain number of wavelet components (WCs), if the spectral content of the fECG signal is not strictly concentrated in one of the levels of the decomposition, applying ICA to these WCs we will take advantage of the increased redundancy, because the event that was visible in one signal (the original channel) is now visible in more that one signal (the wavelet components). In case the spectral content of the fECG signal is concentrated only in a certain level of the wavelet decomposition, ICA could focus on the same level wavelet components, working much better than processing the entire dataset that includes also frequencies not involved in fECG signal.

The block diagram of WICA for fECG extraction is depicted in Figure 2: the first stage is a wavelet decomposition that splits each channel until breathing activity is isolated in the approximation (in this paper, the band of the signal was 0-128Hz and the decomposition was stopped the sixth level, because breathing and other very low frequency activity were isolated in the 0-2Hz wavelet component), this way, Wavelet Transform projects the data into a n-dimensional space where ICA is performed. The basis of this new space consists in the scaling function and the wavelet functions, where n-1 is the number of *levels* of the decomposition, and the scaling and wavelet functions depend on the chosen *wavelet family*. Once the raw data have been so projected into the n-dimensional space, if fetal beat was detectable in a certain WC, every WC belonging to the same decomposition level was selected for the new dataset to be passed through ICA. In the following, we will provide details about the wavelet decomposition and MERMAID algorithm.

1.2.1. Wavelet Decomposition.

The wavelet expansion relative to the *wavelet mother* $\psi(t)$ and the *scaling function* $\varphi(t)$ of a signal $x(t)$ has the following expression [4]:

$$x(t) = \sum_{k} c_{j_0 k}\varphi_{j_0 k}(t) + \sum_{j=j_0}\sum_{k} d_{jk}\psi_{jk}(t) \tag{1}$$

where j_0 is an arbitrary starting scale. The first term in (1) is the *approximation* at scale j_0 and the second term represents the sum of the *details*.

The approximation coefficients $c_{j_0 k}$ have the expression:

$$c_{j_0 k} = \int x(t)\varphi^*_{j_0 k}(t)dt \tag{2}$$

and

$$\varphi_{j_0 k} = \frac{1}{\sqrt{2^{j_0}}}\varphi\Big(\frac{t - k2^{j_0}}{2^{j_0}}\Big) \tag{3}$$

are called *scaling functions*. The details coefficients are defined by the equation:

$$d_{jk} = \int x(t)\psi^*_{jk}(t)dt \tag{4}$$

and

$$\psi_{jk} = \frac{1}{\sqrt{2^j}}\psi\Big(\frac{t - k2^j}{2^j}\Big) \tag{5}$$

are called *wavelet functions*. In this paper *Biorthogonal* family is adopted due to its similarity to ECG shape [4].

1.2.2. MERMAID algorithm for ICA.

Suppose that two independent sources s_1 and s_2 are mixed through the matrix A and that the observed mixtures z_1 and z_2 are so generated. ICA is a computational method for separating a multivariate signal into additive subcomponents, assuming the mutual statistical independence of the source signals. ICA consists in two steps: whitening and rotation. Therefore, in order to perform ICA, the observed data $\mathbf{z}$ will be whitened, producing the signals $\mathbf{x}$, then $\mathbf{x}$ will be rotated to give the estimated sources $\mathbf{y}$.

If we have an observed vector $\mathbf{z}$ that results from the mixing of N sources (source vector $\mathbf{s}$ with N components), if $\mathbf{x}$ is the whitened version of $\mathbf{z}$, the relationship between $\mathbf{x}$ and $\mathbf{z}$ is $\mathbf{x} = \mathbf{W}^T\mathbf{z}$, where $\mathbf{W}$ is the whitening transform that has the following expression:

$$W = \Phi\Lambda^{-1/2} \tag{6}$$

where Φ is the matrix of the eigenvectors of the autocorrelation matrix of $\mathbf{z}$ and Λ is the corresponding matrix of the eigenvalues.

The elements of **y** represent the estimated independent components, they depend on whitening and on the rotation matrix $R(\Theta)$ through the expression:

$$\mathbf{y} = R(\Theta)\mathbf{x} \tag{7}$$

According to [2] the only adaptive part is the rotation matrix $R(\Theta)$, where Θ is a $N(N-1)/2$x1 vector, whose elements Θ_{ij} are the rotation angles between each pair of estimated sources y_i and y_j. For each pair of sources, therefore for each separation angle Θ_{ij}, a Givens rotation matrix R_{ij} is defined as follows: it is a $(N\text{x}N)$ identity matrix whose (i,i), (i,j), (j,i) and (j,j) elements are replaced by $R_{ij}(i,i) = cos\theta_{ij}$, $R_{ij}(i,j) = -sin\theta_{ij}$, $R_{ij}(j,i) = sin\theta_{ij}$ and $R_{ij}(j,j) = cos\theta_{ij}$ respectively, where $i = \{1, 2, ..., N\}$ and $j = \{i+1, ..., N\}$. The rotation matrix R is the product of the rotations matrices Rij :

$$R(\Theta) = \prod_{i=1}^{N-1} \prod_{j=i+1}^{N} R_{ij}(\theta_{ij}) \tag{8}$$

While adapting the rotation matrix $R(\Theta)$ we adapt the estimated independent components **y**, according to (7). The α-order Renyi's mutual information for *n* random variables $y_1, ..., y_n$ is defined as:

$$I_{R_\alpha(y)} = \frac{1}{\alpha-1} log \int_{-\infty}^{+\infty} \frac{f_Y^\alpha(y)}{\prod_{i=1}^{N-1} f_{Y_i}(y_i)^{\alpha-1}} dy \tag{9}$$

where α is a free parameter, $f_Y(y)$ is the joint probability density function (pdf) of y and $f_{Y_i}(y_i)$ is the marginal pdf of y_i. It is non-negative and it is equal to zero only if the random variables are independent, that is if the joint pdf is equal to the product of the marginal pdf's. The α-order Renyi's entropy of a random variable *y* has the following expression:

$$H_{R_\alpha}(y) = \frac{1}{1-\alpha} \log \int_{-\infty}^{+\infty} f_Y^\alpha(y) dy = \frac{1}{1-\alpha} log E[f^{\alpha-1}(y)] \tag{10}$$

it is worth to point out that, in order to transform the first member of (10) into the second one, there was no need of any approximation because it was enough to use the definition of expected value. The relationship between the joint Renyi's entropy and the sum of the Renyi's marginal entropies of a random vector **y** is:

$$\sum_{i=1}^{n} H_{R_\alpha}(y_i) - H_{R_\alpha}(\mathbf{y}) = \frac{1}{\alpha-1} \log\{\frac{\int_{-\infty}^{+\infty} f_Y^\alpha(\mathbf{y})d\mathbf{y}}{\int_{-\infty}^{+\infty} \prod_{i=1}^{N-1} f_{Y_i}^\alpha(y_i)dy}\} \tag{11}$$

the right-hand member of the Equation (11) does not exactly coincide with the Renyi's mutual information (9), but it is also minimized if and only if the joint pdf of the variable **y** is equal to the product of the marginal pdf's, therefore if and only if y_i are statistically independent. Since the joint entropy is invariant to rotations, we can discard it in the cost function, if it was not possible to discard the joint entropy we should have to keep in mind that computing a N-dimensional pdf requires a number of data samples which increases exponentially with N. We can minimize the mutual information while minimizing the first term in the left-hand member of the Equation (11) and the cost function is reduced to [2]:

$$J = \sum_{i=1}^{n} H_{R_\alpha}(y_i) \tag{12}$$

The pdf's are estimated by the Parzen windowing method:

$$f_{Y_i}(y_i) = \frac{1}{N}\sum_{i=1}^{n} k_\sigma(y - y_i) \tag{13}$$

where k_σ is the kernel function, N is the number of samples. We chose a Gaussian kernel (G) with zero mean and variance σ^2, with $\sigma = 0.25$, according to [2], and we set $\alpha = 2$ (Renyi's quadratic entropy). When we substitute the estimated pdf (13) in (10):

$$H_{R_{\alpha_2}}(y_i) = -log\frac{1}{N^2}\sum_{j=1}^{n}\sum_{k=1}^{n} G(y_i(j) - y_i(k), 2\sigma^2) \tag{14}$$

If we substitute (14) into (12), the cost function J is detailed for quadratic Renyi's entropy (sub-gaussian and super-gaussian sources would be equally emphasized) and for the Gaussian kernel (in general, the optimal kernel function is a function of the source distributions but this relationship is still unknown, however, some experimental test demonstrated that Gaussian kernel ensures better performances [2]). It is worth emphasizing that, thanks to Parzen windowing and kernel approximation, no apriori assumption is made about the pdf of the data, the distribution is learnt *directly from samples*.

Once we have substituted (14) in (12), by taking the derivative of (12) with respect to θ_{ij} we obtain the learning rule. Moreover, introducing the MERMAID-SIG (Minimum Renyi's Mutual Information-Stochastic Information Gradient) modification [2], the complexity is reduced whereas the performance is not affected, the learning rule of the neural network will have the following expression:

$$\Delta\theta_{ij} = -\sum_{k=1}^{N} \frac{\sum_{n=1}^{L} G(y_k(n) - y_k(n-1), 2\sigma^2)(y_k(n) - y_k(n-1))(\nabla \mathbf{R}_{ij})_k^T(\mathbf{x}(n) - \mathbf{x}(n-1))}{\sum_{n=1}^{L} G(y_k(n) - y_k(n-1), 2\sigma^2)} \tag{15}$$

where $y_k(n)$ is the $k-th$ estimated source at time n, $\mathbf{x}(n)$ is the (N x 1) whitened observation at time n, L is the width of the Parzen window and $\nabla \mathbf{R}_{ij})_k^T$ is the transposed k-th column of $\nabla \mathbf{R}_{ij})$.

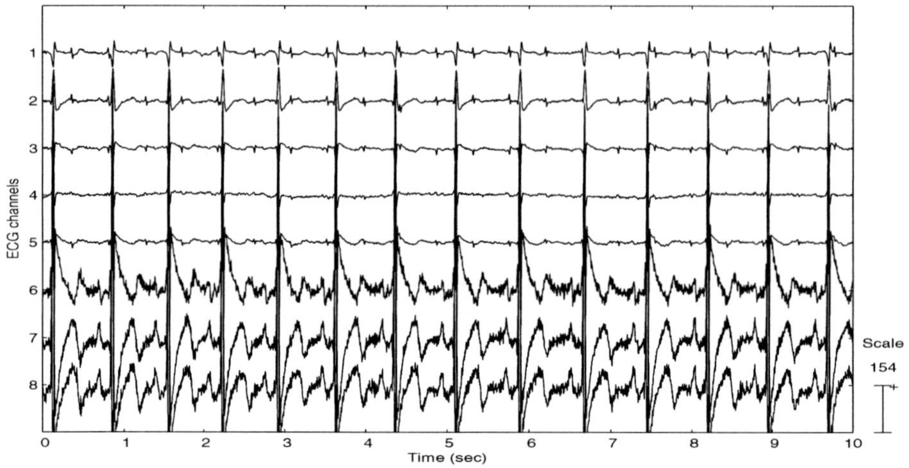

Figure 3. Multichannel ECG recordings collected simultaneously by 8 sensors placed on the mother abdomen (channels 1-5) and thorax (channels 6-8), the data were sampled at 250Hz.

The weights are updated every L samples and the update equation is:

$$\Theta(n+1) = \Theta(n) - \eta\Delta\Theta(n) \tag{16}$$

where η is the learning rate and $\Delta\Theta$ is the vector whose elements are $\Delta\Theta_{ij}$.

2. Fetal Electrocardiogram extraction

2.1. Data description

The data (Figure 3) consist in multichannel ECG recordings collected simultaneously by 8 sensors placed on the mother abdomen (channels 1-5) and thorax (channels 6-8), the data were sampled at 256Hz and are from the Database for the Identification of Systems (for more details see De Moor B.L.R. (ed.), DaISy: Database for the Identification of Systems, Department of Electrical Engineering, ESAT/SISTA, K.U.Leuven, Belgium). The recordings are shown in Fig. 2, the maternal ECG (mECG) is clearly visible, whereas the fECG is barely visible because mECG and artifacts (mother breathing, noise, contractions, etc.) overwhelm it. Therefore, the collected data are an unknown mixing of the electromagnetic fields generated by the two heart dipoles and other artifactual sources.

2.2. fECG extraction

The dataset described in 2.1 was first processed by MERMAID only (Method-1), implemented as described in Section 1.2.2. The same dataset was also processed by W-ICA, where ICA was carried out by INFOMAX (in the following named Method-2) and by Wavelet-ICA, where ICA was carried out by MERMAID (in the following named Method-3).

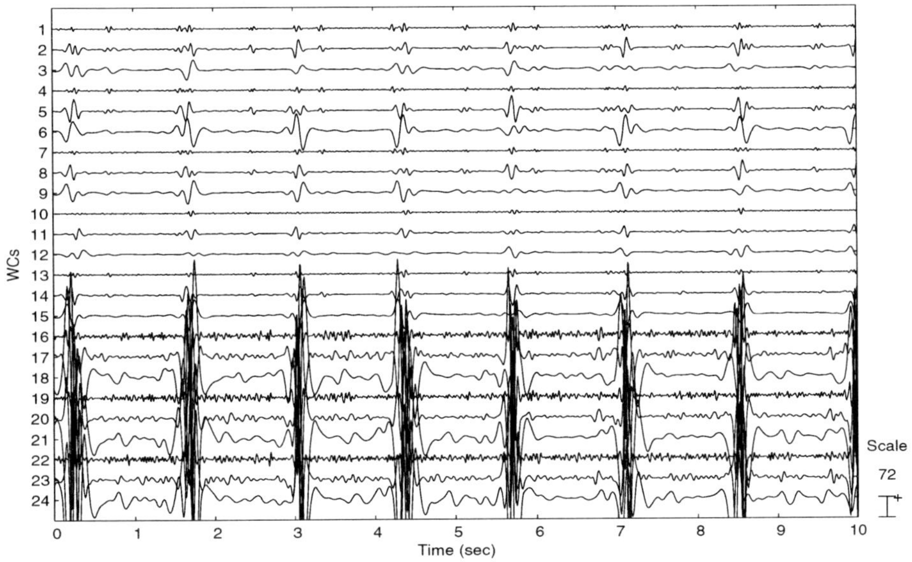

Figure 4. The wavelet components selected for ICA processing.

Method-1 consists in applying MERMAID directly to the 8-channels ECG dataset. Method-2 and Method-3 included wavelet decomposition, prior to ICA, as detailed in Section 1.2.

The number of levels was set at 6 because the frequency band of fECG signal was $0 - 128Hz$ and, splitting it 6 times, we could obtain an approximation whose frequency band was approximately $0 - 2Hz$ and isolated the breathing artifact that was not selected for ICA processing, as well as the WCs accounting for high frequency noise. Figure 4 shows the wavelet components selected for ICA, that is the WCs associated to the levels where fECG was detectable.

Figure 5.a shows the fECG extracted by Method-1 (fECG-1), whereas Figure 5.b and 5.c show the fECG extracted by Method-2 (fECG-2) and by Method-3 (fECG-3). We can point out that Method-3 seems to work better than either MERMAID and WICA with INFOMAX, in fact, fECG-3 is not affected by breathing artifact, as fECG-1 is, and it its shape is more ECG like than fECG-2 is.

3. Conclusions

In this paper the issue of fetal electrocardiogram (fECG) extraction for fetal health monitoring during pregnancy was addressed. Fetal ECG can be considered independent from maternal ECG and from every other bio-electromagnetic source that generate fields that propagate through the tissue and that are collected at the surface of the mother abdomen together with fECG itself. Therefore, in literature, Independent Component Analysis (ICA) has been exploited to extract fECG. Wavelet-ICA (WICA), a technique that merges Wavelet decomposition and INFOMAX algorithm for Independent Component Analysis, was proposed by the authors to enhance fetal ECG extraction. In this paper, we propose to empower WICA performing ICA by MERMAID algorithm, that showed

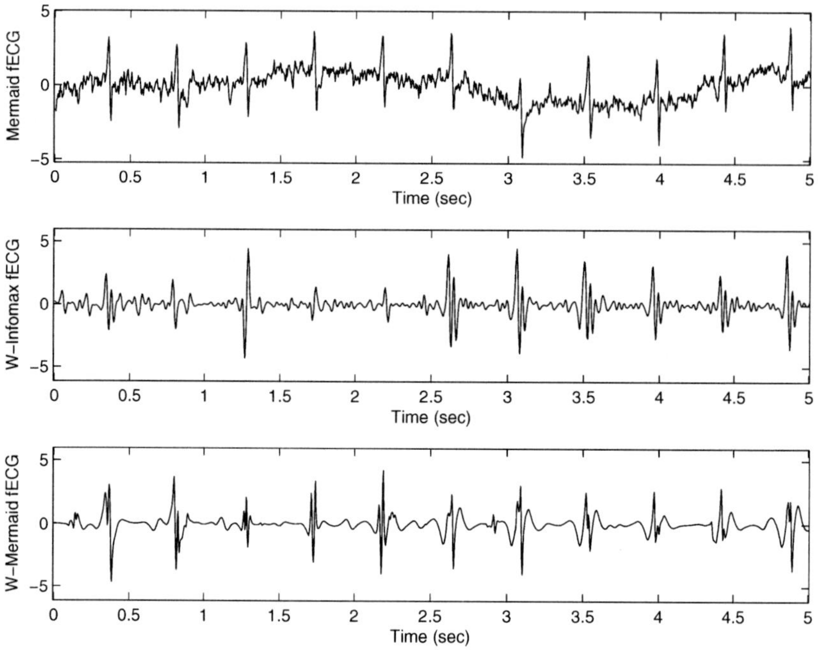

Figure 5. Fetal ECG extracted by: MERMAID, W-ICA whre ICA is performed by INFOMAX and W-ICA where ICA is performed by MERMAID.

to outperform INFOMAX and other well known ICA algorithms. Thus wavelet decomposition, exploited not as a mere pre- or post-processing tool, but as an integral part of the separation process, projects the dataset into a higher dimensional space where MERMAID works. An 8-channels fECG recording was analysed and Wavelet-MERMAID technique showed the best performance. In the future, a realistic fECG model will be built and WICA will be optimized in order to ensure the best fetal ECG shape extraction.

References

[1] T.P. Jung, S. Makeig, T.W. Lee, M.J. McKeown, G. Brown, A.J. Bell, T.J. Sejnowski, Independent Component Analysis of Biomedical Signals, *The 2nd International Workshop on Independent Component Analysis and Signal Separation*, (2000), 633–644.

[2] Erdogmus D., Hild K. E. II, Principe J. C. Blind source separation using Renyi's marginal entropies. *Neurocomputing* **49**, (2002), 25–38.

[3] T.W. Lee, M. Girolami, T.J. Sejnowski, Independent Component Analysis using an extended infomax algorithm for mixed sub-Gaussian and super-Gaussian sources, *Neural Computation*, **11(2)**, (1999),606–633.

[4] Daubechies I., Ten Lectures on Wavelets, *Society for Industrial and Applied Mathematics* (1992).

[5] K.G. Rosén, I. Amer-Wahlin, R. Luzietti, H. Norén, Fetal ECG waveform analysis, *Best Practice & Research Clinical Obstetrics and Gynaecology* **18(3)**, (2004), 485–514.

[6] L. De Lathauwer, B. De Moor, J. Vandevalle, 'Fetal electrocardiogram extraction by blind source subspace separation, *IEEE Trans. Biomedical Engineering*, **47(5)**, (2000), 567–572.

[7] B. Azzerboni, F. La Foresta, N. Mammone, F.C. Morabito, A New Approach Based on Wavelet-ICA Algorithms for Fetal Electrocardiogram Extraction, *Proceedings of The 13th European Symposium on Artificial Neural Networks* (ESANN 2005), 193-198, Bruges, Belgium, April 27–29, 2005.

[8] V. Vigneron, A. Paraschiv-Ionescu, A. Azancot, O. Sibony, C. Jutten, Fetal Electrocardiogram Extraction Based On Non-Stationary ICA And Wavelet Denoising, *ISSPA 2003*.

[9] P. Gao, E.C. Chang, L. Wyse, Blind Separation of fetal ECG from single mixture using SVD and ICA, ICICS-PCM 2003.

[10] F. Vrins, C. Jutten, M. Verleysen, Sensors Array and Electrode Selection for Non-Invasive Fetal Electrocardiogram Extraction by Independent Component Analysis, *LNCS* **3195**, (2004), 1017–1024.

[11] D.E. Marossero, D. Erdogmus, N.R. Euliano, J.C. Principe, K.E. Hild II, Independent Components Analysis For Fetal Electrocardiogram Extraction: A Case For The Data Efficient Mermaid Algorithm, *The 2003 IEEE International Workshop on Neural Networks for Signal Processing*, IWNNSP 2003.

[12] B. Azzerboni, G. Finocchio, M. Ipsale, F. La Foresta, F.C. Morabito, A New Approach to Detection of Muscle Activation by Independent Component Analysis and Wavelet Transform, *LNCS* **2486**, (2002), 109–116.

[13] B. Azzerboni, M. Carpentieri, F. La Foresta, F.C.Morabito, Neural-ICA and Wavelet Transform for Artifacts Removal in surface EMG, *The 2004 International Joint Conference on Neural Networks*, (IJCNN 2004), 3223–3228.

New Directions in Neural Networks
B. Apolloni et al. (Eds.)
IOS Press, 2009

doi:10.3233/978-1-58603-984-4-60

Classification of DNA microarray data with Random Projection Ensembles of Polynomial SVMs

Alberto BERTONI [a], Raffaella FOLGIERI [a] Giorgio VALENTINI [a]
[a] *DSI - Dip. Scienze dell' Informazione, Università degli Studi di Milano, Italy*
e-mail: {bertoni,folgieri,valentini}@dsi.unimi.it

Abstract. In this paper we propose and experimentally analyze ensemble methods based on random projections (as feature extraction method) and SVM with polynomial kernels (as learning algorithm). We show that, under suitable conditions, polynomial kernels are approximately preserved by random projections, with a degradation related to the square of the degree of the polynomial. Experimental results with Random Subspace and Random Projection ensembles of polynomial SVMs, support the hypothesis the low degree polynomial kernels, introducing with high probability lower distortions in the projected data, are better suited to the classification of high dimensional DNA microarray data.

Keywords. supervised ensembles, Johnson-Lindenstrauss lemma, DNA microarrays, polynomial kernels

1. Introduction

The exploration of methods to solve classification problems characterized by high dimensionality and low cardinality of data is a task particularly important in class prediction with microarray data. A typical problem in gene expression data is the so called 'curse of dimensionality' [2]: data set are composed by a small number of classified examples of large dimension. Machine learning algorithms and particularly SVMs [6] [1] [5] [8] represent the state-of-the-art in gene expression data analysis. Other methods have been used, such as Bagging and Boosting [22] and feature selection or extraction methods (see Golub [12]), or feature subsampling proposed by T. K. Ho [11].

In the paper we propose Random Projection ensemble of SVMs, with the aim to improve the accuracy of classification.

We can summarize our approach as follows:

1. we perturb data by random projections
2. we apply a learning algorithm on this data (in our case SVMs with linear, gaussian and polynomial kernels)
3. finally we use the majority voting technique to obtain the 'consensus' classifier.

The objectives of this work are twofold. First of all, we compare ensemble methods based on Random Projections with the classical Random Subspace approach. Random Subspace, originally proposed by Ho [11], is a technique related to feature subsampling. This technique has some analogy with Random Projection; nevertheless, there are important differences. For instance, Random Subspace does not verify the Johnson-Lindenstrauss lemma [21].

The second objective of this work consists in exploring whether a L_2 norm preserving technique based on random projections can work even with algorithms that use kernels as similarity measures. In particular we consider the dependence of the distortion induced by random projections from the degree of the polynomial kernel.

The paper is organized as follows. In Section 2, after recalling the JL lemma, we study which properties of the polynomial kernels are approximately preserved by random projections. In particular we show that with high probability, the kernel applied to the compressed data is ϵ-closed to the optimal solution if we project in space of dimension $d' = O(\alpha^2 \cdot \frac{\lg N}{\epsilon^2})$, where α is the degree of polynomial kernel.

In Section 3 we present an ensemble algorithmic scheme by which the hypotheses are obtained by applying a learning algorithm to the data perturbed by random projections, and the final hypothesis is constructed by majority voting. Two types of random projections are considered: Random Subspace and PMO (Plus Minus One) projections [19], and as learning algorithm we applied SVMs with polynomial kernels.

In Section 4 we experimentally analyze the quality of the solutions of the proposed algorithm on real world clinical data. Particularly, we use two data set from literature: the *Colon adenocarcinoma* data set [14] and the *Leukemia* data set, with two variants of leukemia by analyzing the expression level of 7129 different genes [12].

The conclusions end the paper, after discussing the experimental results and the relationships between the accuracy of the Random Projection ensembles of polynomial SVMs and the degree of polynomial kernel.

2. Random embeddings and polynomial kernels.

First of all, we recall the basic ideas and results on the random projections. Roughly speaking, as random projection we intend a random linear map $\mu : R^d \to R^{d'}$ that approximately preserves the distance between fixed point. In this context, the main result is the so called Johnson-Lindenstrauss lemma: given N vector $\{x_1, ..., x_N\}$ of dimension d, if $d' = O(\frac{\lg N}{\epsilon^2})$ then with high probability a projection μ on a random subspace of dimension d' preserves the distances between x_i and x_j, for all i,j, up to a 'distortion' ϵ.

The main item we analyze in this section is the effect of a random projection on a polynomial kernel, in order to understand whether the Johnson Lindenstrauss lemma can be extended to polynomial kernels.

We recall that a polynomial kernel of degree α is $K_\alpha(x, y) = (x, y)^\alpha$, where (x,y) is the inner product between x and y. Polynomial kernels are useful to trans-

form data, in order to successively apply linear separators such as a perceptron or a SVM algorithm. In our experiments we use polynomial kernels of various degrees (1-9) for the SVMs used as learning algorithms.
First of all, we observe that in a Hilbert space the inner product can be obtained by means of the norm, as follows:

$$(x, y) = \frac{||x+y||^2 - ||x-y||^2}{4}$$

Suppose x,y $\in R^d$. Let P be a random embedding from R^d to $R^{d'}$. For d'=$\frac{4}{\epsilon^2}$ with high probability it holds:

$$1 - \epsilon \leq \frac{||P(x+y)||^2}{||x+y||^2} \leq 1 + \epsilon$$

and:

$$1 - \epsilon \leq \frac{||P(x-y)||^2}{||x-y||^2} \leq 1 + \epsilon$$

So, respectively, we can write:

$$(1 - \epsilon)||x + y||^2 \leq ||P(x + y)||^2 \leq (1 + \epsilon)||x + y||^2$$

$$-(1 + \epsilon)||x - y||^2 \leq -||P(x - y)||^2 \leq -(1 - \epsilon)||x - y||^2$$

By summing the two inequalities we obtain:

$$\begin{gathered} ||x + y||^2 - ||x - y||^2 - \epsilon(||x + y||^2 + ||x - y||^2) \leq \\ \leq ||P(x + y)||^2 - ||P(x - y)||^2 \leq \\ \leq ||x + y||^2 - ||x - y||^2 + \epsilon(||x + y||^2 + ||x - y||^2) \end{gathered}$$

that is:
$(x, y) - \epsilon\frac{||x||^2+||y||^2}{2} \leq (Px, Py) \leq (x, y) + \epsilon\frac{||x||^2+||y||^2}{2}$

For normalized vectors ($||x|| = ||y|| = 1$) we will have, with high probability, $(x, y) - \epsilon \leq (Px, Py) \leq (x, y) + \epsilon$, and this implies:

$$|(Px, Py) - (x, y)| \leq \epsilon$$

Setting $A = (Px, Py)$ and $B = (x, y)$:
$|A^\alpha - B^\alpha| = |A - B| \cdot |A^{\alpha-1} + A^{\alpha-2}B + ... + AB^{\alpha-2} + B^{\alpha-1}| \leq \epsilon \cdot \alpha$
In fact, $|A - B| < \epsilon$; moreover by the Schwartz disequality:
$|A| = |(Px, Py)| \leq ||Px|| \cdot ||Py|| \leq ||x|| \cdot ||y|| = 1$, because P is a projection.
Similarly: $|B| = |(x, y)| \leq ||x|| \cdot ||y|| = 1$
It follows that, for $d' = \frac{4}{\epsilon^2}$, with high probability:

$$|K_\alpha(x, y) - K_\alpha(P_x, P_y)| \leq \epsilon \cdot \alpha$$

Equivalently, for $d' = \frac{4\alpha^2}{\epsilon^2}$:

$$|K_\alpha(x, y) - K_\alpha(P_x, P_y)| \leq \epsilon$$

If we suppose that we have a training set $< (x_1, y_1), ..., (x_N, y_N) >$ on which to apply a learning algorithm such as perceptron or SVM with kernel K_α, the degradation of the quality is related to $d' = O(\alpha^2 \cdot \lg N/\epsilon^2)$, evidencing a quadratic dependency in the degree of the polynomial.

3. The algorithmic scheme

In this section we present the algorithmic scheme by which several instances of data perturbed by means of random projections are used to train an ensemble of SVMs. The high-level pseudo-code is the following:

Random Subspace Ensemble Algorithm

`Input:`

- A data set $\mathcal{D} = \{(\boldsymbol{x}_j, y_j) | 1 \leq j \leq m\}$, $\boldsymbol{x}_j \in \mathcal{X} \subset \mathbb{R}^d$, $t_j \in \mathcal{C} = \{0, 1\}$
- A randomized projection procedure $Projection$
- a *weak* learning algorithm $\mathcal{L}$
- subspace dimension $n < d$
- number of the base learners I

`Output:`

- Final hypothesis $h_{ran} : \mathcal{X} \rightarrow \mathcal{C}$ computed by the ensemble.

`begin`

for $i = 1$ to I

begin

$D_i =$ `Projection`$(\mathcal{D}$, n)

$h_i = \mathcal{L}(D_i)$

end

$h_{ran}(\boldsymbol{x}) = \arg\max_{t \in \mathcal{C}} card(\{i | h_i(\boldsymbol{x}) = t\})$

`end.`

4. Experimental results

To perform all the experiments we used two data sets from literature:

1. The *Colon adenocarcinoma* data set, composed of 2000 genes and 62 samples: 40 colon tumor samples and 22 normal colon tissue samples [14].
2. The *Leukemia* data set, that treats the problem of recognizing two variants of leukemia by analyzing the expression level of 7129 different genes. The data set consists of 72 samples, with 47 cases of Acute Lymphoblastic Leukemia (ALL) and 25 cases of Acute Myeloid Leukemia (AML), split into a training set of 38 tissues and a test set of 34 tissues.

All the data sets have been treated following the same pre-processing procedures reported in [14,12]

We developed new C++ classes and applications for random subspace ensembles extending the *NEURObjects* library [16]. The experiments have been executed by means of the C.I.L.E.A. Avogadro cluster of Xeon dual processor workstations [17].

We classified the above DNA microarray data using the methods listed below:

- single SVMs
- Random Subspace (RS) projection ensemble of SVMs
- Feature Selection Random Subspace (FS-RS) projection ensemble of SVMs (using the Golub feature selection method)
- Random Projection (RP) ensemble of SVMs

In Section 2 we showed that the distortion ϵ induced by random projections in polynomial kernels is proportional to the degree of the polynomial. In the experiments we investigated whether these distortions are related to the accuracy of the ensembles. More precisely we applied polynomial kernels with degree ranging from 1 to 9 in order to verify a degradation of the performance with high degree polynomial ensembles. We experimentally compared RS, RP and FS-RS polynomial SVM ensembles, using single SVMs as baseline classifiers, and cross-validation techniques to estimate the generalization error.

Results of comparison among Random Projection ensemble, single SVMs and Golub Feature Selection RS ensemble showed that in general that RP ensembles obtain results equal or better than RS-ensembles.

In Table 1 and 2 are shown the best results obtained with ensembles of polynomial kernel SVM, by varying the degree of the polynomial kernel.

Table 1. Colon data set: Comparison between Golub Feature Selection Random Subspace ensemble and Random Subspace Ensemble of SVMs results obtained with polynomial kernel.

COLON data set: average errors								
SVMs with polynomial kernel								
	poly degree	C value	Test err	St dev	Training err	St dev	Sens.	Spec.
RS ens	2	10	0.1429	0.0123	0.0831	0.0026	0.8696	0.8500
Single SVMs	1	1	0.1300	0.0201	0.0910	0.0369	0.8261	0.8900
FS RS ens	2	10	0.0968	0.0913	0	0	0.8636	0.9167
PMO RP ens	1	0.001	0.1129	0	0.0768	0	0.8636	0.9000

Table 2. Leukemia data set: Comparison between Golub Feature Selection Random Subspace ensemble and Random Subspace Ensemble of SVMs results obtained with polynomial kernel.

LEUKEMIA data set: average error								
SVMs with polynomial kernel								
	poly degree	C value	Test err	St dev	Training err	St dev	Sens.	Spec.
RS ens	2	10	0.0274	0.0712	0	0	1	0.9200
Single SVMs	3	1	0.0376	0.0040	0.0006	0.0013	0.9828	0.6120
FS RS ens	1	1000	0.0417	0.0151	0	0	0.9787	0.9260
PMO RP ens	1	10	0.0230	0.0140	0.0072	0.0100	1	0.7980

With the Colon data set (Table 1) we achieved the best results for polynomial degree 2 and 1 with respectively RS and RP ensembles. In this case there is a significant difference between the accuracy of the two methods (in favor of RP) at 0.05 significance level.

With the Leukemia data set we obtained the minimum test error for the polynomial degree 1 with RP ensembles, and similar results have been achieved with RS ensemble using a 2-degree polynomial kernel.

Note that with the Colon data set, adding a feature selection step before the random subspace procedure, we substantially reduce the classification error, while with the Leukemia data set we have an increment of the estimated generalization error.

5. Conclusions

In this work we showed that distances between points computed by polynomial kernels are approximately preserved by random projections, up to a degradation proportional to the square of the degree of the polynomial. More precisely, for the polynomial kernels we proved that, if we suppose to have a training set $<(x_1, y_1), ..., (x_N, y_N)>$ on which to apply a learning algorithm such as perceptron or SVM with polynomial kernel of degree α, the degradation of the quality is related to $d' = O(\alpha^2 \cdot \lg N/\epsilon^2)$, evidencing a quadratic dependency on the degree of the polynomial.

Considering that the best results have been achieved with RS and RP ensembles with 1-2 degree polynomial SVMs as base learners, our preliminary experimental results support the hypothesis that low degree polynomial kernels are better suited to the classification of gene expression data.

References

[1] Pomeroy, S. et al.: Gene Expression-Based Classification and Outcome Prediction of Central Nervous System Embryonal Tumors. Nature **415** (2002) 136–142

[2] Bellman, R.: Adaptive Control Processes: a Guided Tour. Princeton University Press. New Jersey. 1961

[3] Bauer, E. and Kohavi, R.: An empirical comparison of voting classification algorithms: Bagging, Boosting and variants. Machine Learning. **36** (1999) 105–139

[4] Novikov, P.S.: On the countable separability of analytic sets. Dokl. Akad. Nauk SSSR. **34 : 3** (1934) 145-149

[5] Guyon, I., Weston, J., Barnhill, S., Vapnik, V.: Gene Selection for Cancer Classification using Support Vector Machines. Machine Learning **46** (2002) 389–422

[6] Vapnik, V. N.: Statistical Learning Theory. Wiley, New York (1998)

[7] Duda, R.O., Hart, P.E. and Stork, D. G.: Pattern Classification, 2nd edn, D.G. Wiley, New York (2000)

[8] Brown, M. et al.: Knowledge-base analysis of microarray gene expression data by using Support Vector Machines. PNAS **97** (2000) 262–267

[9] Furey, T., Cristianini, N., Duffy, N., Bednarski, D., Schummer, M., Haussler, D.: Support Vector Machine classification and validation of cancer tissue saples using microarray expression data. Bioinformatics **16** (2000) 906–914

[10] Bertoni, A., Folgieri, R., Valentini, G.: Random subspace ensembles for the bio-molecular diagnosis of tumors. Neurocomputing **63C** (2005) 535–539

[11] Ho, T.: The Random Subspace method for constructing decision forests. IEEE Transactions on Pattern Analysis and Machine Intelligence **20** (1998) 832–844

[12] Golub, T., et al.: Molecular Classification of Cancer: Class Discovery and Class Prediction by Gene Expression Monitoring. Science **286** (1999) 531–537

[13] Guyon, I., Elisseeff, A.: An Introduction to Variable and Feature Selection. Journal of Machine Learning Research **3** (2003) 1157–1182

[14] Alon, U. et al.: Broad patterns of gene expressions revealed by clustering analysis of tumor and normal colon tissues probed by oligonucleotide arrays. PNAS **96** (1999) 6745–6750

[15] Skurichina, M., Duin, R.: Bagging, boosting and the Random Subspace method for linear classifiers. Pattern Analysis and Applications **5** (2002) 121–135

[16] Valentini, G., Masulli, F.: NEURObjects: an object-oriented library for neural network development. Neurocomputing **48** (2002) 623–646

[17] Arlandini, C.: Avogadro: il CILEA oltre il muro del teraflop. Bollettino del CILEA (2004)

[18] Valentini, G.: Gene expression data analysis of human lymphoma using support vector machines and output coding ensembles. Artificial Intelligence in Medicine, Elsevier **26** (2002) 283–306

[19] Bertoni A., Valentini, G.: Randomized maps for assessing the reliability of patients clusters in DNA microarray data analyses. Artificial Intelligence in Medicine, Elsevier **37(2)** (2006) 85–109

[20] Breiman, L.: Bagging predictors. Machine Learning **24** (1996) 123–140

[21] W.B. Johnson and J. Lindenstrauss: Extensions of Lipshitz mapping into Hilbert space. In Conference in modern analysis and probability, volume 26 of Contemporary Mathematics, Amer. Math. **137** (1984) 189–206

[22] Dettling, M., Buhlmann, P.: Boosting for tumor classification with gene expression data. Bioinformatics **19** (2003) 1061–1069

[23] Breiman, L.: Using convex pseudo-data to increase prediction accuracy. Technical Report 513. Statistics Department, U.C. Berkeley (1998)

[24] Freund, Y., Schapire, R.,E.: A decision-theoretic generalization of on-line learnings and an application to boosting. Journal of computer and system sciences **55** (1997) 119–139

[25] Kleinberg, E.: On the Algorithmic Implementation of Stochastic Discrimination. IEEE Transactions on Pattern Analysis and Machine Intelligence **22** (2000) 473–490

[26] Noble, W. S.: Support vector machine applications in computational biology. In Schoelkopf, B., Tsuda, K., and Vert, J., editors. Kernel Methods in Computational Biology, pages 71-92, MIT Press (2004)

[27] Cristianini, N., Shawe-Taylor, J.: An introduction to Support Vector Machines and other kernel based methods. Cambridge University Press, Cambridge, UK (2000).

[28] Achlioptas,D.: Random Matrices in Data Analysis. Proceedings of ECML'04(2004) 1–8

New Directions in Neural Networks
B. Apolloni et al. (Eds.)
IOS Press, 2009

doi:10.3233/978-1-58603-984-4-67

An Embedded Fingerprints Classification System based on Weightless Neural Networks

V.CONTI[a], C.MILITELLO[a], F.SORBELLO[a] and S.VITABILE[b]
[a]*Dipartimento di Ingegneria Informatica*
Università degli Studi di Palermo
Viale delle Scienze, Ed. 6, 90128 Palermo, ITALY
{conti, militello, sorbello}@unipa.it
[b]*Dipartimento di Biotecnologie Mediche e Medicina Legale,*
Università degli Studi di Palermo
Via del Vespro, 90127 Palermo, ITALY
vitabile@unipa.it

Abstract. Automatic fingerprint classification provides an important indexing scheme to facilitate efficient matching in large-scale fingerprint databases in Automatic Fingerprint Identification Systems (AFISs). The paper presents a new fast fingerprint classification module implementing on embedded Weightless Neural Network (RAM-based neural network). The proposed WNN architecture uses directional maps to classify fingerprint images in the five NIST classes (Left Loop, Right Loop, Whorl, Arch and Tented Arch) without anyone enhancement phase. Starting from the directional map, the WNN architecture computes the fingerprint classification rate. The proposed architecture is implemented on Celoxica RC2000 board employing a Xilinx Virtex-II 2v6000 FPGA and it is computationally few expensive regards execution time and used hardware resources. To validate the goodness of proposed classificator, three different tests have been executed on two databases: a proprietary and FVC database. The best classification rate obtained is of 85.33% with an execution time of 1.15ms.

Keywords. Embedded Fingerprint Classification, Weightless Neural Network, RAM based Neural Networks, Directional Map, FPGA.

Introduction

In a fingertip, the fingerprint image is composed by ridges and valleys which forms unique geometric pattern in the skin [1]. Fingerprints are formed by a set of ridge lines which run parallel and show some micro-characteristics, called minutiae. With more details, the point where the ridge line terminates is called endpoint, while the point where the ridge line intersects another ridge line is called bifurcation [6]. Other fingerprint features are the macro-characteristics, which are regions of fingerprint image where the ridge line flow is irregular. The points in these particular zones are called delta and core: he delta point is the center of a triangular edge pattern, while the core point is the center of a circular edge pattern on a fingerprint image. This pair of macro-characteristics is frequently used for fingerprint classification. Many works have been proposed in literature and many researchers are working in this field to better the fingerprint identification systems. In [2] the authors, after distortion and contrast reducing phases, have extracted the directional map from original fingerprint. From fingerprint directional map, the macro-characteristics (or singularity points) have been extracted and the image classified using topological and numerical consideration about them. In [3] the authors proposed a structural approach that uses relational graph. The fingerprint directional map is segmented in regions by minimizing the variance of the element directions within the regions. From the segmentation of the directional map a relational graph compactly summarizing the macro-structure of the fingerprint is derived. Others classification approaches [4][5] are based on artificial intelligence techniques. The authors use a neural network as decisional state for classification. All these systems are software-based and one of their main drawback is the high classification time.

In this work, the authors propose an embedded fingerprint classification system implementing a Weightless Neural Network (WNN) to reduce the classification time. The proposed system extracts the directional map from original fingerprint image, without noise reduction and contrast enhancement phase and classifies the fingerprints into five classes: Left Loop, Right Loop, Whorl, Arch and Tented Arch. The proposed system is implemented on Celoxica RC2000 board employing a Xilinx Virtex-II 2v6000 FPGA.

The paper is structured as follows. In Section 1 Weightless Neural Networks are presented. In Section 2 the proposed neural classification architecture is described. In Section 3 the experimental results, in terms of classification rates, hardware resources and execution time, are shown. Finally in the last section some conclusions are reported.

1. Weightless Neural Networks

Weightless Neural Networks, known as RAM-based networks, are a class of methods for building pattern recognition systems. Unlike other neural network methods, they train very rapidly and can be implemented in simple hardware structures [5][7]. RAM-based neural networks belong to the memory-based architectures. A RAM-based neural network consists of a set of Look Up Tables (LUTs) that store the image numeric features (like classic neural network weights). Each LUT samples a number of data from the input space. In Fig. 1 the traditional scheme of a RAM-based neural network, where the 0 or 1 values are used as numeric features and stored in the RAMs (LUTs). A value of 1 corresponds to a specific feature in the training set for the class: this value is obtained from the AND bitwise among all bits in the same position in each input vector. As illustrated in Fig. 1, in the testing phase, the output vectors from each LUT, correspondents to a given input, are compared with the input vector (using the AND bitwise) and subsequently, among all discriminators, a Winner-Takes-All decision is taken to perform the input pattern classification (Table 1). In the section 3 more details will be given.

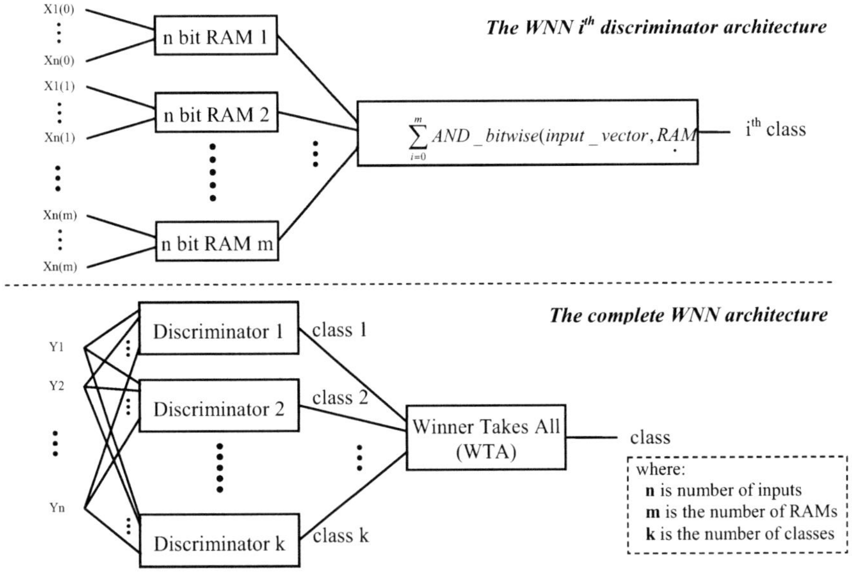

Figure 1. The general scheme of a RAM-based neural network. The discriminator k corresponds to different object classes, while the RAM m corresponds to different patterns of the sampled input data.

Table 1. WNN i^th discriminator scheme. For each input value, a bit is selected and sent to appropriate RAM. The sum of all RAMs represents the output of the discriminator.

	Bits of Input Vector	Discriminator i^th
n bit RAM 1	$X_1(0) \ldots X_n(0)$	010101....1
n bit RAM 2	$X_1(1) \ldots X_n(1)$	111101....0
...	...	...
n bit RAM m	$X_1(m) \ldots X_n(m)$	000101....0
Output		$\sum_{i=0}^{m} AND\_bitwise(input\_vector, RAM_i)$

The above description can be mathematical proofed [8]. Let m be the total number of RAMs (LUTs) in the system, and let S_c describes the set of training examples for class C. Furthermore, let X denote an training example and let Y a testing example. A given example will address a specific column of each RAM. Let $a_i(Y)$ the column in the i_{th} LUT addressed by an example Y. The class assignment given to the example Y is then given by:

$$\arg\max_{c}\left[\sum_{i=1}^{m}\theta\left(\sum_{X\in S_c}\delta_{a_i(X),a_i(Y)}\right)\right] \quad (1)$$

Where $\delta_{i,j}$ is Kronecker delta ($\delta_{i,j} = 1$ if $i = j$ and 0 otherwise), $\theta(z) = 1$ if $z \geq 1$, $\theta(z) = 0$ if $z < 1$.

The input space sampled by a RAM-based network is normally assumed to be binary. If the inputs are real or integer values a representation to change from non-binary values into binary values is applied [9].

2. The Proposed Neural Classification Architecture

The system classifies the fingerprint images into the 5 NIST standard classes: Right Loop, Left Loop, Whorl, Arch and Tented Arch (Fig. 2). With more details, the system extracts the directional map from original fingerprint image, without noise reduction and contrast enhancement. The only directional map is used as input in the RAM-based neural network for fingerprint classification.

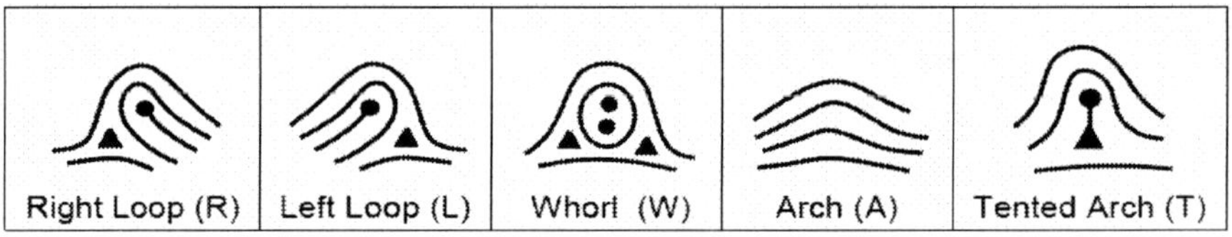

Figure 2. The five fingerprint classes considered in this work: right loop, left loop, whorl, arch and tented arch.

2.1. The Directional Map Extraction

In the directional map, every element represents the local orientation of the ridges in the original gray-scale image [2]. The extracted directions could result different from the predominant direction extracted in the neighbor zones. The algorithm phases are now described.

The direction $dir(i, j)$ of the point (i, j) is defined by the following equation:

$$dir(i, j) = min \sum_{k=1}^{L} \left[level(i_k, j_k) - level(i, j) \right] \qquad (2)$$

where $level(i, j)$ and $level(i_k, j_k)$ indicate the gray level of the point (i, j) and (i_k, j_k) respectively, while L is the number of selected pixels in this calculation along a considered direction. In this paper, 32 directions (from 0° to 180°) have been chosen, while a number of $L = 16$ pixels along the direction has been considered.

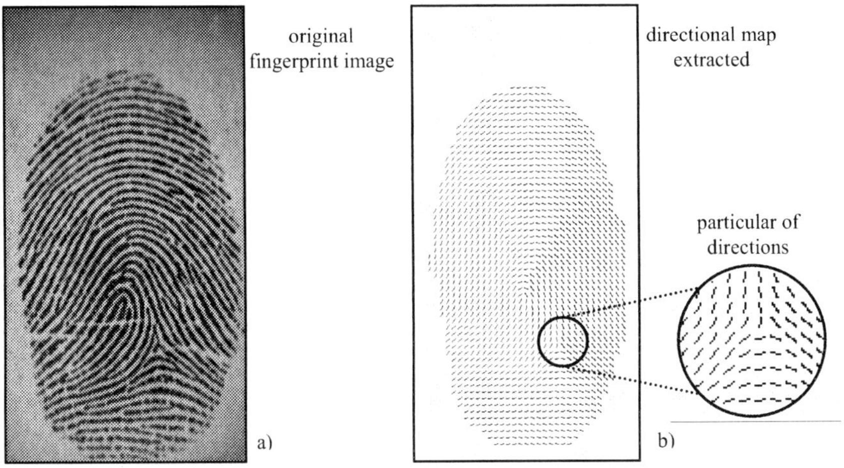

Figure 3. The directional map extraction result: a) the original fingerprint image, b) the extracted directional map.

Using the equation (2), the directions of the single pixels are found. Moreover in every 8x8 pixel block, the direction with greater frequency will be attributed to the considered block. The possible presence of noise in the image used could generate directions in noisy blocks very different respect their neighbor directions. This could cause mistakes in the characteristics extraction phase; therefore a smoothing algorithm has been applied on the directional map. This is achieved by calculating the directional histogram. The directional histogram is obtained from a comparison of direction of an area of 3x3 blocks. The final direction of the central block of the considered area was replaced by the higher frequency direction, in the directional histogram, of the neighboring blocks. The reduced size of directional map decreases the approach complexity. Fig. 3 shows the directional map extraction result: Fig 3a) is the original fingerprint image while Fig 3b) its directional map.

2.2. The Weightless Neural Networks Characteristics

The proposed architecture has the following characteristics: the input vector is sampled in n=30 blocks; each block is connected to bit-plain RAM unit inputs. In this work 32 different directions and m=5 bit-plain have been considered respectively. For each bit-plain, the output of all RAMs are individually summed up with the same input vector and subsequently is applied a bit Weighted Average (bitWA). Finally, a Winner-Takes-All (WTA) block gives the final class [10]. The proposed weightless neural network is depicted in Fig. 4.

In this works, the proposed architecture classifies five fingerprint classes. In the training phase, each discriminator trains itself with the input data of its own class. In the testing phase, each discriminator responds with the number of matched sub-patterns. The pattern is classified accordingly with the highest output of the 5 discriminators.

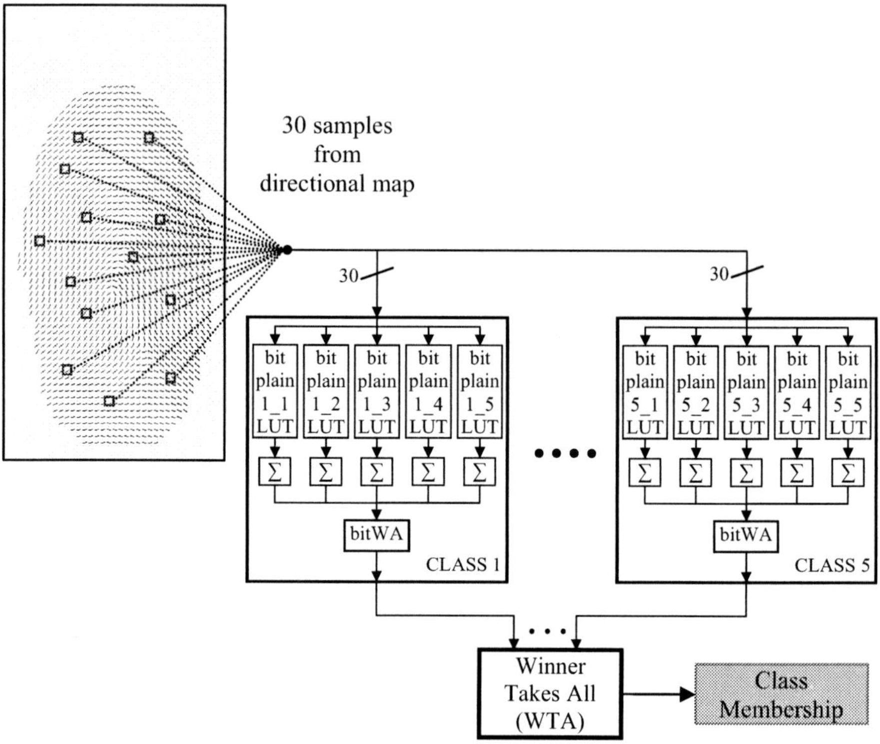

Figure 4. The proposed Weightless Neural Network architecture. For each class five bit-plain ("*class*"_"*bit plain number*") are used to represent the fingerprint features scheme.

3. Experimental Results

The whole described system has been implemented using the Celoxica RC2000 board [12]. The RC2000 provides an environment for the development of high performance FPGA based applications.

The RC2000 is equipped with a FPGA Virtex-II 2v6000 device on a high performance reconfigurable PMC (PCI Mezzanine Card). Features include high speed PCI interface, external memory, high density I/O, programmable clocks, temperature monitoring, battery backed encryption and flash boot facilities. A complete cross API platform with support for WinNT/2000/XP, Linux and VxWorks provides access to the full functionalities of the hardware features. The board is equipped with 6 SRAM independent banks, SDRAM and Flash (16MBytes). On board clock generator provides a synchronous local bus clock for the PCI interface and the Virtex-II FPGA. A second clock is provided for user applications and can be controlled by software. Both clocks are programmable and can be used by the Virtex Clock. The local bus clock works between 400 kHz and 66 MHz, while the user clock until to 100MHz. In our trials, the clock has been fixed at 70 MHz considering timing and delays of the FPGA system implementation.

The tests have been performed on two different databases with images of 296x560 pixels:

- a proprietary database, composed by 484 fingerprint images acquired with the scanner Biometrika FX2000 [11];
- the FVC2002/DB2_B database [14], composed by 80 fingerprint images.

3.1. Classification Analysis

Two different series of test have been performed, after training phase performed using 30 images of each class:

- a test on 4 classes using the proprietary database, considering 120 images for training phase and the remaining 334 images for testing phase (Table 2). The tented arch haven't been computed because the number of these images is only 30;
- a test on a subset of 54 images from FVC database, not considering the images with less half fingerprint (Table 3). In the original FVC database only 3 classes are present (arch and tented arch classes are not present).

Table 2. Classification results on proprietary database, considering 30 images of each class for training. The tended arch haven't been computed because the number of these images is only 30.

Class	Correct Classification	Total Image Number	Classification Rate
Right Loop	141	160	88.13%
Left Loop	76	84	90.48%
Whorl	58	75	77.33%
Tented Arch	not computable	not computable	not computable
Arch	10	15	66.67%
TOTAL	**285**	**334**	
AVERAGE			**85.33%**

Table 3. Classification results on FVC2002 database, considering 30 images of each class for training.

Class	Correct Classification	Total Image Number	Classification Rate
Right Loop	14	18	77.78%
Left Loop	13	16	81.25%
Whorl	14	20	70.00%
Tented Arch	not available	not available	not available
Arch	not available	not available	not available
TOTAL	**41**	**54**	
AVERAGE			**75.93%**

Subsequently, to check the performance of the proposed architecture, another test on 5 classes using the proprietary database has been performed. This test, consists of

100 images for training phase (20 images for each class) and the remaining 384 images for testing phase (Table 4).

Table 4. Classification results on proprietary database, considering 20 images of each class for training.

Class	Correct Classification	Total Image Number	Classification Rate
Right Loop	142	170	83.53%
Left Loop	85	94	90.43%
Whorl	59	85	69.41%
Tented Arch	10	10	100.00%
Arch	12	25	48.00%
TOTAL	**308**	**384**	
AVERAGE			**80.20%**

3.2. Resources Analysis

The used development tools are the Celoxica DK4 [12] and the Xilinx ISE [13]. These platforms allow the development of the Handel-C code and the netlist used to generate the *.bit* file for the FPGA configuration. The reports produced by these tools allow resource analysis required by the fingerprint elaboration chain. In particular, the compilation of the Handel-C code by DK4 tool produces a EDIF netlist having the characteristics shown in Table 5.

Table 5. Resources utilization

Type of Resources	Used Resources Number	Total Resources Number	Used Resources Percentage
Number of Flip Flops	2,166	67,584	3.20 %
Number of LUTs	3,954	67,584	5.8 %
Number of Slice	3,613	33,792	10.6 %

3.3. Execution Time

The whole WNN architecture has been accomplished by using FPGA Virtex-II device. The system clock was experimentally fixed at 70Mhz and the obtained clock cycles number to complete the classification process was of 80,738. The execution time to classify each image has been calculated considering the image already loaded in the board memory of the RC2000 board, and it was 1.15ms.

Conclusions

This work presents an automated method for fingerprint classification based on WNN using only the directional map. The proposed architecture classifies the fingerprints into five classes: Left Loop, Right Loop, Whorl, Arch and Tented Arch. This system, unlike the present literature, uses the acquired fingerprint image without noise reduction and contrast enhancement phase. Both in the training phase and in the testing phase, the input values of directional image are randomly selected to avoid roto-translation problems.

The proposed approach, based only on binary value of features management (AND bitwise, sum and comparison), realizes an easier neural network architecture to implement on hardware devices, respect a traditional MLP architecture. The whole system, implemented on Celoxica RC2000 board equipped with a Xilinx Virtex-II 2v6000 FPGA, is, in fact, characterized by low execution time and hardware resources employment. The best classification rate on a proprietary database composed by 484 fingerprint images is 85.33% with an execution time of 1.15ms.

References

[1] A.K. Jain, L. Hong, and R. Bolle, On-Line Fingerprint Verification IEEE Trans. Pattern Analysis and Machine Intelligence, vol. 19, no. 4, pp. 302-314, Apr. 1997

[2] Meltem Ballan and F. Ayhan Sakarya, "A Fingerprint Classification Technique Using Directional images", proc. of the Thirty-First Asilomar Conference on Signal, System and Computer, 1997, Vol. 1, pp. 101-104, 2-5 Nov 1997

[3] D. Maltoni and D. Maio, "A structural Approach To Fingerprint Classification" proc. of the 13th International Conference on Pattern Recognition, ICPR'96, Vol. 3, pp. 578-585, 25-29 August 1996

[4] M. Kamijo, "Classifying Fingerprint Images Using Neural Network: Deriving The Classification State", IEEE International Conference on neural networks, 1993, Vol. 3, pp. 1932-1937, 28 March-1April 1993

[5] H. V. Neto and D.L. Borges, "Fingerprint Classification with Neural Networks", proc. of 4th IEEE Brazilian Symposium on Neural Networks, pp. 66–72, 3-5 December 1997

[6] D. Maltoni and D. Maio, "Neural Network based minutiae filtering in fingerprints", proc. of 14th International Conference on Pattern Recognition", Vol. 2, pp. 1654-1668, 1998

[7] Y. Tang, W. Pan, H. Li, Y. Xu; "Fuzzy Naive Bayes classifier based on fuzzy clustering", proc. of IEEE International Conference on System, Man and Cybernetics, Vol. 5, 2002

[8] R. Rohwer and M. Morciniec 1996, "A theoretical and experimental account of n-Tuple classifier performance", proc. of Neural Computation, vol. 8, no3, pp. 629-642, 1996, ISSN 0899-7667

[9] R. J. Mitchell, J. M. Bishop, S. K. Box and J. F. Hawker 1995, "Comparison of methods for processing grey level data in weightless networks" proc. of Weightless Neural Network Workshop, WNNW95, pp. 76-81

[10] V. Conti, D. Perconti, S. Romano, G. Tona, S. Vitabile, S. Gaglio, F. Sorbello, "Fast Fingerprints Classification only using the Directional Image" proc. of 11th LNAI International Conference on Knowledge-Based and Intelligent Information & Engineering Systems, Vietri sul Mare, 12-14 september 2007, B. Apolloni et al. (Eds.): KES 2007/WIRN 2007, Part I, LNAI 4692, pp. 34–41, 2007, Springer-Verlag Berlin Heidelberg 2007

[11] Biometrika, http://www.biometrika.it/

[12] Celoxica Ltd, http://www.celoxica.com

[13] Xilinx Inc., http://www.xilinx.com

[14] FVC Databases http://bias.csr.unibo.it/

New Directions in Neural Networks
B. Apolloni et al. (Eds.)
IOS Press, 2009

doi:10.3233/978-1-58603-984-4-76

Discovering regression data quality through clustering methods

Dario MALCHIODI [a], Simone BASSIS [a] and Lorenzo VALERIO [a]
[a] *University of Milan, Department of Computer Science, Via Comelico 39/41, 20135 Milan, Italy*
`{malchiodi,bassis,valerio}@dsi.unimi.it`

Abstract. We propose the use of clustering methods in order to discover the quality of each element in a training set to be subsequently fed to a regression algorithm. The paper shows that these methods, used in combination with regression algorithms taking into account the additional information conveyed by this kind of quality, allow the attainment of higher performances than those obtained through standard techniques.

Keywords. data quality, regression, clustering, SVM

Introduction

Regression methods, as well as other inferential techniques, are based on the assignment of equal importance to each observation of the model. Real world data sets, on the contrary, contain several observations to be considered with different importance: most notably, *outliers*, as observations "which appear to be inconsistent with the remainder of the set of data" [5]. Anyway, the concept of "quality" goes beyond the mere existence of outliers, and precisely delineates two important veins:

1. The possibility of handling other categories of observations rather than normal ones and outliers. Remarkably, the latter however do convey information, for we know that they *do not* describe the model we are trying to infer. Thus, in the realm of regression outliers define points which should not be close to the output of the inferential procedure. Moreover, as observations could have been measured with different equipments, or in different conditions, or be affected by some sort of subjective judgment, we can think of regular observations having different importance, as well as *irrelevant* observations actually being uncorrelated with the model under investigation.
2. The challenge of considering a richer information than that related to the crisp membership of one observation to the regular or outlier categories. Also in light with previous point, we can envision different degrees of importance in each of the observation categories, in line for instance with the habit of using box & whiskers plots [13] in order to find mild and severe outliers.

The field of *relevance learning*, defined as the study and application of inferential procedures exploiting quantitative measures for the quality of each observation, came only recently to the attention of researchers [2,18,7,8]. This work presents some preliminary experimentations about the use of clustering procedures aimed at discovering the quality of a data set when this information is missing. The paper is organized as follows: Section 1 introduces the concept of *data quality* and proposes a broad criterion for its numerical quantification; Section 2 describes how existing clustering procedures may be used in order to infer the quality of a given data set; Section 3 elaborates on how to exploit the discovered quality, while Section 4 illustrates some preliminary experiments. Finally, the last section is devoted to concluding remarks.

1. Measuring quality in regression problems

The starting point of every regression procedure is a set of observations, randomly drawn according to an unknown probability measure P, whose general form is:

$$\mathbf{z} = \{z_1, \ldots, z_m\} = \{(x_1, y_1), \ldots, (x_m, y_m)\} \subseteq Z = X \times Y \tag{1}$$

where X and Y are given spaces, whose elements x_i and y_i are called patterns and labels, respectively, while the pair z_i gathering them is called observation. The output of the procedure is a *regressor* $\ell \quad X \mapsto Y$ which should be able to approximate the value of a label as a function of the corresponding pattern, both on the observations in $\mathbf{z}$ and on new observations drawn from P.

The aim of this work is that of associating $\mathbf{z}$ to another set $\{r_1, \ldots, r_m\} \subset \mathbb{R}$, where for each i the quantity r_i measures the quality of i-th observation w.r.t. the whole dataset $\mathbf{z}$. More precisely, in order to deal with the algorithm described in Section 3, we will assign the following meaning to the numerical values for r_i:

- values close (in either direction) to 0 will denote *relevant* observations. Said in other words, the more r_i is close to 0, the more (x_i, y_i) represents an important observation, i.e. the better we expect that $\ell(x_i)$ approximates y_i;
- high positive values will denote *irrelevant* observations, i.e. the higher will be a positive r_i, the less we expect that ℓ is influenced by i-th observation;
- low negative values will denote outliers, i.e. the lower will be a negative r_i, the less we expect that $\ell(x_i)$ is a good approximation of y_i.

2. Quality discovery through clustering methods

In the following two subsections we propose the application of two clustering methods outputting as a fallout a measure of the quality of each clustered data. The rationale behind both approaches stands in the fact that we expect regular observations to group in clusters geometrically closer one another than with the outliers' position. In the rest of this section, for the sake of simplicity we will directly refer to each observation as a point $z_i \in Z$, thus looking for clusters in $Z = X \times Y$. We will come back to the notation involving patterns and labels in Section 3.

2.1. Support vector clustering

The basic idea underlying the support vector clustering method, introduced in [22,6], consists in: i) mapping data in a new space H (typically having a higher dimension than Z), and ii) finding a small sphere in the latter space possibly enclosing the data images. This is obtained through solving the following constrained optimization problem:

$$\min R^2 + C \sum_{i=1}^{m} \xi_i \tag{2}$$

$$||\Phi(z_i) - a||^2 \leq R^2 + \xi_i \quad i = 1, \ldots, m \tag{3}$$

$$\xi_i \geq 0 \quad i = 1, \ldots, m \tag{4}$$

where $\Phi \quad Z \mapsto H$ is the function used to map data in H, $a \in H$ and R denote respectively the center and radius of the enclosing sphere, $\{\xi_i\}$ denote the slack variables accounting for the possibility that some points are not included in the sphere, and $C > 0$ balances the optimization process.

As usual with support vector methods, the solution of (2-4) is obtained mixing duality theory [12] with the additional expedient, known as kernel trick [1], of introducing a kernel function $k(z_1, z_2) = \Phi(z_1) \cdot \Phi(z_2)$ computing the inner product in H between two images of Φ. Summing up, we get the following problem:

$$\max \sum_{i=1}^{m} k(z_i, z_i)\beta_i - \sum_{i,j=1}^{m} k(z_i, z_j)\beta_i\beta_j \tag{5}$$

$$0 \leq \beta_i \leq C \quad i = 1, \ldots, m \tag{6}$$

where $\{\beta_i\}$ are the lagrange multipliers of the constraints in (3). Denoted with $\beta_1^*, \ldots, \beta_m^*$ the optimal values for (5-6), the quantity

$$R^2(z) = k(z, z) - 2 \sum_{i=1}^{m} k(z_i, z)\beta_i^* + \sum_{i,j=1}^{m} k(z_i, z_j)\beta_i^*\beta_j^* \tag{7}$$

can be used to compute the distance in H from the image of z through Φ and the center of the bounding sphere optimizing (5-6); moreover, simple inspection of the KKT complementary conditions [12] reveals that:

- if $\beta_i^* = 0$, the image of z_i falls within the sphere boundary;
- if $0 < \beta_i^* < C$ the image of z_i falls on the sphere boundary, so $R^2(z_i)$ equals the optimal value R^* of the sphere squared radius;
- if $\beta_i^* = C$, the image of z_i lies outside the sphere (and this condition can occur only when $C < 1$).

Thus the sphere optimizing (5-6) can be pictured as a cluster gathering the images in H through Φ of the relevant z_is. This sphere induces on Z a cluster with a different shape, depending on k.

The support vector clustering procedure can be straightforwardly applied to discover data quality as follows: starting from the available observations $\{z_1, \ldots, z_m\}$, find the solution of (5-6), then estimate the quality of z_i, according to its meaning introduced in Section , with the quantity:

$$r_i = \begin{cases} R^2(z_i) & \text{if } R^2(z_i) \leq R^* \\ R^* - R^2(z_i) & \text{otherwise} \end{cases} \quad (8)$$

In order to be able to run the procedure, two parameters must be fixed beforehand, namely C and k. Concerning the latter, as noted in [23] a good choice is that of gaussian kernels

$$k(z_i, z_j) = \mathrm{e}^{-q\|z_i - z_j\|^2} \quad (9)$$

which in turn introduces a new parameter $q > 0$ related to the kernel width. A good value of C should enable the discovery of outliers: as asymptotically on m the quantity $p = \frac{1}{mC}$ tends to the fraction of points lying outside the sphere in H [21], we propose to set

$$C = \frac{1}{mp} \quad (10)$$

being p the fraction of expected outliers, detected with simple procedures such as those based on box & whiskers plots [13] or with more refined solutions as those proposed in [17].

2.2. *Shared Nearest Neighbor clustering*

The basic idea Shared Nearest Neighbor clustering, for short SNN, relies on the identification of representative points within the dataset, also called *core points*, around which to build clusters of possibly different sizes and shapes without bother on the determination of their number. Although originally introduced in the 70's [14], it is only in the last years that many researchers exploited its main rationale providing methods for identifying core points working regardless of the dimensionality of the data and still maintaining a good level of invariance to variations in density [10]. To achieve this twofold target, suitable definitions of similarity and density must be introduced inducing clusters representing uniform regions w.r.t. their neighborhood, no matter which density (high, medium or low) characterizes these sorrounding areas.

According to these considerations, a clever way to define similarity $s_{ij} = s(z_i, z_j)$ between two points z_i and z_j [14] is by counting how many points they share in their k-nearest neighbor list (for short NN_k), the latter containing the k points nearest to z_i and z_j respectively, on the basis of a suitable metric (e.g. the Euclidean distance):

$$s_{ij} = \#\left\{\mathrm{NN}_k(z_i) \cap \mathrm{NN}_k(z_j)\right\}, \quad (11)$$

where $\#A$ denotes the cardinality of the set A. Of course the greater is the number of shared points and the higher is the similarity between z_i and z_j. As for density $\phi_\epsilon(z)$ around a point z, it can be defined in terms of the number of points lying in an ϵ-radius area centered in z. Since here we focus on similarity measures rather than distance-based ones, the above ϵ-neighboring area is identified in terms of those points having similarity greater than ϵ from the center z. In formulas:

$$\phi_\epsilon(z) = \#\left(\tilde{z} \in \mathbf{z} \;\; s(z, \tilde{z}) > \epsilon\right). \tag{12}$$

The overall SNN clustering algorithm, an extension of the well-known density-based clustering algorithm DBSCAN [20], proceeds by classifying points as either: i) *core points* z_cs as those having density $\phi_\epsilon(z_c) > \pi$, for a suitable π; ii) *border points* z_bs as those, within the remaining points, having similarity $s(z_b, z_c) > \epsilon$ for at least a core point z_c; and iii) *noise points* or *outliers* z_o as the remaining ones, i.e. those having similarity $s(z_o, z_c) \leq \epsilon$ for each core point z_c. The main steps of the procedure are listed in Algorithm 1.

Algorithm 1 SNN clustering algorithm

Given a distance matrix D, where d_{ij} is the distance between z_i and z_j according to a fixed metric, the dimension k of the nearest neighbor list, thresholds ϵ and π,

1. Compute the sparsified similarity matrix $S = s_{ij}$ according to (11)
2. **for** each $z \in \mathbf{z}$, compute its density $\phi_\epsilon(z)$ following (12)
3. Generate subsets $\mathbf{z}_c$ of core points, $\mathbf{z}_b$ of border points and $\mathbf{z}_o$ of outliers:
   3.1 **for** each $z \in \mathbf{z}$, **if** $\phi_\epsilon(z) > \pi$ **then** put z in $\mathbf{z}_c$
   3.2 **for** each $z \in \mathbf{z} \setminus \mathbf{z}_c$, **if** $\exists z_c(z_c \in \mathbf{z}_c \wedge s(z, z_c) > \epsilon)$ **then** put z in $\mathbf{z}_b$
   3.3 **for** each $z \in \mathbf{z} \setminus (\mathbf{z}_c \cup \mathbf{z}_b)$, put z in $\mathbf{z}_o$
4. Form clusters:
   4.1. **for** each $z_1, z_2 \in \mathbf{z}_c$, **if** $s(z_1, z_2) > \epsilon$ **then** place z_1, z_2 in the same cluster
   4.2. **for** each $z_b \in \mathbf{z}_b$, assign z_b to the nearest core point's cluster

Usually parameters ϵ and π are defined as a fraction of k. Intuitively the higher is k and the fewer is the number of discovered clusters, while an increase in π (identifying more reliable core points) can be compensated by an increase in the value of ϵ allowing a less conservative merging of core points.

In order to compute data quality we may rely on the shared nearest neighbor similarity notion explained earlier in this section and compute the quality of a point z in terms of a kind of *per cluster* density, restricting its computation on the sole points of the cluster z belongs to. The intuition is that the more a core or border point z is representative of its cluster, the higher is the number of points in the same cluster similar to z. *Vice versa*, the more an outlier z is dissimilar from the various clusters' border or core points, and the higher is the per cluster density of z w.r.t. its overall density. According to the definition of data quality provided in Section 1 and denoting with $\phi_{\epsilon,\kappa}(z_i)$ the density of z_i computed on the κ-th cluster, we get:

$$r_i = \begin{cases} 1 - \frac{\phi_{\epsilon,\kappa}(z_i)}{\phi_\epsilon(z_i)} & \text{if } z_i \in \mathbf{z}_c \cup \mathbf{z}_b \\ -\frac{\phi_{\epsilon,o}(z_i)}{\phi_\epsilon(z_i)} & \text{if } z_i \in \mathbf{z}_o \end{cases} \tag{13}$$

As $\phi_{\epsilon,\kappa}(z_i) \leq \phi_\epsilon(z_i)$ by definition, r_i lies in the range $-1, 1$ having highest attractive (repulsive) behavior in 0^+ (-1), while being substantially ineffective around $r_i = 1$.

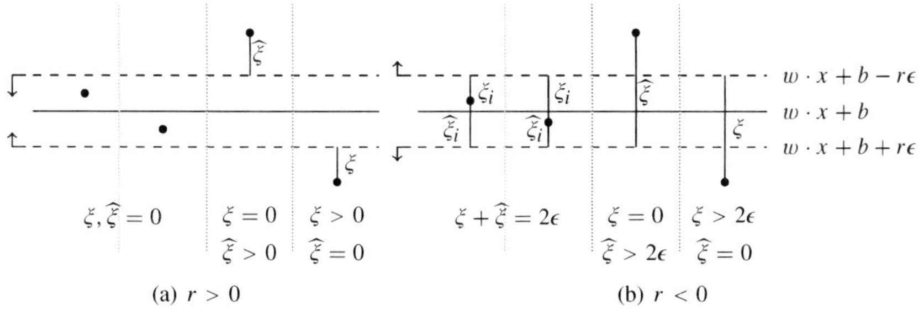

Figure 1. The geometrical interpretation of the proposed SVM regression variant.

Note that, although this is the approach used in Section 4, clever methods may be introduced for computing data quality, by embedding, for instance, shared nearest neighbor similarity in Silhouette-like indices [16], measuring how well matched is a point to the others in its own cluster versus how well matched it would be if it was moved to another cluster.

3. Exploiting data quality

Once data quality $\{r_i, i = 1, \dots, m\}$ has been estimated according for instance to the procedures described in Section 2, the information it conveys can be exploited in order to obtain a robust solution for the related regression problem, for instance via *weighted least square regression* [19]. We recently proposed a variant of the support vector regression ϵ-insensitive method, which we refet to as RSVR [3], accepting $\{r_i, i = 1, \dots, m\}$ as additional input [4] which, starting from a sample as in (1), considers the following constrained optimization problem:

$$\min \frac{1}{2}||w||^2 + C \sum_{i=1}^{m} \left(\xi_i + \widehat{\xi}_i\right), \tag{14}$$

$$y_i \geq w \cdot x_i + b - r_i\epsilon - \xi_i \quad \forall i = 1, \dots, m, \tag{15}$$

$$y_i \leq w \cdot x_i + b + r_i\epsilon + \widehat{\xi}_i \quad \forall i = 1, \dots, m, \tag{16}$$

$$\xi_i + \widehat{\xi}_i \geq h_i \quad \forall i = 1, \dots, m, \tag{17}$$

$$\xi_i, \widehat{\xi}_i \geq 0 \quad \forall i = 1, \dots, m, \tag{18}$$

which represents an extension of the SVM ϵ-insensitive regression algorithm [9], aiming at finding a regression line (w, b) both as flat and as close as possible to each observation (ξ_i and $\widehat{\xi}_i$ measure the drift of i-th observation from a tube of width ϵ centered on the regression line, while $C > 0$ balances the optimization process). The proposed variant is characterized by a different ϵ-tube for each pattern, where the quality of the latter is related to the width of the tube. Moreover, h_i equals 0 when $r_i \geq 0$ and $\rho - 2\epsilon r_i$ otherwise, for a fixed value $\rho > 0$, so that the constraints (17) are redundant when $r_i > 0$ and forbid that i-th observation falls inside the tube when $r_i < 0$ (see Fig. 2 for a geometrical interpretation of the constraints). In other words, (14-18) is tailored in order to exploit data quality $\{r_i\}$ as introduced in Section 1.

The dual formulation of the proposed variant implementing the kernel trick allowing for the search of nonlinear regressors is the following:

$$\max \; -\frac{1}{2}\sum_{i,j=1}^{m}(\alpha_i-\widehat{\alpha}_i)\;(\alpha_j-\widehat{\alpha}_j)\,x_i\cdot x_j-\sum_{i=1}^{m}(\alpha_i-\widehat{\alpha}_i)\,y_i$$

$$-\sum_{i=1}^{m}(r_i\epsilon+h_i)\,(\alpha_i+\widehat{\alpha}_i) \tag{19}$$

$$\textstyle\sum_{i=1}^{m}(\alpha_i-\widehat{\alpha}_i)=0, \tag{20}$$

$$0\le\alpha_i\le C, \tag{21}$$

$$0\le\widehat{\alpha}_i\le C, \tag{22}$$

being α_i and $\widehat{\alpha}_i$ the lagrangian multipliers associated to the original formulation's constraints. Once the optimal values for these multipliers have been determined, the regressor is found as usual with SVMs, i.e. through exploitation of duality and KKT conditions.

4. Numerical experiments

We preliminary tested the proposed methodology on the Iris Plants data set created by R. A. Fisher [11], which is one of the best known data sets to be found in the pattern recognition literature. It is constituted by a set of records describing 3 classes of plants: Iris Setosa, Versicolor and Virginica. For each class 50 instances are reported in terms of four canonical features: sepal and petal length and width. For the sake of visualization we extracted the first three principal components of the data set [15] and run both clustering procedures described in Section 2 in order to discover the quality of each data item. More in detail, concerning the SVC algorithm, we computed C according to (10) and experimentally set q to 6. As for the SNN Clustering procedure, we experimentally set k to 7 and consequently derived the values for the remaining parameters [10]. The pictures in Fig. 2 illustrate the obtained results: each point represents an observation, colored according to the class it belongs to; moreover each point size is related to the corresponding quality (the smaller the size, the less relevant is the observation). The two pictures show that the discovered quality moderately depends on the chosen clustering procedure. On the basis of the obtained quality we run RSVR algorithm relying on a linear regressor and exploiting a polynomial kernel of third degree. In both cases we selected the free parameters after some experimentation, namely $C = 100, \epsilon = 0.01$ in the former case, and $C = 1, \epsilon = 0.1$ in the latter. Figure 3 illustrates the obtained regressors. In order to evaluate the latter we used them to automatically assign each observation to the three classes in the data set: namely, given a generic observation we assigned it to the class corresponding to the nearest regressor w.r.t. the Euclidean distance. Table 1 summarizes the results of the classification.

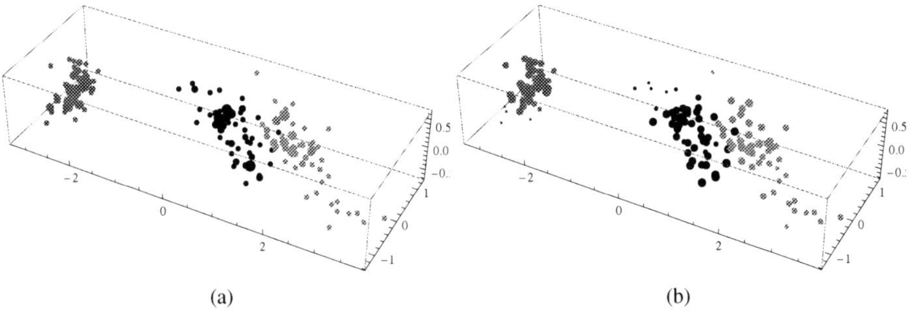

Figure 2. Data quality discovered using: (a) SVC, and (b) SNN Clustering algorithms. Bullets represent observations in the Iris data set, colored according to the class they belong to; moreover each point size is related to the corresponding quality (the smaller the size, the less relevant is the observation).

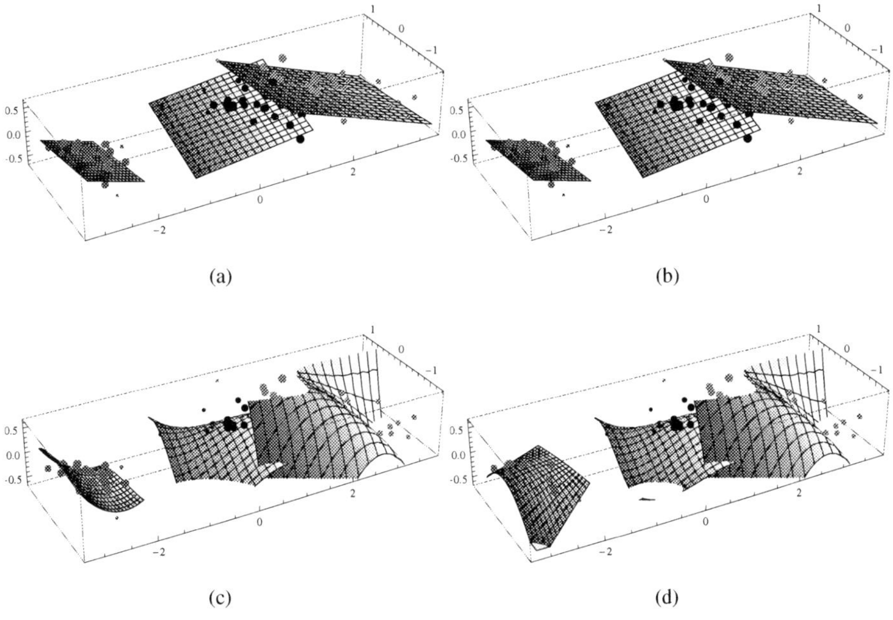

Figure 3. Regressors in output to the proposed procedure. The first and second row report respectively linear and polynomial regressors, while first and second column refer respectively to SVC and SNN Clustering.

5. Conclusions

In this paper we proposed the use of standard clustering procedures for discovering quality in data sets for regression problems. We used the extracted quality exploiting special versions of a regression algorithm tailored as for dealing with this enriched information and compared the results with standard regression techniques. The obtained performance is interesting and delineates future research directions, mainly related to a deeper experimentation phase also involving the use of different clustering procedures. Moreover, the proposed technique of training quality-based regressor specialized for each given

	linear	polynomial
SVC + RSVR	22	12
SNNC + RSVR	22	19
SVR	20	15
LSE	52	16

Table 1. Number of misclassifications when points are assigned to the class corresponding to the nearest linear / polynomial regressor computed according to four different algorithms: Support Vector Clustering with Relevance SVR (SVC + RSVR), Shared Nearest Neighbor Clustering with Relevance SVR (SNNC + RSVR), Support Vector Regression (SVR) and Least Square Estimate (LSE).

class offers attractive comparisons within the field of ensemble learning which is worth exploring.

References

[1] M. Aizerman, E. Braverman, and L. Rozonoer. Theoretical foundations of the potential function method in pattern recognition learning. *Automation and Remote Control*, 25:821–837, 1964.

[2] B. Apolloni and D. Malchiodi. Embedding sample points relevance in SVM linear classification. In V. Torra, Y. Narukawa, A Valls, and J. Domingo-Ferrer, editors, *Modeling Decision for Artificial Intelligence. Third International Conference MDAI 2006. Tarragona, Spain, April 2006. CD Proceedings*, 2006.

[3] B. Apolloni, D. Malchiodi, and L. Valerio. Relevance regression learning with support vector machines. In *Proceedings of WCNA 2008*, 2008. in press.

[4] Bruno Apolloni, Dario Malchiodi, and Luca Natali. A modified SVM classification algorithm for data of variable quality. In *Knowledge-Based Intelligent Information and Engineering Systems 11th International Conference, KES 2007*, pages 131–139, Berlin Heidelberg, 2007. Springer-Verlag.

[5] V. Barnett and T. Lewis. *Outliers in Statistical Data*. Wiley, 3rd edition, 1995.

[6] Asa Ben-Hur, David Horn, Hava T. Siegelmann, and Vladimir Vapnik. Support vector clustering. *Journal of Machine Learning Research*, 2:125–137, 2001.

[7] S. W. Christensen, I. Sinclair, and P. A. S. Reed. Designing committees of models through deliberate weighting of data points. *Journal of Machine Learning Research*, 4:39–66, 2003.

[8] K. Crammer, M. Kearns, and J. Wortman. Learning from data of variable quality. In *Proceedings of NIPS 2005*, 2005. in press.

[9] Harris Drucker, Chris J.C. Burges, Linda Kaufman, Alex Smola, and Vladimir Vapnik. Support vector regression machines. In *Advances in Neural Information Processing Systems 9*, pages 155–161. MIT Press, 1997.

[10] L. Ertoz, M. Steinbach, and V. Kumar. Finding clusters of different sizes, shapes, and densities in noisy, high dimensional data. In *SIAM International Conference on Data Mining (SDM'03)*, 2003.

[11] R.A. Fisher. The use of multiple measurements in taxonomic problems. *Annual Eugenics, Part II*, 7:179–188, 1936. Also in *Contributions to Mathematical Statistics* (John Wiley, NY, 1950).

[12] R. Fletcher. *Practical Methods of Optimisations*. John Wiley & Sons, Chichester, second edition, 1987.

[13] Michael Frigge, David C. Hoaglin, and Boris Iglewicz. Some implementations of the boxplot. *The American Statistician*, 43(1):50–54, 1989.

[14] R. A. Jarvis and E. A. Patrick. Clustering using a similarity measure based on shared nearest neighbors. *IEEE Transactions on Computers*, C-22(11):1025–1034, 1973.

[15] I. T. Jolliffe. *Principal Component Analysis*. Springer Verlag, 1986.

[16] L. Kaufman and P. Rousseeuw. *Finding groups in data: an introduction to cluster analysis*. Wiley, New York, 1990.

[17] M. Last and A. Kandel. Automated detection of outliers in real-world data. In *Proceedings of the Second International Conference on Intelligent Technologies (InTech'2001), Bangkok, Thailand, November, 27-29, 2001*, pages 292–301, 2001.

[18] D. Malchiodi. Embedding sample points uncertainty measures in learning algorithms. *Nonlinear Analysis*, 2(2):635–647, 2008.

[19] T.P. Ryan. *Modern Regression Methods*. Wiley, New York, 1997.

[20] J. Sander, M Ester, H. P. Kriegel, and X Xu. Density-based clustering in spatial databases: The algorithm GDBSCAN and its applications. *Data Minining and Knowledge Discovery*, 2(2):169–194, 1998.

[21] B. Schölkopf, R. C. Williamson, A. J. Smola, J. Shawe-Taylor, and J. Platt. Support vector method for novelty detection. In *Advances in Neural Information Processing Systems 12: Proceedings of the 1999 Conference*, pages 582–588, 2000.

[22] Bernhard Schölkopf, John C. Platt, John Shawe-Taylor, Alex J. Smola, and Robert C. Williamson. Estimating the support of a high-dimensional distribution. *Neural Computation*, 13(7):1443,1471, 2001.

[23] D. M. J. Tax and R. P. W. Duin. Support vector domain description. *Pattern Recognition Letters*, 20:1991–1999, 1999.

Chapter 2

Models

New Directions in Neural Networks
B. Apolloni et al. (Eds.)
IOS Press, 2009

doi:10.3233/978-1-58603-984-4-89

A Flexible Natural Gradient Approach to Blind Separation of Complex Signals

Michele SCARPINITI [1], Daniele VIGLIANO, Raffaele PARISI and Aurelio UNCINI
Infocom Department, "Sapienza" University of Rome

Abstract. In this paper a natural gradient approach to blind source separation in complex environment is presented. It is shown that signals can be successfully reconstructed by a network based on the so called generalized splitting activation function (GSAF). This activation function, whose shape is modified during the learning process, is based on a couple of bi-dimensional spline functions, one for the real and one for the imaginary part of the input, thus avoiding the restriction due to the Louiville's theorem. In addition recent learning metrics are compared with the classical ones in order to improve the speed convergence.
Several experimental results are shown to demonstrate the effectiveness of the proposed method.

Keywords. Blind Source Separation, Natural Gradient, Complex nonlinear functions, Spline functions

Introduction

In the last years an increasing interest in blind separation of complex signal has arisen both in linear [1,2,3,4] and nonlinear environment [5]. It is very important to consider the complex nature of data in problems where both amplitude and phase recovery is essential [6]. A very meaningful case of application is in digital radio communications, where complex envelopes are complex signals.
One of the main issues in designing complex neural networks is the choice of the activation function. Let $f(z)$ be the complex activation function (AF) with $z \in \mathbb{C}$. It is known that $f(z)$ should be nonlinear and bounded and its partial derivatives should exist and be bounded [7].
Unfortunately the analytic and boundedness characteristics are in contrast with the Liouville's theorem [8]. In other words $f(z)$ should be defined as a nonlinear complex function that is bounded almost everywhere in the complex domain $\mathbb{C}$ [2,9].
Recently in [7,10,11,12] it has been introduced a complex neural network using a bi-dimensional (2D) spline function in order to define a new class of flexible AFs, called generalized splitting activation functions (GSAF), which are bounded and (locally) analytic, suitable to define a new class of complex domain neural networks.
In this paper we expand on the generalized splitting AF and derive a natural gradient learning rule [13]. In addition new riemannian metrics [14,15] are tested in order to prove

[1]Corresponding Author: Infocom Department, "Sapienza" University of Rome, via Eudossiana 18, 00184 Roma; E-mail: michele.scarpiniti@uniroma1.it.

their effectiveness in our approach providing several experimental results. This work shows the improvement in speed convergence resulting in the use of a flexible activation function.

The paper is organized as follows: section 1 introduces the blind signal separation (BSS) problem; section 2 shows the problem of choosing a complex activation function; this problem is solved by introducing the generalized splitting function performed by a couple of bi-dimensional spline functions described in section 3. Section 4 describes the natural gradient approach and some modifications; finally section 5 shows some experimental results.

1. Blind Signal Separation in the Complex Environment

Let us consider a vector $\mathbf{s}[n] = \{s_1[n], \ldots, s_N[n]\}^T$ of N complex sources at time n ($\mathbf{s}[n] \in \mathbb{C}^{N\times 1}$); the h-th source can be expressed as $s_h[n] = s_{Rh}[n] + js_{Ih}[n]$. The goal of BSS realized by conventional ICA is to recover the complex signal $\mathbf{s}[n]$ from some observations of the complex mixture $\mathbf{x}[n] = \{x_1[n], \ldots, x_N[n]\}^T$. In this paper the linear and instantaneous mixing model is extended to the complex domain by assuming

$$\mathbf{x[n]} = \mathbf{As[n]} \tag{1}$$

where $\mathbf{A}$ is the $N \times N$ complex-valued mixing matrix, such that $a_{i,j} \in \mathbb{C}$.

The recovering system consists of a complex-valued separating matrix $\mathbf{W}$ which must be estimated to generate independent component outputs

$$\mathbf{y[n]} = \mathbf{Wx[n]} \tag{2}$$

where $\mathbf{y}[n]$ is an estimate of the true source vector $\mathbf{s}[n]$, and its components are as independent as possible.

The de-mixing network is realized through a single layer perceptron shown in figure 1, while the de-mixing algorithm is based on output independence criterion [16]. This approach performs separation by minimization of the mutual information of the network output $\mathbf{y}[n]$ (MMI approach) or by maximization of joint entropy of the network output $\mathbf{y}[n]$ (ME approach). In this paper the ME approach is proposed: it usually allows for simple learning rules and it is closely related to the other approaches based on information theory or high order statistic [17].

We apply the learning algorithm proposed by Bell & Sejnowski [16], known as the INFOMAX principle. Maximizing the joint entropy of the output vector $\mathbf{y}$ (ME approach) we can derive the following learning algorithm

$$\Delta\mathbf{W} = \eta_W[(\mathbf{W}^H)^{-1} + 2\mathbf{g}\mathbf{x}^H] \tag{3}$$

where η_W is the learning rate, a real and positive constant and $\mathbf{g}$ is defined as a derivative function of the activation function (see section 3). Eq. (3) is the final expression of the generalized algorithm proposed by Bell & Sejnowski.

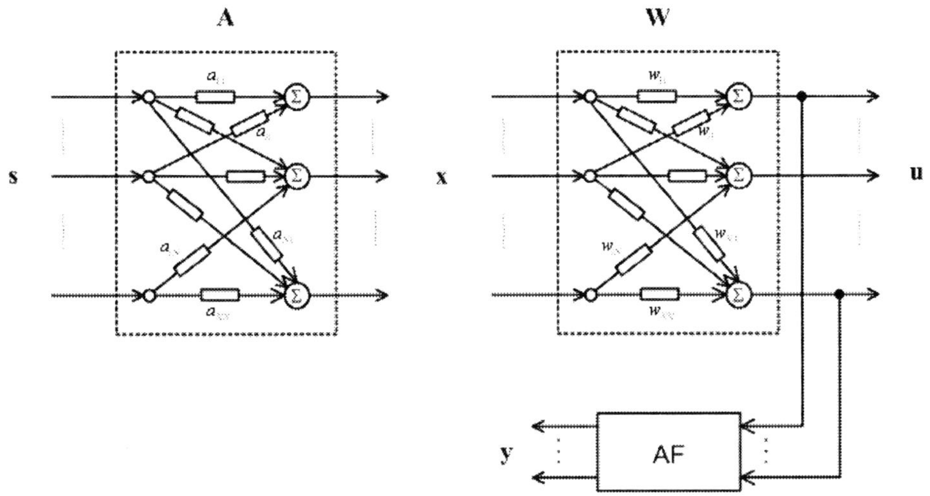

Figure 1. The mixing/de-mixing model

2. The Complex Activation Function

Let $f(z)$ be the complex activation function with $z \in \mathbb{C}$ and $z = x + jy$. According with the need to have complex derivative $f'(z)$ of the activation function without specifying a domain in order to derive the back-propagation rule, the most critical issue is the trade off between the boundedness and analyticity of the nonlinear functions in complex domain $\mathbb{C}$. If the domain is taken to be $\mathbb{C}$, then such functions are called entire. The problem on the existence of an activation function which is both entire and bounded is stated by the Liouville's theorem [8], which asserts that the only bounded and differentiable function is the constant function.

Directly from this theorem follows that entire functions are not suitable activation functions.

Now we can consider the expression of a complex function in relation to the real and imaginary part:

$$f(z) = f(x, y) = u(x, y) + jv(x, y) \tag{4}$$

where the two functions $u(x, y)$ and $v(x, y)$ called real part and imaginary part of the function, are bounded and differentiable, so we can assume $u_x = \frac{\partial u}{\partial x}$, $u_y = \frac{\partial u}{\partial y}$, $v_x = \frac{\partial v}{\partial x}$ and $u_y = \frac{\partial v}{\partial y}$.

In this way Georgiou & Koutsougeras [8] identified five desirable properties of a fully complex activation function:

1. (4) is nonlinear in x and y;
2. $f(z)$ is bounded;
3. the partial derivatives u_x, u_y, v_x and v_y exist and are bounded;
4. $f(z)$ is not entire;
5. $u_x v_y \neq v_x u_y$.

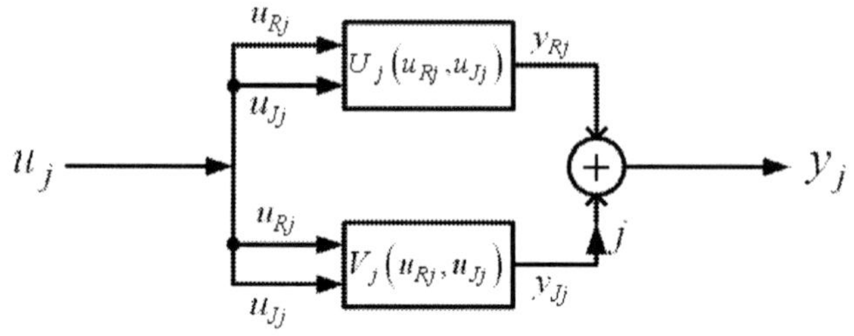

Figure 2. The generalized splitting activation function (GSAF)

Note that by Liouville's theorem, the second and the fourth conditions are redundant. Using this fact Kim & Adali [9] reduced the above conditions into four conditions given below:

1. (4) is nonlinear in x and y;
2. $f(z)$ should have no singularities and be bounded for all z in a bounded set;
3. the partial derivatives u_x, u_y, v_x and v_y exist and are bounded;
4. $u_x v_y \neq v_x u_y$. If not, then $f(z)$ is not a suitable activation function except in the following cases:
   - $u_x = v_x = 0$ and $u_y \neq 0, v_y \neq 0$;
   - $u_y = v_y = 0$ and $u_x \neq 0, v_x \neq 0$

Note that both sets of conditions above emphasize boundedness of an activation function and its partial derivatives, even when the function is defined in a local domain of interest. By Liouville's theorem the cost of this restriction is that a bounded activation function cannot be analytic, which consequently lets the complex activation function to approximate the partial derivatives. A lot of functions proposed for complex neural networks violate the second and third boundedness requirements of both sets of conditions above for the presence of singular points, which hardly pose a problem in learning [2,9].
The last restriction $u_x v_y \neq v_x u_y$ was originally imposed to guarantee continuous learning, but this condition is unnecessary for fully complex functions. This because the fully complex functions satisfy the Cauchy-Riemann equations, which are a necessary condition for a complex function to be analytic at a point $z \in \mathbb{C}$ [8].
Recent works [2] have shown that, for the multilayer perceptron (MLP), a complex counterpart of the universal approximation theorem can be shown with activation functions that are entire (analytic for all values of z) but bounded only almost everywhere, i.e. the elementary transcendental function (ETF). In the case of infomax, since the network is single layer, and the output of the first layer is not used beyond the optimization stage, the problem is simpler.
Following these considerations Vitagliano & al. [7] proposed a complex neural network based on bi-dimensional spline AF.
Considering the complex function (4) it is possible to express both real and imaginary part as bi-dimensional real functions $u(x, y)$ and $v(x, y)$, which must be bounded and differentiable, with bi-dimensional splines. This AF is known as generalized splitting activation function (GSAF), see figure 2.

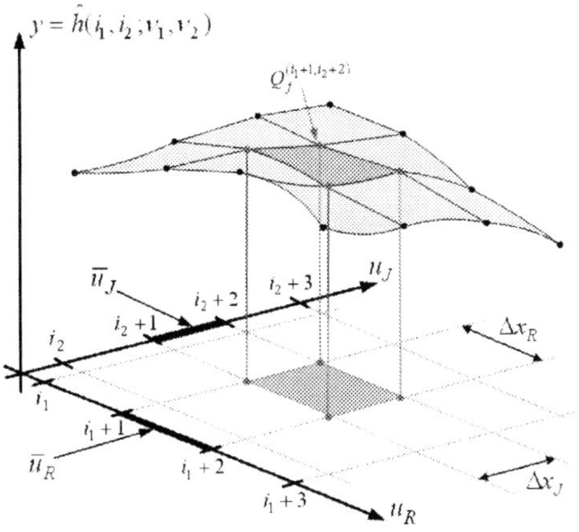

Figure 3. An example of 2D CR-spline

3. Spline approximation neuron

In the last years a great interest in the intelligent use of the activation functions has been oriented to reduce hardware complexity and improve the generalization ability. The Spline mono-dimensional neuron is a LUT-based activation function which can solve this problem [18]. The spline neuron performs the interpolation of the LUT values, which represent the samples of the function for a fixed abscissas. The interpolation scheme involves only four control points, nearest to the point to be adapted, selected on the base of the parameter i: the span index that selects which tract of the adaptive function is used; the position of the abscissa with respect to the inner interval of control points has been specified by the local parameter u [18]. This scheme guarantees a continuous first derivate and the capability to locally adapt the curve. A detailed dissertation on spline activation neuron is out of the scope of this section, see [10,18] for more details.

The mono-dimentional spline neuron can be generalized to realize bi-dimensional functions as hyper-surface interpolation of control points using higher order interpolants [10]. In particular piecewise of splines are here employed in order to render the hyper-surface continuous in its partial derivatives. The entire approximation is represented through the concatenation of local functions each centered and controlled by 4^2 control points, which lie on a regular 2D grid in $\mathbb{R}^2$, defined over the region $0 \leq u_1, u_2 \leq 1$ (see figure 3), and in matrix formulation it is expressed as follows:

$$y = \hat{h}(i_1, i_2; u_1, u_2) = \mathbf{T_2M}(\mathbf{T_1MQ})^T \tag{5}$$

where $\mathbf{T}_k = \left[u_k^3 \; u_k^2 \; u_k \; 1\right]$, $\mathbf{M}$ is a matrix that selects which basis is chosen (*Catmull-Rom (CR)* or *B-Spline*) and $\mathbf{Q}$ is a 2-dimensional structure called the local control points.

Now the idea is to use the expression (5) to realize the real and imaginary function in (4), as introduced in [12]. The data path of our generalized splitting activation function is shown in figure 4.

Since the activation function is a flexible one and its shape is changed during the learning, a learning rule is due. We again adopt the INFOMAX algorithm, maximizing the joint

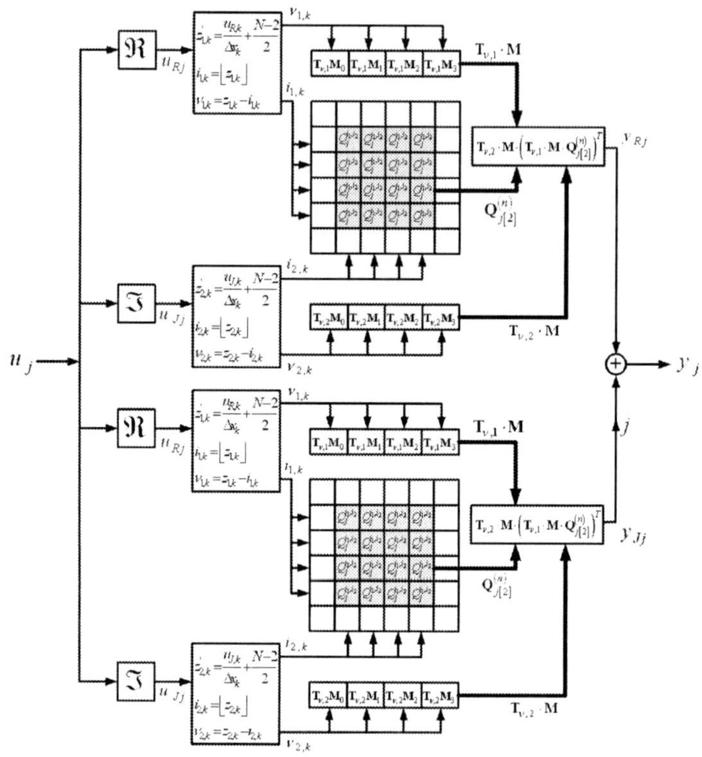

Figure 4. Data path of GSAF

entropy of the network output $\mathbf{y}$ with respect the control points Q_j of the AF. We obtain (see appendix A in [12]):

$$\begin{aligned}\Delta Q_{j,i_R+m_R,i_J+m_J} &= 2\eta_{\mathbf{Q}}\cdot \\ \cdot\Bigg(&\frac{\left(\mathbf{T}_{2j}\cdot\mathbf{M}\cdot\left(\dot{\mathbf{T}}_{1j}\cdot\mathbf{M}\cdot\mathbf{Q}_{jR}\right)^T\right)\left(\mathbf{T}_{2j}\cdot\mathbf{M}_{m_J}\cdot\left(\dot{\mathbf{T}}_{1j}\cdot\mathbf{M}_{m_R}\right)^T\right)}{\left(\mathbf{T}_{2j}\cdot\mathbf{M}\cdot\left(\dot{\mathbf{T}}_{1j}\cdot\mathbf{M}\cdot\mathbf{Q}_{jR}\right)^T\right)^2+\left(\dot{\mathbf{T}}_{2j}\cdot\mathbf{M}\cdot\left(\mathbf{T}_{1j}\cdot\mathbf{M}\cdot\mathbf{Q}_{jR}\right)^T\right)^2}+ \\ &+\frac{\left(\dot{\mathbf{T}}_{2j}\cdot\mathbf{M}\cdot\left(\mathbf{T}_{1j}\cdot\mathbf{M}\cdot\mathbf{Q}_{jR}\right)^T\right)\left(\dot{\mathbf{T}}_{2j}\cdot\mathbf{M}_{m_J}\cdot\left(\mathbf{T}_{1j}\cdot\mathbf{M}_{m_R}\right)^T\right)}{\left(\mathbf{T}_{2j}\cdot\mathbf{M}\cdot\left(\dot{\mathbf{T}}_{1j}\cdot\mathbf{M}\cdot\mathbf{Q}_{jR}\right)^T\right)^2+\left(\dot{\mathbf{T}}_{2j}\cdot\mathbf{M}\cdot\left(\mathbf{T}_{1j}\cdot\mathbf{M}\cdot\mathbf{Q}_{jR}\right)^T\right)^2}\Bigg)\end{aligned} \tag{6}$$

where $\mathbf{M}_k$ is a matrix in which all the elements are zero, except the k-th column which is equal to the k-th column of $\mathbf{M}$, $\dot{\mathbf{T}}_k = \begin{bmatrix}3u_k^2 & 2u_k & 1 & 0\end{bmatrix}$ and where η_Q is the learning rate.

4. Natural Gradient Adaptation

The stochastic gradient technique is widely used in literature for maximizing or minimizing a cost function. It is a very simple approach but, if data lies in a Riemannian space $\mathcal{S} = \{\vartheta \in \mathbb{C}\}$, the convergence can be very slow or the solution can fall in a local

solution.
To avoid these problems the natural gradient is introduced [13,19] for an arbitrary functional $J(\vartheta)$ defined in the space $\mathcal{S}$:

$$\tilde{\nabla} J(\vartheta) = G^{-1}(\vartheta)\nabla J(\vartheta) \tag{7}$$

where $\nabla J(\vartheta)$ is the standard stochastic gradient, $G^{-1}(\vartheta)$ is the inverse of the metric tensor and $\tilde{\nabla} J(\vartheta)$ is the natural gradient.
Amari has demonstrated in [13] that the inverse of the metric tensor in (7) is a very simple expression in the Lie group, i.e. the space of invertible matrices $\mathbf{W}_{\mathbf{n}\times\mathbf{n}}$, namely $GL(n, \mathbb{R})$. It is simply

$$\tilde{\nabla} J(W) = \nabla J(W) W^T W \tag{8}$$

Using (8) the ME algorithm (3) becomes the following one:

$$\Delta\mathbf{W} = (\mathbf{I} + 2\mathbf{g}\mathbf{u}^H)\mathbf{W} \tag{9}$$

This algorithm is numerically more efficient than the classical one since that it avoids the inversion of the $\mathbf{W}$ matrix.
In addition some new riemannian metrics are introduced in [14] and [15], in order to improve the convergence speed. The authors introduced four additional and alternative algorithms in a riemannian space. The new idea is based on an alternative natural gradient formulation, imposing that the inner product in a riemannian space be invariant under translation in such space. In this way five different natural gradient expression can be derived:

$$\tilde{\nabla}_R J(W) = \nabla J(W) W^T W \tag{10}$$

$$\tilde{\nabla}_L J(W) = W W^T \nabla J(W) \tag{11}$$

$$\tilde{\nabla}_{LR} J(W) = (W W^T) \nabla J(W) (W^T W) \tag{12}$$

$$\tilde{\nabla}_{RR} J(W) = \nabla J(W) (W^T W^T W W) \tag{13}$$

$$\tilde{\nabla}_{LL} J(W) = (W W W^T W^T) \nabla J(W) \tag{14}$$

namely the right natural gradient (10), which is the standard natural gradient (8) introduced in [13], the left natural gradient (11), the right/left natural gradient (12), the right/right natural gradient (13) and the left/left natural gradient (14) rispectively.
Using (11)-(14) the ME algorithm (3) becomes:

$$\Delta\mathbf{W} = \mathbf{W}(\mathbf{I} + 2\mathbf{W}^H\mathbf{g}\mathbf{x}^H) \tag{15}$$

$$\Delta\mathbf{W} = \mathbf{W}\mathbf{W}^H(\mathbf{I} + 2\mathbf{g}\mathbf{u}^H)\mathbf{W} \tag{16}$$

$$\Delta\mathbf{W} = (\mathbf{I} + 2\mathbf{g}\mathbf{u}^H)\mathbf{W}^H\mathbf{W}\mathbf{W} \tag{17}$$

$$\Delta\mathbf{W} = \mathbf{W}\mathbf{W}\mathbf{W}^H(\mathbf{I} + 2\mathbf{W}^H\mathbf{g}\mathbf{x}^H) \tag{18}$$

It should be noted that algorithms (16)-(18) do not satisfy the equivariance property.

5. Results

In order to test our architecture, we used a 8-PSK (Phase Shift Keying) signal, a uniform noise signal and a 4-QAM Quadrature Amplitude Modulation) signal, each with 1000 samples. In all the experiments we use the following parameters: the learning rate for the $\mathbf{W}$ matrix is set to $\eta_W = 0.0001$, while the learning rate for the spline control points is set to $\eta_Q = 0.0005$. The spline step is $\Delta = 0.3$ and the algorithm runs for 100 epochs. The results are mean over 30 runs.

In order to provide a mathematical evaluation of the output separation, different indexes of performance are available in literature. In this paper the signal to interference ratio (SIR) S_j of the j-th source was adopted [20]; the index was presented in real environment but in this work it has been extended to a complex environment:

$$S_j = 10\log\left[E\left\{\left(|y|_{\sigma(j),j}\right)^2\right\} \Big/ E\left\{\sum_{k\neq j}\left(|y|_{\sigma(j),k}\right)^2\right\}\right] \tag{19}$$

In (19) $y_{i,j}$ is the i-th output signal when only the j-th input signal is present, while $\sigma(j)$ is the output channel corresponding to the j-th input.

Another way to evaluate the performance of the algorithm is to analyze the matrix product $\mathbf{WA}$ which has to be close to the product of a diagonal matrix and a permutation matrix. Thus according to the desired solution to BSS problem, only one element in each row and column can be substantially a non zero element.

Let us assume h_{ij} the elements of the matrix $\mathbf{H} = \mathbf{WA}$, we can define the following performance index [21]:

$$S = \sum_{i=1}^{N}\left(\frac{\sum_{j=1}^{N}|h_{ij}|^2}{\max_p\left[|h_{ip}|^2\right]} - 1\right) + \sum_{j=1}^{N}\left(\frac{\sum_{i=1}^{N}|h_{ij}|^2}{\max_p\left[|h_{pj}|^2\right]} - 1\right) \tag{20}$$

This index is positive and it is equal to zero only for perfect separation.

The results of the first experimental test are summarized in the following table 1.

We perform a second test using a 16-PSK (Phase Shift Keying) signal, a 4-QAM (Quadrature Amplitude Modulation) signal and a 16-QAM signal, each with 1000 samples. In all the experiments we use the previous parameters. The results of this test are summarized in the following table 2.

Table 1. Results of the first test

Gradient	**SIR** (dB)			**Sep. Index**	**Convergence**
	s_1	s_2	s_3	$\times 10^{-3}$	(epochs)
Standard	37,99	8,11	22,96	238	50
Right	50,48	40,05	34,35	2,29	25
Left	42,73	18,55	24,02	33	30
Right/left	39,24	33,14	37,26	1,63	15
Left/left	9,37	9,56	9,55	752	20
Right/right	45,41	34,45	40,40	1,041	23

Table 2. Result of the second test

Gradient	**SIR** (dB)			**Sep. Index**	**Convergence**
	s_1	s_2	s_3	$\times 10^{-3}$	(epochs)
Standard	30,02	17,08	20,40	62	60
Rigth	35,95	42,61	29,85	3,46	35
Left	34,71	10,87	5,98	45	25
Right/left	33,22	13,70	10,11	2,03	35
Left/left	17,68	21,57	12,06	380	15
Right/right	23,87	38,10	23,21	2,10	30

Table 1 shows that the standard stochastic gradient provides a quite good separation performance, but the learning is slow: it is stable after about 50 epochs. Better is the solution with the standard natural gradient (right natural gradient): the value of SIR is higher and the learning is faster (about 25 epochs). More performance is the use of right/left and right/right natural gradient: good SIR and very fast (about 15 and 23 epochs respectively); while worst is the case of left and left/left natural gradient: bad SIR, but quite fast (better than the standard stochastic gradient).
Softly worst are the results in the second test (table 2), due to the presence of two similar distributed signals (8-PSK and 16-PSK), but the trend is similar to the first test.
The use of the generalized splitting activation function realized with the bi-dimensional spline functions improve more the convergence speed with respect a fix function, comparing our tests with the ones in [15].

6. Conclusion

This paper introduces a natural gradient approach to the blind separation of complex sources extending to the complex domain the well-known INFOMAX algorithm. In addition some new riemannian metrics [15] are tested and demonstrate the improving in speed of convergence.
Furthermore, the convergence speed is improved choosing an activation function of the de-mixing network implemented with a couple of bi-dimensional and adaptive cubic functions, whose shape is changed during the learning [11] and [12].
Several tests have been performed to verify the effectiveness of the proposed approach and demonstrate that it can easily solve the problem of separating complex signals. The quality of the separation has been evaluated in terms of the SIR and Separation Index which are widely diffused in literature.

References

[1] Eriksson, J., Koivunen, V.: Complex random vectors and ica models: identifiability, uniqueness, and separability. Information Theory, IEEE Transactions on **52**(3) (March 2006) 1017–1029

[2] Adali, T., Kim, T., Calhoun, V.: Independent component analysis by complex nonlinearities. In: Acoustics, Speech, and Signal Processing, 2004. Proceedings. (ICASSP '04). IEEE International Conference on. Volume 5. (17-21 May 2004) 525–528

[3] Calhoun, V., Adali, T.: Complex infomax: convergence and approximation of infomax with complex nonlinearities. In: Neural Networks for Signal Processing, 2002. Proceedings of the 2002 12th IEEE Workshop on. (4-6 Sept. 2002) 307–316

[4] Theis, F.J.: Uniqueness of complex and multidimensional independent component analysis. Signal Processing **84** (2004) 951–956

[5] Vigliano, D., Scarpiniti, M., Parisi, R., Uncini, A.: A flexible blind source recovery in complex nonlinear environment. In: Intelligent Control, 2006. IEEE International Symposium on, Munich, Germany (October 4-6 2006) 3059–3063

[6] Calhoun, V., Adali, T., Pearlson, G., van Zijl, P., Pekar, J.: Independent component analysis of fmri data in the complex domain. Magnetic Resonance in Medicine **48** (2002) 180–192

[7] Vitagliano, F., Parisi, R., Uncini, A.: Generalized splitting 2d flexible activation function. In: Lecture Notes in Computer Science. Volume 2859. (May 2003) 165–170

[8] Georgiou, G., Koutsougeras, C.: Complex domain backpropagation. IEEE Transaction on Circuit and System **39**(5) (May 1992) 330–334

[9] Kim, T., Adali, T.: Fully complex backpropagation for constant envelope signal processing. In: Neural Networks for Signal Processing X, 2000. Proceedings of the 2000 IEEE Signal Processing Society Workshop. Volume 1. (11-13 Dec. 2000) 231–240

[10] Solazzi, M., Uncini, A.: Regularising neural networks using flexible multivariate activation function. Neural Networks **17** (2004) 247–260

[11] Scarpiniti, M., Vigliano, D., Parisi, R., Uncini, A.: Generalized flexible splitting function outperforms classical approaches in blind signal separation of complex environment. In: Proc. of DSP2007, Cardiff, U.K. (July 1-4 2007) 215–218

[12] Scarpiniti, M., Vigliano, D., Parisi, R., Uncini, A.: Generalized splitting functions for blind separation of complex signals. Neurocomputing **71** (2008) 2245–2270

[13] Amari, S.I.: Natural gradient works efficiently in learning. Neural Computation **10** (1998) 251–276

[14] Arcangeli, A., Squartini, S., Piazza, F.: An alternative natural gradient approach for ica based learning algorithms in blind source separation. In: Proceedings of EUSIPCO 2004, Vienna, Austria (2004) 593–596

[15] Squartini, S., Piazza, F., Shawker, A.: New riemannian metrics for improvement of convergence speed in ica based learning algorithms. In: Proc. IEEE International Symposium on Circuits and Systems ISCAS 2005. Volume 4. (2005) 3603–3606

[16] Bell, A.J., Sejnowski, T.J.: An information-maximisation approach to blind separation and blind deconvolution. Neural Computation **7** (1995) 1129–1159

[17] Lee, T.W., Girolami, M., Bell, A.J., Sejnowski, T.J.: A unifying information-theoretic framework for independent component analysis. Computer & Mathematics with applications **39**(11) (June 2000) 1–21

[18] Uncini, A., Piazza, F.: Blind signal processing by complex domain adaptive spline neural networks. Neural Networks, IEEE Transactions on **14**(2) (March 2003) 399–412

[19] Haykin, S., ed.: Unsupervised Adaptive Filtering, Volume 1: Blind Signal Separation. Volume 1. John Wiley & Sons, Inc. (2000)

[20] Shobben, D., Torkkola, K., Smaragdis, P.: Evaluation of blind signal separation methods. In: In Proc. of ICA and BSS, Aussois, France (Jenuary, 11-15 1999) 239–244

[21] Amari, S., Cichocki, A., Howard, H.: A new learning algorithm for blind signal separation. Advances in Neural Information Processing Systems **8** (1996) 757–763

New Directions in Neural Networks
B. Apolloni et al. (Eds.)
IOS Press, 2009

doi:10.3233/978-1-58603-984-4-99

Single Channel Polyphonic Music Transcription

ANGELO CIARAMELLA [a,1]
[a] *Dept. of Applied Sciences University of Naples "Parthenope", Isola C4, Centro Direzionale I-80143, Napoli, Italy*

Abstract. This work aims to propose a novel model to perform automatic music transcription of polyphonic audio sounds. The notes of different musical instruments are extracted from a single channel recording by using a non-linear Principal Component Analysis Neural Network. The estimated components (waveforms) are classified by using a dictionary (i.e. database). The dictionary contains the features of the notes for several musical instruments (i.e. probability densities). A Kullback-Leibler divergence is used to recognize the extract waveforms as belonging to one instrument in the database. Moreover, considering the weights of the Neural Network a MUSIC frequency estimator is used to obtain the frequencies of the musical notes. Several results are proposed to show the performance of this technique for the transcription of mixtures of different musical instruments, real songs and recordings obtained in a real environment.

Keywords. Non-linear Principal Component Analysis, Polyphonic Sound, Musical Transcription

Introduction

Musical transcription of audio data is the process of converting a musical recording or performance into a musical score, or equivalent representation. Transcribing a piece of music implies a number of high-level tasks:

- estimating the pitch and timing of individual notes
- estimating the tempo, metre and key of each section of the piece
- identifying and labeling ornamentations
- recognizing the instruments being played
- segregating voices according to the instrument that played them and to their function (i.e. melody, accompaniment, etc.)

These tasks, already complicated for highly trained individuals such as musicians and musicologists, have proven extremely difficult for computers. Relatively successful methods have been proposed for monophonic signals, i.e. when only one note is at a time. However, success has been more evasive for the analysis of polyphonic signals, i.e. presenting a multiplicity of notes and, possibly, instruments at a time. At its simplest, the

[1]Corresponding Author: Dept. of Applied Sciences University of Naples "Parthenope", Isola C4, Centro Direzionale I-80143, Napoli, Italy, e-mail: angelo.ciaramella@uniparthenope.it

issue of transcribing music, except for information related to timbre and instrumentation, can be reduced to knowing the fundamental frequency, start time, duration and loudness of individual musical notes in the recording.
In literature polyphonic music transcription systems rely on the analysis of information in the frequency domain [14,15,18]. In fact, in [10] the transcription of polyphonic sounds of a single instrument is obtained by using an iterative calculation of the predominant frequency in separated frequency bands. Moreover, based on frequency information in [13] the author uses a blackboard system (e.g. database system) to extract the scores of a single known instrument. In [12] a Bayesian probability network for the grouping of supportive frequency-domain evidence is used. In [16] both Hidden Markov Model and spectral feature vectors are used to describe chord sequences in piano music signals. In [18] and [8] the authors proposed a system to extract drum tracks from polyphonic music using Independent Subspace Analysis (ISA) in the frequency domain. In [17] the authors presented a methodology based on non-negative matrix factorization to analyze polyphonic musical passages comprised by notes that exhibit a harmonically fixed spectral profile (i.e. piano notes). In [1] some solutions for automatic piano transcription using both frequency and time-domain features are proposed. However, relying on the analysis of the frequency-domain data has some disadvantage [1,11]. The resolution limitations of most time-frequency representations can badly effect the frequency localization of spectral components. This is emphasized by the polyphony of the signal: when more than one note is present, peaks related to different frequencies can lie in the same frequency bin and therefore are not uniquely identifiable. The problem becomes worse when the polyphony increases, often increasing the number of estimation errors. Overlapping between the different harmonic (or nearly harmonic) series is also produced by the presence of harmonic relations between sounds (i.e. harmonicity). This phenomena sharply diminishes the chances of resolving the mixture of notes in the signal.
The aim of this work is to propose novel ways of automatically extracting note events from simple polyphonic sounds, i.e. real recordings including an undetermined number of notes at a time played by a single or by multiple instruments. The proposed approach is based on the estimation of the waveform of the notes for each single instrument (e.g. information about timbre, attack, etc..). The musical score transcription of different instrumental sources is obtained from a single channel recording. In other words, the aim is to estimate the independent components from a single channel mixture [2,7,19]. In [2] the authors introduced an approach to estimate the independent sources of single channel mixtures by studying the embedding space of the signal (i.e. embedding dimension and time lag).
In this work the separation of the notes from audio files is obtained by using a non-linear Principal Component Analysis (PCA) Neural Network (NN) [2,4,6]. The estimated components (waveforms) are recognized as belonging to one known musical instrument by querying a dictionary of features (database). This database, in fact, contains the features extracted from single notes of several instruments. In this paper, as features, we simply use a probability density of the notes but a different and more complex measure can be used (i.e. High Frequency Content [1]). To classify one separated component to one instrument in the database, we compare both the densities by using a Kullback-Leibler divergence. Furthermore, the weights of the NN related with the components recognized as belonging to one musical instrument are used to calculate the frequencies of the single notes by using the MUSIC (MUltiple SIgnal Classfication) frequency estimator [4,6].

The paper is organized as follows. In Section 1 we introduce the non-linear PCA Neural Network approach. In Section 2 the proposed transcription scheme is detailed. Moreover in Section 3 we show some experimental results obtained on realistic and real audio data.

1. PCA Neural Networks

PCA is a widely used technique in data analysis. Mathematically, it is de fined as follows. Let $\mathbf{C} = E(\mathbf{x}\mathbf{x}^T)$ be the covariance matrix of L-dimensional zero mean input data vectors $\mathbf{x}$. The i-th principal component of $\mathbf{x}$ is defined as $\mathbf{x}^T\mathbf{c}(i)$, where $\mathbf{c}(i)$ is the normalized eigenvector of $\mathbf{C}$ corresponding to the i-th largest eigenvalue $\lambda(i)$. The subspace spanned by the principal eigenvectors $\mathbf{c}(1), \ldots, \mathbf{c}(M), (M < L))$ is called the PCA subspace (of dimensionality M). We note that the PCA can be neurally realized in various ways [9,4,6].

In this paper we use a PCA NN that is a one layer feedforward NN which is able to extract the principal components of the stream of input vectors. Typically, Hebbian type learning rules are used, based on the one unit learning algorithm originally proposed by Oja. Many different versions and extensions of this basic algorithm have been proposed during the recent years [4,6,9]. The structure of the PCA NN can be summarised as follows: there is one input layer and one forward layer of neurons totally connected to the inputs; during the learning phase there are feedback links among neurons, that classify the network structure as either hierarchical or symmetric. After the learning phase the network becomes purely feedforward. The hierarchical case leads to the well known GHA algorithm; in the symmetric case we have the Oja's subspace network.

PCA neural algorithms can be derived from optimization problems; in this way the learning algorithms can be further classified in linear PCA algorithms and non-linear PCA algorithms. As defined in [4,6] in order to extract the principal components we use a non-linear PCA NN that derives from the robust generalization of variance maximisation where the objective function $f(t)$ is assumed to be a valid cost function, such as $\ln\cosh(t)$. The general algorithm is described in figure 1.

2. Musical Transcription Scheme

In this Section we introduce the general scheme of the proposed model for the musical transcription of polyphonic audio sounds.

Initially a dictionary of features must be defined. It contains information about the notes of different musical instruments. It is used, successively, to classify the single extract components as belonging to one musical instrument. The features used in this work are extracted from the notes by using a non-parametric density estimator (histogram). In figure 1a the A_4 note of a piano in time domain is plotted and in figure 1b its corresponding histogram. Can be noted that for a fixed musical instrument the histograms have a similar behavior, how shown in figure 1c. Here we have plotted the histograms for some notes of the fourth octave of a piano. Moreover, can be noted that the densities of a musical note, estimated with different phases, describe a similar distribution. This effect is visualized in figure 1d where are compared the densities obtained from the note A_4 of

Algorithm 1 Non-linear PCA Algorithm

1: Initialize the number of output neurons m. Initialize the weight matrix $\mathbf{W} = [\mathbf{w}_1, \ldots, \mathbf{w}_m]$ with small random values. Initialize the learning threshold ϵ, the learning rate μ and the α parameter.
Reset pattern counter $k = 1$.

2: Input the $n - th$ pattern

$$\mathbf{x}_n = [x(n), x(n+1), \ldots, x(n + (q-1))]$$

where q is the number of input components .

3: Calculate the output for each neuron $y_i = \mathbf{w}_i^T \mathbf{x}_n$. $\forall i = 1, ..., m$

4: Modify the weights using the following equation

$$\mathbf{w}_i(k+1) = \mathbf{w}_i(k) + \mu_k g(y_i(k)) \mathbf{e}_i(k)$$

$$\mathbf{e}_i(k) = \mathbf{x}_i - \sum_{j=1}^{I(i)} y_j(k) \mathbf{w}_j(k)$$

$$\mathbf{w}_i(k+1) = \frac{\mathbf{w}_i(k+1)}{\|\mathbf{w}_i(k+1)\|}$$

where in the hierarchical case we have $I(i) = i$. In the symmetric case $I(i) = m$, the error vector $\mathbf{e}_i(k)$ becomes the same $\mathbf{e}_i$ for all the neurons.

5: UNTIL the number of pattern is not empty GO TO 2

6: Convergence test:
IF $C_T = \frac{1}{2} \sum_{i=1}^{m} \sum_{j=1}^{m} (w_{ij} - w_{ij}^{old})^2 < \epsilon$
THEN GO TO 8
ELSE

$$\mathbf{W} = (\mathbf{W}\mathbf{W}^T)^{\frac{1}{2}} \mathbf{W}$$

$$\mathbf{W}^{old} = \mathbf{W}$$

7: $k = k + 1$; GO TO 2.

8: END

a piano with different delays (delay $\Delta T = 500 - 1000 - 5000$ samples).
Successively, given a sound signal the next step is to apply a non-linear PCA NN to obtain a number of fixed components or independent waveforms. For each estimated component we calculate its probability density and then we compare it with the densities of the musical instruments contained in the database. To calculate the similarity between the densities we use the Kullback-Leibler (KL) divergence. The KL divergence is defined

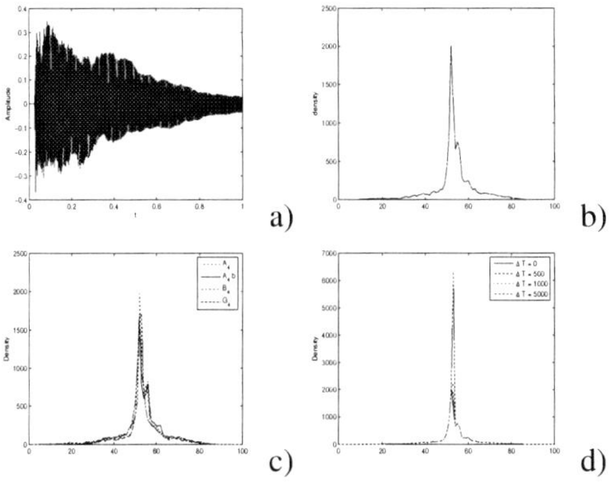

Figure 1. Piano A_4 note: a) time domain; b) histogram; c) histogram of several piano notes; d) comparison between histograms of the same musical note but with different phases.

between two discrete n-dimensional probability density functions $\mathbf{p} = [p_1 \dots p_n]$ and $\mathbf{q} = [q_1, \dots, q_n]$ as

$$KL(\mathbf{p}, \mathbf{q}) = \sum_{i=1}^{n} p_i \log\left(\frac{p_i}{q_i}\right) \tag{1}$$

This is known as the relative entropy. It satisfies the Gibbs' inequality

$$KL(\mathbf{p}||\mathbf{q}) \geq 0 \tag{2}$$

where equality holds only if $\mathbf{p} \equiv \mathbf{q}$. In general $KL(\mathbf{p}||\mathbf{q}) \neq KL(\mathbf{q}||\mathbf{p})$. In our experiments we use the symmetric version that can be defined as

$$KL = \frac{KL(\mathbf{p}||\mathbf{q}) + KL(\mathbf{q}||\mathbf{p})}{2}. \tag{3}$$

The next step consists in the estimation of the frequencies considering all the components recognized as belonging to a musical instrument. We directly use the weights of the PCA NN to obtain the frequency information related with the notes. We simply calculate the Power Spectrum Density (PSD) by using the MUSIC (MUltiple SIgnal Classificator) estimator[4]. MUSIC takes as input the weight matrix columns related with the components recognized as belonging to one instrument. The estimated signal frequencies are obtained as the peak locations of the function of the following equation

$$PSD(f) = \frac{1}{\left(M - \sum_{i=1}^{M} |\mathbf{e}_f^H \mathbf{w}_i|^2\right)} \tag{4}$$

where M is the number of selected components associated to one instrument, w_i is the i-th NN weight vector, and e_f^H is the vector

$$\mathbf{e}_f^H = \left[1, e_f^{j2\pi f t_0}, \dots, e_f^{j2\pi f t_{L-1}}\right] \tag{5}$$

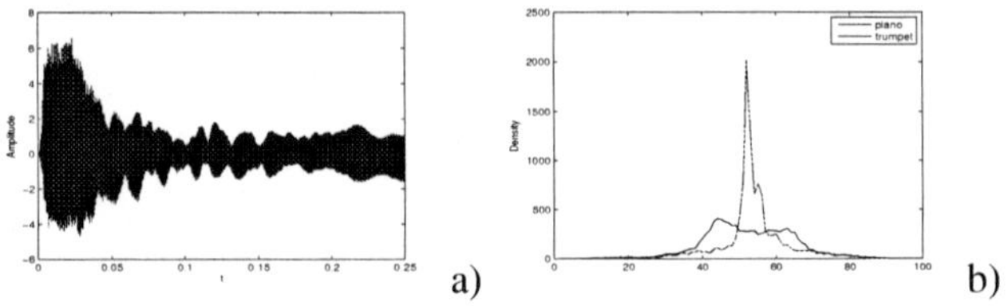

Figure 2. a) A_4 note of the trumpet ; b) histograms of the A_4 note for the piano and the trumpet.

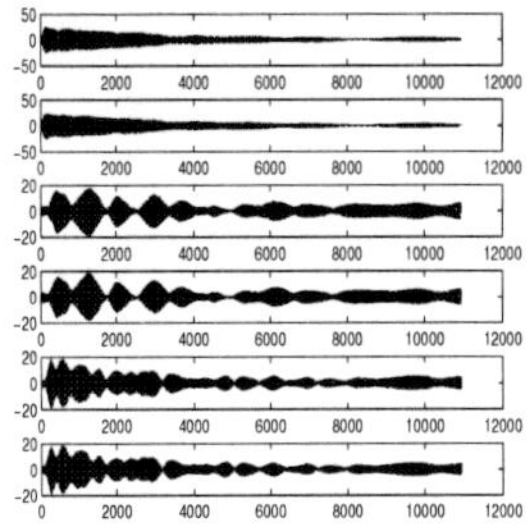

Figure 3. PCA NN estimated components.

where $t_0, t_1, \ldots, t_{L-1}$ are the first L components of the temporal coordinates of the signal. We note that when f is the frequency of the i-th sinusoidal component, $f = f_i$, we have $\mathbf{e} = \mathbf{e}_i$ and $PSD(f) \rightarrow \infty$. In practice we have a peak near and in correspondence of the component frequency. Estimate are related to the highest peaks. The highest frequency is extracted and used to obtain the frequency of the note. In the next Section several experiments will be proposed to clarify the overall process.

3. Experimental results

Now we detail some experimental results obtained applying the described scheme on synthetic and real data.
In a first experiment we consider two different musical instruments that play the same note. We observe that also for this simple experiment the separation is not simple for the approaches that use only frequency information. The proposed approach, instead, uses information related with the waveform of a specific musical instrument (e.g. envelope, attack, sustain, decay, etc..).
In the experiment we consider the A_4 note of a piano and the same note for a trumpet. In this case we have a dictionary that contains the histograms of the C_4 note for both the instruments. In figure 2a we plot the waveform of the trumpet and in figure 2b the histograms of this sound and of the piano note. We observe that the densities are independent and that they could be considered as super- and sub-Gaussian distributions.
Now we apply the PCA NN to estimate six independent components (see figure 3). Successively, the histograms are calculated for each single extract waveform. After the comparison with the histograms contained in the database we classify the first two components as piano and the other four as trumpet. In figure 4a we plot the sources classified

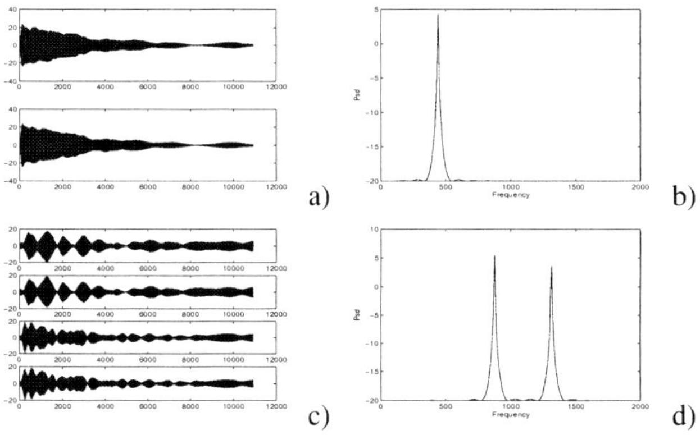

Figure 4. Extract sources: a) time domain (piano); b) *HFC* obtained with the MUSIC estimator (piano); c) time domain (trumpet); b) *HFC* obtained with the MUSIC estimator (trumpet).

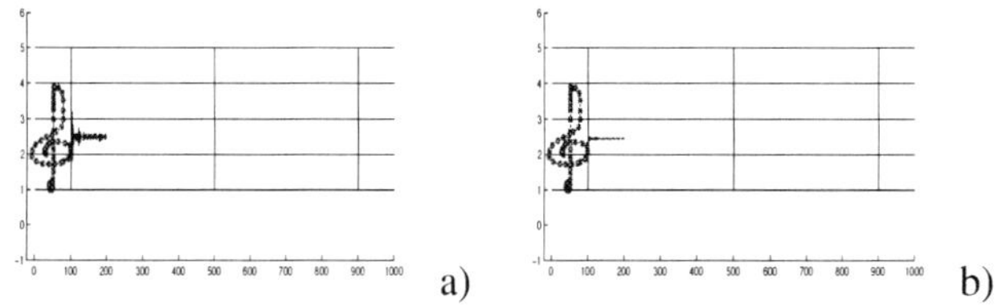

Figure 5. Pentagram: a) piano; b) trumpet.

as piano and in figure 4b the *PSD* obtained with the MUSIC estimator. In figure 4c and figure 4d we plot the sources classified as trumpet and the *PSD* obtained by MUSIC. We note that in this last case the *PSD* has two frequencies but with the same information (the fundamental frequency and one harmonic frequency). Moreover, we developed a system that automatically displays the notes on a pentagram and that associate, for each instrument, the position corresponding to the recognized frequency (also the waveform, in this case). In 5a and 5b, in fact, we visualize the estimated waveforms in the positions corresponding to the estimate frequencies, for the piano and the trumpet, respectively.
Now we show a second experiment in which we consider different musical notes in the fourth octave for the piano (A_4, G_4, C_4, D_4, E_4, F_4, B_4) and a single note for the trumpet (A_4). Aim of this experiment is to demonstrate that a perfect separation is achieved also varying the fundamental frequency of the waveform. Also in this case we consider a database that contains the histograms of the C_4 note for both the instruments. The one-dimensional recording is plotted in figure 6a.
In this case, to separate the notes, we divide the mixture in different contiguous frames and for each of them we apply the same analysis previously described (each frame is of 5000 samples). Also in this case we apply the PCA NN approach and we extract the histograms from the single components. Successively, we recognize the waveforms querying the database. The obtained pentagrams are showed in figure 6b and 6c for the piano and the trumpet, respectively.

Now we observe that in literature most approaches are applied on synthesized data. Here we show the results obtained on a real jazz song (shuffle), "Blue Room" played by Chet Baker. In this recording there are four different instruments that are a drum set,

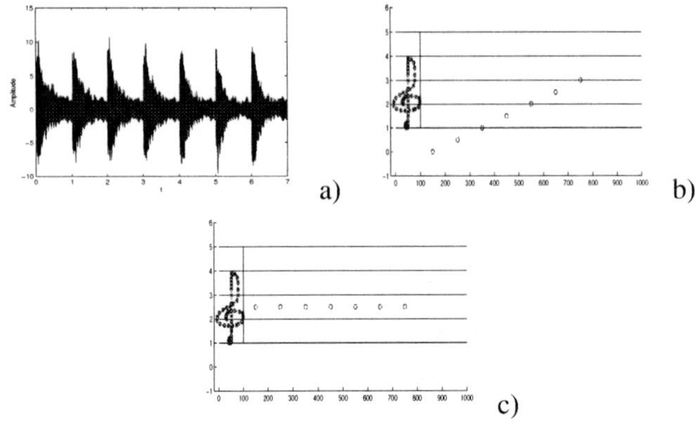

Figure 6. a) piano and trumpet mixture; b) piano pentagram; c) trumpet pentagram.

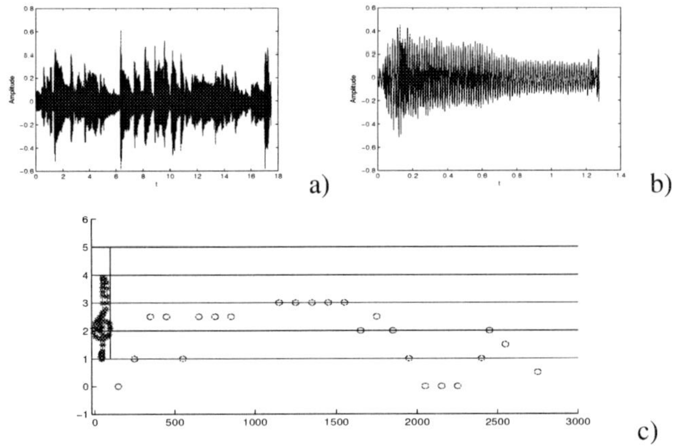

Figure 7. Blue room song: a) extract sequence; b) waveform stored in the database; c) pentagram with the extract notes.

a piano, a bass and a trumpet. Here we present the extraction of the trumpet musical score. In figure 7a we show the sequence of the song that we analyze and in figure 7b the waveform of the trumpet related with the histogram that is stored in the database. In figure 7c we visualize the pentagram obtained for the trumpet score. We observe that in our analysis the notes are normalized in the fourth octave.

Moreover, we show the results obtained considering a real recorded song in a real environment. The recording is obtained using one microphone. In this case the song is "Shadows" played by the Kismet rock band. We have one drum set, a bass, two guitars (accompaniment and solo) and one voice. Here we present the extraction of the snare and kick bass drums of the drum set. In figure 8a we show the sequence that we analyze and in figure 8b and 8c we plot the sequences of the both snare and kick bass drums in the database, respectively. In figure 8d is presented the pentagram with the notes associated to these drum set components.

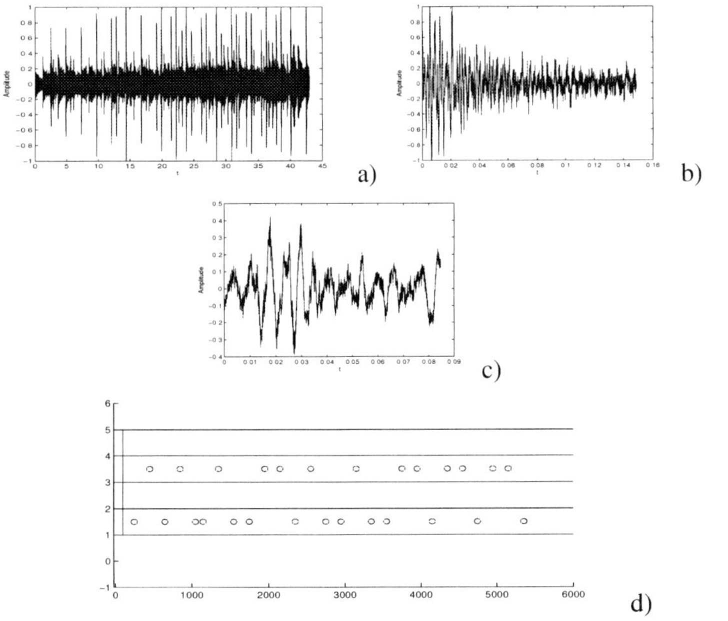

Figure 8. Shadows song: a) extract sequence; b) snare drum in the database; c) kick bass drum in the database; d) pentagram with the extract notes.

4. Conclusions

In this work we introduced a model to perform automatic musical transcription of polyphonic sounds. The transcription is obtained on a single channel mixture by using a non-linear PCA NN. The PCA NN permits to obtain different independent waveforms that can be associated to a specific instrument. To associate the waveforms to one instrument a database system has been considered. This system contains a dictionary of probability densities. Moreover, the frequencies of the notes are obtained directly by using a MUSIC frequency estimator on the recognized and classified components.

From the proposed experimental results we observed that the system is able to extract both frequency and temporal information from a mixture of signals and, in this, way to obtain an appreciable transcription of different musical instruments.

There are several directions that can be followed to validate and to optimize the model. For example to add in the process further information as the start time, duration, loudness and to apply onset detection to segment the signals. Moreover, to use MPEG-7 sound recognition descriptors to obtain a robust database system and to introduce constrained non-linear PCA NN to automatically extract sequences from the recordings.

References

[1] J.P. Bello, L. Daudet, M. B. Sandler, Automatic Piano Transcripion Using Frequency and time-domain Information, IEEE Transaction on Multimedia, 2006.

[2] A. Ciaramella, A. Eleuteri, L. Giordano, L. Milano, R. Tagliaferri, Music Score Transcription from Single Channel Mixtures Proceedings of ICA Research Network Workshop (ICARN 2006), Liverpool, UK 18 - 19 September 2006.

[3] A. Ciaramella, E. de Lauro, S. De Martino, M. Falanga, R. Tagliaferri, Complexity of Time Series Associated to Dynamical Systems Inferred from Independent Component Analysis,Physical Review E. 72, 046712-1/14 (2005).

[4] A. Ciaramella, et al. , A Multifrequency Analysis of Radio Variability of Blazars, Astronomy& Astrophysics Journal, vol. 419, Page(s): 485-500, 2004.

[5] F. Acernese, A. Ciaramella, S. De Martino, R. De Rosa, M. Falanga, R. Tagliaferri, Neural Networks for Blind-Source Separation of Stromboli Explosion Quakes, IEEE Transactions on Neural Networks, Volume: 14, Issue: 1, Page(s): 167-175, Gennaio 2003.

[6] R. Tagliaferri, A. Ciaramella, L.Milano, F. Barone, G. Longo, Spectral Analysis of Stellar Light Curves by Means of Neural Networks, Astronomy and Astrophysics Supplement Series vol. 137, Page(s): 391-405, 1999.

[7] M. Davies and C. James Source Separation Using Single Channel ICA, Proceedings of ICA Research Network Workshop (ICARN 2006), Liverpool, UK 18 - 19 September 2006.

[8] D. FitzGerald, B. Lawlor, E. Coyle, Prior Subspace Analysis for Drum Transcription, Audio Engineering Society, 114th Convention, Amsterdam, 2003.

[9] A. Hyvärinen, J. Karhunen and E. Oja, *Independent Component Analysis*, (Wiley-Sons, Inc., 2001).

[10] A. Klapuri, T. Virtanen, J. M. Holm, Robust Multipitch Estimation for the Analysis and Manipulation of polyphonic Musical Signals, Proceedings of the COST-G6 Conference on Digital Audio Effects, 2000.

[11] A. Klapuri, Number Theoretical Means of Resolving a Mixture of Several Harmonic Sounds, Proceedings of the European Signal Processing Conference, 1998.

[12] K. Kashino, K. Nakadai, T. Kinoshita, H. Tanaka, Application of Bayesian Probability Network to Music Scene Analysis, Computational Auditory Scene Analysis, 1998.

[13] K.D. Martin, A Blackboard System for Automatic Transcription of Simple Polyphonic Music, Tech. Report. 385, MIT Media Lab., Perceptual Computing Section, 1996.

[14] J. A. Moorer, On the transcription of musical sound computer, Computer Musical Journal, vol. 1, no. 4, pp. 32-38, 1977.

[15] M. Piszczalski, B. A. Galler, Automatic Music Transcription, Computer Musical Journal, vol. 1, no. 4, pp. 24-31, 1977.

[16] C. Raphael, Automatic Transcription of Piano Music, Proceedings of the 3rd International Conference on Music Information Retrieval, 2002.

[17] P. Smaragdis, J. C. Brown, Non-Negative Matrix Factorization for Polyphonic Music Transcription, Proceedings of the IEEE Workshop on Applications of Signal Processing to Audio and Acoustics, 2003

[18] C. Uhle, C. Dittmar, T. Sporer, Extraction of Drum Tracks from Polyphonic Music using Independent Subspace Analysis, Proceedings of 4th International Symposium on Independent Component Analysis and Blind Source Separation, 2003.

[19] Gil-Jin Jang, Te-Won Lee, A Maximum Likelihood Approach to Single-channel Source Separation, Journal of Machine Learning Research 4: 1365-1392 (2003).

New Directions in Neural Networks
B. Apolloni et al. (Eds.)
IOS Press, 2009

doi:10.3233/978-1-58603-984-4-109

Genetic Regulatory Networks and Neural Networks

Roberto Serra[1], Alex Graudenzi[1], Marco Villani[1]

[1] *Department of Social, Cognitive and Quantitative Sciences, Modena and Reggio Emilia University, via Allegri 9, I-42100 Reggio Emilia*
{roberto.serra, alex.graudenzi, marco.villani}@unimore.it

Abstract. The discussion on the neural networks paradigm casted a bright light on the notion of network and on what we may define as the "dynamical systems approach". The rebounds of this emphasis involved, during the years, the most disparate scientific areas, such as biology, social sciences and artificial life, contributing to reinforce the foundations of the complex systems science.

In this work we will discuss about a particular network model, i.e. random Boolean networks, which have been introduced to represent the gene regulatory mechanism, and we will comment on the similarities and the differences with the model of neural networks.

Moreover, we will present the results of the analysis of the dynamical behaviour that random Boolean networks show in presence of different sets of updating function and discuss on the concepts of criticality and biological suitability of such a model.

Keywords: genetic networks, neural networks, random Boolean networks, canalyzing functions, criticality.

1 Introduction

One of the reasons of the explosion of interest in neural networks in the 80's, apart from their (high) applicability to various challenging problems and their (limited) resemblance to biological neural circuits, was to be found in their promise to provide an approach to intelligence radically different from the then prevailing symbolic one.

Particular emphasis was given to the differences between human cognition and that of a computer: "parallel processing" and "distributed systems" were among the major keywords of the time.

However, there was also a perhaps complementary reason of interest, i.e. the idea that *dynamical systems* may provide a powerful principle of self-organization, which might be applied to the artificial simulation of cognitive processes [1, 2]. But if this is the case, then the strict adherence to "neuron-like" elements is no longer at the heart of the approach, whose core should indeed be found in the use of dynamical systems.

Classifier systems [3] appeared particularly intriguing in this respect, as they tried in a sense to bridge the gap between dynamical and symbolic processing. It was also proven ([1, 4, 5]) that they can be formally regarded as equivalent to a (quite peculiar) kind of neural network.

The "dynamical systems approach" to AI later became a major trend in the 90's, although it took a meaning different from that described in [1].

Another major role for which the neural network movement must be credited is that *networks* were put at the center of the stage with great emphasis. And networks provide indeed a very effective (although not all-encompassing) representation of complex systems. Networks had already been previously used in AI (semantic nets, Petri nets) but they later became a major focus of attention in many areas of complex systems, including biology, economics and artificial life.

In this paper we will comment on a particular network model, i.e. that of random Boolean networks (briefly, "RBN"), which were introduced by S. Kauffman [6, 7] in order to describe the interactions among genes in a cell, and on their relationship with neural networks. In section 2 we will introduce the RBN model and we will comment on the similarities and the differences with neural nets.

It is also interesting to recall that techniques to develop learning procedures for RBNs had been proposed in the past in the NN literature and in one of the first Vietri workshops [8].

RBNs have been recently used by our group [9, 10] and others [11, 12] to investigate a very bold and important claim, i.e. that living beings (and, more generally, evolving systems) tend to reach states which can be broadly called "critical" [7]. The evidences regarding this aspect are briefly reviewed in section 3. A key role is played by the dynamical regime in which biological genetic networks operate, which is compared to that of RBNs.

The initial model ("classical" RBNs) allow every kind of Boolean function at each node, but it has recently been shown that the (few) biological circuits which have been investigated in detail present a strong bias in favour of a limited set of such functions, which are called "canalyzing" [13] – briefly, "C". For reasons discussed in section 4, these functions are not fully satisfying, and we propose here a new class of functions, which will be called "biologically-plausible" (shortly, "P"). Another interesting set of restricted Boolean functions is that of linear separable ones ("S"), which is directly inspired by neural nets.

If a RBN has two inputs the three sets of functions (C, S and P) coincide, and this indeed the case which has been most widely studied. We have therefore analyzed the case where more inputs are present, and have shown that the three sets are indeed different. In section 4 we discuss these issues and show the relationships among these different sets.

Restricting the set of Boolean functions profoundly affects the dynamics of the network and, as it has been stressed above, the dynamical properties are particularly important. Therefore section 5 is dedicated to an analysis of the effect of these restrictions on the dynamics. The final section presents critical comments and indications for further work.

2 Random Boolean networks and neural networks

There are some excellent reviews and books on RBNs [6, 7, 14] so we will briefly summarize here only their main features. Let us consider a network composed of N genes, or nodes, which can take either the value 0 (inactive) or 1 (active). In a classical RBN each node has the same number of incoming connections k, and its k input nodes are chosen at random with uniform probability among the remaining N-1 nodes (multiple connections from the same node and self-connections being prohibited). It then turns out that the distribution of outgoing connections per node follows a Poisson distribution.

The output (i.e. the new value of a node) corresponding to each set of values of the input nodes is determined by a Boolean function, which is associated to that node, and which is also chosen at random, according to some probability distribution. The simplest choice is that of a uniform distribution among all the possible Boolean functions of k_{in} arguments. Both the topology and the Boolean function associated to each gene do not change in time (in the "quenched" model which will be considered here). The network dynamics is discrete and synchronous.

In order to analyze the properties of an ensemble of random Boolean networks, different networks are synthesized and their dynamical properties are examined. While individual realizations may differ markedly from the average properties of a given class of networks [15] one of the major results is the discovery of the existence of two different dynamical regimes, an ordered and a disordered one, divided by a "critical zone" in parameter space. Attractors are always cycles in finite RBNs: in the ordered regime their length scales as a power of N, moreover in this regime the system is stable with respect to small perturbations of the initial conditions. In the disordered regime the length of the cycles grows exponentially with N, and small changes in initial conditions often lead to different attractors. For fixed N, the most relevant parameter which determines the kind of regime is the connectivity per node, k: one typically observes ordered behaviour for small k, and a disordered one for larger k. The parameter which determines whether a network is in the ordered or in the disordered regime is the so-called Derrida parameter, which measures the rate at which nearby initial states diverge. Let q be the probability that, choosing at random a node of the network and switching the value of only one of its inputs, the state of the chosen node changes. Then the Derrida parameter λ is given by

$$\lambda \equiv kq \qquad [2.1]$$

For a more detailed discussion, the reader is referred to [6, 14, 15, 16].

The main similarity of RBNs with Boolean neural networks is the fairly obvious fact that in both cases there are Boolean nodes and a connection network. In NNs one often uses asynchronous update, but this is not always required. The main differences are then:

– the topology, which is random in RBNs and either fully connected or structured in NNs,

– the updating function: while RBNs allow arbitrary Boolean functions, NNs allow only separable ones.

It is appropriate to remark that, as it is well known, each Boolean function can be realized by a Boolean neural net, but in the case of non-separable functions this would require the introduction of fictitious nodes, which do not correspond to a gene. We will exclude such fictitious nodes from our, therefore the set of functions is limited in NNs with respect to RBNs.

There is of course also a major difference which is related to the purpose of the two different systems: in NNs there is a learning stage which is absent in the most frequent works on RBNs ([8] being an exception).

3 Criticality in random Boolean networks and in real genetic networks

The experiments discussed below are described in [17], while the theoretical analyses are discussed in depth in [9, 10]: the reader interested in a deeper understanding of these topics is referred to these works.

Hughes and co-workers [17] have performed several experiments where a single gene of *S. Cerevisiae* has been knocked-out and, using DNA-microarrays, have compared the expression levels of all the genes of such perturbed cells with those of normal, wild-type cells.

The knock-out experiment can be simulated *in silico* by comparing the evolution of two RBNs which start from identical initial conditions, except for the fact that one gene (the "knocked-out" one) is clamped permanently to the value 0 in the network which simulates the perturbed cell. The results of both experiments and simulations can be described by the distribution of "avalanches", where the size of an avalanche is the number of genes which are modified in a given experiment. In order to compare continuous experimental data with the results of Boolean models it is necessary to define a threshold for the former, so that two expression levels are considered "different" if their ratio exceeds the threshold. The initial simulations were performed using a classical RBN with 2 input connections per node, restricting the set of Boolean functions to the so-called canalyzing ones, for reasons which will be detailed in Section 4.

The comparison of the simulation results with the experimental distribution of avalanches is really good. This was fairly surprising, since the simplest model with practically no parameters, where all nodes have an equal number of inputs (a condition which is certainly not satisfied in real cells) was used.

It was then possible to analytically determine that the distribution of avalanches in RBNs, as long as they involve a number of genes which is much smaller than the total number of nodes in the network, depends only upon the distribution of outgoing links: that's why a simple model with an equal number of input links per node actually works well.

Let p_n be the probability that an avalanche involves n nodes, and let $p_{out}(k)$ be the probability that a node has k outgoing connections. It can be proven that all the p_n can be found from the knowledge of the "outgoing" moment generating function F:

$$F = \sum_{m=0}^{N-1} q^m p_{out}(m) \qquad [3.1]$$

In classical RBN $p_{out}(k)$ is Poissonian, and in this case it can be proven that

$$F = e^{-\lambda} \qquad [3.2]$$

Here λ is the Derrida exponent defined in Eq. 2.1, which also determines the network dynamical regime. Therefore, the distribution of avalanches depends only upon a single parameter, namely the Derrida exponent. The simple model which we had used in our simulations had a value of this parameter slightly smaller than the critical one, and this turned out to be a fortunate choice.

As suggested in [11] the dependency of the distribution of avalanches on λ can then be used to try to infer the value of the parameter which corresponds to it in real cells, and which should discriminate between ordered and disordered states.

Among the different cases which have been considered, the best agreement (according the well-known χ^2 index) with experimental data is provided by the case where $\lambda=6/7$, slightly smaller than the critical value 1. This supports the suggestion that life forms tend to exist at the critical state or in the ordered region, close to criticality [7]. Note however that, since only a single data set is presently available, it would be inappropriate to draw definite conclusions concerning this point.

See also [12] for a different way to apply RBNs to the problem of ascertaining whether cells are critical by studying time courses of gene expression levels.

4 Constraining the set of Boolean functions

While the initial RBN model made use of all the allowed Boolean functions, it was soon realized that biological circuitry may have difficulties in implementing some of those functions, like e.g. the XOR. Kauffman then proposed to consider networks where all the Boolean functions were canalyzing. A function is said to be canalyzing if there is at least one value of one of its inputs which determines the output. Note that this feature, specifically referred to inhibition, could be found also in the original McCulloch-Pitts model of NNs.

It was later found that, when one tries to model real gene circuits with a Boolean approach, one indeed finds a strong bias in favour of canalyzing functions [13].

On the other hand, biological plausibility may suggest also a different kind of restriction. Usually a gene either favours or opposes the expression of another gene located downstream. However, if all the Boolean functions are allowed, it may be that the same gene can play both roles, depending upon the values of the other input genes. Consider for example the case of a node X which receives three inputs, A, B, and C. Suppose that the input configuration (0,0,0) leads to a new activation value 0, while if the input is (1,0,0) then X takes the value 1. Then A activates X. But if all the Boolean functions are allowed, it may be e.g. that (0,1,1) leads to 1 and (1,1,1) to 0: in this case "turning A on" would have the opposite effect. In order to exclude these unrealistic behaviours we define the set of biologically plausible (P) functions as follows.

For a given gene of the net, let i be one of its input genes, and let R_i collectively denote the other input genes. Let $X_i \in \{0,1\}$ be the value of the i-th input gene and let $Y_i \in \{0,1\}^{k-1}$ be the set of values of input genes in R_i. Let also Z denote the (new) value of the chosen gene, computed according to the given Boolean function. For ease of notation we will write $Z = Z(X_i, Y_i)$. Then a function is in P iff, for every i, the following conditions are satisfied:

$$\text{If } \exists i : Z(1,Y_i) > Z(0,Y_i) \Rightarrow \forall j : Z(1,Y_j) \geq Z(0,Y_j)$$

$$\text{If } \exists i : Z(1,Y_i) < Z(0,Y_i) \Rightarrow \forall j : Z(1,Y_j) \leq Z(0,Y_j)$$

In the first case i is an activator, in the second one an inhibitor. The rule states that an activator (inhibitor) can never become an inhibitor (activator) although it allows it to be non influential in the case of other values of Y_i.

A third kind of possible restriction of the set of Boolean functions is inspired by analogy with neural nets, and is also biologically plausible. Indeed, it seems that in some cases different controlling genes provide additive contributions of different importance, like in the usual neural models. In this case one can introduce synaptic weights and define the update rule as follows

$$X_i(t+1) = H\left(\sum W_{ij} X_j - \theta_i\right) \qquad [4.1]$$

Where H is the Heaviside function: H(I)=1 if I>0, H(I)=0 otherwise.

Although it cannot be excluded that also multiplicative nets could be biologically sound, we will omit their treatment in this paper.

As it has been observed, the three sets of canalyzing, biologically plausible and separable functions (respectively C, P, S) coincide in the case of two input connections, where only two out of 16 functions are excluded (namely the XOR and its negation). By adding a subscript to indicate the number of inputs, this finding can expressed as

$$C_2 = P_2 = S_2 \qquad [4.2]$$

In the case k=3 one finds that the sets of plausible and separable functions are identical, while that of canalyzing functions is different, so

$$C_3 \neq P_3 = S_3 \qquad [4.3]$$

Note also that C is neither a subset nor a superset of P. The number of functions belonging to the different classes is given in Tab.1

Number of functions which are not in $P \cup C$	128
Number of functions in P (=S)	104
Number of functions in C	120
Number of functions in $P \cap C$	96
Number of functions in $P - C$	8
Number of functions in $C - P$	24

Table 1: number of functions of different types for k=3

5 Dynamics with restricted sets of Boolean functions

As it has been observed, the dynamics of RBNs is particularly important. In order to analyze the effects of the different kinds of restrictions separately we discuss here the case with three inputs per node.

It is known that Boolean nets with three inputs per node, in the case where all the Boolean functions are allowed (with uniform probability), are in the disordered regime, and finding their attractors may require prohibitively long times.

We analyzed a number of different networks belonging to the various classes by fixing a maximum allowable length for the transient and for the attractor cycle. For different initial conditions, we analyzed (for networks belonging to the different classes defined in section 4) the average frequency with which an attractor is reached (within the limits of the search) for every initial condition and the frequency with which an attractor is reached for at least one initial condition. We also analyzed the number of different attractors (computed of course for those networks which have reached an attractor) and their period.

The major results are summarized in Table 2 below.

Set of allowed Boolean functions (uniform probability)	An attractor is always reached	An attractor is reached at least once (not always)
All the functions	0.06	0.72
Functions in C	0.97	0.03
Functions in P	1	-
Functions in C and not in P	0.23	0.75
Functions in P and not in C	-	0.70

Table 2: frequency of different dynamical behaviours for different network types. The parameters of the simulations are as follows: each network is composed by 100 nodes, each node has 3 input connections; for every set of networks 100 different realizations are analyzed, considering for each one 100.000 different initial conditions. The search for an attractor ends after 3000 time steps, and the maximum length of the attractor which can be found is 500 steps. In the second column, the fraction of networks where an attractor is reached for every initial condition; in the third column, the fraction of networks for which an attractor is reached for at least one initial condition, but not for all of them (the remaining fraction of networks is necessarily given by those networks which never reach an attractor for any initial condition).

It is apparent that the set of canalyzing and the of plausible functions present a much more ordered behaviour than that of the set of all the possible Boolean functions. However, this higher degree of order is likely to derive mostly from those functions which are both in S and in P: the degree of order of the functions which belong only to one of the two classes is indeed much lower than that of those which belong to both. Actually, by using functions which are both in P and in C one obtains results which are almost indistinguishable (given the limitations on the simulations) from those of the functions which are in P.

The analysis of the data concerning the average number of different attractors and their average length is complicated in those cases where an attractor is rarely reached. By looking at the data (not shown here), the major observation is that, on the average, the attractors of the networks whose functions have no restrictions are rather analogous in terms of length to those of the networks whose functions are in P – C and in C – P, but significantly higher than those who belong to $P \cap C$.

6 Conclusions

On the basis of the results obtained for k=3, one might be tempted to guess that the two sets C_k and P_k coincide also for values of the connectivity higher than 3. However, this turns out not to be the case. Indeed, if a function is separable, then if gene A is e.g. an activator for gene X in a given configuration, it means that the corresponding synaptic weight is positive, so A can never be an inhibitor. Therefore if a function is in S then it is also in P. But the opposite needs not be the case, since a function may be in P even if it is not additive. An example of a 4-input function which is in P but not separable is given by the function "0000010111001101" (where the different ciphers describe the output corresponding to the 16 input configurations, ordered from 0000 to 1111).

Therefore, the sets of restricted Boolean functions which have been introduced are indeed distinct and, as it has been shown above, the choice of different sets profoundly affects the dynamics. Note that some other efforts to indentify the criteria for choosing biological meaningful functions have been interestingly carried out, as, for instance, in [18].

However, in order to reach definitive conclusions about this important general issue, more detailed studies of real biological systems are needed. In our case, for example, it would be deeply interesting to analyze existent biological circuits in order to understand whether functions which are not in P are ever observed.

References

1. Serra, R., Zanarini, G.: Complex systems and cognitive processes. Springer, Heidelberg (1990)
2. Weisbuch, G.: Complex Systems Dynamics. Addison-Wesley, Redwood City, USA (1990)
3. Holland, J. H., Holyoak, K.J., Nisbett, R.E., Thagard, P.R.: Induction. Processes of Inference, Learning and Discovery. MIT Press, Cambridge, MA (1986)
4. Compiani, M., Montanari, D., Serra, R., Valastro, G.: Classifier systems and neural networks. In E. Caianiello (ed): Parallel architectures and neural networks, pp. 105-118. World Scientific, Singapore (1989)
5. Forrest, S., Miller, J.H: Emergent behavior in classifier systems. Physica D 42, 213-227 (1990)
6. Kauffman, S.A.: The origins of order. Oxford University Press (1993)
7. Kauffman, S. A.: At home in the universe. Oxford University Press (1995)
8. Patarnello, S., Carnevali, P.: Learning networks of neurons with Boolean logic. Europhysics letters 4, 503-508 (1987)
9. Serra, R., Villani, M., Semeria, A. : Genetic network models and statistical properties of gene expression data in knock-out experiments. J. Theor. Biol. 227, 149-157 (2004)
10. Serra, R., Villani, M., Graudenzi, A., Kauffman, S.A. : Why a simple model of genetic regulatory networks describes the distribution of avalanches in gene expression data. J. Theor. Biol. 249 : 449-460 (2007)
11. Ramo, P., Kesseli, J., Yli-Harja, O.: Perturbation avalanches and criticality in gene regulatory networks. J. Theor. Biol. 242, 164 (2006)
12. Shmulevich, I., Kauffman, S.A., Aldana, M.. Eukaryotic cells are dynamically ordered or critical but not chaotic. Proc. Natl Acad. Sci. 102, 13439–13444 (2005)
13. Harris, S.E., Sawhill, B.K., Wuensche, A., Kauffman, S.A.: A model of transcriptional regulatory networks based on biases in the observed regulation rules. Complexity 7, 23-40 (2002)
14. Aldana, M., Coppersmith, S., Kadanoff, L.P.: Boolean Dynamics with Random Couplings, in E. Kaplan, J.E. Marsden, K.R. Sreenivasan (eds.), Perspectives and Problems in Nonlinear Science. Springer Applied Mathematical Sciences Series (2003)
15. Bastolla, U., Parisi, G.: The modular structure of Kauffman networks. Physica D 115, 219-233 (1998)
16. Socolar, J.E.S., Kauffman, S.A.: Scaling in Ordered and Critical Random Boolean Networks. Phys. Rev. Let. 90 (2003)
17. Hughes, T.R. et al.: Functional discovery via a compendium of expression profiles. Cell 102, 109-126 (2000)
18. Raeymaekers L.: Dynamics of Boolean networks controlled by biologically meaningful functions, J. Theor. Biol. 218, 331-341 (2002)

New Directions in Neural Networks
B. Apolloni et al. (Eds.)
IOS Press, 2009

doi:10.3233/978-1-58603-984-4-118

An Experimental Comparison of Kernel Clustering Methods

Maurizio FILIPPONE [a] Francesco MASULLI [b,c] Stefano ROVETTA [b]

[a] *Department of Computer Science, University of Sheffield, Sheffield, United Kingdom*
[b] *Department of Computer and Information Sciences, University of Genoa, and CNISM, Genova Research Unit, Genova, Italy*
[c] *Center for Biotechnology, Temple University, Philadelphia, USA*

Abstract. In this paper, we compare the performances of some among the most popular kernel clustering methods on several data sets. The methods are all based on central clustering and incorporate in various ways the concepts of fuzzy clustering and kernel machines. The data sets are a sample of several application domains and sizes. A thorough discussion about the techniques for validating results is also presented. Results indicate that clustering in kernel space generally outperforms standard clustering, although no method can be proven to be consistently better than the others.

Keywords. Kernel methods, Clustering, Experimental comparison, Fuzzy clustering, Performance indexes for clustering

1. Introduction

In this paper, we compare the performances of some among the most popular kernel clustering methods [7] on several data sets. In particular, we compare the clustering algorithms in feature space, clustering with the kernelization of the metric, Support Vector Clustering, and three standard methods: K-means, FCM-I, and FCM-II. The motivation supporting such experimental comparison lies in the fact that these recent clustering models have not been sufficiently validated in applications by the authors. The data sets included in the present study are well known among the Machine Learning community. All the data sets are labeled. Some of them can be found in the UCI repository [1], while one of them is a bioinformatic data set. We decided to include a variety of data sets differing from cardinality, dimensionality, and number of classes. The comparison is done on the basis of three performance indexes, in particular: misclassifications, normalized mutual information, and conditional entropy.

In the next sections we briefly describe the methods compared, the data sets, and the performance indexes. Section 5 shows the results, and the last section is devoted to a discussion about them.

2. Methods

2.1. K-means

This is the standard K-means clustering algorithm [13], included as a baseline method. The initialization is random, and it is made by selecting the position of the centroids among the patterns to cluster. The only input is the number c of clusters to be found.

2.2. FCM-I and FCM-II

These algorithms are two flavours of Fuzzy c-means, differing in the objective function they address. The fuzzy c-means algorithm (FCM-I) [4] identifies clusters as fuzzy sets. In the original formulation, it minimizes the functional:

$$J(U,V) = \sum_{h=1}^{n} \sum_{i=1}^{c} (u_{ih})^m \|\mathbf{x}_h - \mathbf{v}_i\|^2 \tag{1}$$

with respect to the membership matrix U and the codebook V with the constraints $\sum_{i=1}^{c} u_{ih} = 1$. The parameter m controls the fuzziness of the memberships and often it is set to two; for high values of m the memberships tend to be equal, while for m close to one we obtain crisp memberships as in K-means. By a Lagrangian approach, the update equations are obtained as follows:

$$u_{ih} = \left[\sum_{j=1}^{c} \left(\frac{\|\mathbf{x}_h - \mathbf{v}_i\|}{\|\mathbf{x}_h - \mathbf{v}_j\|}\right)\right]^{(m-1)/2} \qquad \mathbf{v}_i = \frac{\sum_{h=1}^{n} (u_{ih})^m \mathbf{x}_h}{\sum_{h=1}^{n} (u_{ih})^m} \tag{2}$$

The method that hereinafter is referred to as FCM-II is a variation [3][14] where a maximum entropy criterion is introduced in the objective function by adding the penalty term

$$\lambda \sum_{h=1}^{n} \sum_{i=1}^{c} u_{ih} \ln(u_{ih}) \tag{3}$$

and fixing $m = 1$. The centroids are still updated with the previous equation, while the membership update is as follows:

$$u_{ih} = \frac{\exp\left(-\frac{\|\mathbf{x}_h - \mathbf{v}_i\|^2}{\lambda}\right)}{\sum_{j=1}^{c} \exp\left(-\frac{\|\mathbf{x}_h - \mathbf{v}_j\|^2}{\lambda}\right)} \tag{4}$$

In FCM-I we have to set the number of clusters c and the fuzziness m. In FCM-II we have to set the number of clusters c and the fuzziness λ.

2.3. FCM-I-fs and FCM-II-fs

These are kernel methods. They are respectively Fuzzy c-means I in feature space and Fuzzy c-means II in feature space [7].

Clustering in feature space is made by mapping each pattern using the mapping function $\Phi()$ defined (possibly only implicitly) by the kernel $K(\mathbf{a}, \mathbf{b}) = \Phi(\mathbf{a})\Phi(\mathbf{b})$, and computing centroids $\mathbf{v}_i^{\Phi}$ in feature space. Distances can be computed by means of the kernel trick.

In both algorithms, we have to select the number of clusters c and the kernel function along with its parameters. In the following, we will use the Gaussian kernel with standard deviation σ. In FCM-I fs we have to set the fuzziness m, while in FCM-II fs we have to set the fuzziness λ.

2.4. FCM-I-km and FCM-II-km

These kernel methods are respectively Fuzzy c-means I with the kernelization of the metric [15] and the Fuzzy c-means II with the kernelization of the metric.

Methods based on kernelization of the metric look for centroids in input space and the distances between patterns and centroids is computed by means of kernels:

$$||\Phi(\mathbf{x}_h) - \Phi(\mathbf{v}_i)||^2 = K(\mathbf{x}_h, \mathbf{x}_h) + K(\mathbf{v}_i, \mathbf{v}_i) + 2K(\mathbf{v}_i, \mathbf{x}_h) \tag{5}$$

In both algorithms we have to select the number of clusters c and the kernel function along with its parameters. In the following, we will use the Gaussian kernel with standard deviation σ. In FCM-I fs we have to set the fuzziness m, while in FCM-II fs we have to set the fuzziness λ.

2.5. SVC

This is the Support Vector Clustering algorithm [2]. The aim of this approach is to look for an hypersphere centered in $\mathbf{v}$ containing almost all data, namely allowing some outliers. The support vector description of data in the kernel-induced space leads to possibly non-linear surfaces separating the clusters in the original space. A labeling algorithm is necessary to assign the same label to the patterns belonging to the same region.

We have to select the parameter C (or ν) and the kernel function along with its parameters. In the following, we will use the Gaussian kernel with standard deviation σ. We set $C = 1$, in order to avoid outlier rejection that is not handled by the other comparing algorithms. The algorithm will automatically find the number of clusters.

3. Performance Indexes

A common problem in evaluating clustering methods is related to the unsupervised nature of the method. Cluster attribution cannot be univocally determined, as opposed to supervised classification, hence it cannot be summarized by a percentage of correct attributions. Moreover, different algorithms and different runs of a given algorithm may produce cluster differing in composition and sometimes in number, and, even when very similar, clusters may be ordered differently from run to run, making it harder to match two clustering results. The following performance indexes are a collection of criteria to evaluate clustering performance, that also exploit supervised information available for the data sets. Therefore, we will only select datasets for which a target is available. By proposing several indicators, the reliability of the results is somewhat increased.

Let $X = \{\mathbf{x}_1, \ldots, \mathbf{x}_n\}$ be a labeled data set composed of n patterns. Let's denote the class labels with t_i, belonging to the set of the possible realizations $\mathcal{T} = \{t_1, \ldots, t_b\}$. The class labels can be considered as the realization of a random variable T. Applying a clustering algorithm to the elements of X, we obtain the cluster labels z_i that can be seen as the realization of a random variable Z. Here z_i belongs to the set of possible realizations $\mathcal{Z} = \{z_1, \dots, z_c\}$. In this context, it is possible to apply some statistical tools to analyze the dependence between these two random variables.

3.1. Simple Match

A simple choice could be the match between the two realizations. In order to do that, we have to take into account two things: in general c and b are not equal and the sets of labels $\mathcal{T}$ and $\mathcal{Z}$ might be different. For these reasons we need to rearrange the cluster labels according to a univoque criterion. A natural choice is to match as much as possible the class labels. In other words, we need to transform the cluster label with a function $\pi_k : \mathcal{Z} \to \mathcal{T}$ such that $\pi_k(z_i) = t_j$. In this way we obtain the new cluster labels vector $\{t'_1, \dots, t'_n\}$. Now it is possible to compute the match between the two label vectors. We will use the misclassification [12]:

$$\mu = \#\{t'_i \neq t_i\} \tag{6}$$

and the accuracy:

$$\psi = \#\{t'_i = t_i\}/n \tag{7}$$

Among all the permutations π_k, we select the one leading to the minimum value of μ.

3.2. Preliminary definitions for entropy based scores

Let's define the confusion matrix:

		Cluster Labels			
		z_1	z_2	$\cdots$	z_c
Class Labels	t_1	a_{11}	a_{12}	$\cdots$	a_{1c}
	t_2	a_{21}	a_{22}	$\cdots$	a_{2c}
	$\vdots$	$\vdots$	$\vdots$	$\ddots$	$\vdots$
	t_b	a_{b1}	a_{b2}	$\cdots$	a_{bc}

Each entry a_{ij} of the confusion matrix contains the number of times that the clustering algorithm assigned the cluster label z_j to the pattern $\mathbf{x}_i$ having class labels t_i. On the basis of the confusion matrix, the following probabilities can be defined:

$$\begin{aligned} p(t_i) &= \frac{|t_i|}{n} = \frac{\sum_r a_{ir}}{n} \\ p(z_j) &= \frac{|z_j|}{n} = \frac{\sum_r a_{rj}}{n} \\ p(t_i, z_j) &= \frac{a_{ij}}{n} \end{aligned} \tag{8}$$

Entropy for the random variables T and Z is defined as follows:

$$H(T) = \sum_i p(t_i) \log(p(t_i)) \tag{9}$$

$$H(Z) = \sum_j p(z_j) \log (p(z_j)) \tag{10}$$

The joint entropy of T and Z is:

$$H(T,Z) = -\sum_{ij} p(t_i, z_j) \log (p(t_i, z_j)) \tag{11}$$

We will use the following two entropy based scores to assess the quality of the clustering results: Conditional Entropy $H(T|Z)$ and Normalized Mutual Information $I_{\mathrm{N}}(T,Z)$.

3.3. Conditional Entropy

The Conditional Entropy $H(T|Z)$ is a measure of the uncertainty of a random variable T given the value of the random variable Z [6]. It is defined as:

$$H(T|Z) = \sum_j p(z_j) H(T|Z = z_j) = -\sum_j p(z_j) \sum_i p(t_i|z_j) \log (p(t_i|z_j)) \tag{12}$$

Applying some transformations, it is possible to rewrite the Conditional Entropy:

$$H(T|Z) = H(T,Z) - H(Z) = -\sum_{ij} p(t_i, z_j) \log (p(t_i, z_j)) + \sum_j p(z_j) \log (p(z_j)) \tag{13}$$

Intuitively, if the two random variables are identical, knowing the realization of Z gives no uncertainty about T, leading to a null conditional entropy. On the contrary, if the two random variables are independent, there is still uncertainty in the value of T given Z. Formally, in the dependent case, $p(t_i|z_j) = 1$ leading to $H(T|Z) = 0$. In the independent case, $p(t_i|z_j) = p(t_i)$ leading to $H(T|Z) = H(T)$. The Conditional Entropy is zero when each cluster found contains pattern from a single class. This can be useful to check the purity of the cluster labels Z with respect to the class labels T. On the other hand, the method is biased when the number of clusters c is very large. In the extreme case when we assign one pattern per cluster, the Conditional Entropy results $H(T|Z) = 0$.

3.4. Normalized Mutual Information

The mutual information between two discrete random variables T and Z is [6]:

$$I(T,Z) = \sum_{ij} p(t_i, z_j) \log \left(\frac{p(t_i, z_j)}{p(t_i) p(z_j)} \right) \tag{14}$$

The mutual information measures the information shared by two discrete random variables: it measures how much knowing one of these variables reduces our uncertainty about the other. Intuitively, if the two random variables are independent, knowing the realization of one of them does not give any information about the other and viceversa; their mutual information is zero. If the two random variables are identical, the realization of one of them determines the value of the other and viceversa. As a result, the mutual information is the same as the uncertainty contained in either one of the random variables, that is their entropy. Formally, if they are uncorrelated, it is possible to factorize the joint probability $p(t_i, z_j) = p(t_i) p(z_j)$ leading to $I(T,Z) = 0$. If they are identical, $I(T,Z)$ reduces to the entropy $H(T) = H(Z)$, since $p(x,y) = p(x) = p(y)$. These considerations show that the mutual information is dependent on the data set; in other words, the upper bound is not independent from the considered problem. It is possible to normalize $I(T,Z)$ in the interval $[0,1]$ using the following [6]:

$$I_{\mathrm{N}}(T,Z) = \frac{I(T,Z)}{\sqrt{H(T)H(Z)}} \tag{15}$$

In this way, a value of $I_{\mathrm{N}}(T,Z)$ close to one means high correlation between cluster and class labels, a value near zero means independence.

4. Data Sets

As noted earlier, all data sets are labelled, so that we can exploit the supervised information for ease of cluster evaluation.

4.1. Iris

(150 patterns of dimension 4, 3 classes.) This is one of the most popular data sets studied by the Machine Learning community [8,5]. The data set contains three classes of 50 patterns each; each class refers to a type of iris plant. One class is linearly separable from the other two that are overlapped. The features are four: sepal length, sepal width, petal length, and petal width.

4.2. Breast

(683 patterns of dimensio 9, 2 classes.) The Breast Cancer Wisconsin (Original) Data Set was obtained by the University of Wisconsin Hospitals, Madison from Dr. William H. Wolberg [16]. The samples were analyzed in different moments, since they were received periodically. The data set is composed by 699 nine-dimensional patterns, labeled as benign or malignant. Since there are some missing values, we decided to remove the corresponding patterns, obtaining 683 patterns. The class distribution is 65% for the benign class and 35% for the Malignant class.

4.3. Ecoli

(336 patterns of dimension 7, 8 classes.) Contains the protein localization sites of a E. coli [11]. The 336 patterns are described by seven features, and are classified in eight classes. Three of these classes contain less than five patterns.

4.4. Glass

(214 patterns of dimension 9, 6 classes.) This data set contains 214 patterns related to the analysis of types of glass. The nine features describing each pattern are the refractive index and the concentration of eight chemical elements (Na, Mg, Al, Si, K, Ca, Ba, and Fe). The type of glass can be one among six: building windows float processed, building windows non float processed, vehicle windows float processed, containers, tableware, and headlamps.

4.5. Lung

(32 patterns of dimension 54, 3 classes.) The data set was published in Ref. [10]. It contains 32 54-dimensional patterns that can belong to one out of three types of pathological lung cancers. The Authors give no information about the individual variables.

5. Results

The methods presented in Section 2 have been tested on the data sets described in Section 4. The number of classes can give some guidelines on the selection of the number of clusters. It is worth noting, however, that in general the number of clusters and the number of classes might be not related to each other. A typical example is the Iris data set, where the two overlapped classes are very likely to be identified as one cluster by a clustering algorithm. In other situations, it is possible to use some prior information about the number of clusters. To perform a fair comparison among the methods, we used the same number of clusters for all of them. Some algorithms find the natural number of clusters given a particular set of parameters. In this case, we set the parameters in order to have a selection of the wanted number of clusters by the algorithm. We tested the methods varying all the parameters in a wide range; we report the results for the selection giving the best performances. For the algorithms starting with a random initialization, the results are averaged over 20 runs; in Table 1 each score is reported along with its standard deviation.

6. Discussion

By inspecting the experimental results, it is possible to see that there are no methods that perform better or worse than the others in general.

Concerning clustering methods using kernels, in general, we can see that the methods in feature space perform better than methods with the kernelization of the metric. Clustering with the kernelization of the metric, in some situations give very poor results, especially when the number of clusters is very high. SVC has been used only with $C = 1$, i.e., without the rejection of the outliers. This fact affected the results that are not very good in general. On the other hand, this choice was necessary to compare its results with the other methods that do not handle an outlier class.

An important result, that is clear from the experimental validation, is that clustering in kernel induced spaces outperform standard clustering algorithms. This is one of the motivations that support the interest of the Machine Learning community for these recent clustering techniques. On the other hand, the methods based on kernels require the tuning of the kernel or the adjacency function. In many applications, we found that the values of the standard deviation of such functions lead to good performances only in a narrow interval.

The results therefore show that it is very difficult to identify the best approach in terms of accuracy, and a similar conclusion (although not considered in this study) applies to computational efficiency.

Iris				
Method	Parameters	ψ (μ)	$I_N(T,Z)$	$H(T \mid Z)$
FCM-I-fs	$c = 3, \sigma = 0.6, m = 1.2$	0.947, 0.000 (8.0, 0.0)	0.845, 0.000	0.172, 0.000
FCM-II-fs	$c = 3, \sigma = 0.6, \lambda = 0.1$	0.923, 0.017 (11.5, 2.6)	0.810, 0.024	0.214, 0.029
FCM-I-km	$c = 3, \sigma = 3, m = 2.4$	0.907, 0.000 (14.0, 0.0)	0.766, 0.000	0.260, 0.000
FCM-II-km	$c = 3, \sigma = 5, \lambda = 0.2$	0.913, 0.000 (13.0, 0.0)	0.745, 0.000	0.283, 0.000
SVC	$c = 3, C = 1, \sigma = 0.35$	0.680, 0.000 (48.0, 0.0)	0.736, 0.000	0.453, 0.000
FCM-I	$c = 3, m = 2.4$	0.900, 0.000 (15.0, 0.0)	0.758, 0.000	0.270, 0.000
FCM-II	$c = 3, \lambda = 5.4$	0.913, 0.000 (13.0, 0.0)	0.745, 0.000	0.283, 0.000
K-means	$c = 3$	0.860, 0.083 (21.1, 12.5)	0.733, 0.061	0.309, 0.087

Breast				
Method	Parameters	ψ (μ)	$I_N(T,Z)$	$H(T \mid Z)$
FCM-I-fs	$c = 3, \sigma = 7.2, m = 1.2$	0.972, 0.003 (18.9, 2.2)	0.702, 0.039	0.103, 0.014
FCM-II-fs	$c = 2, \sigma = 8, \lambda = 0.35$	0.972, 0.000 (19.0, 0.0)	0.814, 0.000	0.116, 0.000
FCM-I-km	$c = 2, \sigma = 0.1, m = 1.2$	0.653, 0.000 (237.0, 0.0)	0.009, 0.000	0.646, 0.000
FCM-II-km	$c = 2, \sigma = 0.01, \lambda = 0.02$	0.652, 0.000 (238.0, 0.0)	0.007, 0.000	0.646, 0.000
SVC	$c = 3, C = 1, \sigma = 3.75$	0.652, 0.000 (238.0, 0.0)	0.018, 0.000	0.646, 0.000
FCM-I	$c = 2, m = 1.2$	0.960, 0.000 (27.0, 0.0)	0.748, 0.000	0.166, 0.000
FCM-II	$c = 2, \lambda = 400$	0.972, 0.000 (19.0, 0.2)	0.812, 0.002	0.118, 0.001
K-means	$c = 2$	0.960, 0.000 (27.0, 0.0)	0.748, 0.000	0.166, 0.000

Ecoli				
Method	Parameters	ψ (μ)	$I_N(T,Z)$	$H(T \mid Z)$
FCM-I-fs	$c = 7, \sigma = 0.6, m = 1.6$	0.732, 0.001 (90.0, 0.2)	0.459, 0.001	0.731, 0.002
FCM-II-fs	$c = 7, \sigma = 0.8, \lambda = 0.09$	0.727, 0.009 (91.8, 2.9)	0.455, 0.012	0.739, 0.022
FCM-I-km	$c = 7, \sigma = 0.1, m = 1.2$	0.446, 0.000 (186.0, 0.0)	0.046, 0.000	1.446, 0.000
FCM-II-km	$c = 7, \sigma = 0.1, \lambda = 0.002$	0.443, 0.000 (187.0, 0.0)	0.045, 0.000	1.448, 0.000
SVC	$c = 7, C = 1, \sigma = 0.22$	0.446, 0.000 (186.0, 0.0)	0.148, 0.000	1.450, 0.000
FCM-I	$c = 7, m = 1.6$	0.724, 0.001 (92.8, 0.4)	0.458, 0.004	0.738, 0.007
FCM-II	$c = 7, \lambda = 0.06$	0.720, 0.009 (94.1, 3.1)	0.453, 0.015	0.746, 0.025
K-means	$c = 7$	0.705, 0.016 (99.0, 5.4)	0.429, 0.024	0.790, 0.047

Glass				
Method	Parameters	ψ (μ)	$I_N(T,Z)$	$H(T \mid Z)$
FCM-I-fs	$c = 6, \sigma = 1, m = 1.4$	0.623, 0.019 (80.8, 4.1)	0.408, 0.006	0.856, 0.013
FCM-II-fs	$c = 6, \sigma = 0.8, \lambda = 0.2$	0.624, 0.010 (80.5, 2.2)	0.381, 0.012	0.898, 0.018
FCM-I-km	$c = 6, \sigma = 2, m = 1.2$	0.463, 0.000 (115.0, 0.0)	0.074, 0.000	1.391, 0.000
FCM-II-km	$c = 6, \sigma = 10, \lambda = 0.001$	0.393, 0.000 (130.0, 0.0)	0.039, 0.000	1.451, 0.000
SVC	$c = 6, C = 1, \sigma = 1.3$	0.379, 0.000 (133.0, 0.0)	0.129, 0.000	1.443, 0.000
FCM-I	$c = 6, m = 1.8$	0.610, 0.002 (83.4, 0.5)	0.363, 0.001	0.946, 0.0009
FCM-II	$c = 6, \lambda = 1.2$	0.614, 0.038 (82.5, 8.2)	0.343, 0.027	0.976, 0.0349
K-means	$c = 6$	0.571, 0.015 (91.7, 3.2)	0.404, 0.022	0.948, 0.026

Lung				
Method	Parameters	ψ (μ)	$I_N(T,Z)$	$H(T \mid Z)$
FCM-I-fs	$c = 3, \sigma = 4, m = 1.2$	0.563, 0.000 (14.0, 0.0)	0.300, 0.000	0.760, 0.000
FCM-II-fs	$c = 3, \sigma = 6, \lambda = 0.1$	0.581, 0.029 (13.4, 0.9)	0.290, 0.028	0.777, 0.024
FCM-I-km	$c = 3, \sigma = 70, m = 2$	0.553, 0.035 (14.3, 1.1)	0.293, 0.048	0.788, 0.054
FCM-II-km	$c = 3, \sigma = 10, \lambda = 0.06$	0.603, 0.015 (12.7, 0.5)	0.328, 0.005	0.754, 0.009
SVC	$c = 4, C = 1, \sigma = 1.9$	0.500, 0.000 (16.0, 0.0)	0.173, 0.000	0.970, 0.000
FCM-I	$c = 3, m = 2.2$	0.548, 0.030 (14.5, 0.9)	0.285, 0.061	0.790, 0.065
FCM-II	$c = 3, \lambda = 5$	0.633, 0.042 (11.8, 1.3)	0.363, 0.000	0.707, 0.011
K-means	$c = 3$	0.538, 0.024 (14.8, 0.8)	0.279, 0.055	0.796, 0.055

Table 1. Clustering results on all datasets.

Acknowledgments

We thank Giorgio Valentini for the useful suggestions provided while discussing this work.

References

[1] A. Asuncion and D. J. Newman. UCI machine learning repository, 2007.

[2] A. Ben Hur, D. Horn, H. T. Siegelmann, and V. Vapnik. Support vector clustering. *Journal of Machine Learning Research*, 2:125-137, 2001.

[3] G. Beni and X. Liu. A least biased fuzzy clustering method. *IEEE Transactions on Pattern Analysis and Machine Intelligence*, 16(9):954-960, 1994.

[4] J. C. Bezdek. Pattern Recognition with Fuzzy Objective Function Algorithms. Kluwer Academic Publishers, Norwell, MA, USA, 1981.

[5] R. O. Duda and P. E. Hart. *Pattern Classification and Scene Analysis*. Wiley, 1973.

[6] Xiaoli Z. Fern and Carla E. Brodley. Random projection for high dimensional data clustering: A cluster ensemble approach. In Tom Fawcett and Nina Mishra, editors, *ICML*, pages 186–193. AAAI Press, 2003.

[7] Maurizio Filippone, Francesco Camastra, Francesco Masulli, and Stefano Rovetta. A survey of kernel and spectral methods for clustering. *Pattern Recognition*, 41(1):176–190, January 2008.

[8] Ronald A. Fisher. The use of multiple measurements in taxonomic problems. *Annals Eugenics*, 7:179–188, 1936.

[9] M. Girolami, Mercer kernel based clustering in feature space, *IEEE Trans. Neural Networks* 13 (3) (2002), pp. 780-784.

[10] Zi Q. Hong and Jing Y. Yang. Optimal discriminant plane for a small number of samples and design method of classifier on the plane. *Pattern Recognition*, 24(4):317–324, 1991.

[11] Paul Horton and Kenta Nakai. A probabilistic classification system for predicting the cellular localization sites of proteins. In *Proceedings of the Fourth International Conference on Intelligent Systems for Molecular Biology*, pages 109–115. AAAI Press, 1996.

[12] Tilman Lange, Volker Roth, Mikio L. Braun, and Joachim M. Buhmann. Stability-based validation of clustering solutions. *Neural Computation*, 16(6):1299–1323, 2004.

[13] S. Lloyd. Least squares quantization in PCM. *IEEE Transactions on Information Theory*, 28:129-137, 1982. Reprinted from Bell Laboratories technical note, 1957.

[14] S. Miyamoto and M. Mukaidono, Fuzzy C-Means as a regularization and maximum entropy approach, *Proceedings of the Seventh IFSA World Congress*, Prague, 86-91, 1997.

[15] Zhong D. Wu, Wei X. Xie, and Jian P. Yu. Fuzzy c-means clustering algorithm based on kernel method. *Computational Intelligence and Multimedia Applications, 2003.*

[16] W. H. Wolberg and O. L. Mangasarian. Multisurface method of pattern separation for medical diagnosis applied to breast cytology. *Proceedings of the National Academy of Sciences,U.S.A.*, 87:9193–9196, 1990.

New Directions in Neural Networks
B. Apolloni et al. (Eds.)
IOS Press, 2009

doi:10.3233/978-1-58603-984-4-127

Diffusion Learning and Regularization

Marco GORI [a]
[a] *Dipartimento di Ingegneria dell'Informazione, University of Siena, Via Roma, 56 53100 Siena, Italy*
{marco}@dii.unisi.it

Abstract. Most of the emphasis in machine learning has been placed on parametric models in which the purpose of the learning algorithm is to adjust weights mainly according to appropriate optimization criteria. However, schemes based on a direct data inference, like for instance K-nearest neighbor, have also become quite popular. Recently, a number of people have proposed methods to perform classification and regression that are based on different forms of diffusion processes from the labelled examples. The aim of this paper is to provide motivations for diffusion learning from the continuum setting by using Tikhnov's regularization framework. Diffusion learning is discussed in both the continuous and discrete setting and an intriguing link is established between the Green function of the regularization operators and the structure of the graph in the corresponding discrete structure. It is pointed out that an appropriate choice of the smoothing operators allows one to implement a regularization that gives rise to Green functions whose corresponding matrix is sparse, which imposes a corresponding structure on the graph associated to the training set. Finally, the choice of the smoothness operator is given a Bayesian interpretation in terms of prior probability on the expected values of the function.

Keywords. kernel machines, machine learning, regularization

1. Introduction

The reconstruction of a surface given a collection of examples has a impressive number of applications and has been successfully attacked using regularization frameworks in which the errors with respect to the desired values and some smoothness figure are jointly penalized [2]. This framework has been nicely adopted in machine learning to devise a theory of approximation that has become popular especially for an in-depth understanding of radial basis functions networks [1]. The regularization framework for learning is revisited to provide a statistical interpretation related to the one proposed in [1]. The analysis of differential operators for regularization suggests that one can construct Green functions that are exactly null outside a bounded characteristic domain. This gives rise to sparse Gram matrices that contributes to speed up the computation to determine the solution of the Euler-Lagrange equation. It is shown that solution can be thought of as a diffusion process with nice physical counterparts in problems like the determination of gravitational (electrostatic) field or the bending of a thin plate. The most important contribution of the paper is to show that such a diffusion process is very much related to what has been proposed in the discrete setting for graphical domains (see e.g. [3,4]). Basically, it is shown that the classic continuous variational framework gives rise to the same equations that are derived in the discrete setting by appropriate choices of the smoothness operator.

This paper is organized as follows. In the next section we review the Tikhnov regularization while in section 3 we discuss some of the most popular finite smoothness operators. In section 4 we discuss how to construct appropriate Green functions, while in section 5 the concept of semi-parametric regularization is introduced. In section 6, we present the main contribution of the paper concerning the link between discrete and continuous regularization. and, finally, some conclusions are drawn in section 7.

2. Tikhnov regularization with infinite training set

Beginning from Tikhnov regularization theory, we introduce a related variational framework to determine $f(x)$ by

$$f(x) = \arg\min_{f \in \mathcal{F}} \left\{ \int_{\mathcal{L}} p_L(x) w_L(x) \ell(x, y, f(x)) dx + \lambda r \left(\int_{\Omega} p(x) \parallel Df \parallel^2 dx \right\} \right) \tag{1}$$

where $\ell(x, y, f(x)$ is the loss function, $r(\cdot)$ is a strictly monotonic increasing function, $p(x)$ is the density of the data probability distribution, $p_L(x)$ is the density of the training set, $w_L(x)$ is a weight to express the trust of the supervised pair $(x, y(x))$ and D is the differential operator that is used for smoothing the function. In the literature, the case which is normally taken into account is the one in which there are a finite number of examples $\{(x_k, y_k),\ k = 1, \ldots, n\}$ for which $p_L(x) = \sum_{k=1}^{n} \delta(x - x_k)$. We can solve equation 1 by the usual computation of the variation determined by replacing f with $f + h$, by imposing the boundary condition on the variation $\forall x \in \partial\Omega: \quad h(x) \equiv 0$.

For the first term, when restricting to first-order variations and posing $p_L^w \doteq p_L(x) w(x)$ with we get:

$$\int_{\mathcal{L}} p_L^w(x) \ell(x, y, f + h(x)) dx \equiv \int_{\mathcal{L}} p_L^w(x) \left(\ell(x, y, f(x)) + \ell'_f(x, y, f(x)) h(x) \right) dx$$

and, therefore, the variation is $\int_{\mathcal{L}} p_L^w \ell'_f(x, y, f(x)) h(x) dx$. When using the notation of the L^2 Hilbert space we have

$$\delta \left(\int_{\mathcal{L}} p_L^w(x) \ell(x, y, f(x)) dx \right) = \int_{\mathcal{L}} p_L^w(x) \ell'_f(x, y, f(x)) h(x) dx \tag{2}$$

$$= \int_{\mathcal{L}} \frac{p_L^w(x)}{p(x)} \ell'_f(x, y, f(x)) h(x) p(x) dx \tag{3}$$

$$= < \frac{p_L^w(x)}{p(x)} h, \ell'_f(x, y, f(x)) > \tag{4}$$

For the variation of the regularization term we can use the Hilbert space notation again. Since D is linear

$$\begin{aligned} r(< D(f+h), D(f+h) >) &= r(< Df + Dh, Df + Dh >) \\ &= r(\| Df \|^2 + 2 < Df, Dh > + \| f \|^2) \\ &\equiv r(\| Df \|^2 + 2 < Df, Dh >) \\ &\equiv r(\| Df \|^2) + 2r'(\| Df \|^2) < Df, Dh > \end{aligned}$$

Hence,

$$\delta\left(r(\| Df \|^2)\right) = 2r'(\| Df \|^2) < Df, Dh > \tag{5}$$

The necessary condition for the extreme turns out to be

$$< h, \frac{p_L^w}{p} \ell'_f > + 2r'(\| Df \|^2)\lambda < Dh, Df >= 0$$

Let D^* be the adjunct operator of D, that is $< Du, v >=< u, D^* v >$. If we choose, $u = Df$ and $v = h$ we get $< Df, Dh >=< Dh, Df >=< h, D^* Df >$ and, therefore,

$$< h, \frac{p_L^w}{p} \ell'_f > + 2r'(\| Df \|^2)\lambda < h, D^* Df > .$$

Since, this holds for any variation h, we end up in the classic Euler-Lagrange equation:

$$D^* Df + \frac{p_L^w}{2p\lambda r'(\| Df \|^2)} \ell'_f = 0 \tag{6}$$

Let us restrict attention to the case of linear r and $p_L(x) = p(x)$. Furthermore, let us assume that we only trust a finite training set, so that $w(x) = \sum_{k=1}^n \delta(x - x_k)$ and, therefore,

$$D^* Df + \frac{1}{2\lambda} \sum_{k=1}^{n} \delta(x - x_k) \ell'_f(x_k, y_k, f(x_k)) = 0 \tag{7}$$

Let $\rho(x) \doteq -\frac{1}{2\lambda} \sum_{k=1}^n \delta(x - x_k)\ell'_f(x_k, y_k, f(x_k))$. Let $L = D^\star D$ be and let us assume that the kernel space of the operator is $\{0\}$, that is the only function $h(x)$ such that $Lh(x) = 0$ is $h(x) \equiv 0$. Under this assumption, if $g(x)$ is the Green function of L then $f = g \otimes \rho$. More explicitly

$$f(x) = \sum_{k=1}^{n} w_k g(x, x_k) \tag{8}$$

where

$$w_k = -\frac{1}{2\lambda} \ell'_f(x_k, y_k, f(x_k)) \tag{9}$$

Notice that this holds provided that there exists no function $\psi(\cdot)$ such that $T\psi(x) = 0$, apart from $g(x, x_k)$ for which $Tg(x, x_k) = 0, \ \forall x \in \Omega - \{x_k\}$. The case in which this condition is violated is treated in Section 5.

Let us consider the quadratic and the logistic loss functions.

- QUADRATIC LOSS FUNCTION
  In this case, from $\ell(x, y, f(x)) = (y - f(x))^2$ we get $\ell'_f(x_k, y_k, f(x_k)) = 2(f(x_k - y_k)$ which, in turn, yields $w_k = \frac{y_k - f(x_k)}{\lambda}$ When introducing the Green matrix G such that $G[i, j] = g(x_i, x_j)$ we get

$$(G + \lambda I)w = y. \tag{10}$$

  By inverting $R = G + \lambda I$ we find w and, finally, $f(x)$ by equation 8.
- LOGISTIC LOSS FUNCTION
  In this case, from $\ell(x, y, f(x)) = \ln(1 + \exp(-yf(x))$, from equation 9, by inverting $\ell'_f(x_i, y_i, f(x_i))$ for all $i = 1, \ldots, n$we get

$$f(x_i) = \frac{1}{y_i} \ln \left(\frac{y_i}{2\lambda w_i} - 1 \right).$$

  When pairing this equation with 8, finally, we get

$$\sum_{j=1}^{n} g(x_i, x_j) w_j = \frac{1}{y_i} \ln \left(\frac{y_i}{2\lambda w_i} - 1 \right).$$

  which holds for all $i = 1, \ldots, n$.

Finally, we show that in the classic case of finite training set the overall index 1 which expresses the solution as a variational problem can be converted into the finite space of the weight parameter w.
When using the representer theorem given by equation 8 for the first (fitting) term we get

$$\begin{aligned} \sum_{i=1}^{n} \ell(x_i, y_i, f(x_i) &= \ell(x_i, y_i, \sum_{j=1}^{n} w_j g(x_i, x_j)) \\ &= \mathcal{L}(x, y, Gw) \end{aligned}$$

For the second term

$$
\begin{aligned}
\int_{\Omega} p(x) r(\| Df \|^2) dx &= r(< Df, Df >) \\
&= r(< D \sum_{i=1}^{n} w_i g(x, x_i), D \sum_{j=1}^{n} w_j g(x, x_j) >) \\
&= r(< \sum_{i=1}^{n} w_i Dg(x, x_i), \sum_{j=1}^{n} w_j Dg(x, x_j) >) \\
&= r(\sum_{i=1}^{n} \sum_{j=1}^{n} < Dg(x, x_i), Dg(x, x_j) > w_i w_j) \\
&= r(\sum_{i=1}^{n} \sum_{j=1}^{n} < g(x, x_i), D^{\star} Dg(x, x_j) > w_i w_j) \\
&= r(\sum_{i=1}^{n} \sum_{j=1}^{n} < g(x, x_i), \delta(x, x_j) > w_i w_j) \\
&= r(\sum_{i=1}^{n} \sum_{j=1}^{n} < g(x_i, x_j) > w_i w_j) \\
&= r(w' G w).
\end{aligned}
$$

Finally, the variational problem 1 turns out to be equivalent to

$$
\arg \min_{w \in \mathcal{W}} \left(\mathcal{L}(x, y, Gw) + \lambda r(w' G w) \right) \tag{11}
$$

and, therefore, because of equation 8, the variational problem is converted into an optimization problem in $I\!R^n$.

3. Finite regularization operators

We review three different cases that turns out to be useful to better understand general issues on how to construct appropriate Green functions.

GRADIENT OPERATOR
Let $D = \nabla$ be. We have $\nabla \cdot (h \nabla f) = \nabla f \cdot \nabla h + h \nabla^2 f$ and, therefore, when considering the boundary condition $\forall x \in \partial\Omega : \quad h(x) \equiv 0$, we get

$$
\begin{aligned}
\int_{\Omega} \nabla f \cdot \nabla h &= \int_{\Omega} \left[\nabla \cdot (h \nabla f) - h \nabla^2 f \right] dx \\
&= \int_{\partial\Omega} \nabla \cdot (h \nabla f) \times \boldsymbol{r} dS - \int_{\Omega} h \nabla^2 f dx \\
&= - \int_{\Omega} h \nabla^2 f dx
\end{aligned}
$$

An interpretation of this equation can be given in terms of the adjoint operator of ∇. Let $v = \nabla f$ and $u = h$ be. The above equations can be rewritten as $< \nabla u, v >=< u, (-\nabla) \cdot \nabla v >$, and, therefore, $D^\star = \nabla^\star = -\nabla \cdot$. Finally, in this case the Euler-Lagrange equations 6 becomes $\nabla^2 f - \rho f = \rho y$ where $\rho(x) = p_L^w(x)/p(x)\lambda$. In the special case in which ρ is constant, this is the Helmholtz equation that represent a diffusion process. Interestingly, when considering the classic finite training set with the corresponding singular probability distribution the Helmholtz equation becomes $\nabla^2 f = 0$, since the adjoint equation 12 does require that f is continuous with its derivatives. There are well-known physical counterparts of this phenomenon for instance in the case of gravitational and electrostatic fields in which concentrated masses and charges yield explosion of the potential. This comes from noting that for $m > 2$, the Green function is $f(x) = (\| x \|)^{2-m}$ and, therefore, $\lim_{x \to x_k} f(x) = \infty$. However, we can immediately realize that the Helmholtz equation assumes that one knows the target $y(x)$ in Ω, which is obviously an unreasonable hypothesis in the problem at hand. As already pointed out, a more reasonable assumption is that the supervision is available in $\Omega_s \subset \Omega$, thought this requires to populate supervision in the small set Ω_s by a noisy model. In any case, the ∇ operator gives rise to singularity unless a distributed distribution of labels is used. Notice that in this case, $L = \nabla^2$ has linear functions in its kernel

$$f(x) = \sum_{k=0}^{n} w_k x_k$$

When imposing the consistency on the training set we find that $f(x) = w'x$, where $w \in I\!R^{m+1}$, that can be discovered by solving

$$\arg\min_{\alpha} \left(\mathcal{L}(x, y, w'x) + \lambda w^2 \right). \tag{12}$$

This derives straightforwardly from carrying out an analysis similar to 11. Notice that we cannot apply directly equation 11 since it derives from assuming that $Ker(L) = \{0\}$, which is violated in this case.

LAPLACIAN OPERATOR

Let $D = \nabla^2 = \Delta$ be. We have

$$\nabla \cdot (\nabla u \cdot v) = v \nabla^2 u + \nabla u \cdot \nabla v$$
$$\nabla \cdot (\nabla v \cdot u) = u \nabla^2 v + \nabla v \cdot \nabla u$$

and

$$\int_\Omega \nabla \cdot (\nabla u \cdot v) = \int_{\partial\Omega} v \cdot \nabla u dx$$
$$= \int_\Omega v \nabla^2 u dx + \int_\Omega \nabla u \cdot \nabla v dx.$$

Since $\forall x \in \partial\Omega \;\; v(x) = 0$

$$\int_{\partial\Omega} \nabla v \cdot \nabla u \ dx = < \nabla u, \nabla v >$$

$$= - \int_{\Omega} v \nabla^2 u dx$$

$$= - < v, \nabla^2 u >$$

If we exchange u with v we get $< \nabla u, \nabla v >= - < u, \nabla^2 v >$ and, finally,

$$< v, \nabla^2 u >=< \nabla^2 u, v >=< u, \nabla^2 v > \tag{13}$$

that is Δ is self-adjoint. Hence, the corresponding Euler-Lagrange equation 6 becomes the biharmonic equation [1].

$$\Delta^2 f - \frac{1}{\lambda} \sum_{k=1}^{n} \delta(x - x_k)(y(x_k) - f(x_k) = 0 \tag{14}$$

This is the biharmonic equation which occurs in physics for the problem of modeling the thin-plate deformation (thin plate spline) [2]. The position of the thin plate results in the minimization of the bending energy $1/2(\Delta f)^2$. The Green function of the square Laplace operator Δ^2 is $r^2 \log r^2$ and, unlike for the ∇ operator, we have that $\lim_{r \to 0} r^2 \log r^2 = 0$, that is the approximation does not present singularities in Ω, apart from the points of the training set.

4. Characteristic Green functions

Let us consider the infinite dimensional regularization operator $D = \odot$ defined by

$$\odot f = [\alpha_o^{1/2} d^o, \alpha_1^{1/2} d^1, \cdots, \alpha_h^{1/2} d^h, \cdots] \tag{15}$$

where $d^{2m} = \Delta^m = \nabla^{2m}$ and $d^{2m+1} = \nabla\nabla^{2m}$ for $m = 0, 1, \cdots$. The corresponding regularization term is

$$\| \odot f \|^2 = \int_{\Omega} dx \sum_{h=0}^{\infty} \alpha_h \left(d^h f(x)\right)^2$$

Now we find the adjoint $(\odot)^\star$ of $\odot$. We need to discuss even and odd coordinates of $\odot$ separately. For *even* coordinates we easily conclude that d^{2m} is self-adjoint. This can be proven by induction on m.

- *Basis of induction*: For $m = 1$, $d^2 = \nabla^2$. According to equation 13, d^2 is self-adjoint.

[1]Emile Leonard Mathieu (1835-1890) was the first who addressed in full the mathematical properties of the biharmonic equationeral relations for linear partial differential equations with constant coefÞcients. For $m = 1$ this fourth-order equation yields the natural cubic splines.

[2]The equation arises also for modeling liquid flows.

- *Induction step*: Since ∇^2 is self-adjoint (basis of induction), and because of the induction hypothesis $< \nabla^{2(m-1)}u, v >=< u, \nabla^{2(m-1)}v >$, we have

$$\begin{aligned} < \nabla^{2m}u, v > &= < \nabla^2(\nabla^{2(m-1)}u), v > \\ &= < \nabla^{2(m-1)}u, \nabla^2 v > \\ &= < u, \nabla^{2(m-1}\nabla^2 v > \\ &= < u, \nabla^{2m}v > . \end{aligned}$$

For odd coordinates of $\odot$ we prove that the adjoint of ∇^{2m+1} is $-\nabla^{2m+1}$.

- *Basis of induction*: For $m = 1$, we have $d^1 = \nabla$. According to equation 12, $\nabla^\star = -\nabla\cdot$
- *Induction step*: When using the basis and the induction we get

$$\begin{aligned} < \nabla^{2m+1}u, v > &= < \nabla\nabla^{2m}u, v > \\ &= < \nabla^{2m}u, -\nabla \cdot v > \\ &= < u, -\nabla^{2m}\nabla \cdot v > \\ &= < u, -\nabla^{2m+1}v > . \end{aligned}$$

We conclude that

$$T = D^\star D = \odot^\star\odot = \sum_{m=0}^{\infty}(-1)^m \alpha_m \nabla^{2m} \tag{16}$$

As a consequence, the Green function satisfies $(\odot^\star\odot)g(x) = \delta(x)$. When using the Fourier transform we get

$$\sum_{m=0}^{\infty} \alpha_h(\omega\cdot\omega)^h G(\omega) = 1,$$

and, therefore,

$$g(x) = \int_\Omega d\omega \frac{e^{j\omega\cdot x}}{\sum_{m=0}^{\infty}\alpha_m(\omega\cdot\omega)^h} \tag{17}$$

This equation can nicely be used to "designńń a desired Green function by appropriate choice of the coefficients α_h. As a special case we find the Green functions associated with the ∇ and ∇^2 differential operators. In particular, we get the Gaussian function $g(x) = \exp(-x^2/2\sigma^2)$ when choosing

$$\alpha_h = \frac{\sigma^{2h}}{h!2^h}$$

The operator $(\odot^\star\odot)$ makes it possible to design Green functions that, unlike the Gaussian, are null outside a given domain $\Gamma \subset \Omega = I\!R^n$. Given the desired Green function, one must determine α_h such that

$$G(\omega) = \frac{1}{\sum_{h=0}^{\infty}\alpha_m(\omega\cdot\omega)^h}$$

5. Semi-parametric regularization

In the general case, the solution of Euler-Lagrange equations is given by an extension of the representer theorem in which

$$f(x) = \psi(x) + \sum_{k=1}^{n} w_k g(x, x_k)$$

and $T\psi(x) = 0$. If we consider the T operator expressed by equation 16 we conclude that by an appropriate choice of α_h the additional term $\phi(\cdot)$ can be any polynomial. It is worth mentioning that the case in which $f(x)$ admits a unique representation in the kernel basis, that is $\psi(x) = 0$, imposes an immediate condition on the T operator. Let us consider the case $\psi(x) = p_r(x)$ is a polynomial of degree r. Then

$$T = D^{\star}D = \odot^{\star} \odot p_r = \sum_{m=0}^{\infty} (-1)^m \alpha_m \nabla^{2m} \left(\sum_{j=0}^{r} \gamma_j \right)$$

6. Diffusion learning in discrete and continuous structures

A possible numerical method to determine the weights w that leads to the solution of the regularization problem is use iterative schemes like Gauss-Siedel's and Jacobi's, that is

$$w(t+1) = -\frac{G}{\lambda} w(t) + \frac{y}{\lambda} \tag{18}$$

which converges to the solution $w^{\star} = (\lambda I + G)^{-1} y$. Notice that the matrix G/λ can always lead to a stable system by an appropriate choice of λ. The equation 18 corresponds to a diffusion process that propagates the labels y to the final fix-point $w^{\star}$. If G is sparse, the diffusion process can easily be understood and related to discrete methods operating on graphs (see e.g. [3]). In particular, we can calculate $f(\cdot)$ on the training examples that correspond with the graph in the discrete setting. Hence, we can construct an iterative scheme for $f(\cdot)$ as follows:

$$\begin{aligned} f(t+1) &= Gw(t+1) \\ &= -\frac{1}{\lambda} G\left(Gw(t) - y\right) \\ &= -\frac{1}{\lambda}\left(Gf(t) - G \cdot y\right). \end{aligned}$$

We can easily see $f(t)$ is stable and converges to

$$\begin{aligned} f^{\star} &= (\lambda I + G)^{-1} G y \\ &= [G(\lambda I G^{-1} + I)]^{-1} G y \\ &= (I + \lambda G^{-1})^{-1} y. \end{aligned}$$

Now let if we rewrite these equations by using the following transformations

$$\alpha = \frac{\lambda}{1+\lambda}$$
$$S_\Omega = I - G^{-1}$$

we get

$$f^\star = (1-\alpha)\,(I - \alpha S_\Omega)^{-1}\, y$$

Now, let us consider the case $D = \nabla$. The matrix G is the Gram matrix corresponding to the Green function that is solution of $\nabla^2 g(x) = \delta(x)$. If we consider the regular graph obtained by connecting each training example with each other, $x_i \sim x_j$, then the Laplacian equation for $g(x)$ can be approximated on the nodes of the graph by means of approximatation

$$L_\Omega g(x_i, x_j) = (0, \ldots, 0, 1, 0, \ldots, 0)'$$

where, the only 1 is located in the $j-th$ position and L_Ω is the Laplacian of the graph. When writing this equation for all nodes of the graph we get $L_\Omega G = I$ and, consequently $G^{-1} = L_\Omega$. Since $L_\Omega = I - S_\Omega$ we can attribute a specific meaning to $S_\Omega = I - L_\Omega = I - G^{-1}$. In particular, since the inverse of a sparse matrix is sparse we can easily conclude that if G is sparse then S_Ω is also sparse. That is in the case of sparse G, deriving from the specific structure of the differential operator $D^\star \cdot D$, then the corresponding regular graph of the discrete counterpart assumes a structure given by S_Ω which is now sparse, too. This establishes an intriguing link with the case of graphical diffusion treated in [3] and shows that in the continuous setting a diffusion processes similar to the case of discrete structures represented by graphs takes place.

Notice that the Euler-Lagrange equation 6 is itself the manifestation of a diffusion process associated to the operator $D^\star \cdot D$. However, while this is well-known in physics for operators like ∇ and Δ, the same interpretation is not straightforward for the differential operator $\odot$, which accumulates infinite differential terms.

Finally we can adopt the Bayesian framework as an interpretation of the solution of the proposed regularization problem. If $y \in I\!R^n$ is the set of targets attached to the value of $f(\cdot)$ and $f \in I\!R^n$ is the value reached by the function, following [1], we can determine $P(f|y)$ by

$$P(f|y) = \frac{P(y|f) \cdot P(f)}{P(y)} \propto P(y|f) \cdot P(f)$$

Now, if we make the hypothesis of Gaussian distribution, the likelihood is

$$P(y|f) \propto \exp\left(-\frac{\mathcal{L}(x, y, f)}{2\sigma^2}\right).$$

If no other explicit prior is given, one can consider to introduce the smoothness constraints. If we consider again a Gaussian hypothesis distribution, we can introduce the prior

$$P(f) \propto \exp\left(-\frac{1}{2} < f, D^{\star}Df >\right) = \exp\left(-\frac{1}{2} < f, Lf >\right)$$

Therefore, the maximization of the posterior gives rise to the minimization of

$$\begin{aligned} E &= \frac{\mathcal{L}(x,y,f)}{2\sigma^2} + \frac{1}{2} < f, Lf > \\ &\propto \mathcal{L}(x,y,f) + \lambda < f, Lf > \end{aligned}$$

7. Conclusions

This paper provides an introduction to diffusion learning in the continuum setting and gives some insights on the connections with the discrete counterpart of learning in graphical domains. After having provided the classic variational framework of regularization, it is proven that it gives rise to a diffusion process that can be directly interpreted by the associated Euler-Lagrange equations. Moreover, it is shown that this process can be nicely approximated by graphical diffusion thorough the examples of the training set and that the structure of the Green function which is inherited from the differential smooth operators yields a corresponding graphical structure in the graphical discrete approximation.

References

[1] Tomaso Poggio and Federico Girosi. A theory of networks for approximation and learning. Technical report, MIT, 1989.

[2] A.N. Tikhnov and V. Y. Arsenin. *Solution of ill-posed problems*. W.H. Winston, Washington, D.C., 1977.

[3] Denyong Zhou and Bernard Schoelkopf. A regularization framework for learning from graph data. In *Workshop on Statistical Relational Learning*, 2004.

[4] Denyong Zhou and Bernard Schoelkopf. Regularization on discrete spaces. In *Lecture Notes in Computer Science - Pattern Recognition*, pages 361–368, 2005.

New Directions in Neural Networks
B. Apolloni et al. (Eds.)
IOS Press, 2009

doi:10.3233/978-1-58603-984-4-138

Sources of asymmetric randomness

Bruno APOLLONI [a] and Simone BASSIS [a]
[a] *University of Milan, Department of Computer Science, Via Comelico 39/41, 20135 Milan, Italy*
{apolloni,bassis}@dsi.unimi.it

Abstract. In view of discussing the genuine roots of the connectionist paradigm we toss in this paper the *non symmetry* features of the involved random phenomena. Reading these features in terms of *intentionality* with which we drive a learning process far from a simple random walk, we focus on elementary processes where trajectories cannot be decomposed as the sum of a deterministic recursive function plus a symmetric noise. Rather we look at nonlinear compositions of the above ingredients, as a source of genuine non symmetric atomic random actions, like those at the basis of a training process. To this aim we introduce an extended Pareto distribution law with which we analyze some intentional trajectories. With this model we issue some preliminary considerations on elapsed times of training sessions of some families of neural networks.

Keywords. Algorithmic Inference, Pareto distribution, neural networks

Introduction

Discovering a law ruling Nature requires managing features that are common to its application field. Without any philosophical pretension, we may identify them with properties with a certain degree of uniformity. It may refer to *invariance* of physical laws [14], uniformity of organic systems [11] or constancy of living systems' morphology [5], and so on. Under a logical perspective all of them share the minimal feature of symmetry as both a fairness guarantee and a universality prerequisite. Moving from static laws to algorithms, their correctness has been customary tossed in terms of homogeneity: the algorithm is correct since it produces a correct output for whatever input, with the understatement that an extended form of symmetry now concerns the tool for processing data and not the phenomenon generating them. Recently, the connectionist paradigm and more in general the granular computation framework moved a step ahead in the consideration of symmetry constraints versus benefits. Within this framework, an algorithm is satisfactory if it works well on a certain set of inputs, not necessarily coinciding with the input universe. To be useful, however, we expect that this set covers a wide family of instances that we may encounter in the real world. Now, with this strategy algorithms are tailored on data, thus producing statistics, by definition. The study of statistics, however, is tightly connected to the study of probabilistic models, in turn heavily biased by symmetry constraints as antidotes to lack of knowledge. This opens a hiatus in the above sequence toward the symmetry release.

As a matter of fact, in spite of: i) indices such as Vapnik-Chervonenkis dimension [13] that are clear indicators of lack of symmetry in classes of functions (whenever are

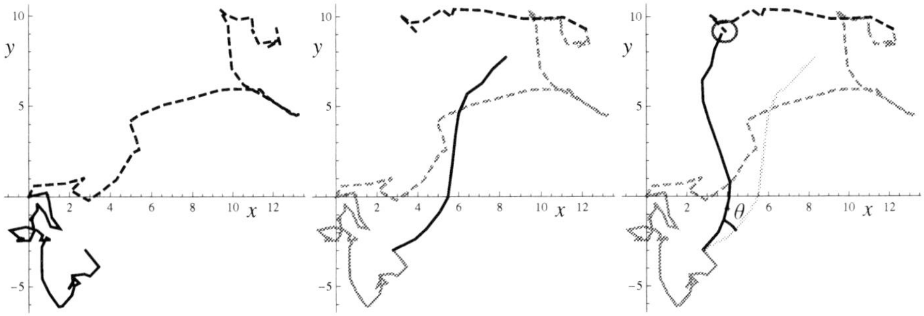

(a) (b) (c)

Figure 1. Joint traces of two cars (plain and dashed curve respectively) when (a) both move according to a Brownian motion behavior; (b) the former moves only in one quadrant (absolute value of the Brownian motion components) from a trigger time on; and (c) an oracle rotates this trajectory toward the other car with some approximation (quantified by the raw of a proximity circle).

less than ∞), ii) practitioner concepts such as negentropy to denote the diversity from basic Gaussian phenomena [7], or iii) swarm intelligence methods to identify preferential directions in a complex search problem [8], most statistical analyses of computational problems are still based on uniform, Gaussian and negative exponential variables that are the template descriptors of the most symmetric phenomena [1].

In this paper we move in the direction of filling the mentioned gap between algorithms and statistical models. We do this using a toy model whose results we preliminarly apply to the class of single and multilayer perceptrons trained with customary supervised learning algorithms.

1. Putting intention in crashing a bumper car

Assume you are playing with bumper machines in an amusement park. You wander in the paddock until, time to time, you decide to hit a given car that is ignoring your willingness. For the sake of simplicity we may assume the trajectory of each car to be a plane Brownian motion before the chase triggering. Thus, with the reference frame in Fig. 1(a), indexing with $i = 1, 2$ the cars whose histories we are following, we have [2]

$$X_i(t) \sim \mathcal{N}_{0,\sqrt{t}}; \qquad Y_i(t) \sim \mathcal{N}_{0,\sqrt{t}} \tag{1}$$

Then you, seating in the first car, decide at time τ to reach and crash the second car. The questioned variable records the instant $T > \tau$ when you succeed. In the case study where cars are points in the plane, in order to identify this instant we must specify: i) an operational definition of the cars' rendevouz since the probability of exact matching is 0, and ii) the symmetry break introduced by the chase intention. The chase effectiveness depends on the capability of orienting your motion in the direction of the target, which

[1]Note that the constance of the former is moulded in the other two distributions just as a consequence of cumulating much many uniform phenomena giving rise to either crowded events (in the domain of Gaussian variables) or distinguishable events (in the domain of negative exponential distributions) [15].

[2]By default, capital letters (such as U, X) will denote random variables and small letters (u, x) their corresponding realizations.

corresponds to converting a part of the motion along the cars' connecting line from symmetric to oriented moves. Mathematically, orientation corresponds to taking the absolute value of the elementary steps in that direction, so as to work with Chi distributed addends in place of Gaussian ones (see Fig. 1(b)). In order to overcome analytical complications we propose this simple scheme. As the difference between two Gaussian variables is a Gaussian variable too, we may use (1) also to describe the components of the distance Δ between the two cars before τ. We just need to multiply them by $\sqrt{2}$ so as $X_\Delta(t) \sim \mathcal{N}_{0,\sqrt{2t}}$ and similarly for $Y_\Delta(t)$. Moreover, if we move to polar coordinates (r, θ) with $x = r\cos\theta$, $y = r\sin\theta$, the density function f_Δ of Δ becomes

$$f_\Delta(r, \theta) = \frac{1}{4\pi t} r e^{-\frac{r^2}{4t}} \tag{2}$$

which looks for the joint density function of (R, Θ), with R a Chi variable with 2 degrees of freedoms scaled by a factor $\sqrt{2t}$ and Θ a variable uniformly distributed in $0, 2\pi)$. Our assumption on pursuit is that, with reference to the distances D_1 and D_2 of the two cars from the position of the first one at time τ, you are able to maneuver Θ_1 from τ on, so that when $D_1 = D_2$ also $\Theta_1 = \Theta_2$ (see Fig. 1(c)). As mentioned before, *per se* the probability of a match between two points representing the cars is null. Thus your task is unrealistic. However intentionality recovers feasibility thanks to the fact that in practice it is enough that the angles are sufficiently close to entangle the two cars. The actual correspondence with the pursuit dynamics is facilitated by some free coefficients which will be embedded in the model.

With this assumption we are interested in the time t when $D_1 = D_2$. Given the continuity of the latter we may measure only a probability density with t. Said in other words, at any change of the sign in the difference $D_1 - D_2$ with the running of the two cars, it will correspond a matching time as a specification of a continuous variable T. Since both D_1 and D_2 scale with the square of a time, expressing their dependence on the *trigger time* τ and the *pursuit time* t, we have:

$$D_1(t) = \sqrt{t}\chi_{2_1}; \qquad D_2(t) = \sqrt{2\tau + t}\chi_{2_2} \tag{3}$$

with $f_{\chi_2}(z) = ze^{-\frac{z^2}{2}}$, obtaining after equating $D_1(t)$ with $D_2(t)$

$$1 = \frac{D_1(t)}{D_2(t)} = \frac{\chi_{2_2}}{\chi_{2_1}} \frac{\sqrt{2\tau + t}}{\sqrt{t}} \tag{4}$$

under the condition $\chi_{2_2} \geq \chi_{2_1}$. Denoting with T the random variable with specifications t and $\mathcal{T}$ with specifications τ, this equation finds a stochastic solution in the random variable

$$V = \frac{T}{\mathcal{T}} = 2\left(\frac{\chi_{2_1}^2}{\chi_{2_2}^2} - 1\right)^{-1} \tag{5}$$

which follows the same distribution law of the ratio between two unconstrained Chi square variables, i.e. an F variable with parameter (2, 2) [6], whose c.d.f. reads

$$F_V(\upsilon) = 1 - \frac{1}{1+\upsilon} I_{0,\infty)}(\upsilon) = \frac{\upsilon}{1+\upsilon} I_{0,\infty)}(\upsilon) \tag{6}$$

where $I_{a,b}(x)$ is the indicator function of x w.r.t. the interval a, b, thus being 1 for $a \leq x \leq b$, 0 otherwise.

2. A very general way of maintaining memory in a time process

Let us make some general considerations about processes with memory. Starting from a very beginning, for any *ordered* variable T, such that only events on their sorted values are of interest to us, the following *master equation* holds

$$\mathrm{P}(T > t|T > k) = \mathrm{P}(T > a|T > k)\mathrm{P}(T > t|T > a) \quad \forall k \leq a \leq t \tag{7}$$

It comes simply from the fact that in the expression of the conditional probability

$$\mathrm{P}(T > t|T > k) = \frac{\mathrm{P}(T > t)}{\mathrm{P}(T > k)} = \frac{g(t)}{g(k)} \tag{8}$$

we may separate the conditioned variables from the conditioning ones. While (7) denotes the time splitting in the fashion of Chapmann–Kolmogorov theorem [9] as a general property of any sequence of data, equation (8) highlights that events $(T > t)$ and $(T > k)$ are by definition never independent. What is generally the target of the memory divide in random processes is the time $t - k$ between two events. In this perspective, the template of memoryless phenomena descriptor is the Poisson process, whose basic property is $\mathrm{P}(T > t) = \mathrm{P}(T > a)\mathrm{P}(T > t - a)$, if $t > a$. It says that if a random event (for instance a hard disk failure) did not occur before time a and you ask what will happen within time t, you must forget this past story (it does not mean that the disk became either more robust or weaker), since your true question concerns whether or not the event will occur at a time $t - a$. Hence your true variable is $\tau = T - a$, and the above property is satisfied by the negative exponential distribution law with $\mathrm{P}(T > t) = \mathrm{e}^{-\lambda t}$, for constant λ [3], since with this law (7) reads

$$\mathrm{e}^{-\lambda(t-k)} = \mathrm{e}^{-\lambda(a-k)}\mathrm{e}^{-\lambda(t-a)} \tag{9}$$

and the property that $\frac{g(t)}{g(k)}$ in (8) equals $g(t-k)$ is only owned by the exponential function.

On the contrary you introduce a memory of the past (a-long) if you cannot separate $T - a$ from a. In this paper we are called to consider the very simple cases where this occurs because the time dependence is of the form $\tau = (T/a)^{\beta}$. The simplest solution of (7) is represented by $\mathrm{P}(T > t|T > k) = (t/k)^{-\alpha}$ so that the master equation reads

$$(t/k)^{-\alpha} = (t/a)^{-\alpha}(a/k)^{-\alpha} \tag{10}$$

Note that this distribution, commonly called Pareto distribution, is defined only for $t \geq k$, with $k > 0$ denoting the true time origin, where α identifies the distribution with the

[3] variants with $\lambda = 1/\beta(t)$ allow simple adaptation the law to more complex phenomena when $\beta(t)$ is not far to be a constant.

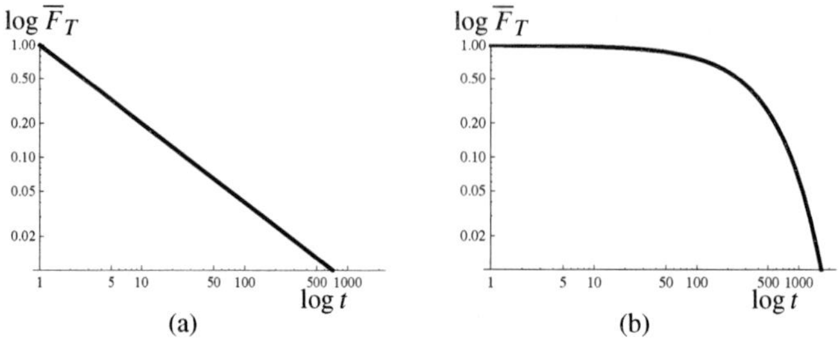

Figure 2. Complementary c.d.f. LogLogPlot when T follows: (a) a Pareto law; (b) a Negative Exponential exponential law.

scale of its logarithm. The main difference with the negative exponential distribution is highlighted by the LogLogPlots of the complementary cumulative distribution function (c.c.d.f.) tail in Fig. 2: a line segment with a Pareto curve (see picture (a)) in contrast with a more than linearly decreasing curve with the exponential distribution (picture (b)).

We recover the distribution of V coming from the bumper car model by extending (6) as follows

$$F_V(\upsilon) = 1 - \frac{b}{b + (\upsilon/c + 1)^a} \tag{11}$$

that we call *shifted* Pareto, with b and c playing the role of both scale and shift parameters. The latter stands for a key feature of a memory dependent model; the former of a memoryless framework. The exponent a plays a role similar to α's (but nothing to do with the memory length as in (10)). With this formula we aim to approximately capture many variants of υ, as for both modeling variations and model adaptation to real data. For instance we almost recover

$$F_V(\upsilon) = \frac{2\upsilon^{\frac{2}{\alpha}}}{\upsilon^{\frac{2}{\alpha}} + (\upsilon + 2)^{\frac{2}{\alpha}}} I_{0,\infty)}(\upsilon) \tag{12}$$

obtained by extending the dependence on t from square root to a generic power $1/\alpha$. Though somewhat structurally different from (12), (11) almost coincides with (12), both taking the form (6) when $\alpha = 2$ in the latter expression, and $a = b = c = 1$ and $\upsilon = \upsilon - 1$ in the former; but we may get satisfactory approximations in a relatively wide range of parameters. Moreover V in (11) ranges from $-c$ to $+\infty$. Hence, when we refer to a variable in $0, +\infty)$, we use the truncated version of (11) that is given by

$$F_V(\upsilon) = 1 - \frac{(b+1)}{b + (\upsilon/c + 1)^a} \tag{13}$$

To obtain the pursuit times we need to multiply υ by the trigger time, and to add the latter to the product in order to obtain the contact times. In the next section we will see that both contact times and intercontact times remain approximately in the same family, provided we have a suitable distribution law of the trigger times. We will also study some manageable deviations from this model.

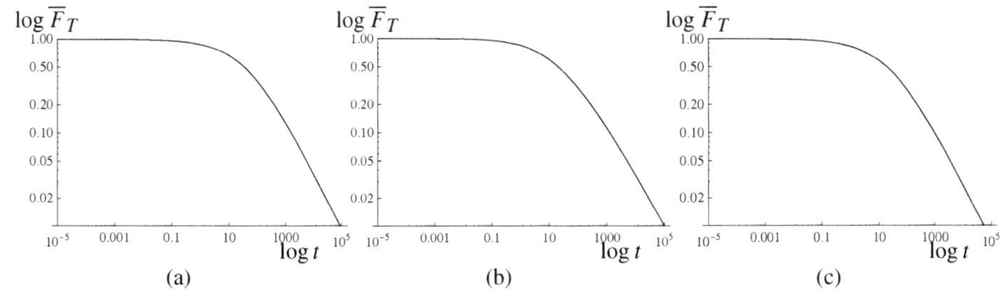

Figure 3. Complementary c.d.f. LogLogPlot of contact times with a trigger time varying according to distribution law: (a) uniform ; (b) Pareto; and (c) negative exponential.

3. The timing of the intentional process

From our model we are left with a power law describing the ratio between pursuit and trigger times. Since $t = \upsilon\tau$, to complete the description of contact times we need a model for the trigger time too. Let $f_{\mathcal{T}}$ be its probability distribution function (p.d.f.), defined in a range $(\tau_{\text{inf}}, \tau_{\text{sup}})$. Since $t+\tau = (\upsilon+1)\tau$, we obtain F_W with $W = T + \mathcal{T}$ by computing

$$F_W(w) = \int_{\tau_{\text{inf}}}^{\max\{w,\tau_{\text{sup}}\}} F_V(w/\tau - 1) f_{\mathcal{T}}(\tau)\mathrm{d}\tau \tag{14}$$

With many families of $\mathcal{T}$ p.d.f.s the shape of V c.d.f. transfers to W, as shown in Figs. 3(a) to (c).

For instance, for a Pareto distributed trigger time:

$$F_{\mathcal{T}}(\tau) = 1 - \tau^{-\lambda} \tag{15}$$

with $c = 1$ we have the expression

$$F_W(w) = 1 - {}_2\mathcal{F}_1\left(1, \frac{\lambda}{a}; \frac{a+\lambda}{a}; -\frac{w^a}{b}\right), \tag{16}$$

where ${}_2\mathcal{F}_1$ is the Hypergeometric2F1 function defined as ${}_2\mathcal{F}_1(a,b;c;z) = \sum_{k=0}^{\infty} \frac{(a)_k (b)_k}{(c)_k} \frac{z^k}{k}$, with $(a)_k = a(a+1)(a+2)\cdots(a+k-1)$ being the rising factorial.

3.1. Intentionality in learning

Following a random walk trajectory, in a very sharp way we identify absence of memory with symmetry of the next move's distribution around 0. Whereas brain activity is commonly denoted by a symmetry break as a symptom of an intentionality of the move linked to the memory of the past history. In particular, learning definitely needs a management of past history. With connectionist models this functionality emerges from a wise mix of random walk in the learner state space and a gently bias toward attractors representing the *correct state* we expect of the trained device. Hence the analogy with bumping cars is more or less tight depending on the incidence of the two parts, in turn determined by the hardness of the learning task. In a very schematic way, our conjecture is that the more difficult is the learning task, so more relevant is the random walk components of the training evolutions in order to discover new tracks toward attractors. From a statistical perspective this means an increment of the shift term b in (11), while a characterizes the difficult of the intentional part *per se*. Structural artifacts, such as bias in the dynamics, correlations and alike, introduce drifts from the template distribution. To check this conjecture we: i) create databases of learning times with different learning task complexity, and ii) synthesize data through curves in the mentioned families of distribution laws, estimated through standard Algorithmic Inference procedures.

3.1.1. The databases.

Learners are represented by either single perceptrons (SP) or three layer perceptrons (TP). Tasks are represented by either fix (FF) or random functions (RF). For each task we train $m = 301$ randomly initialized learners, stopping the training session when the mean square error is less than $\varepsilon = 0.01$. The learning algorithm is standard gradient descent with backpropagation in case of three-layer perceptron. Namely we have the following benchmarks:

SPFF A perceptron with 5 inputs is trained on a fixed singleton.

SPRF A perceptron with 5 inputs is trained on a randomly formed singleton.

TPFF$_1$ A three-layer perceptron with 5 input nodes, 3 hidden nodes and 1 output node is trained on the set of 5 instances having a unitary code in input (say $\{0, 1, 0, 0, 0\}$) and its positional translation divided by 6 (say 0.333) as output.

TPFF$_2$ A three-layer perceptron with 2 hidden nodes and 4 both input and output nodes is trained to mirroring the set of the four unitary codes.

TPRF A three-layer perceptron with 2 hidden nodes and 4 both input and output nodes is trained to mirroring a set of four randomly generated binary strings.

3.1.2. Estimating the time distribution laws.

We have three parameters a, b and c to be estimated in (11). Their joint estimate definitely proves difficult in a conventional (either frequentist or Bayesian) framework. Hence we decide to adopt a modern statistical framework called *Algorithmic Inference* [3] with an estimate procedure ruling out through the following steps.

1. *Sampling mechanism.* It consists of a pair $\langle \Psi, g_\theta \rangle$, where the *seed* Ψ is a random variable without unknown parameters, while the *explaining function* g_θ is a function mapping from samples of Ψ to samples of the random variable X we are interested in. Thanks to the inverse probability theorem [10] we have that by using the uniform variable U in 0, 1 as a seed Ψ the explaining function for T distributed according to (13) is:

$$t = c\left(\frac{1+bu}{1-u}\right)^{\frac{1}{a}} - c. \tag{17}$$

2. *Master equations.* The actual connection between the model and the observed data is tossed in terms of a set of relations between statistics on the data and unknown parameters that come as a corollary of the sampling mechanisms. With these relations we may inspect the values of the parameters that could have generated a sample with the observed statistic from a particular setting of the seeds. Hence, if we draw seeds according to their known distribution – uniform in our case – we get a sample of compatible parameters in response [3]. In order to ensure this sample clean properties, it is enough to involve sufficient statistics w.r.t. the parameters [12] in the master equations. Unluckily, because of the shift terms, the parameters are so embedded in the density function of T that we cannot identify such statistics for them. Rather we focus on the statistics $t_{\mathrm{med}} = t_{(\lfloor m/2+1 \rfloor)}$, $s_1 = \sum_{i=1}^{m} \left| t_{(i)}/t_{\mathrm{med}} - 1 \right|^r$ and $s_2 = \sum_{i=\lfloor m/2+1 \rfloor}^{m} \log \left(t_{(i)}/t_{\mathrm{med}} \right)$, where $t_{(i)}$ denotes the i-th item within the sample sorted in ascending order, and propose the following master equations having analogous notation for $u_{(i)}$ and u_{med}

$$t_{\mathrm{med}} = c \left(\frac{1 + b u_{\mathrm{med}}}{1 - u_{\mathrm{med}}} \right)^{\frac{1}{a}} - c \tag{18}$$

$$s_1 = \sum_{i=1}^{m} \left| \left(\frac{\left(\frac{1+b u_{(i)}}{1-u_{(i)}} \right)}{\left(\frac{1+b u_{\mathrm{med}}}{1-u_{\mathrm{med}}} \right)} \right)^{\frac{1}{a}} - 1 \right|^r \tag{19}$$

$$s_2 = \sum_{i=\lfloor \frac{m}{2}+1 \rfloor}^{m} \log \left(\frac{1 + b u_{(i)}}{1 - u_{(i)}} \right) - \log \left(\frac{1 + b u_{\mathrm{med}}}{1 - u_{\mathrm{med}}} \right) + \log c^{\lfloor \frac{m}{2}+1 \rfloor} \tag{20}$$

We cannot state a general course of these statistics with the parameters. However, in the field we expect to find solution this course is monotone in a and b, with a tilting attitude of c. In a greater detail, the true ratio term in s_1 and s_2 should be $\left(\left(\frac{1+b u_{(i)}}{1-u_{(i)}} \right)^{\frac{1}{a}} - 1 \right) / \left(\left(\frac{1+b u_{\mathrm{med}}}{1-u_{\mathrm{med}}} \right)^{\frac{1}{a}} - 1 \right)$, that we approximately simplify as in (19) to make the solution easier. Moreover last term in (20) does not derive from the explaining function of T. Rather, it is added to introduce a shaking in the numeric search of solution, in the assumption that c is close to 1, hence its logarithm to 0, while shifts from this value raises t_{med} and decreases s_2. To achieve the first condition together with a suitable range of values, we normalize the t_is with a wise shift and rescaling. We also trigger r, ruling a balance between second and third statistics, so that to avoid disastrous paths followed by the search algorithm leading to diverge. This denotes the fact that at the moment, because of the difficulties of the involved numerical optimization tasks, the estimation procedure is not completely automatic.

Embedding the found parameters in (13) we obtain a population of random curves to contrast with the empirical ones as in Fig. 4.

Here we report a confidence region [2] where we expect to lie with confidence 0.90 the c.c.d.f. curve compatible with the experimental data according to our model. The curves are rendered in LogLog coordinates like the previous figures. The confidence region is derived from the empirical population through a *peeling method,* as detailed

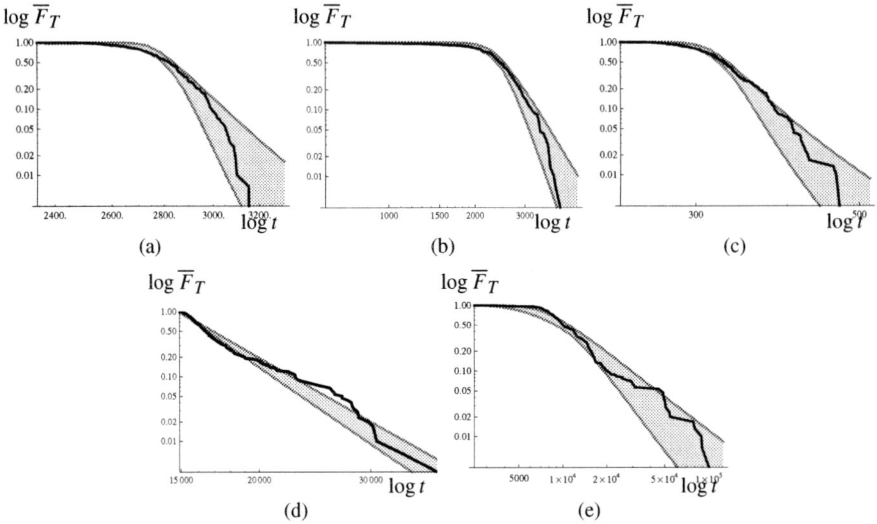

Figure 4. Learning time plots for the benchmarks: (a) → SPFF, (b) → SPRF, (c) → TPFF_1, (d) → TPFF_2, (e) → TPRF. Shadow region: 0.90 confidence region; black curve: empirical distribution. Rendering in LogLog representation.

in [2], in short by discarding the most external curves up to a percentage of 10%. This picture seems to sustain our conjecture. We may conclude that the task of TPFF_1 is more simple than those of perceptrons, as both for the random walks and for the intentional part. The mirroring task introduces further artifacts connected with the tight structure it induces. Intentionality seems to start since the beginning of the training session (TPFF_2 seems ruled by a pure Pareto distribution), but other phenomena add variously oriented humps. These features also witness that, in spite of some abundance of parameters, the shifted Pareto model is not a cover that is adaptable to describe any benchmark.

We finally remark that the use of Pareto distribution for modeling intentional processes is not new. A clever example is represented by the analysis of the intercontact times in opportunistic networks [4,1].

References

[1] B. Apolloni, S. Bassis, and S. Gaito. Fitting opportunistic networks data with a pareto distribution. In Bruno Apolloni, Robert J. Howlett, and Lakhmi C. Jain, editors, *Knowledge-Based Intelligent Information and Engineering Systems 11th International Conference, KES 2007, XVII Italian Workshop on Neural Networks, Vietri sul Mare, Italy, September 12-14, 2007*, Lecture Notes in Artificial Intelligence 4694, pages 812–820, Berlin Heidelberg, 2007. Springer-Verlag.

[2] B. Apolloni, S. Bassis, S. Gaito, and D. Malchiodi. Appreciation of medical treatments by learning underlying functions with good confidence. *Current Pharmaceutical Design*, 13(15):1545–1570, 2007.

[3] B. Apolloni, D. Malchiodi, and S. Gaito. *Algorithmic Inference in Machine Learning*. Advanced Knowledge International, Magill, Adelaide, 2nd edition, 2006.

[4] A. Chaintreau, P. Hui, J. Crowcroft, C Diot, R. Gass, and J. Scott. Impact of human mobility on the design of opportunistic forwarding algorithms. In *Proceedings of the 25th IEEE International Conference on Computer Communications (INFOCOM)*, Barcelona, Spain, 2006.

[5] A. C. Elitzur. Constancy, uniformity and symmetry of living systems: the computational functions of morphological invariance. *BioSystems*, 43:41–53, 1997.

[6] M. A. Fisher. On the mathematical foundations of theoretical statistics. *Philosophical Transactions of the Royal Society of London Ser. A*, 222:309–368, 1925.
[7] A. Hyvärinen, J. Kahunen, and E. Oja. *Independent Component Analysis*. John Wiley&Sons, 2001.
[8] J. Kennedy, R. C. Eberhart, and Y. Shi. *Swarm Intelligence*. Morgan Kaufmann Publishers, San Francisco, 2001.
[9] A. Papoulis. *Probability, Random Variables, and Stochastic Processes*. McGraw-Hill, New York, 2nd edition, 1984.
[10] V. K. Rohatgi. *An Introduction to Probablity Theory and Mathematical Statistics*. Wiley Series in Probability and Mathematical Statistics. John Wiley & Sons, New York, 1976.
[11] E. Schrodinger. *What is life?* Cambridge University Press, Cambridge, 1945.
[12] S. Stigler. Studies in the history of probability and statistics. xxxii: Laplace, fisher and the discovery of the concept of sufficiency. *Biometrika*, 60(3):439–445, 1973.
[13] V. Vapnik. *Statitical Learning Theory*. John Wiley & Sons, New York, 1998.
[14] E. Wigner. Invariance in physical theory. *Proceedings of the American Philosophical Society*, 93(7), 1949.
[15] S. S. Wilks. *Mathematical Statistics*. Wiley Publications in Statistics. John Wiley, New York, 1962.

New Directions in Neural Networks
B. Apolloni et al. (Eds.)
IOS Press, 2009

doi:10.3233/978-1-58603-984-4-148

Random projections preserving the Hamming distance between words

Stefano ARCA [a], Alberto BERTONI [a] and Giuseppe LIPORI [a]

[a] *University of Milan, Department of Computer Science, Via Comelico 39/41, 20135 Milan, Italy*

{arca,bertoni,lipori}@dsi.unimi.it

Abstract. Random projections in the Euclidean space reduce the dimensionality of the data approximately preserving the distances between points. In the hypercube it holds a weaker property: random projections approximately preserve the distances within a certain range.

In this note, we show an analogous result for the metric space $\langle \Sigma^d, d_H \rangle$, where Σ^d is the set of words of length d on alphabet Σ and d_H is the Hamming distance.

Introduction

The term random projection refers to a technique of transforming a set of vectors from a high-dimensional space to a low-dimensional one by means of a random matrix. Since some properties of interest are (approximately) preserved by the application of suitable random matrices, while the data-dimension is reduced, this technique turns out to be a useful tool in many areas, including approximation algorithms for NP-hard optimization problems, information retrieval [1], supervised and non-supervised learning, stability based methods [2].

In this context, the basic result for the Euclidean space is the Johnson-Lindenstrauss Lemma [3]: given N points, with high probability their pairwise distances are preserved, up to a distortion ϵ, by random projections to a subspace of dimension $k = O(\log N/\epsilon^2)$. This geometric idea has been used for finding approximate solutions to problems such as Max cut, Max k-cut [4], Minimum Coloring [5], Nearest Neighbor [6], and Clustering.

Random projections have been studied also for the hypercube $\mathbb{Z}_2^d$ with Hamming distance. In this case a "random projection" is realized by means of a random $d \times k$ matrix R, where each component is independently set to be 1 with probability p and 0 with probability $1 - p$, for a fixed parameter p $(0 < p < 1)$. In this case it is possible to prove that, by choosing a suitable value for p, the distances within a certain range are approximately preserved, while distances outside this range can be only distorted away from the range. This result is considerably weaker than Johnson-Lindenstrauss Lemma; however, it turns out to be useful for the nearest neighbor problem [7] and for the approximate clustering.

In this paper we consider the set Σ^d of words of length d on a finite alphabet Σ, with Hamming distance $d_H(x_1x_2\ldots x_d, y_1y_2\ldots y_d)$, defined as the number of indices i for which $x_i \neq y_i$. Since Σ can be represented as a subset of $\mathbb{Z}_q$, for a prime q sufficiently large, w.l.g. instead of Σ^d we can consider the vector space $\mathbb{Z}_q^d$ on the field $\mathbb{Z}_q$, together with the Hamming distance. Analogously to the case of the hypercube, we can realize random projections by means of random $d \times k$ matrices R, where each component is independently set to be s ($s \neq 0$) with probability $p/(q-1)$ and 0 with probability $1-p$, for a fixed parameter p ($0 < p < 1$). We are able to extend the results on random projections obtained for the hypercube; in particular we prove that, by choosing a suitable value p, the distances within a certain range are approximately preserved, while distances outside this range can be only distorted away from the range.

The remainder of the paper is organized as follows: in Sec. 2 we evaluate the distribution of a particular random projection from $\mathbb{Z}_q^d$ to $\mathbb{Z}_q$; in Sec. 3 we propose a mapping from an alphabet Σ to $\mathbb{Z}_q$ and we extend to words the result holding for points in the hypercube; in Sec 4 we draw some conclusions and we point out possible developments of the work.

1. Introduction

The term random projection refers to a technique of transforming a set of vectors from a high-dimensional space to a low-dimensional one by means of a random matrix. Since some properties of interest are (approximately) preserved by the application of suitable random matrices, while the data-dimension is reduced, this technique turns out to be a useful tool in many areas, including approximation algorithms for NP-hard optimization problems, information retrieval [1], supervised and non-supervised learning, stability based methods [2].

In this context, the basic result for the Euclidean space is the Johnson-Lindenstrauss Lemma [3]: given N points, with high probability their pairwise distances are preserved, up to a distortion ϵ, by random projections to a subspace of dimension $k = O(\log N/\epsilon^2)$. This geometric idea has been used for finding approximate solutions to problems such as Max cut, Max k-cut [4], Minimum Coloring [5], Nearest Neighbor [6], and Clustering.

Random projections have been studied also for the hypercube $\mathbb{Z}_2^d$ with Hamming distance. In this case a "random projection" is realized by means of a random $d \times k$ matrix R, where each component is independently set to be 1 with probability p and 0 with probability $1-p$, for a fixed parameter p ($0 < p < 1$). In this case it is possible to prove that, by choosing a suitable value for p, the distances within a certain range are approximately preserved, while distances outside this range can be only distorted away from the range. This result is considerably weaker than Johnson-Lindenstrauss Lemma; however, it turns out to be useful for the nearest neighbor problem [7] and for the approximate clustering.

In this paper we consider the set Σ^d of words of length d on a finite alphabet Σ, with Hamming distance $d_H(x_1x_2\ldots x_d, y_1y_2\ldots y_d)$, defined as the number of indices i for which $x_i \neq y_i$. Since Σ can be represented as a subset of $\mathbb{Z}_q$, for a prime q sufficiently large, w.l.g. instead of Σ^d we can consider the vector space $\mathbb{Z}_q^d$ on the field $\mathbb{Z}_q$, together with the Hamming distance. Analogously to the case of the hypercube, we can realize random projections by means of random $d \times k$ matrices R, where each component is independently set to be s ($s \neq 0$) with probability $p/(q-1)$ and 0 with probability $1-p$, for a fixed parameter p ($0 < p < 1$). We are able to extend the results on random projections obtained for the hypercube; in particular we prove that, by choosing a suitable value p, the distances within a certain range are approximately preserved, while distances outside this range can be only distorted away from the range.

The remainder of the paper is organized as follows: in Sec. 2 we evaluate the distribution of a particular random projection from $\mathbb{Z}_q^d$ to $\mathbb{Z}_q$; in Sec. 3 we propose a mapping from an alphabet Σ to $\mathbb{Z}_q$ and we extend to words the result holding for points in the hypercube; in Sec 4 we draw some conclusions and we point out possible developments of the work.

2. Random projections in $\mathbb{Z}_q$

In this section we consider a random projection of vectors from $\mathbb{Z}_q^d$ to $\mathbb{Z}_q$, with q prime, and evaluate the probability of the projection to be different from zero as a function of the number of non-zero components of the original vector. In the following, all the operations on elements of $\mathbb{Z}_q$ are in arithmetic modulo q.

Lemma 1. *Let* $\mathbb{Z}_q = \langle \{0, 1, \ldots, q-1\}, +, \cdot \rangle$ *be the usual field of size q, (q prime) and let* r_i $(i = 1, \ldots, d)$, *be i.i.d. random variables with*

$$Prob\{r_i = s\} = \begin{cases} 1-p & \text{if } s = 0 \\ \frac{p}{q-1} & \text{if } s = 1 \ldots q-1 \end{cases}$$

if $\mathbf{x} = (x_1, x_2, \ldots, x_d)$ *is a vector* $\mathbf{x} \in \mathbb{Z}_q^d$, *then*

$$Prob\left\{ \sum_{i=1}^{d} r_i \cdot x_i \neq 0 \right\} = \frac{q-1}{q} \left(1 - \left(1 - \frac{q}{q-1} p \right)^{|\mathbf{x}|_H} \right)$$

where $|\mathbf{x}|_H = |\{i | x_i \neq 0\}|$ *and p is s.t.* $\frac{q}{q-1} \cdot p < 1$.

Proof. Let Y_t be the stochastic process defined as:

$$Y_t = \sum_{k=1}^{t} (r_k \cdot x_k), \quad t \in [1, \ldots, d]$$

that is:

$$Y_t = Y_{t-1} + r_t \cdot x_t$$

Y_t is a finite Markov Chain with state space $S = \{0, 1, .., q-1\} = \mathbb{Z}_q$, the process is not time-homogeneous with transition matrices $M_{ij}(x_t) = Prob\{Y_t = j | Y_{t-1} = i\}$, with $i, j \in S$, depending on x_t and determined as follows:

$$\begin{aligned}
&if\ x_t = 0 \quad M_{ij}(x_t) = I \\
&if\ x_t \neq 0 \quad M_{ij}(x_t) = Prob\left\{r_t = (j-i) \cdot x_t^{-1}\right\} \\
&\qquad\qquad\qquad\quad = \begin{cases} Prob\{r_s = 0\} = 1-p & if\ i = j \\ Prob\{r_s \neq 0\} = p/(q-1) & if\ i \neq j \end{cases} \\
&\qquad\qquad\qquad\quad = \alpha \cdot Q + (1 - \alpha \cdot I)
\end{aligned}$$

where $\alpha = \frac{q}{q-1} \cdot p$ and $Q_{ij} = \frac{1}{q}$.

Given the input vector $\mathbf{x} = (x_1 \dots x_d)$ and the probability vector $\mathbf{a}$ representing the initial state, (that is $a_i = Prob\{Y_0 = s_i\}$), then the probability that the chain is in state s_i after d steps is the ith entry in the vector $\mathbf{b}$ given by:

$$\begin{aligned}
\mathbf{b} &= \mathbf{a} \cdot [M(x_1) \cdot M(x_2) \cdots M(x_d)] \\
&= \mathbf{a} \cdot [\alpha \cdot Q + (1-\alpha) \cdot I]^{|\mathbf{x}|_H} \\
&= \mathbf{a} \cdot \left[\sum_{i=0}^{|\mathbf{x}|_H} \binom{|\mathbf{x}|_H}{i} Q^i \alpha^i (1-\alpha)^{|\mathbf{x}|_H - i} \right] \\
&= \mathbf{a} \cdot \left[(1-\alpha)^{|\mathbf{x}|_H} I + Q \sum_{i=1}^{|\mathbf{x}|_H} \binom{|\mathbf{x}|_H}{i} \alpha^i (1-\alpha)^{|\mathbf{x}|_H - i} \right] \\
&= \mathbf{a} \cdot \left[(1-\alpha)^{|\mathbf{x}|_H} I + Q \left(\sum_{i=0}^{|\mathbf{x}|_H} \binom{|\mathbf{x}|_H}{i} \alpha^i (1-\alpha)^{|\mathbf{x}|_H - i} - (1-\alpha)^{|\mathbf{x}|_H} \right) \right] \\
&= \mathbf{a} \cdot \left[(1-\alpha)^{|\mathbf{x}|_H} I + Q \left(1 - (1-\alpha)^{|\mathbf{x}|_H} \right) \right] \\
&= \mathbf{a} \cdot D
\end{aligned}$$

using the binomial expansion and observing that the matrix Q is idempotent ($Q^i = Q$). Then:

$$Prob\left\{ \sum_{i=1}^{d} r_i \cdot x_i \neq 0 \right\} = Prob\{Y_d \neq 0\} = \sum_{i \neq 1} b_i$$

for the initial state we have $Prob\{Y_0 = 0\} = 1$ and $Prob\{Y_0 \neq 0\} = 0$ that leads to $\mathbf{a} = [1, 0, \dots, 0]$; then the probability searched is the sum of the first row of the matrix D describing the process without its first element:

$$\sum_{i \neq 1} b_i = \sum_{j \neq 1} D(1, j) = \frac{q-1}{q} \left(1 - \left(1 - \frac{q}{q-1} p \right)^{|\mathbf{x}|_H} \right)$$

□ □

3. Random projections of words

In this section we exploit the result of the previous section to prove a theorem on random projections of words, which is a generalization of the well known result on random projections of hypercube vertices.

Let us consider the words in Σ^d, where Σ is an alphabet of n symbols. The Hamming distance of two such words $\mathbf{y}, \mathbf{z}$ is defined as

$$d_H(\mathbf{y}, \mathbf{z}) = |\{i | y_i \neq z_i, 1 \leq i \leq d\}| \tag{1}$$

In order to apply the results of Lemma 1 to words, one can define a mapping from Σ to $\mathbb{Z}_q$, being q the smallest prime s.t. $n \leq q$. If n is not prime, one is guaranteed that q will not exceed $2n - 1$ and all the $q - n$ elements that have no pre-image in Σ will not be used in coding.

If $\mathbf{u}, \mathbf{v} \in \mathbb{Z}_q^d$ are the vectors coding the words $\mathbf{y}, \mathbf{z}$, then it immediately follows that $d_H(\mathbf{y}, \mathbf{z}) = |\mathbf{u} - \mathbf{v}|_H$.

It holds the following:

Theorem 1. *Let $0 \leq \epsilon \leq 1/q$ and $1 \leq l \leq d$. Let each entry of a $d \times k$ matrix R be chosen independently within $\mathbb{Z}_q$ with distribution:*

$$Prob\{r_{ij} = s\} = \begin{cases} 1 - p & \text{if } s = 0 \\ \frac{p}{q-1} & \forall s \neq 0 \end{cases}$$

where $p = \frac{\epsilon^2}{l}(q-1)$. Let $\mathbf{u}, \mathbf{v} \in \mathbb{Z}_q^d$ and $\mathbf{u}', \mathbf{v}' \in \mathbb{Z}_q^k$ be obtained as

$$\mathbf{u}' = R^T \mathbf{u}, \ \ \mathbf{v}' = R^T \mathbf{v}$$

then it exists a constant C such that with probability at least $1 - 2e^{-C\epsilon^4 k}$,

(a) *If* $|\mathbf{u} - \mathbf{v}|_H < \frac{l}{2q}$, *then* $|\mathbf{u}' - \mathbf{v}'|_H < (1+\epsilon)\frac{kpl}{2q}$

(b) *If* $\frac{l}{2q} \leq |\mathbf{u} - \mathbf{v}|_H \leq \frac{l}{q\epsilon}$, *then* $(1-\epsilon)kp \leq \dfrac{|\mathbf{u}' - \mathbf{v}'|_H}{|\mathbf{u} - \mathbf{v}|_H} \leq (1+\epsilon)kp$

(c) *If* $|\mathbf{u} - \mathbf{v}|_H > \frac{l}{q\epsilon}$, *then* $|\mathbf{u}' - \mathbf{v}'|_H > (1-\epsilon)\frac{kpl}{q\epsilon}$

Proof. (Sketch) Note that by substituting $q = 2$ one gets exactly the theorem for vectors in $\mathbb{Z}_2^d$ that has been already proven in [1]. The proof of the generalization result follows the same arguments of the original proof:

First of all, let $\mathbf{r}_j$ be the j-th row of the projection matrix R^T, $j = 1, \ldots, k$, and let E_j be the event that the projection of **x** according to that row is different from zero, i.e. $\mathbf{r}_j \cdot (\mathbf{u} - \mathbf{v}) \neq 0$. Being the entries of R i.i.d., $Prob\{E_j\}$ is the same for all rows and we call it simply $Prob\{E\}$. From Lemma 1, substituting $\mathbf{x} = (\mathbf{u} - \mathbf{v})$, it follows immediately that

$$Prob\{E\} = \frac{q-1}{q}\left(1 - \left(1 - \frac{q}{q-1}p\right)^{|\mathbf{u}-\mathbf{v}|_H}\right)$$

Note that, according to the definition of p, the value $\frac{q}{q-1} \cdot p \leq \frac{1}{ql} < 1$, hence $Prob\{E\}$ is well defined and it is a monotonically increasing function of $|\mathbf{u} - \mathbf{v}|_H$. The demonstration of each case $(a) - (c)$ proceeds from the hypothesis much alike in [1], using the fact that

$$p|\mathbf{u} - \mathbf{v}|_H - p^2|\mathbf{u} - \mathbf{v}|_H^2 \leq Prob\{E\} \leq p|\mathbf{u} - \mathbf{v}|_H$$

and by applying the Chernoff multiplicative bound. □ □

The main difference with respect to the original formulation is the dependence on q of the projection error ϵ, of the probability p, and of the interval length $\left[\frac{l}{2q}, \frac{l}{q\epsilon}\right]$ in which the Hamming distance is approximately preserved. Also the C constant depends on q in a way that the bound on probability gets looser with the increase of the alphabet length.

4. Conclusions and future work

In this note we have presented a preliminary work that generalizes to words the result holding for random projections of hypercube points. The bound on probability derived applying the Chernoff inequality is quite loose as it depends on the fourth power of ϵ. Regarding future works we intend to improve the dependency on ϵ of the bounds in Theorem 1 and to apply the result obtained to algorithms for Approximate Nearest Neighbor and Clustering on textual data.

References

[1] Santosh Vempala, S.: The random projection method. DIMACS. American Mathematical Society

[2] Bertoni, A., Valentini, G.: Model order selection for bio-molecular data clustering. BMC Bioinformatics **8 (Suppl. 3)**

[3] Johnson, W., Lindenstrauss, J.: Extensions of lipshitz mapping into hilbert space. Contemporary Mathematics **26** (1984) 189–206

[4] Frieze, A., Jerrum, M.: Improved approximation algorithms for max k-cut and max bisection. Algorithmica **18** (1997) 61–67

[5] Karger, D., Motwani, R., Sudan, M.: Improved graph coloring via semidefinite programming. JACM **45(2)** (1998) 246–265

[6] Kleinberg, J.: Two algorithms for nearest-neighbor search in high-dimensions. Proc. of STOC (1998) 599–608

[7] Kushilevitz, E., Ostrovsky, R., Rabani, Y.: Efficient search for approximate nearest-neighbor in high-dimensional spaces. SIAM J. comp. **30(2)** (2000) 457–474

New Directions in Neural Networks
B. Apolloni et al. (Eds.)
IOS Press, 2009

doi:10.3233/978-1-58603-984-4-154

Notes on Factor Graphs

Francesco PALMIERI [a,1],
[a] *Dipartimento di Ingegneria dell'Informazione, Seconda Università di Napoli, Italy*

Abstract. Many applications that involve inference and learning in signal processing, communication and artificial intelligence can be cast into a graph framework. Factor graphs are a type of network that can be studied and solved by propagating belief messages with the sum/product algorithm. In this paper we provide explicit matrix formulas for inference and learning in finite alphabet Forney-style factor graphs, with the precise intent of allowing rapid prototyping of arbitrary topologies in standard software like MATLAB.

Keywords. Bayesian Networks, Artificial Intelligence, Propagation of Belief, MATLAB

Introduction

Bayesian inference on graphs, pioneerd by Pearl [1], has become over the last few years a very popular and promising paradigm for approaching many problems in communication, signal processing and artificial intelligence [4]. In fact, when a problem can be formulated in the form of a graph, it is very appealing to study the variables involved as part of an interconnected system whose equilibrium point is the solution. The obvious similarities with the working of the nervous system give this paradigm an extra motivation. The literature on this topic is now quite vast and various authors have tried to provide graphical forms and transformation methods to allow agile design of algorithms for inference and learning. A comprehensive list of references is beyond the scope of these notes and we advice the interested reader to look at some recent excellent reviews such as [4] also for connections to Hidden Markov Models and to turbo and LDPC decoding.

In these notes we report the results of our work of translation, for graphs with finite-dimensional alphabets, of the sum-product algoritm into explicit matrix formulas. The expressions that follow are crafted with the precise intent of allowing rapid programming in standard software like MATLAB. Our approach follows the propagation of belief in directed graphs in Forney-style Factor Graphs (FFG) [3]. Rapid prototyping in simulating our inference networks will help us to understand better the intrinsec functioning of the paradigm and will give us ideas on how to deal with more complicated topologies.

1. The matrix setup

Factor graphs [3][4], are much simpler to study than Bayesian networks because of their direct correspondence to signal flow-graphs used in communication, control and signal

[1]Corresponding Author: Francesco Palmieri, Dipartimento di Ingegneria dell'Informazione, Seconda Università di Napoli, via Roma 29, 81031 Aversa (CE), Italy; E-mail: francesco.palmieri@unina2.it.

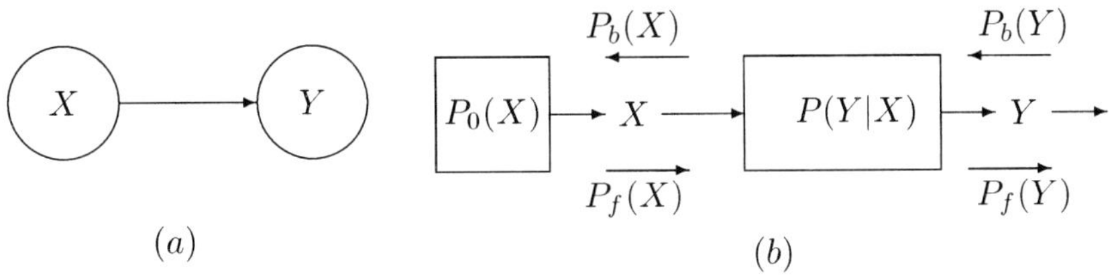

Figure 1. A two-variable directed graph in Bayesian (a) and in factor-graph (b) form

processing. Factor graphs allows a much clearer definition and manipulation of forward and backward messages by assigning each random variable to a branch (rather than to a node as in Bayesian graphs). The various blocks in the system describe the transformations (*factors*).

The simplest example of a directed graph involving two random variable X and Y is depicted in Figure 1 both in Bayesian and in factor-graph form. To introduce our notation, we assume that in our example values of X and Y belong to the two finite alphabets

$$\mathcal{X} = \{x_1, x_2, .., x_{N_X}\}; \quad \mathcal{Y} = \{y_1, y_2, ..., y_{N_Y}\}. \tag{1}$$

The N_X-dimensional column vector $P_0(X)$ contains the apriori probabilities for X, and the $N_X \times N_Y$ matrix $P(Y|X)$ contains all the conditional probabilities in the direction of the arrow

$$P_0(X) = \begin{pmatrix} P_0(x_1) \\ P_0(x_2) \\ . \\ . \\ . \\ P_0(x_{N_X}) \end{pmatrix}; \tag{2}$$

$$P(Y|X) = \begin{pmatrix} P(y_1|x_1) & P(y_2|x_1) & \dots & P(y_{N_Y}|x_1) \\ P(y_1|x_2) & P(y_2|x_2) & \dots & P(y_{N_Y}|x_2) \\ . & . & \dots & . \\ P(y_1|x_{N_X}) & P(y_2|x_{N_X}) & \dots & P(y_{N_Y}|x_{N_X}) \end{pmatrix}. \tag{3}$$

The messages are computed as

$$P_f(X) = P_0(X); \quad P_f(Y) = P(Y|X)^T P_f(X); \quad P_b(X) = \frac{P(Y|X)P_b(Y)}{|P(Y|X)P_b(Y)|}, \tag{4}$$

where $|\xi|$ denotes the sum of the elements of vector ξ. The distribution of X that uses all the available information is given by the *product rule*

$$P(X) = \frac{P_f(X) \odot P_b(X)}{P_f^T(X)P_b(X)} \stackrel{def}{=} P_f(X) \stackrel{N}{\odot} P_b(X), \tag{5}$$

where $\xi \odot \eta$ is the Hadamard product (element-by-element) between ξ and η and $\xi \overset{N}{\odot} \eta$ is its normalized version (sum equal to one). [2]

The model of Figure 1 can be associated to a classical noisy communication channel and can be used in various modalities. For examples, if we want to infer X from an observation of the output $Y = y_j$, we "clamp" Y forcing $P_b(Y) = \delta_j(Y) \overset{def}{=} (0, 0, .., 0, \underbrace{1}_{jth}, 0, .)^T$. It is straighforward to verify that $P(X)$, computed from backpropagation and from the product rule, is the aposteriori distribution of X given $Y = y_j$.

We have a different scenario if no observation is available at the output. In this case $P_b(Y)$ is the uniform distribution $P_b(Y) = \frac{1}{N_Y}(1, 1, .., 1)^T \overset{def}{=} U(Y)$. After backpropagation of $P_b(Y)$ and application of the product rule we get $P(X) = P_0(X)$ and $P(Y) = P(Y|X)^T P_0(X)$.

In the most general case a backward distribution may be available in Y. Such information can be backpropagated across the block to make inferences on X.

To help the reader to build his/her own arbitrary graph, we have reported in Figure 2 a collection of items like "sources," "open branches" and "clamps," with their relative message definitions. For example, a source feeds a branch with apriori information, while an open branch backpropagates no information with its backward message being just a uniform distribution. If X insists on a open branch $P(X) = P_f(X) \overset{N}{\odot} U(X) = P_f(X)$. Furthermore, when we need to constrain a variable X to a specific value (clamp to $X = x_j$) we have to split that branch-variable into two new separated terminal branches (X_r and X_l) with relative backward and forward messages being delta vectors, as shown in Figure 2. Note that in a split branch $P_f(X_l)$ and $P_b(X_r)$ are useless because

$$P(X_l) = P_f(X_l) \overset{N}{\odot} \delta_j(X_l) = \delta_j(X_l); \tag{6}$$

$$P(X_r) = P_b(X_r) \overset{N}{\odot} \delta_j(X_r) = \delta_j(X_r). \tag{7}$$

A word of caution must be given about using the product rule on a generic branch variable when some elements of the two vector-messages are null, because their product may result into a null vector. In such a case we have *incompatible messages*, i.e. clamps somewhere in the system have been set to impossible configurations.

When we build our graphs we have to deal also with multiples outgoing branches. Fig 3 shows a single variable X that branches out into two directions. For each branch, following Forney's suggestion [3], the factor graph is transformed by introducing as many variables as branches, each one of them with its own forward and backward message. The outgoing messages are simply the product of the incoming ones. In the three branch case of Figure 3

$$P_b(X_1) = P_b(X_2) \overset{N}{\odot} P_b(X_3); \quad P_f(X_2) = P_f(X_1) \overset{N}{\odot} P_b(X_3); \tag{8}$$

$$P_f(X_3) = P_f(X_1) \overset{N}{\odot} P_b(X_2). \tag{9}$$

[2] In our formulas we include normalization to make messages valid distributions, although this is not strictly necessary. Some authors avoid normalization leaving the final results valid up to a constant. We prefer maintaining all vectors normalized also for numerical stability.

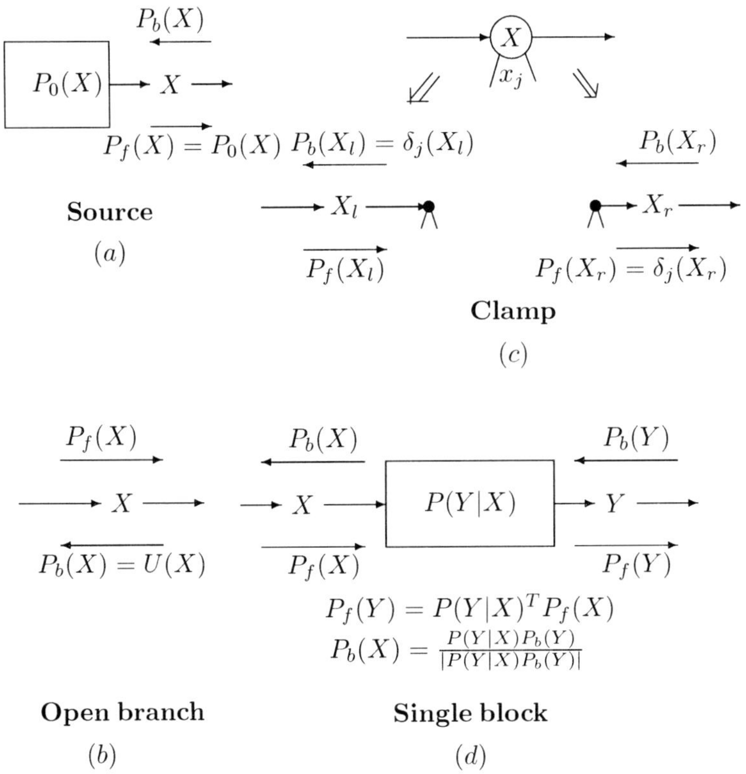

Figure 2. Messages for a source (a) and for an open branch (b); (c) messages for a clamp $X = x_j$ that splits a branch-variable into two terminal branches; (d) messages for a single block.

The rule is immediately generalized to an arbitrary number of outgoing branches.

A more complicated situation arises when more branches converge on the same node. In Figure 4 it is shown the simplest case of two branches that converge to a new variable Z that belongs to the finite alphabet $\mathcal{Z} = \{z_1, ..., z_{N_Z}\}$. The $(N_X N_Y) \times N_Z$ matrix $P(Z|XY)$ represents the function and it must account for all possible pairs XY

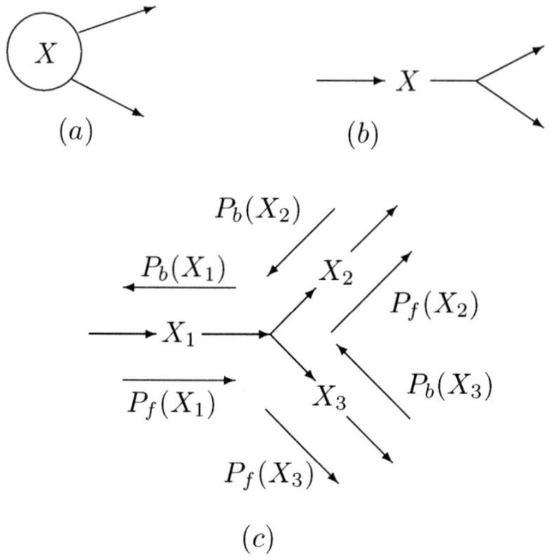

Figure 3. An outgoing multiple branch is transformed into a set of variables with different forward and backward messages: (a) Bayesian graph; (b) Factor-graph; (c) Transformed factor-graph.

$$P(Z|XY) = \begin{pmatrix} P(z_1|x_1, y_1) & \ldots & P(z_{N_Z}|x_1, y_1) \\ . & \ldots & . \\ P(z_1|x_1, y_{N_Y}) & \ldots & P(z_{N_Z}|x_1, y_{N_Y}) \\ P(z_1|x_2, y_1) & \ldots & P(z_{N_Z}|x_2, y_1) \\ . & \ldots & . \\ P(z_1|x_2, y_{N_Y}) & \ldots & P(z_{N_Z}|x_2, y_{N_Y}) \\ . & \ldots & . \\ . & \ldots & . \\ P(z_1|x_{N_X}, y_1) & \ldots & P(z_{N_Z}|x_{N_X}, y_1) \\ . & \ldots & . \\ P(z_1|x_{N_X}, y_{N_Y}) & \ldots & P(z_{N_Z}|x_{N_X}, y_{N_Y}) \end{pmatrix}. \tag{10}$$

If the variables X and Y were considered jointly with $(N_X N_Y)$-dimensional forward and backward vectors

$$\begin{aligned} P_f(XY) &= (P_f(x_1, y_1)...P_f(x_1, y_{N_Y})P_f(x_2, y_1)...P_f(x_2, y_{N_Y})... \\ &\qquad ...P_f(x_{N_X} y_1)...P_f(x_{N_Y} y_{N_Y}))^T, \\ P_b(XY) &= (P_b(x_1, y_1)...P_b(x_1, y_{N_Y})P_b(x_2, y_1)...P_b(x_2, y_{N_Y})... \\ &\qquad ...P_b(x_{N_X} y_1)...P_b(x_{N_Y} y_{N_Y}))^T, \end{aligned} \tag{11}$$

the block is like a single-input/single-output block with

$$P_f(Z) = P(Z|XY)^T P_f(XY); \quad P_b(XY) = \frac{P(Z|XY)P_b(XY)}{|P(Z|XY)^T P_b(XY)|}. \tag{12}$$

Clearly this is incompatible with the graph structure on which information is carried separately on the two branches. Therefore we must make the fundamental assumption that: *variables X and Y are marginally independent*, even though they are conditionally dependent on Z. Equivalently the converging branches must belong to a tree [4] (to verify that a structure is a tree, we cut any branch and verify that it results in two separate trees).

Under the independence assumption, the forward formula is

$$P_f(Z) = P(Z|XY)^T \left(P_f(X) \otimes P_f(Y)\right), \tag{13}$$

where $\otimes$ denotes the Kronecker product.

To derive the backward formulas we have to introduce the *marginalizers*

$$M_1 = \left(\underbrace{\begin{matrix} \overbrace{1\,1 \ldots 1}^{m}\,0\,0 \ldots 0 \,.\,.\ldots.\, 0\,0 \ldots 0 \\ 0\,0 \ldots 0\,1\,1 \ldots 1 \,.\,.\ldots.\, 0\,0 \ldots 0 \\ \ldots\ldots \quad \ldots\ldots \quad \ldots\ldots \quad \ldots\ldots \\ 0\,0 \ldots 0\,0\,0 \ldots 0 \,.\,.\ldots.\, 1\,1 \ldots 1 \end{matrix}}_{n \cdot m} \right) = I_n \otimes \mathbf{1}_m^T, \tag{14}$$

$$M_2 = \left(\underbrace{\begin{matrix} \overbrace{1\,0 \ldots 0}^{m}\,1\,0 \ldots 0 \,.\,.\ldots.\, 1\,0 \ldots 0 \\ 0\,1 \ldots 0\,0\,1 \ldots 0 \,.\,.\ldots.\, 0\,1 \ldots 0 \\ \ldots\ldots \quad \ldots\ldots \quad \ldots\ldots \quad \ldots\ldots \\ 0\,0 \ldots 1\,0\,0 \ldots 1 \,.\,.\ldots.\, 0\,0 \ldots 1 \end{matrix}}_{n \cdot m} \right) = \mathbf{1}_m^T \otimes I_n, \tag{15}$$

where $\mathbf{1}_m \stackrel{def}{=} (\underbrace{1, 1, \ldots, 1}_{m})^T$. The matrix M_1 multiplied by an nm-dimensional vector sums in order m consecutive elements at a time returning an n-dimensional vector. Similarly M_2 multiplied by an nm-dimensional vector sums every m elements returning an m-dimensional vector. These operations applied to a vector representing the joint density of X and Y, return their respective marginal distributions.

Conversely, we can verify that the transposed M_1^T and M_2^T are *replicators*, because applied to an n-dimensional and to an m-dimensional vector respectively, give nm-dimensional vectors with consecutive and interlaced replicae. An immediate consequence is that given two vectors ξ and η,

$$M_1^T \xi \odot M_2^T \eta = \xi \otimes \eta. \tag{16}$$

The backward formulas are derived to be

$$P_b(X) = M_1 \left[(P(Z|XY)P_b(Z)) \overset{N}{\odot} M_2^T P_f(Y) \right]; \tag{17}$$

$$P_b(Y) = M_2 \left[(P(Z|XY)P_b(Z)) \overset{N}{\odot} M_1^T P_f(X) \right]. \tag{18}$$

The formulas are then generalized to N incoming branches as in Figure 5. The incoming variable are mutually independent and they belong to the finite alphabets $\mathcal{X}_1, \mathcal{X}_2, \ldots, \mathcal{X}_N$ of sizes $N_1, N_2, \ldots, N_N$. Forward propagation gives

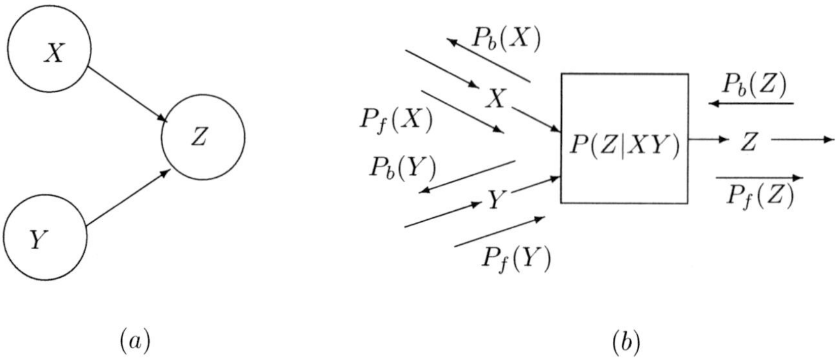

Figure 4. Two incoming branches in a: (a) Bayesian graph form; (b) Factor-graph form.

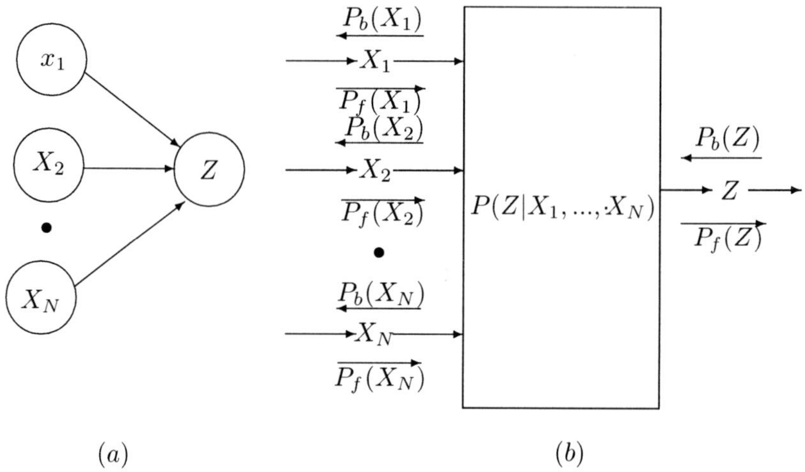

Figure 5. N incoming branches in a: (a) Bayesian graph form; (b) Factor-graph form.

$$P_f(Z) = P(Z|X_1...X_N)^T \left(P_f(X_1) \otimes P_f(X_2) \otimes ... \otimes P_f(X_N)\right), \tag{19}$$

where $P(Z|X_1...X_N)$ is an $(N_1 N_2 \cdots N_N) \times N_Z$ matrix containing the conditional probabilities. The joint variable $X_1 X_2 ... X_N$ belongs to the ordered set $\mathcal{X}_1 \times ... \times \mathcal{X}_N$ and the marginalizers $M_1, M_2, ..., M_N$ for an $(N_1 N_2 \cdot ... \cdot N_N)$-dimensional vector are

$$M_j = \mathbf{1}_{N_1}^T \otimes ... \otimes \mathbf{1}_{N_{j-1}}^T \otimes I_{N_j} \otimes \mathbf{1}_{N_{j+1}}^T \otimes ... \otimes \mathbf{1}_{N_N}^T, \quad j = 1, ..., N. \tag{20}$$

The replicators are just their transposed. The backward equations are

$$P_b(X_j) = M_j \Big[(P(Z|X_1...X_N)P_b(Z)) \overset{N}{\odot} (M_1^T P_f(X_1) \odot ... \\ ... \odot M_{j-1}^T P_f(X_{j-1}) \odot M_{j+1}^T P_f(X_{j+1}) \odot ... \odot M_N^T P_f(X_N)) \Big] \\ j = 1, ..., N. \tag{21}$$

2. Running the inference

The formulas provided above should be sufficient for the reader to draw his/her own graph and quickly program a simulation. The first step is to fill up the function matrices and the source vectors. Note that the function nodes can also be deterministic, i.e. they can be just fixed correspondence maps. The second step is to inizialize all messages. It is good practice to initialize them all to uniform distributions to avoid divisions by zero. The third step is updating. Even though special update scheduling around any system can be deviced, it is adviced to update the messages all together before using the new values.

Particular attention must be paid to clamping. In fact when we simulate observations we must be careful to clamp to *compatible values*. In fact, if we mistakenly impose incompatible deterministic values, all-zero messages and distributions may arise with meaningless overflows.

It is well known that convergence is guaranteed for all graphs with no cycles in a number of steps equal to the diameter of the graph [7]. In graphs with cycles, the same algorithm will run, but the results may only be approximate inferences. Also oscillations may emerge [7]. Relevant examples of successful use of the algorithm in graphs with cycles are in decoding turbo and LDPC codes [4].

3. Learning

Factor graphs are most appealing in the applications where the function blocks are only partially known, or not available at all. In such cases the system is typically presented with examples and the system block matrices must be learnt with the EM-algorithm. The explicit steps to follow are:

(1) Initialize all unknown function matrices to uniform distributions. For a generic block

$$P(Z|X_1X_2...X_N)[0] = \mathbf{1}_{N_1N_2..N_N} \otimes \frac{1}{N_Z}\mathbf{1}_{N_Z}^T, \tag{22}$$

and for a generic source

$$P_0(X)[0] = \frac{1}{N_X}\mathbf{1}_{N_X}. \tag{23}$$

(2) Given the nth example, clamp all the known branches to the example values. Set all the messages for the other branches to uniform distributions;

(3) (E-step) Run the inference algorithm to convergence and compute from the product algorithm the distribution on each branch;

(4) (M-step) Update the function matrices according to the running mean, i.e. for a generic block

$$\begin{aligned} P(Z|X_1X_2...X_N)[n] = & \tfrac{n}{n+1} P(Z|X_1X_2...X_N)[n-1] \\ & + \tfrac{1}{n+1} \left(P(X_1)[n] \otimes ... \otimes P(X_N)[n]\right) P(Z)[n]^T, \end{aligned} \tag{24}$$

and for a generic (unknown) source

$$P_0(X)[n] = \frac{n}{n+1} P_0(X)[n-1] + \frac{1}{n+1} P(X)[n]. \tag{25}$$

(5) Back to step (2) until all examples have been used.

References

[1] J. Pearl, *Probabilistic Reasoning in Intelligent Systems*, 2nd ed. San Francisco: Morgan Kaufmann, 1988.

[2] Kschischang F.R., B.J. Frey, H.A. Loeliger, "Factor Graphs and the Sum-Product Algorithm," *IEEE Trans. on Information Theory*, Vol. 47, N. 2, pp. 498-519, February 2001.

[3] G. D. Forney, Jr., "Codes on graphs: normal realizations, " *IEEE Trans. Information Theory*, vol. 47, no. 2, pp. 520-548, 2001.

[4] H. A. Loeliger, "An Introduction to Factor Graphs." *IEEE Signal Processing Magazine*, pp. 28-41, Jan 2004.

[5] M. I. Jordan and T.J. Sejnowski, eds., *Graphical Models: Foundations of Neural Computation*, MIT Press, 2001.

[6] Special issue on "The turbo principle: from theory to practice II" of *IEEE J. Select. Areas Comm.*, vol. 19, Sept. 2001.

[7] J. S. Yedidia, W. T. Freeman, and Y. Weiss, "Generalized Belief Propagation." *Advances in Neural Information Processing Systems (NIPS)*, vol. 13, pp. 689-695, December 2000.

Chapter 3

Economy and Complexity Workshop

New Directions in Neural Networks
B. Apolloni et al. (Eds.)
IOS Press, 2009

doi:10.3233/978-1-58603-984-4-165

Safety loading in the annuity pension fund dynamics

Marilena SIBILLO [a,1], Mariarosaria COPPOLA [b], Valeria D'AMATO [b] and Emilia DI LORENZO [b]

[a] *Università di Salerno, Italy*

[b] *Università di Napoli Federico II, Italy, Università di Salerno, Italy and Università di Napoli Federico II, Italy*

Abstract. The portfolio consistency fund studied in the paper is referred to a pension scheme of beneficiaries entering in the retirement state at the same time. It arises from the payment stream consisting in cash flows due at the beginning of each year in case of life of the pensioner: in the deferment period, in the form of premiums entering in the fund, and during the retirement period, in the form of instalments getting out of it. The fund dynamic as function of the time of valuation evolves increasing thanks to the interest maturing on the accumulated fund and decreasing because of the benefits paid to the survivals. Both the mortality trend, determining the number of payments at each time, and the interest maturing on the fund, are considered deterministically unknown at the moment of the contract issue. Stochastic assumptions about the behaviour of the interest rate process and the description of the mortality trend betterment, most likely to be expected in very long periods and in civilized world, provide a dynamic description of the pension scheme and in particular of the pension fund. In the paper we want to deepen the aspect of the financial and demographic basis chosen for premium calculation with respect to the impact on the portfolio fund consistency and on the risk arising from the randomness in the choice of the survival model used for the valuations. To this aim, we will assume for the fund description different projection levels for the survival probabilities and the Vasicek hypotheses for the interest rates maturing on the fund itself; moreover, we will determine the premium amounts introducing different scenarios in a safety loading perspective. As evident, in the premium quantification lower interest rate jointly with higher survival probabilities constitute a form of implied loading. The numerical application presented in the paper shows how the change in the premium calculation conditions affects the portfolio fund consistency in the different scenarios and investigates on the impact they have on the Demographic Model Risk Measure. Useful information for managing aim can be derived.

Keywords. Life insurance, portfolio net value, survival laws, premium calculation

1. The pension annuity fund: safety loadings and risk mapping

The paper regards a pension annuity scheme in its classical form consisting in a portfolio of homogeneous contracts, each being a flow of constant premiums paid by the insureds

[1]Corresponding Author: Marilena Sibillo, Dipartimento di Scienze Economiche e Statistiche, Università di Salerno,via Ponte Don Melillo, Salerno, Italy; E-mail: msibillo@unisa.it

at the beginning of each year during the *deferment period*, started at the contract issue time and ending at the retirement date, and in a flow of constant instalments, that we will suppose anticipated, paid by the insurer to the survivals each year of the time interval beginning from the retirement date on, we will call *annuitization period.*
Pension annuities, due to the saving purposes they follow up, are hardly influenced by both the betterment in the future mortality trend and the random evolution of the financial incomes earned by the portfolio fund period by period. The insurer (or the pension plan) and the insured (or pensioner) interact each other on the basis of the relationship settled at the contract issue time, establishing in particular the constant amount the insured has to pay at the beginning of each year of the accumulation period. A "right" description of the financial and demographic risk drivers governing the future business evolution and a "right" quantification of the insured's engagements are the two pillars on which the insurer can control the business risk arising from the two main risk sources, financial and demographic. In particular, from the demographic point of view supposing well counter-balanced the accidental risk deriving from the random deviations of deaths with respect to their expected value by means of pooling strategies [2], [3], we will strictly refer to the systematic deviations due to the survival betterment.
As well known in the actuarial literature and practice, the premium determined on the basis of the simple equivalence principle (for which the expected loss is zero) inevitably leads to the lack of profit and to a highly probable portfolio loss. The reasonable business management needs the quantification of the implied loading called *safety loading* to sum to the equivalence premium in order to get a convenient cash flow as revenues. In practice the safety loaded premium is given by the equivalence premium determined using technical basis favourable to the insurer [9](pp.118-119). The final amount actually paid by the insured will be the equivalent premium with the safety loading to which successively will be added the expense loadings and taxes.
In the life insurance products and in particular in the specific case of a deferred life annuity, the safety loading affects the interest rates guaranteed to the insured (the lower it is, the higher the premium) and the survival probabilities of paying the instalments (the higher they are, the higher the premium).
In the paper the attention is focussed on the relation between the hypotheses on premium calculation and those ones on the portfolio evolution. The topic is studied in the after-effects it presents on the portfolio fund consistency and on the measure of the risk connected to the mortality assumption chosen for the fund evaluation, the *Demographic Model Risk Measure*, calculated by an opportune risk index.
The layout of the paper is the following. In section 2 we present a synthesis of the main risks affecting a life annuity portfolio, while section 3 is dedicated to the formulas for calculating the consistency of the portfolio fund at a certain time of valuation. In section 4 the Demographic Model Risk Measure is formulated and in section 5 the relationship between safety loadings and fund dynamic is briefly presented. In section 6 the application to specific scenarios is presented and finally in section 7 some conclusions and final remarks are reported.

2. Main risks on the pension annuity portfolio. A brief overview

As a wide literature explains, the two main risk sources influencing a life insurance business have the financial and the demographic nature. For what concerns the portfolio fund evolution in time, the financial risk originates in the randomness of the markets in which the insurer or the pension plan invests. The interest rate process describing the interest maturing on the portfolio fund under consideration, can be described by means of a stochastic model expressing the instantaneous global rate of return on assets in the shape of a short rate, synthetizing the global return on investments got by the insurer and able to provide negative values, coherently with the behaviour of a short rate reflecting the global investment strategy connected to the portfolio.
The demographic risk in the portfolio fund amount is due to the uncertainty in the number of survivors at each defined contract term, i.e. in the number of premiums going in during the accumulation period and out during the retirement interval. This randomness is at the same time due to the accidental deviations of the number of survivors from the expected value at each term (insurance risk) and to the systematic deviations caused by the betterment in mortality, this last risk component known as longevity risk.
Financial risk and systematic demographic risk are insensitive to any pooling strategies, acting in the same sense on each contract in portfolio. Only the accidental demographic risk can be markedly reduced enlarging the number of contracts in homogeneous portfolio [2] . In what follows we will consider the portfolio of homogeneous policies large enough to allow the accidental demographic risk to be negligible in the global portfolio risk mapping. Consequently the longevity risk constitutes the only demographic risk component influencing the portfolio valuations. Managing strategies aiming to control this risk driver are mainly based on projected mortality tables, that is survival tables taking into account the longevity phenomenon, constituting at the moment the most usual and diffused actuarial technique for avoiding underestimation of future costs due to a number of survivals systematically higher than the expected one. The insurer has to choose one of the survival tables taking into account the betterment in the mortality trend and this circumstance gives origin to another risk driver, consisting in the risk connected to the choice of the survival table. This risk component has the nature of a model risk and can be measured by an opportune risk index.
Let us now have a look to the premium calculation assumptions. The two risk drivers financial and demographic are again crucial. As above said, the *safety loading* refers to both the risk drivers and comes true by means of the use of technical basis favourable to the insurer. In our specific case, the safety loading affects the interest rates guaranteed to the insured, in the sense that the lower it is the higher the premium, and the probabilities of paying the instalments, in the sense that the higher they are, the higher the premium. The premiums paid by the survivors during the deferment period will interact with the stochastic description of the portfolio fund dynamic, and this interplay will determine the fund consistency and the demographic risk behaviour in time.

3. The portfolio fund consistency in a pension annuity assessment: the model

A pension annuity on an individual aged x at issue time consists in a sequence of constant premiums P, paid at the beginning of each contract term in case of the beneficiary's life

up to the retirement date n (*deferment or accumulation period*)and in a sequence of level benefits R starting at the beginning of the retirement period (*annuitization period*) and paid to the insured at each contract term if living. We assume the benefits paid at the beginning of each year. The premiums are deposited in a fund earning interest term by term (cf.[8]).
We consider a portfolio of N_0 persons having the same age x, going in the pension plan above described and reaching the retirement state at the same time n, that is at the age $x+n$.
During the premium payment phase, the portfolio gets richer thanks to the payment of P made at the beginning of each period, say k ($k = 1, 2, ..., n$), by the N_k survivals at that time. These deposits earn a random financial interest rate i_k^* in the time period $(k-1, k)$. From time n on, the survivals receive the constant benefit R at the beginning of each contract term, until the contractor is alive.
Indicating by Z_k the portfolio fund consistency at time k, [5], we can write:

$$Z_k = Z_{k-1}(1+i_k^*) + N^k P \ \ if \ \ k = 1, ..., n-1 \text{ deferement period}$$

and (1)

$$Z_k = Z_{k-1}(1+i_k^*) - N^k R \ \ if \ \ k = n, ..., \omega - x \text{ annuitization period}$$

From formulas 1 it is clear how the premium amount is entailed in the evolution of the fund and interplays with the stochastic assumptions describing the future evolution of the fund itself.
Indicating by $_{n}/\ddot{a}_x$ the present value of an anticipated unitary life annuity on x deferred of n years and by $\ddot{a}_{x,n}$ the present value of an anticipated unitary and immediate life annuity on x with duration n, the premium is calculated on the basis of the following formula:

$$P = \frac{_{n}/\ddot{a}_x}{\ddot{a}_{x,n}} \qquad (2)$$

In formula 2 both the interest rate and the survival assumptions, that is the technical basis loadable for safety purposes, are involved.
Formulas 1 in the annuitization phase can be written in the following more explicit form, with ω the ultimate life time:

$$Z_{n+m} = [\textstyle\sum_{i=0}^{n-2} N^i P \prod_{j=i+1}^{n-1}(1+i_j^*) + N^{n-1}P]\{\prod_{l=n}^{n+m}(1+i_l^*)+$$

$$-[\textstyle\sum_{r=n}^{n+m-1} N^r R \prod_{q=r+1}^{n+m}(1+i_q^*) + N^{n+m}R]\} \ \ m = 1, ..., \omega-(x+n) \qquad (3)$$

and

$$Z_n = Z_{n-1}(1+i_n^*) - N^n R$$

4. The Demographic Model Risk Measure

The systematic demographic risk source lies in the choice of the survival law suitable to represent the evolution of the survival phenomenon, in particular for the age class

represented in the specific portfolio. In this way the survival table will be consider as a random variable T, whose variability is due to the existence of several models able to represent the longevity phenomenon in the survival probabilities. Which demographic model could, better than others, describe the effective evolution of the survival trend in the future is the critical question. A model risk arises, concerning exactly the choice of the survival table. Among the demographic models proposed in literature for describing the number of survivors at the payment terms, the actuary has to choose a good model, able to capture the decreasing trend of the survival phenomenon as an age function but contextually its increasing trend as function of the reference time.
The random variables *"curtate future lifetime of the i^{th}contractor"* $(i = 1, ..., N^0)$ represent the number of future years completely lived by the ith contractor belonging to the pension plan before his death [1]: as usually made in literature, we suppose those variables independent and identically distributed and independent on the financial process investing the portfolio fund.
The demographic model risk [4] will be measured by the following index:

$$DMRM = Var_T[E[Z_k]] \tag{4}$$

quantifying the variability of the fund consistency Z_k due to the randomness in the projection level of the survival law, averaging out the effects of the financial risk source (i.e. interest rate process); by conditioning the variance on T, we mean to calculate the fund variability due to the randomness in the choice of the survival function used to determine the survival probabilities. The index in (4) is a measure of the demographic model risk impact on the portfolio value in k. For further details on the risk decomposition for a portfolio of life annuity, see for example [2] and [3].

5. Safety loading and the portfolio fund

The valuation system within which we work concerns the fund description during the annuitization phase and is developed at the issue time, when the contractual assumptions are settled; in our perspective this means when the financial and demographic hypotheses are fixed both for the premium calculation and for the fund time evolution description. From the demographic point of view, it is obvious that a higher degree of projection in the survival law used for premiums produces higher amounts in the fund during the accumulation phase: in a safety loading perspective, the pension planning has to settle a projection level for the premium higher than the projection level assumed in the fund description. Similar considerations can be done from the financial point of view: in the premium quantification the guaranteed interest rates used for premiums has to be fixed lower than the fund earning capacity.
In what follows we inspect the impact that different relationships between the premium hypotheses in a safety loading perspective and those ones made on the fund achieve in the fund evolution description and in the dynamics of the demographic model risk index introduced in §4. This aim will be performed by means of numerical evidences got in different scenario assumptions.

6. Scenario testing

6.1. Basic assumptions

Portfolio description

We consider an annuity pension scheme referred to a cohort of $N^0 = 1000$ individuals aged $x = 45$ at time $t = 0$, the contract issue time, and entering in the retirement state at the age of 65, that is 20 years later. For each of them two flows in and out of the portfolio are expected: a sequence of constant premiums P, payable at the beginning of each year up to $t = 20$ in case of the beneficiary's life (*accumulation phase*) and a sequence of fixed constant benefits $R = 100$, payable at the beginning of each year after $t = 20$ (*annuitization phase*), still in case of the beneficiary's life.

Fund consistency: financial assumptions

For describing the fund capitalization stochastic process year by year we adopt the Vasicek model [11]. The solution of the following Stochastic Differential Equation (SDE) is the short interest rate r_t earned by the fund in the form of the instantaneous global rate of return on the assets linked to the portfolio under consideration:

$$dr_t = \alpha(\gamma - r_t)dt + \sigma dW_t \tag{5}$$

In the SDE reported in formula 5 $\{W_t\}$ is a standard Wiener process and α, γ, and σ are positive constants. As known, the SDE solution can provide negative values, coherently with the behaviour of a short rate reflecting the global investment strategy connected to the portfolio, on which we will not make any specific assumption. For this numerical exemplification, as in [8] we assign the following values to the model parameters:$r_0 = 0.05$, $\alpha = 0.1$, $\gamma = 0.04$, $\sigma = 0.01$. The fund value at a certain date $t > n$ feels the increasing effects of the interest earnings from one year to the next one and the decreasing effects of the benefit payments at that time (formulas 3).

Fund consistency: demographic assumptions

We consider three different mortality tables with different degree of projection; they are, listed at increasing projection level:

- the Heligman Pollard law modelled at a *low* projection level(H-P low)
- the Heligman Pollard law modelled at a *medium* projection level (H-P medium)
- the Heligman Pollard law modelled at a *high* projection level (H-P high)

In particular, considering the specific age range in which a pension plan takes place, if $p_x = 1 - qx$ and q_x are respectively the annual survival and mortality rate (that is the probability of an individual aged x respectively to be alive at the age $x+1$ or to die before $x+1$), with the Heligman Pollard law we will model the mortality by the following ratio:

$$\frac{q_x}{p_x} = GH^x \tag{6}$$

Precisely, in formula 6 the third term of Heligman - Pollard law is reported, describing the old - age pattern of mortality [6] and called "odds" by the authors. G expresses the level of senescent mortality and H the rate of increase of senescent mortality itself. The following values assigned to the two parameters (estimated as in [8]) allow us to build three mortality tables at three different degree of projection:

Table 1. Parameters of the Heligman Pollard law

	low	medium	high
G	0.000042	0.000002	0.0000001
H	1.09803	1.13451	1.17215

Premium calculation: hypotheses

In the following numerical applications the premium amount will be calculated in mortality assumptions specified case by case among the preceding three hypotheses; in the first two scenarios the projection level assumed for the premium is higher than that one supposed for the fund evolution (for safety loading purposes) while in the third case no differences are settled (lack of safety loading). The financial component will be considered constant and fixed at various level of the interest rate, from 1% to high values as 4%, the long term mean supposed in the Vasicek model and 5%, the initial rate checked at time 0.

6.2. *Scenario Testing*

Scenario A (lowest demographic assumptions)

Premium calculation assumptions: H-P medium, fixed interest rates: 1%, 1.5%, 2%, 2.5%, 3%, 3.5%, 4%, 4.5%, 5%.

Fund dynamic assumptions: H-P low, Vasicek term structure

Figure 1.

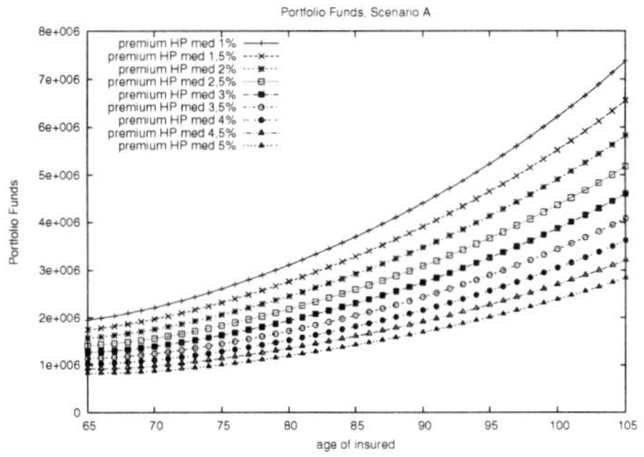

Figure 1 represents the portfolio fund as function of the valuation time in a scenario with the lowest demographic hypotheses for the premium calculation in a safety loading assessment: it shows the increasing trend of the portfolio fund when the premium interest rate decreases. In the scenario A hypotheses no demographic model risk arises: the low projection (H-P medium) assumed for premium means the fund trend describable in the safety loading viewpoint by the H-P low, the only distribution with a lower projection level.

Scenario B (highest premium demographic assumption)

Premium calculation assumptions: H-P high, fixed interest rates: 1%, 4%, 5%.

Fund dynamic assumptions: H-P low, H-P medium, Vasicek term structure.
In these assumptions it can be seen that the fund trend is always higher when the projection level assigned to its evolution is lower. In particular, in the case of low premium interest rates (from 1% to 2%) the trend increases in any of the two demographic assumptions for the fund (H-P low and H-P medium). For higher premium interest rates, the assumption of higher number of survivals (H-P medium) in the fund description, charges more and more in terms of fund consistency. In this case the trend remains almost constant or slightly decreases up to 3.5% and tends to zero when the premium interest rate coincides with the Vasicek long term mean (figure 2b). For higher premium interest rates the decreasing trend leads to negative values of the fund. The valuations considered in

Figure 2.

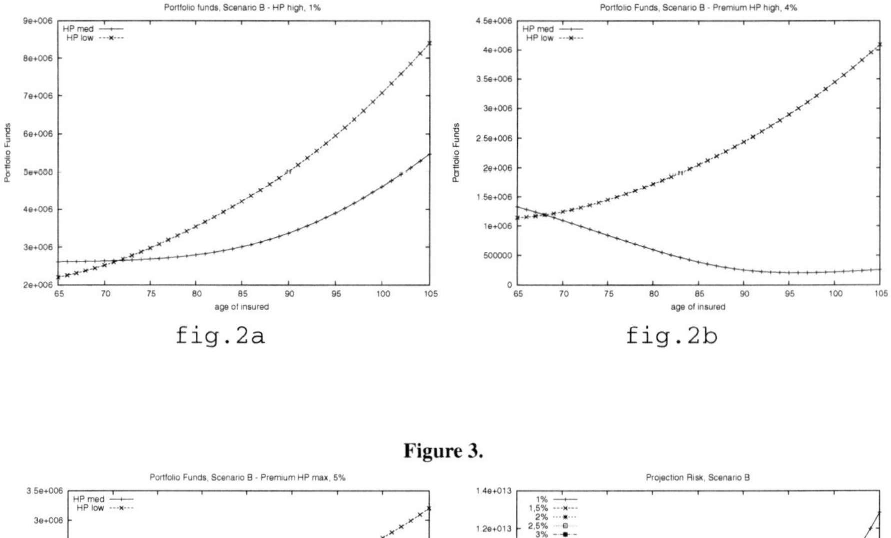

fig.2a fig.2b

Figure 3.

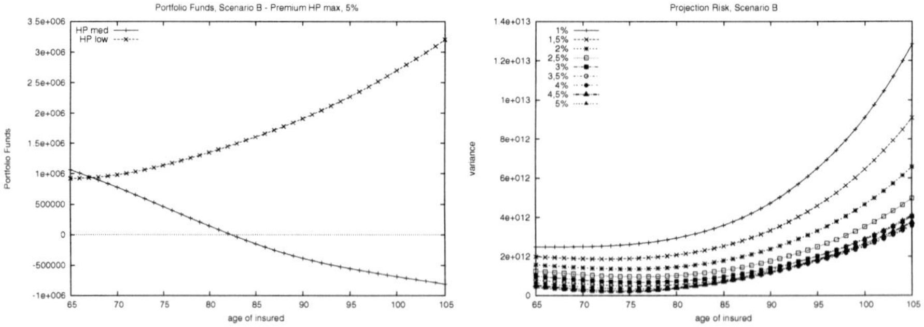

fig.3a fig.3b

scenario B are affected by the randomness in the choice of the survival table in the fund description. The uncertainty consists exactly in the choice of H-P medium or H-P high. In order to provide an example of application, we assume the probabilities of 0.4 and 0.6 to choose respectively H-P low or H-P medium. In the following figure 3b we report the trend of the Demographic Model Risk Measure in the proposed scheme. Figure 3b shows the increasing behaviour of the risk index when the premium interest rates decreases. For higher values of the premium interest rates the risk remains almost null for about 15 years of the annuitization period.

Figure 4.

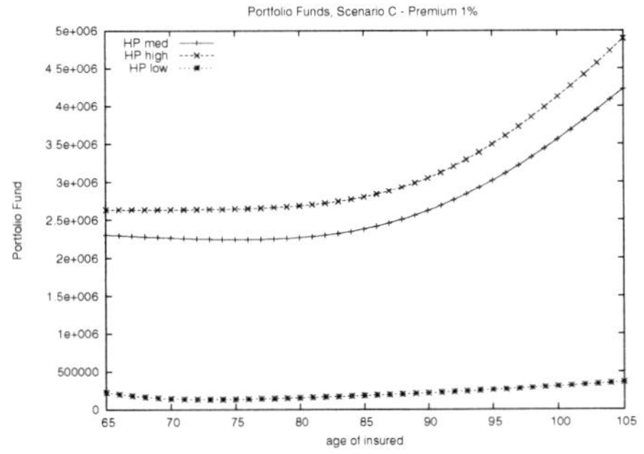

fig.4a

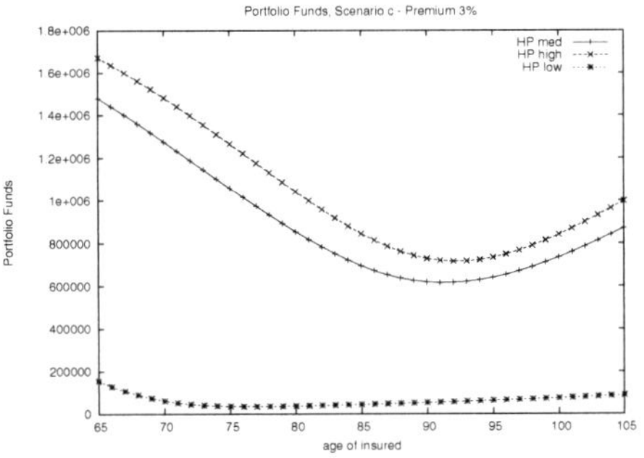

fig.4b

Scenario C (homogeneous premium and fund demographic assumptions)
Premium calculation assumptions: H-P low, H-P medium, H-P high, fixed interest rates: 1%, 4%, 5%.
Fund dynamic assumptions: H-P: low, H-P medium, H-P high, Vasicek term structure.
This case is devoted to the preceding inspection when the same demographic assumptions are considered for both premium calculations and fund description, in a scenario with no demographic safety loading. From the annuitization period beginning the paths are different in the three demographic assumptions and different financial basis.
The figures show the suffering of the fund trend in the case of low demographic hypotheses. In the other two cases, the fund trend strictly increases for low premium interest rates (from 1% to 1.5%); for premium interest rates from 2% to 3.5% the fund trend initially decreases beginning again to increase after about 25 years. For higher premium interest rates the trend is resolutely strictly decreasing becoming negative. The passage to negative values happens earlier when the premium interest rate increases; in particular after about 16 years if the premium interest rate is 5%.

Figure 5.

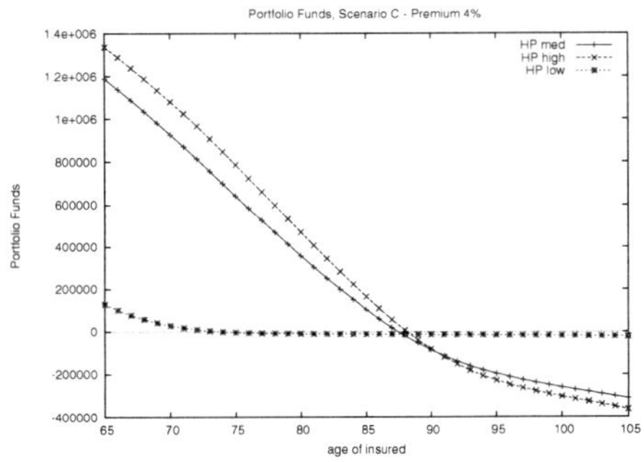

fig.5a

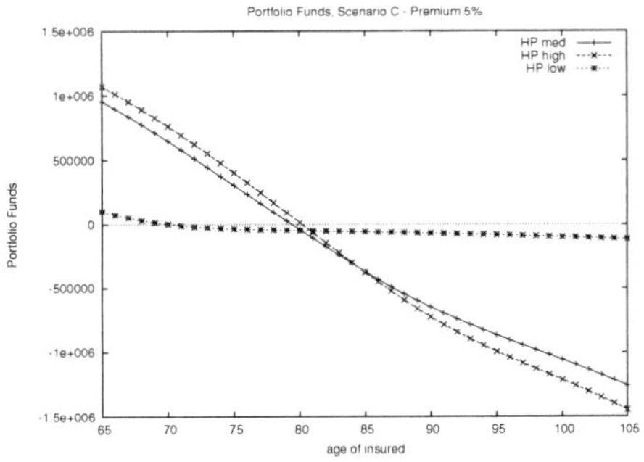

fig.5b

In scenario C hypotheses we can calculate the Demographic Model Risk Measure assuming the following three different probabilities to choose the three different mortality tables above introduced: 0.2, 0.5 and 0.3 respectively to the choice of H-P low, H-P medium and H-P high tables. High premium interest rates cause a meaningless risk.

Figure 6.

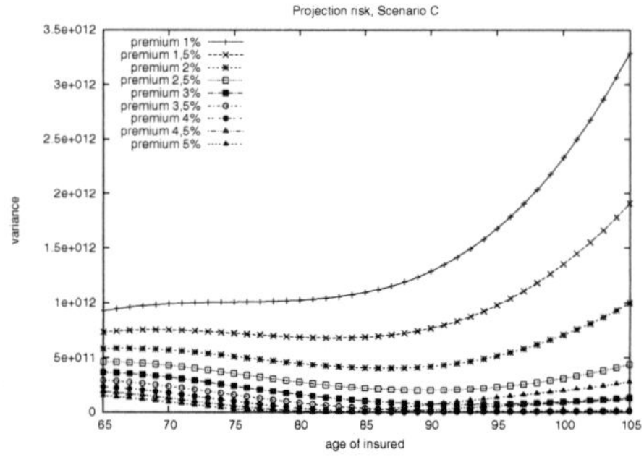

The increasing behaviour with consequently high values for the risk is evident for lower premium interest rates.

7. Final remarks and conclusion

In the paper the interaction between the financial and demographic assumptions made on premium calculation with safety loading purposes and fund consistency behaviour has been inspected in the case of a pension annuity portfolio. The analysis is developed at the issue time, when the level premiums are determined and concerns the fund evolution during the annuitization period. The fund financial component has been modelled by a short term interest rate structure evinced by the Vasicek stochastic differential equation. The resulting interest rates represent the global rate on return on the assets linked to the fund. The premium interest rates have been chosen constant and fixed at different levels, from very low values to the long term mean of the Vasicek process and the initial rate of the process itself. The demographic description has taken into account the longevity phenomenon and has been managed with three different survival laws characterized by different projection degrees.
The analysis remarks the sensibility of the fund consistency to the premium interest rates, increasing when they decrease (financial safety loading), and to the premium projection degree. The fund reaches better performances when the projection degree chosen for premium and fund description are not adjacent.
By the side of the demographic risk index, without demographic safety loading purposes and assuming only the financial safety loading (scenario C) it results meaningful only in the case of premium interest rate very low, that is correspondingly with higher fund values. In this specific case of scenario C hypotheses, the risk index shows the lower values if compared to scenario B. This confirms a profile of lower risk in the hypotheses of homogeneity in the basis chosen for premium and fund.

References

[1] Bowers, N.L.jr, Gerber, H. U., Hickman, J. C., Jones, D. A., Nesbitt, C. J., *Actuarial Mathematics.* Published by The Society of Actuaries **54**, 1997

[2] Coppola, M., Di Lorenzo, E., Sibillo, M., *Risk Sources in a Life Annuity Portfolio: Decomposition and Measurement Tools.* Journal of Actuarial Practice. **8**, Nos. 1 and 2, Absalom Press, 2000, 43–61

[3] Coppola, M., Di Lorenzo, E., Sibillo, M., *Further Remarks on Risk Sources Measuring: the case of a Life Annuity Portfolio.* Journal of Actuarial Practice. **10**, Nos. 1 and 2 Absalom Press, 2002

[4] Coppola, M., D'Amato, V., Di Lorenzo, E., Sibillo, M., *Risk Measurement and Fair Valuation Assessment in the Life Insurance Field.* New Series Book by Springer, Economics: from Tradition to Complexity (to appear). Faggini M., Lux T. Editors, 2007

[5] Coppola, M., D'Amato, V., Di Lorenzo, E., Sibillo, M., *Life Office Management Perspective by Actuarial Risk Indexes.* International Scientific Journal "Investment Management and Financial Innovations" ,**2**, Publishing Company "Business Perspective", 2008

[6] Heligman, L., Pollard, J. H., *The Age Pattern of Mortality.* Journal of the Institute of Actuaries. **107**, 1980, pp.49–80

[7] Lee, R., Carter, L., *Modelling and Forecasting US Mortality.* Journal of the Statistical Association. **87, No.419**, 1992

[8] Olivieri, A., Pitacco, E., *Solvency requirements for pension annuities,* Journal of Pension Economics and Finance. **2**, 2003 pp.127-157

[9] Pitacco E., *Elementi di Matematica delle Assicurazioni*,Ed Lint, Trieste, 2000

[10] Pitacco E., *Survivals Models in Dynamic context: a survey.* Insurace: Mathematics & Economics, **35 no2**,pp. 279-298, 2004

[11] Vasicek, O.: *An Equilibrium Characterization of the Term Structure*, Journal of Financial Economics **5 n02**(1977) pp.177-88

New Directions in Neural Networks
B. Apolloni et al. (Eds.)
IOS Press, 2009

doi:10.3233/978-1-58603-984-4-176

Early Warning Systems: an approach via Self Organizing Maps with applications to emergent markets

Marina RESTA [a,1],
[a] *University of Genova, Italy.*

Abstract. Over the past two decades the globalization of market economies have led to a large number of financial crises in emerging markets. The case of Paraguay in earlier '90 of the past century or, more recently, the crises in Turkey, Argentina, and Far East Asian markets have taught the important lesson that such phenomena, originally arising at local basis, can spread contagiously to other markets as well. At the same time, this made clear the importance of Early Warning System (EWS) models to identify economic and financial vulnerabilities among emerging markets, and, ultimately, to anticipate such events. With this in mind, we have introduced an EWS model based on the powerful clustering capabilities of Kohonen's Self Organizing Maps. Using macroeconomic data of several emerging countries, our analysis has been twofold. We have originally provided a static snapshot of countries in our dataset, according to the way their macroeconomic data cluster in the map. In this way, we were able to capture the (eventual) reciprocities and similarities from various emerging markets. As second step, we have dynamically monitored their evolution path in the map over the time. As main results, we were able to develop a crisis indicator to measure the vulnerability of countries, and we have also provided a proper framework to deduce probabilities of future crises.

Keywords. Early Warning Systems, Self Organizing Maps, Emergent markets

1. Introduction

Over the past two decades a large number of emerging market economies was interested by financial crises whose economic, social and political consequences have been often devastating, especially because instead of remaining bounded to the country where originated, they widely spread to neighbour economies. In order to provide a brief review, moving towards a chronological order, we can start with the crisis of the European Monetary System (EMS) in 1992/1993. In 1994 Latin America knew the so called tequila effect, when the crisis hitting the Mexican economy spred to the neighbouring countries. In the middle of 1997, it was then the turn of many Asian economies (Thailand, Malaysia, Indonesia, the Philippines, Hong Kong, Singapore, Taiwan, and South Korea) that were interested by imbalances originated by the devaluation of the Thai baht. In 1998 the Rus-

[1]Marina Resta, DI.E.M. sezione di Matematica Finanziaria, via Vivaldi 5, 16126 Genova, Italy; E-mail: mresta@unige.it.

sian crisis was really spectacular too: it was the first time that a literature appeared about the bankruptcy of a state. At the dawn of the 2000's financial instability interested Brazil (1999), Argentina (2001, 2003), Turkey (2001), and South Korea (2005).

Early Warning Systems (EWS) emerged then as new tools for policy makers and for regulators, to anticipate whether and when some country or economic sector may suffer a financial crisis, or, more generally, to detect intrinsec economic weaknesses and vulnerabilities. In their general acception, EWS are nothing but econometric models, including both macro and microeconomic variables. Important issues are therefore related to the choice of data to evaluate, and of the underlying methodology to transform financial and macroeconomic indicators. However, since the critical episodes often exhibit various characteristics, the generalization through an economic model to explain all these different cases has been commonly assumed to be not possible, and the remedies have been distinguished according to the sources of the crisis. In particular, the attention of researchers has devoted to the development of EWS focused on the study of the financial contagion channel. Jagtiani et al. [5], for instance, developed an EWS model that provides signals of capital inadequacy in banks; using a range of financial indicators, [6] extracted early signals as well. Discrete choice models with continuous variables on the right-hand side (logit and probit models) have been also popular [1].

Within the framework depicted above, our work is intended to add valuable contributions towards different directions. Firstly, we have analised the situation of a panel of countries under a huge number of indicators, not only of financial type, but also economic, monitoring both internal (local) and external fiscal conditions whose imbalance may compromise the economic and financial stability of a country and its surroundings. In practice, this means to control various type of vulnerability at one time. The tool employed is a non parametric method based on unsupervised neural networks, namely: Self Organizing Maps (SOM). SOMs appeared to be a "natural" tool of investigation to our purposes, since they basically realize a non–linear projection of multi–dimensional data into a bi–dimensional lattice of nodes arranged according to their similarity. This gives us the possibility to exploit the degree of vulnerability of each observed country, and its capability to spread contagiously to neighbour countries. Here the notion of neighbourhood has been assumed into a wider acception, since it can be intended either in a geographical sense, or in the sense to incorporate countries sharing similar features from the economical and financial perspective.

The paper proceeds as follows. Section 2 starts by reviewing Self Organizing Maps. Section 3 after a brief description of the data sample, discusses the results obtained by our methodology. Section 4 then concludes.

2. Some brief remarks on Self Organizing Maps

The Self Organizing Map (SOM) [9] is a projection method based on the principle of space representation through dimension reduction: a finite set of input patterns is represented by means of a number of nodes (neurons), sharing with inputs the same format, and arranged into a mono or bi–dimensional grid; in order to avoid hedges effects, wraparound versions can be also implemented [8,10]. When an arbitrary input is presented to a SOM, a competitive procedure starts, during which a winner or leader neuron is chosen in the map, as the best matching node, according to a metric previously fixed.

A generic step of the procedure may be then summarized as follows: we will refer to the case of a mono–dimensional SOM, but the layout presented can be easily generalized to higher dimensional grids. If $\mathbf{x}(t) = \{x_j(t)\}_{j=1,\ldots,n} \in \mathbb{R}^n$ is the input item presented to a map M with q nodes with weights $\mathbf{m}_i(t) = \{m_{i,j}(t)\}_{j=1,\ldots,n} \in \mathbb{R}^n$, $(i = 1, ..., q)$, i_t^* will be claimed the winner neuron at step t iff:

$$i_t^* = \underset{i \in M}{argmin} \left(\sum_{i \in M} \sum_{j=1}^{n} |x_j(t) - m_{i,j}(t)|^p \right)^{1/p}, \; p \in \mathbb{N} \tag{1}$$

Note that although $p \in \mathbb{N}$, most common choices are for $p = 1$, or $p = 2$. Once the leader has been identified according to Eq. (1), the correction of nodes in the map takes place; if $N_{i^*}(t)$ is the set of neurons in the map belonging to the *neighbourhood* of i^* (in a topological sense), then:

$$\mathbf{m}_i(t+1) = \mathbf{m}_i(t) + h_{i*,i}(t)[\mathbf{x}(t) - \mathbf{m}_i(t)] \tag{2}$$

Here $h_{i^*,i}(\cdot)$ is an interaction function, governing the way the nodes adjust respect to the winning neuron on the grid. Typical shapes for h include the constant function:

$$h_{i^*,i}(t) = \begin{cases} \alpha, \; i = {i^*}_t \vee i \in N_{i^*}(t) \\ 0, \text{ otherwise} \end{cases} \tag{3}$$

with $\alpha \in (0, 1)$, and the Gaussian function:

$$h_{i^*,i}(t) = exp \left\{ -\frac{\sum_{r=1}^{n} |m_{i,r}(t) - m_{i^*,r}(t)|^2}{2} \right\}, \; i = 1, \ldots, q \tag{4}$$

After iterating the procedure over a number of epochs, the map should tend to a steady organized state [3], and neighbouring neurons should represent similar inputs.

3. Case study

3.1. Description of the input set

Our dataset is a $51 \times 49 \times 51$ tensor made up by 51 countries observed through 49 different variables, from the first quarter of 1995 to the third quarter of 2007 (51 records). Table 1 lists the countries included in our panel.

Table 1.Countries belonging to our panel data. The table shows the countries included in our study, the corresponding shortname used, and the dataset they belong to.

Country	ID	Dataset	Country	ID	Dataset	Country	ID	Dataset
Argentina	ARG	WLD1, WLD2	Albania	ALB	WLD1, WLD3	China	CHI	WLD1,WLD4
Brazil	BRA	WLD1, WLD2	Bosnia Herzegovina	BOH	WLD1, WLD3	Hong Kong	HOK	WLD1, WLD4
Chile	CHI	WLD1, WLD2	Croatia	CRO	WLD1, WLD3	South Korea	SKO	WLD1, WLD4
Colombia	COL	WLD1, WLD2	Macedonia	MAC	WLD1, WLD3	Taiwan	TAI	WLD1,WLD4
Paraguay	PAR	WLD1, WLD2	Serbia	SER	WLD1, WLD3	Indonesia	IND	WLD1,WLD4
Peru	PER	WLD1, WLD2	Russia	RU	WLD1, WLD3	Malaysia	MAL	WLD1,WLD4
Uruguay	URU	WLD1, WLD2	Ukraine	UKR	WLD1, WLD3	Philippines	PHI	WLD1,WLD4
Venezuela	VEN	WLD1, WLD2	Armenia	ARM	WLD1, WLD3,WLD4	Thailand	THA	WLD1,WLD4
Bulgaria	BUL	WLD1, WLD3	Azerbaijan	AZE	WLD1, WLD3,WLD4	Vietnam	VIE	WLD1,WLD4
Estonia	EST	WLD1, WLD3	Belarus	BEL	WLD1, WLD3	Singapore	SIN	WLD1,WLD4
Hungary	HUN	WLD1, WLD3	Georgia	GEO	WLD1, WLD3,WLD4	India	IDI	WLD1,WLD4
Poland	POL	WLD1, WLD3	Kazakhstan	KAZ	WLD1, WLD3,WLD4	Pakistan	PAK	WLD1,WLD4
Latvia	LAT	WLD1, WLD3	Kyrgyzstan	KYR	WLD1, WLD3,WLD4	Iran	IRN	WLD1,WLD4
Lithuania	LIT	WLD1, WLD3	Moldova	MOL	WLD1, WLD3	Turkey	TUR	WLD1,WLD4
Romania	ROM	WLD1, WLD3	Tajikistan	TAJ	WLD1, WLD3,WLD4	Egypt	EGY	WLD1, WLD4
Slovakia	SLK	WLD1, WLD3	Turkmenistan	TUK	WLD1, WLD3,WLD4	Tunisia	TUN	WLD1, WLD4
Slovenia	SLO	WLD1, WLD3	Uzbekistan	UZB	WLD1, WLD3,WLD4	Kenya	KEN	WLD1, WLD4

For each country we have reported the corresponding label used in our analysis, and the subgroup for which the country has been taken into account. This point represents one of the key issues of this study. Our aim was in fact two–fold. We were interested to monitor whether or not financial/economic distress can spread over neighbour countries, or even to world scale. To such purpose, we analysed our sample data as a whole (WLD1), but we have also studied subgroups, obtained once WLD1 was split following (straightforward) territorial or economical divisions: this led us to consider Latin American countries (WLD2), Euro–area surrounding countries (WLD3), Asian (or Asian influenced) countries (WLD4).

For what it concerns the variables in use, most of our dataset was extracted from the World Bank database, although some data were taken from the International Monetary Fund (IMF), and from the Organisation for Economic Co–operation and Development (OECD) database. The sample was selected (with respect to choice of both country and time) to maximize data availability; however, some observations are missing for individual variables. Despite from standard approaches to EWS building that focus only on the determinants of a particular crisis type (financial, polytical, economical), our analysis takes into account factors that variously affect the general equilibrium of a country. The variables we have considered belong to four categories:

(i) foreign variables, like interest rates, nominal rate of exchange (with US Dollar assumed as currency benchmark), and foreign direct investment (FDI);
(ii) domestic macroeconomic indicators, such as monetary and fiscal shocks indicators, real Gross Domestic Product (GDP) growth rate, fiscal stance, public debt (% GDP), inflation rate, domestic investment ratios, and M1, M2 indicators;
(iii) external variables, such as over-valuation, the level of indebtedness, fixed–rate vs. floating-rate borrowing, and domestic–currency vs foreign–currency denomination;
(iv) debt components, divided into the amounts lent by commercial banks, confessional, variable–rate; short–term; and lent by multilateral developmentbanks (including the World Bank and regional banks, but not the IMF).

3.2. Discussion of the results

We have originally provided a static snapshot of countries in our dataset, according to the way the corresponding macroeconomic data cluster in the map; to such purpose, WLD1 and WLD2 were trained on hexagonal 35×9 maps, WLD3 and WLD4 on 24×9 maps. The map dimensions vary according to the subgroup of data in use, and they were chosen after a preliminary data snooping procedure, during which we examined the sensitivity of convergence indexes to changes in the number of neurons [2,4]. Figure 1 reports the results obtained on the four groups of data with variables referring to the third quarter of 2007.

Figure 1 is organized with two maps placed on each row: the first map is the classical Uniformity Matrix (U–Matrix), where we have put into evidence the relative importance of each node, whose size have been scaled by the distance matrix calculated from all 49 components. The map on the right hand side is the same U–Matrix where each node shows the countries that belong to it. Looking at the organization of the maps, one can observe that the critierion joined by the SOM algorithm is essentially a geographical one: see for instance Figure 1(a), where Armenia, Moldova and Iran are grouped into

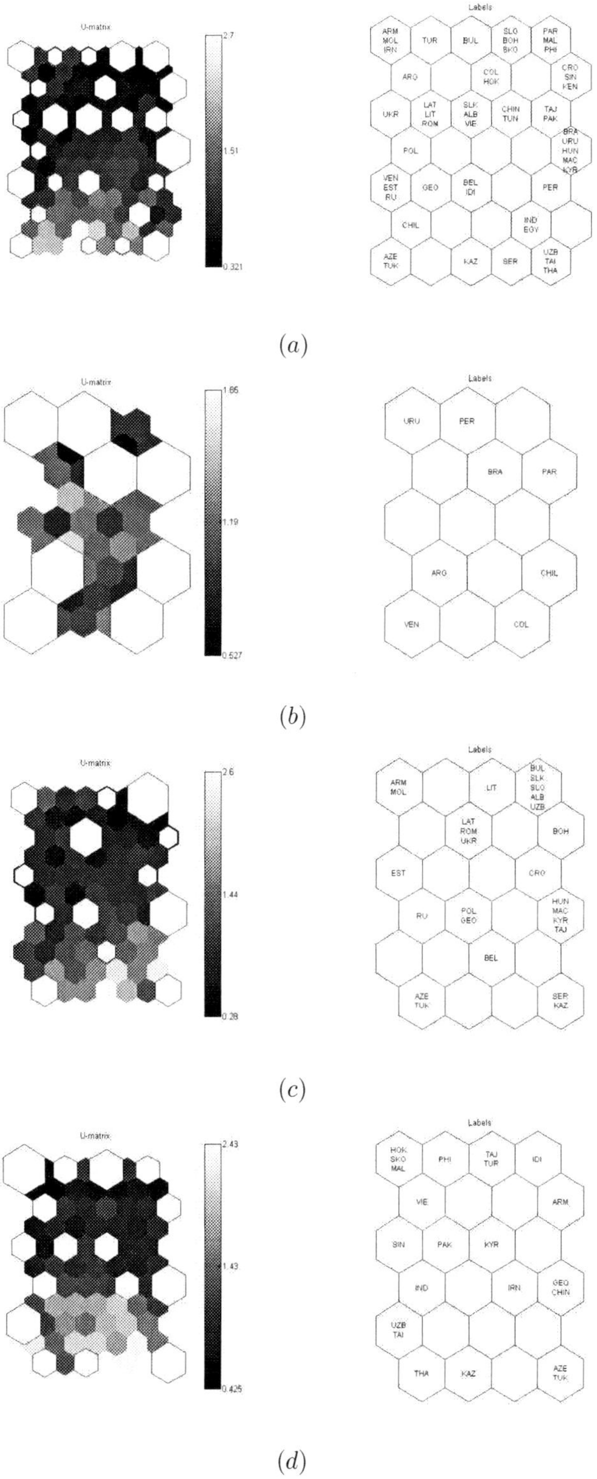

Figure 1. Results for WLD1 (a), and WLD2 (b), WLD3 (c) and WLD4 (d) datasets

Table 2. Probability of crisis in the countries belonging to our sample 8 quarters ahead.

Country	ID	Prob	Country	ID	Prob	Country	ID	Prob
Argentina	ARG	40%	Albania	ALB	55%	China	CHI	40%
Brazil	BRA	45%	Bosnia Herzegovina	BOH	57%	Hong Kong	HOK	55%
Chile	CHI	30%	Croatia	CRO	45%	South Korea	SKO	50%
Colombia	COL	30%	Macedonia	MAC	55%	Taiwan	TAI	50%
Paraguay	PAR	30%	Serbia	SER	55%	Indonesia	IND	55%
Peru	PER	35%	Russia	RU	68%	Malaysia	MAL	65%
Uruguay	URU	35%	Ukraine	UKR	65%	Philippines	PHI	45%
Venezuela	VEN	45%	Armenia	ARM	56%	Thailand	THA	45%
Bulgaria	BUL	20%	Azerbaijan	AZE	60%	Vietnam	VIE	40%
Estonia	EST	20%	Belarus	BEL	60%	Singapore	SIN	48%
Hungary	HUN	20%	Georgia	GEO	61%	India	IDI	40%
Poland	POL	20%	Kazakhstan	KAZ	64%	Pakistan	PAK	70%
Latvia	LAT	20%	Kyrgyzstan	KYR	64%	Iran	IRN	48%
Lithuania	LIT	20%	Moldova	MOL	60%	Turkey	TUR	45%
Romania	ROM	20%	Tajikistan	TAJ	60%	Egypt	EGY	30%
Slovakia	SLK	20%	Turkmenistan	TUK	66%	Tunisia	TUN	30%
Slovenia	SLO	20%	Uzbekistan	UZB	66%	Kenya	KEN	55%

the same cell, and they are surrounded by Turkey (on the right) and by Turkmenistan and Azerbaijan (on the upper bound). This observation holds also for the other maps in Figure 1. Moving to the analysis of nodes, one should note that the maps sub (a) are those with the largest degree of generality, since clusters have been obtained using all the countries in the data sample: we therefore refer our conclusions mostly to such maps. According to the snapshot taken at the third quarter of 2007, nodes in the lower right side of the map refer to countries with reduced default probability. Such probability tends to increase moving to the upper side of the map, from left to right: the outcomes we reported on are somewhat confirmed by looking at the relative position of the countries in the maps sub (b)–(d).

As second step, we have dynamically monitored the evolution path in the map of each country over the available 51 quarters, according to the different levels of significant variables. In this case, we traced the route on the map of each country (through the values of the 49 variables representing the related vector code), and we have inferred the probability of future crises 8 quarters (2 years) ahead. Figure 2 gives an idea of how the procedure works: on the upper side the dynamic route followed by Brazil is traced from 1995 to 2007; the lower part of Figure 2 shows the path of China within the same period. The probabilistic palette to asses the level of vulnerability of various countries in our sample is provided in Table 2.

4. Conclusions

This paper discussed a new Early Warning System (EWS) model, based on Self Organizing Maps (SOMs). Respect to existing EWS models, our model includes both economic and financial variables, and it is therefore better suited to provide signals of alarm respect to a wider range of imbalances and weaknesses a country may be exposed to. Addition-

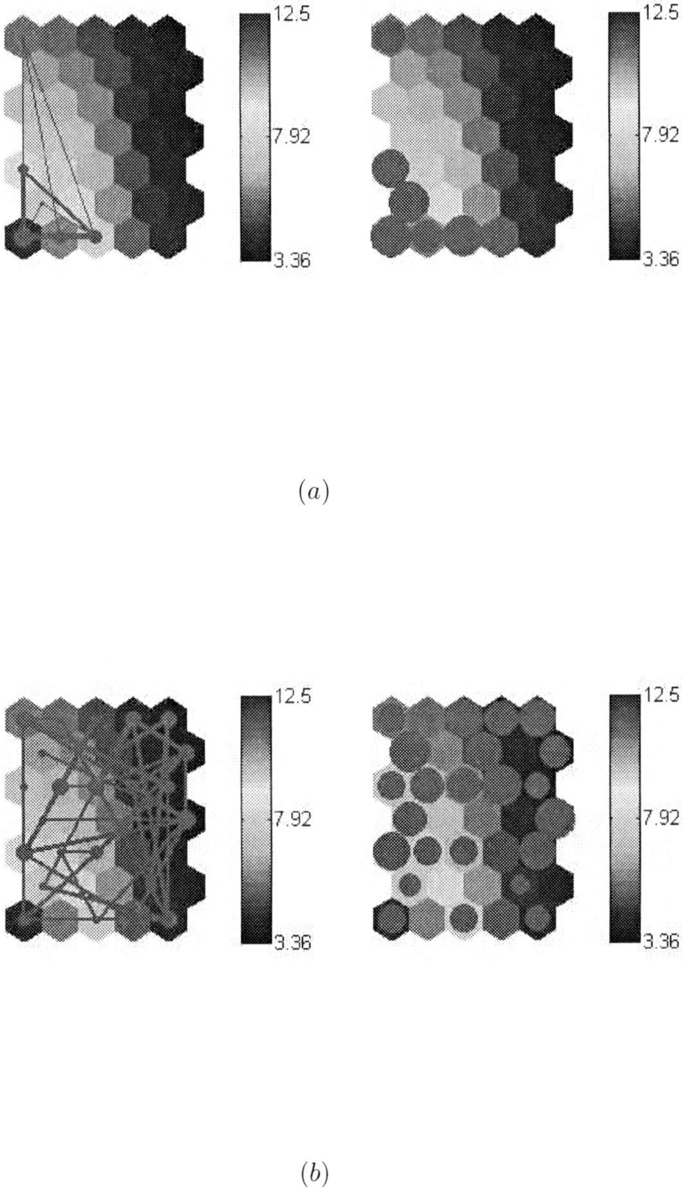

Figure 2. Sample trajectories of Brazil (a) and China (b): the maps in the left hand side show details of the route traced through 51 quarters, the maps in the right hand side report the significance of node joined through the path.

ally, the method we have employed is non parametric, and it performs a non–linear projection of high dimensional input datasets into a bi–dimensional manifolds, thus being more robust than traditional logit or probit models that need preliminary data cleanings.

Our model was tested on data of 51 countries, mostly extracted from the World Bank database, although some data were taken from the IMF, and from the OECD database. We have originally provided a static snapshot of countries in our dataset, fixed to the third quarter of 2007, according to the way their macroeconomic data cluster in the map. In this way, we were able to capture the reciprocities and similarities from various emerging markets. In particular, looking at the results obtained it seems that the local proximity is the major contagion factor of economic vulnerabilities: neighbours are those with highest probability to get imbalanced when a critical event arises in a surrounding country. As second step, we have dynamically monitored countries' evolution path in the map over the time, with each variable observed from the first quarter of 1995 to the third quarter of 2007. Looking at the position changes of each country on the map along time, it has been possibile to infer the probability of future crises two years ahead.

It should be emphasized that the EWS model developed in this paper does certainly not constitute the final step towards a comprehensive EWS model. However, we believe that SOMs represent a new approach to EWS building, and hence the paper can address further steps towards developing more powerful tools for policy-makers in the future.

References

[1] Bussiere M, and M. Fratzscher (2002), Towards a new early warning system of financial crises. *European Central Bank working paper series*, 145, May 2002.

[2] Cattaneo Adorno, M. and M. Resta (2004), Reliability and convergence on Kohonen maps: an empirical study. In: M. Gh. Negoita, R. J. Howlett and L. C. Jain, *Proceedings of Knowledge-Based Intelligent Information and Engineering Systems*, Part I, Lecture Notes in Computer Science, Springer, 426-433.

[3] Cheng, Y. (1997), Convergence and ordering of Kohonen's batch map. *Neural Computation* 9, 1667-1676.

[4] De Bodt, E., Cottrell, M., and M. Verleysen (2002), Statistical tools to assess the reliability of self-organizing maps. *Neural Networks*, 15, 967-978.

[5] Jagtiani J., Kolari J., Lemieux C., and H. Shin (2003), Early Warning Models for Bank Supervision: Simpler Could Be Better. *Federal Reserve Bank of Chicago Economic Perspectives* (Quarter 3): 49Ű60.

[6] Kamin S., Schindler J., and S. Shawna (2001), The Contribution of Domestic and External Factors to Emerging Market Devaluation Crises: An Early Warning Systems Approach. *International Finance Working Paper* No. 711, Board of Governors of the Federal Reserve System.

[7] Kaminsky G. L., Lizondo S., and C. M. Reinhart (1998), Leading Indicators of Currency Crises. *IMF Staff Papers*, 45, No. 1, pp. 1-48.

[8] M. Y. Kiang, U. R. Kulkarni, M. Goul, A. Philippakis, R. T. Chi and E., Turban (1997), Improving the Effectiveness of Self-Organizing Map Networks Using a Circular Kohonen Layer. *Proc. Thirtieth Annual Hawaii Int. Conf. on System Sciences.*

[9] T. Kohonen (1982), *Self-Organizing Maps*, Springer Verlag, Berlin.

[10] C. Y. Liou and W. P. Tai (1999), Conformal self-organization for continuity on a feature map. *Neural Networks*, 12, 893-905.

New Directions in Neural Networks
B. Apolloni et al. (Eds.)
IOS Press, 2009

doi:10.3233/978-1-58603-984-4-185

Optimal partial questioning in large dimensional AHP

Michele FEDRIZZI [a,1], Silvio GIOVE [b]
[a] *University of Trento, Italy*
[b] *University of Venice, Italy*

Abstract. In this paper we propose a flexible method for optimally choosing and sequencing in time a subset of pairwise comparisons between the alternatives in large–dimensional AHP problems. Two criteria are taken into account in defining the choice rule: the fair involvement of all the alternatives in the pairwise comparisons and the consistency of the elicited judgements. The combination of the two criteria guarantees the best reliability of the already collected information. The method indicates at each step the two alternatives to be next compared and stops the process taking into account both the reliability of the already elicited judgements and the necessity of bounding the potentially large number of judgements to be submitted to the decision maker.

Keywords. AHP, Pairwise Comparisons, Consistency.

Introduction

The Analytical Hierarchy Process, AHP, as well as all the other methods based on pairwise comparisons, is characterized by the redundancy of the information collected by comparing each one of the, say N, alternatives with all the others. Far to be an useless procedure, this method guarantees the reliability of the data by means of the compensation of possible contradictory elicited judgements. This means that the pairwise comparison method can suitably manage the unavoidable inconsistency of human judgements. Nevertheless, it is not rare the case when a large number of alternatives are involved in the pairwise comparison process and the nature of the problem does not allow to split them in different further hierarchical levels. In this case it could be necessary, or even unavoidable, to perform only a part of the $N(N-1)/2$ total comparisons, otherwise the expert/decision maker would renounce himself to complete the comparison process or he/she would perform it without accuracy, with the consequence of the non–reliability of the elicited judgements.

On the basis of some suitable criteria, we propose in this paper an iterative algorithm for selecting the comparisons to be sequentially submitted to the decision maker and for deciding when the process must be stopped. The paper is organized as follows: in the section 1 we shortly describe the problem and we set the necessary definitions and

[1]Corresponding Author: Department of Computer Science and Management Studies, University of Trento, Via Inama 5, TN 38100 Trento, Italy; E-mail: michele.fedrizzi@unitn.it

notations. In section 2 we define the choice rule identifying, at each step, the 'next comparison' to be submitted to the expert as well as the stopping rule that brings to end the process. In section 3 we define and study what we call the scoring function, i.e. the 'core' of the selection process. In section 4 we briefly formalize the algorithm and finally, in section 5, we propose some remarks and conclusions.

1. Problem description

Let $\Lambda = \{A_1, A_2, ..., A_N\}$ be a set of N alternatives and let the judgements of a decision maker be expressed by pairwise comparisons of the alternatives. We assume that the reader is familiar with Saaty's approach [8] [9], and we only recall, very briefly, its main features. The decision maker's judgement a_{ij} estimates the preference intensity of alternative A_i over alternative A_j by means of the ratio w_i/w_j and the 1– 9 ratio scale is used to quantify these judgements. The obtained matrix $A = [a_{ij}]$ is positive and reciprocal, $a_{ji} = 1/a_{ij}, \ \forall i, j$ and it is called Pairwise Comparison Matrix, *PCM* in the following. We denote by Ω_N the set of the $N \times N$ pairwise comparison matrices.
A *PCM* $A = [a_{ij}] \in \Omega_N$ is called consistent if and only if

$$a_{ij} = a_{ih}a_{hj} \, , \quad i, j, h = 1, ..., N. \tag{1}$$

As mentioned before, we focus on the case where a large number N of alternatives is given. Having decided that it is unacceptable for the decision maker to perform all the $N(N-1)/2$ comparisons, let us denote by $N^* < N(N-1)/2$ the number of comparisons really submitted to the decision maker. In this case, the final result may be heavily affected by the choice of these N^* comparisons. It becomes therefore a crucial task to introduce a selection process on the basis of some suitable a priori defined optimality criteria. Moreover, the total number N^* of comparisons submitted to the decision maker can either be fixed a priori or, as we suggest, may depend on the achievement, during the comparison process, of a global reliability threshold. More precisely, we propose that the questioning process terminates when a satisfactory compromise is achieved between the number of already submitted comparisons and the reliability of the collected judgements.

Few research works has been done till now on this problem [10], although several papers have faced the related problem of the optimal use of a given incomplete pairwise comparison matrix [1] [2] [3] [4] [5] [6] [7] [11] [12] [13] [14] [15].

2. The choice of the next comparison

This section describes the rule we propose for determining the comparison to be submitted to the expert at every step of the preference elicitation process.

Let us suppose we already performed p pairwise comparisons $\{A_h, A_k\}$ during the questioning process and let us denote this set of pairwise comparisons by Q. Then, p is clearly the cardinality of Q, $p = |Q|$. In the previous section we have denoted by N^* the maximum value achieved by p at the end of the process, so it is $0 \le p \le N^* \le N(N-1)/2$. Let us call 'next comparison' simply the $(p+1)$–*th* comparison, say $\{A_i, A_j\}$.

We propose to determine the next comparison on the basis of two criteria, both referring to the robustness and to the reliability of the set of collected data. The first one is to share as uniformly as possible the comparisons between the alternatives. The second one is to resolve possible inconsistency emerged in previous comparisons. We need some additional notation. Let q_i denote the index set of the alternatives already compared with A_i , $q_i = \{h|\{A_i, A_h\} \in Q\}$. Then, the number of comparisons already involving alternative A_i or alternative A_j is $|q_i| + |q_j|$. This quantity will play an important role in defining the score function in section 3.

For what concerns the consistency evaluation of the already elicited preferences, let us define some relevant quantities. If A_i is compared with A_h, obtaining a_{ih}, and A_h is compared with A_j, obtaining a_{hj}, then A_i is also indirectly compared with A_j, and this indirect comparison is quantified by the product $a_{ih}a_{hj}$ (note that $\frac{w_i}{w_j} = \frac{w_i}{w_h}\frac{w_h}{w_j}$ and refer to (1)). We denote by μ_{ij} the mean value of all indirect comparisons of A_i with A_j,

$$\mu_{ij} = \begin{cases} 0 & \text{if} \quad q_i \cap q_j = \emptyset \\ \frac{1}{|q_i \cap q_j|} \sum_{h \in q_i \cap q_j} a_{ih}a_{hj} & \text{if} \quad q_i \cap q_j \neq \emptyset \end{cases} \tag{2}$$

The mean inconsistency φ_{ij} of the indirect comparisons of A_i with A_j is defined by

$$\varphi_{ij} = \begin{cases} 0 & \text{if} \quad \mu_{ij} = 0 \\ \left[\frac{1}{|q_i \cap q_j|} \sum_{h \in q_i \cap q_j} (a_{ih}a_{hj} - \mu_{ij})^2\right]^{\frac{1}{2}} & \text{if} \quad \mu_{ij} \neq 0 \end{cases} \tag{3}$$

Note that, for $q_i \cap q_j \neq \emptyset$, $\varphi_{i,j}$ is the standard deviation of $(a_{ih}a_{hj})$. Moreover, it is $\varphi_{i,j} = 0$ if and only if all the indirect comparisons $a_{ih}a_{hj}$ of A_i with A_j are performed in a perfectly coherent way, i.e. the correspondent judgements are consistent, $a_{ih}a_{hj} = a_{ik}a_{kj}$, $\forall h, k \in q_i \cap q_j$.

It is convenient to normalize φ_{ij} by calculating its maximum value. Let us then consider a generic set of numbers $\{x_1, x_2, ..., x_n\}$, where $x_i \in [m, M]$. If n is even[2], the maximum standard deviation is obtained when $\frac{n}{2}$ numbers are equal to M and the other $\frac{n}{2}$ are equal to m. In this case, the mean value is $\bar{x} = \frac{1}{n}\sum_i x_i = \frac{1}{2}(m + M)$, and it is easy to prove that the standard deviation is

$$\sigma = \left[\frac{1}{n}\sum_i [x_i - \bar{x}]^2\right]^{\frac{1}{2}} = \frac{1}{2}[M - m].$$

Using Saaty's scale $(\frac{1}{9}, ..., \frac{1}{2}, 1, 2, ..., 9)$, it is $M = 9$ and $m = \frac{1}{9}$. The maximum standard deviation, say σ_M, is therefore

$$\sigma_M = \frac{1}{2}(81 - \frac{1}{81}) \approx 40.49\,, \tag{4}$$

and represents the maximum value of the inconsistency (3). In the next section we will normalize the inconsistency values (3) within the interval $[0, 1]$ by means of (4).

It can be observed that, in general, it is $\varphi_{ij} \neq \varphi_{ji}$, since $a_{ih}a_{hj} \neq a_{jh}a_{hi}$. On the other hand, the choice of the pair of alternatives $\{A_i, A_j\}$ for the 'next comparison' must clearly be independent from their order, $\{A_i, A_j\} = \{A_j, A_i\}$. Therefore, we set

[2] If n is odd a similar result is obtained.

$$\rho_{ij} = \frac{\varphi_{ij} + \varphi_{ji}}{2} \tag{5}$$

to obtain a symmetric measure of the mean inconsistency of the indirect comparisons *between* A_i and A_j.

Note that, from the point of view of graph theory, a pair of alternatives $\{A_i, A_j\}$ can be viewed as an 'arch' connecting the two 'nodes' A_i and A_j. So we consider the terms 'arch' and 'pair of alternatives' as synonyms. Therefore, 'empty arch' means pair of alternatives not already compared.

As mentioned before, the two alternatives for the next comparison are chosen by favoring those ones that rarely appear in the already performed comparisons (small value of $|q_i| + |q_j|$) and those that have been previously involved in inconsistent comparisons (large value of ρ_{ij}, requiring, therefore, clarifying judgements). To this purpose, in the following section a suitable scoring function will be assigned to each *empty* arc (i, j). A high value of the scoring function will indicate a high necessity to compare A_i with A_j, since few comparisons (or not at all) have up to now involved A_i or A_j and/or these comparisons contain some inconsistency. At each step, the arc with the maximum value of the score function will be selected, thus identifying the next comparison.

The procedure will be repeated until, for all the empty arcs, the scoring function becomes smaller than a pre-fixed threshold and the questioning process stops. This means that the utility of a new comparison is overcome by the necessity to maintain the number of questions submitted to the expert sufficiently small.

3. The scoring function

A score $\tau(i, j)$ is assigned to each empty arc (i, j) through a function $F(|q_i|, |q_j|, \rho_{i,j})$ depending on $|q_i|$, $|q_j|$, i.e. the actual number of comparisons involving A_i and A_j respectively, and on the inconsistency measure (5). Such function should privilege low values of at least one between $|q_i|$ and $|q_j|$, but, as a first approximation, we can assume that F depends on $(|q_i| + |q_j|)$ and $\rho_{i,j}$ and not on $|q_i|$ and $|q_j|$ separately[3],

$$\tau(i, j) = F(|q_i| + |q_j|, \rho_{i,j})$$
$$F : N \times \Re \to [0, 1]$$

Referring to the above described criteria, the function F has to be decreasing in the first argument, which is a natural number:

$$F(n + 1, x) < F(n, x), \forall n \in N, \forall x \in \Re \tag{6}$$

and not necessarily increasing in the second one, a real number (see later).

However, if the DM considers more important the robustness of the information than the consistency, he/she can set the following constraint on the function $F(n, x)$:

$$F(n + 1, x_1) \leq F(n, x_2), \tag{7}$$

[3]Even if it seems more realistic that, if *at least* one among $|q_i|$ and $|q_j|$ is low, the score $\tau(i, j)$ should be high.

for every real values x_1 and x_2 of the inconsistency measure. Clearly, such a condition is not necessary and depends on the DM's subjective preference. Furthermore, he can decide to impose (7) only for some values of n.
We propose the following expression for the scoring function F and then we will explain some of its properties,

$$F(|q_i| + |q_j|, \rho_{i,j}) = S(|q_i| + |q_j|)\,[1 + D(|q_i| + |q_j|) \cdot q(\rho_{i,j})]\,. \tag{8}$$

In the sequel, if not strictly necessary, we omit the indices i, j and we use the simpler notation $n = |q_i| + |q_j|$ and $\rho = \rho_{i,j}$. The scoring function (8) can then be written as

$$F(n, \rho) = S(n)[1 + D(n) \cdot q(\rho)]. \tag{9}$$

The first term, $S(n)$ measures the effect of the cardinality of the comparisons involving A_i or A_j. The second term, $[1 + D(n) \cdot q(\rho)]$ plays the role of a *multiplicative* effect due to the inconsistency of the comparisons, and can both increase or decrease the value of $S(n)$ as later described, depending on the value of function $D(n)$. The function $q(\rho)$ normalizes the inconsistency ρ into the interval $[0, 1]$ and it is an increasing real function,

$$q(\rho) : [0, \sigma_M] \rightarrow [0, 1]$$
$$\frac{\partial q}{\partial \rho} > 0$$
$$q(0) = 0, \quad q(\sigma_M) = 1$$

A possible simple definition of $q(\rho)$ is

$$q(\rho) = \frac{\rho}{\sigma_M}.$$

The scoring function $F(n, \rho)$ needs to satisfy the monotonicity property:

$$F(n + 1, \rho) < F(n, \rho). \tag{10}$$

Let us find some sufficient conditions for (10) by rewriting it in the form

$$S(n + 1)[1 + D(n + 1) \cdot q(\rho)] < S(n)[1 + D(n) \cdot q(\rho)], \tag{11}$$

which in turn implies:

$$S(n) - S(n + 1) > q(\rho) \cdot [S(n + 1) \cdot D(n + 1) - S(n) \cdot D(n)]. \tag{12}$$

In particular, for $\rho = 0$, that is for $q(\rho) = 0$, we obtain:

$$S(n) > S(n + 1), \tag{13}$$

implying that $S(n)$ must be decreasing. As specified above, $n = |q_i| + |q_j|$ represents the cardinality of the comparisons involving A_i or A_j. Therefore, condition (13) is coherent with our previous assumptions[4].

[4] Increasing the number of comparisons, the ranking of the arc decreases.

Moreover, from (13) it follows that the the monotonicity condition (11) is satisfied if we assume that also $D(n)$ is decreasing,

$$D(n) > D(n+1)\,. \tag{14}$$

We suggest to assume this property be verified, since it is natural to state that, if n increases, the inconsistency contribution to the scoring function has to decrease[5].

Assuming that a decision maker wants the strict property (7) be satisfied, it is easy to prove the following proposition,

Proposition 1
If the inequality

$$0 \leq D(n+1) \leq \frac{S(n)}{S(n+1)} - 1 \tag{15}$$

holds for every n, then property (7) is satisfied for every inconsistency value in $[0,1]$.

Proof
Since $0 \leq q(\rho) \leq 1$, from (9) it is

$$F(n+1,\rho^*) = S(n+1)[1 + D(n+1)\cdot q(\rho^*)] \leq S(n+1)[1 + D(n+1)]\,.$$

Then, from (15),

$$S(n+1)[1 + D(n+1)] \leq S(n) \leq S(n)[1 + D(n)\cdot q(\rho^{**})] = F(n,\rho^{**})\,,$$

whatever are the inconsistency values ρ^* and ρ^{**} in $[0,1]$, so that the proposition is proved.

In this case, an arc with higher value of $n = |q_i| + |q_j|$ will scored higher than an other one with lower value of $n = |q_i| + |q_j|$, no matter of the inconsistency.

3.1. Specifying the scoring function

In (8) and (9) we do not give single fixed expressions to the functions $S(n)$, $D(n)$, and $q(\rho)$. In order to preserve the flexibility of our proposal, we prefer to clarify how the terms $S(n)$ and $D(n)$ determine the properties of the scoring function (9) and let, for each case under study, the possibility of choosing the most suitable expressions.

The role of function $S(n)$ is twofold. First of all it must fairly share the comparisons among the alternatives. This effect is achieved as long as $S(n)$ is decreasing, since this implies that alternatives rarely compared are favored by higher score. Secondly, function $S(n)$ also contributes, when n increases, to reduce the global value of $F(n,\rho)$ towards its threshold, thus playing the main role in stopping the questioning process.

[5]Even for the inconsistency, if an arc has a large number of comparisons, the inconsistency weights less, given that such arc has to be scored low.

Function $D(n)$ controls the effect of inconsistency $q(\rho)$ on the scoring function $F(n,\rho)$. By choosing $D(n)$ as a positive decreasing function, we tend to clarify inconsistency generated by few comparisons, thus disregarding useless efforts to resolve numerous contradictory indirect comparisons. This last outcome can be enforced by giving negative values to $D(n)$ for large n, thus reversing the effect of having high inconsistency. More precisely, in this case we give a high score to arcs with high inconsistency and low values of n, but we give a very low score to the arcs with large values of both n and $q(\rho)$, since they correspond to an irreparable situation that has to be ignored.

Moreover, particular care must be taken in the choice of the function $q(\rho)$ since it is crucial in determining the role of the consistency in the scoring function (9).

The next section gives a short description, in pseudo-code, of the basic optimizing algorithm which implements the proposed method for comparison selection.

4. The algorithm

The basic algorithm determines at each step the next arc to be inserted, starting from an empty $N \times N$ comparison matrix. The selected arc is the one with maximum value of the scoring function F. Initially, all the arcs exhibit the same value of F, since no connecting arc exists. Subsequently, if more than one arc (i,j) shares the same value of (9), one of them is randomly selected. The algorithm uses two iteratively updated sets of arcs,

- P, the set of the arcs that maximize τ
- Q, the set of the assigned arcs (i.e. performed comparisons) at each process step.

Any arc characterized by the maximum value of $\tau(i,j)$ can be selected for the next comparison. The algorithm stops as soon as the maximum τ of the empty arcs is less than a pre-fixed threshold τ^* (stopping criterion), that is:

$$\tau(i,j) \leq \tau^*, \ \forall\{A_i, A_j\} \notin Q \tag{16}$$

The value τ^* can be tuned from the two pre-defined sequences $S(n), D(n)$. For instance, it can be decided to take as a benchmark a threshold n^* defined in the consistent case ($\rho = 0$) for the sum of the nodes cardinality. More precisely, if all the performed comparisons are consistent, the questioning procedure stops as soon as $|q_i| + |q_j| \geq n^* \ \forall\{A_i, A_j\} \notin Q$. The threshold n^* leads to $\tau^* = S(n^*)$, being $\rho = 0$ in (9), and this value τ^* can then be chosen also for the inconsistent cases. Thus, the basic structure of the proposed algorithm is the following.

BASIC ALGORITHM

$Q = \emptyset$;
repeat:

1. $\tau_{opt} = max\,\{\tau(i,j), \{A_i, A_j\} \notin Q\}$; let P be the set of the corresponding maximizers,
2. Choose randomly an element in P, say $\{A_i, A_j\} \in P$,
3. The DM compares A_i with A_j and assigns the corresponding value $a_{i,j}$. This value is subsequently stored in the comparison matrix

4. $Q \rightarrow Q \cup \{\{A_i, A_j\}\}$,

until $\tau_{opt} \leq \tau^*$

Obviously, if P contains only one arc, say (i, j), then step 2 can be ignored and the DM has to assign, in the step 3, the value $a_{i,j}$.
The basic algorithm interacts continuously with the DM, requiring at each step the insertion of the comparison value for a pair of alternatives. When the algorithm stops, a set of arcs (comparisons) has been assigned, but, necessarily, a certain number of comparisons, precisely $\frac{N(N-1)}{2} - N^*$, are missing. At this point, the incomplete pairwise comparison matrix we obtained can either be completed by means of some known methods [1] [3] [11], or it can directly be used to compute the weight vector for the alternatives [2] [4] [5] [6] [7] [12] [13] [14] [15].

5. Final remarks

The method we have presented is aimed at helping the decision maker in eliciting his/her preferences in large dimensional AHP problems, where it is crucial to bound the excessively large number of questions he/she should answer. We based our proposal on some reasonable criteria trying to obtain a rational questioning process which is suitably flexible to be applied in various contexts; moreover it fulfills different requirements of the decision maker.

What we presented in this paper is a methodological proposal. In order to implement a real world application, it will be necessary an accurate specification of the functions and a fine tuning of the parameters involved in the algorithm. This will be developed in our future research activity.

References

[1] Alonso S., Chiclana F., Herrera F., Herrera–Viedma E., A learning procedure to estimate missing values in fuzzy preference relations based on additive consistency, *tech. rep.*, Department of Comuter Science and Artificial Intelligence, University of Granada, Spain, (2006).

[2] Chen, Q., Triantaphyllou, E.: Estimating Data for Multi–Criteria Decision Making Problems: Optimization Techniques. In P.M. Pardalos and C. Floudas (ed) Encyclopedia of Optimization. Kluwer Academic Publishers, Boston, MA, Vol. 2, (2001)

[3] M. Fedrizzi, S. Giove, Incomplete pairwise comparison and consistency optimization, European Journal of Operational Research, 183, n. 1, 303–313 (2007)

[4] Harker, P.T. Alternative modes of questioning in the analytic hierarcy process, *Mathl Modelling*, 9 (1987) n. 3–5 353–360.

[5] Harker, P.T. Incomplete pairwise comparisons in the analytic hierarcy process, *Mathl Modelling*, 9 (1987) n. 11 837–848.

[6] Kwiesielewicz, M.: The logaritmic least squares and the generalized pseudoinverse in estimating ratios. European Journal of Operational Research, 93, 611–619 (1996)

[7] Nishizawa, K.: Estimation of unknown comparisons in incomplete AHP and it's compensation. Report of the Research Institute of Industrial Technology, Nihon University, n. 77 (2004)

[8] Saaty, T. L.: A scaling method for priorities in hierarchical structures. J. Math. Psychology, 15, 234–281 (1977)

[9] Saaty, T. L.: The Analytic Hierarchy Process. McGraw-Hill, New York (1980)

[10] Setiawan, S.: The effect of initial selections in estimating the missing comparisons in an incomplete AHP matrix. Thesis, Louisiana State University (1998)

[11] Shiraishi, S., Obata, T., Daigo, M.: Properties of a positive reciprocal matrix and their application to AHP. J. Oper. Res. Soc. Japan, 41, 404–414 (1998)

[12] Takeda, E., Yu, P.L.: Assessing priority weights from subsets of pairwise comparisons in multiple criteria optimization problems. European Journal of Operational Research, 86, 315–331 (1995)

[13] van Uden, E.: Estimating missing data in pairwise comparison matrices. In Z. Bubnicki, O. Hryniewicz and R. Kulikowski (ed) Operational and Systems Research in the Face to Challenge the XXI Century, Methods and Techniques in Information Analysis and Decision Making, Academic Printing House, Warsaw, (2002)

[14] Xu, Z.S.: Goal programming models for obtaining the priority vector of incomplete fuzzy preference relation. International Journal of Approximate Reasoning, 36, 261–270 (2004)

[15] Xu, Z.S.: A procedure for decision making based on incomplete fuzzy preference relation. Fuzzy Optimization and Decision Making, 4, 175–189 (2005)

New Directions in Neural Networks
B. Apolloni et al. (Eds.)
IOS Press, 2009

doi:10.3233/978-1-58603-984-4-194

Evaluation of fuzzy quantities by means of a weighting function

Gisella FACCHINETTI [a], Nicoletta PACCHIAROTTI [b]

[a] *Dip. di Economia Politica-Università di Modena e Reggio Emilia-Italia*
[b] *Dip. di Matematica Pura e Applicata-Università di Modena e Reggio Emilia-Italia*

Abstract. We consider here *fuzzy quantities* , i.e. fuzzy sets without any hypothesis about normality nor convexity. Two main topics are examined: the first one consists in defining the evaluation of a fuzzy quantity, in such a way that it may be applied both in ranking and in defuzzification problems. The definition is based on α-cuts and depends on two parameters: a coefficient connected with the optimistic or pessimistic attitude of the decision maker and a weighting function similar to a density function. The second aim is showing that the proposed definition is suitable for defuzzifying the output of a fuzzy expert system: we treat a classical example discussed in [1], using several t-norms and t-conorms in aggregation procedures.

Keywords. Fuzzy sets.Aggregation operators. Evaluation function. Ranking. Defuzzification.

Introduction

In a previous paper [8] we faced the problem of *evaluating* a fuzzy quantity, that is a fuzzy set which does not need to be normal or convex; moreover, by *to evaluate* we mean to associate to the fuzzy set a real number, somehow representing it. Many authors studied this problem with regard to fuzzy numbers ([2], [3], [4], [5], [7], [8], [9], [10], [11], [15]) and it is well-known that it is very important both in optimization problems involving fuzzy functions and in fuzzy control problems, where the ultimate step requires specifically a defuzzification.
The aim of the present paper is twofold. First of all we give here a definition of evaluation which is more general with respect to the one we gave in [8]; it depends on two parameters: a coefficient connected with the optimistic or pessimistic attitude of the decision maker and a weighting function that generalizes the additive measure we used in the previous paper and can be considered as a probabilistic density function. When these two parameters vary, our definition includes a lot of definitions introduced in fuzzy literature.
Regardless of the values of the paramenters, the evaluation always lies in the support of the fuzzy quantity: we hold this property be fundamental, mainly from the point of view of defuzzification problems. Indeed, in such cases the crisp value

we associate to the fuzzy quantity must be strongly connected with the support of the output resulting from the fuzzy control system we are studing.

A second purpose of the present paper is giving an answer to an interesting question suggested by a referee of [8]: he exhorted us to investigate whether our definition is still well posed when the T-norms and the T-conorms used in the aggregation process of the fuzzy control system vary. With such an aim, we consider a classical example of a fuzzy control system and prove that the evaluation we propose is always utilizable and its computation is really simple.

1. Basic definitions and notations

Let X be a universal set ; a fuzzy subset $\tilde{A}$ of X is defined by a function $\mu_{\tilde{A}}(.) : X \to [0,1]$, called membership function. Throughout this paper, X is assumed to be the set of real numbers R and $\mathcal{F}$ the space of fuzzy sets.

Definition 1.1 . The fuzzy set $\tilde{A} \in \mathcal{F}$ is a fuzzy number iff:

1) $\forall \alpha \in [0,1]$ the set $A^{\alpha} = \{x \in R \ : \ \mu_{\tilde{A}}(x) \geq \alpha\}$, which is called α -cut of $\tilde{A}$, is a convex set.

2) $\mu_{\tilde{A}}(.)$ is an upper-semicontinuous function.

3) $supp(\tilde{A}) = \{x \in R : \mu_{\tilde{A}}(x) > 0\}$ is a bounded set in R.

4) height $\tilde{A} = max_{x \in X} \mu_{\tilde{A}}(x) = h > 0$

By conditions 1) and 2), each α-cut is a compact and convex subset of R hence it is a closed interval in R, $A^{\alpha} = [a_L(\alpha), a_R(\alpha)]$. If $h = 1$ we say that the fuzzy number is normal; we denote the set of normal fuzzy numbers by $\mathcal{NFN}$.

If condition 1) fails, we say that $\tilde{A}$ is a **fuzzy quantity** . Finally, $\tilde{A}$ is a crisp number with value m if its membership function is given by $\mu_{\tilde{A}}(x) = 1$ if $x = m$ and $\mu_{\tilde{A}}(x) = 0$ otherwise.

2. Evaluation of non-normal fuzzy numbers

In order either to define ranking procedures and to introduce a defuzzifing method, we propose to associate a real number to a fuzzy set: we call this procedure "to *evaluate* a fuzzy number" . The ranking problem has an obvious meaning, while the second one is the ultimate step in approximate reasoning and consists in the replacement of a fuzzy set with a suitable "crisp" value. Both these problems can be solved associating to a fuzzy set $\tilde{A}$ a real number by means of a function F that maps the set of fuzzy numbers on the real line, where we can use the natural ordering. Therefore we consider these two matters as the same one and it turns unavoidable stating the following Axiom:

The evaluation of the fuzzy number $\tilde{A}$ lies in its support, that is $F(\tilde{A}) \in supp\,\tilde{A}$.

This last is a widely accepted axiomatic condition. Namely, if we really use the evaluation either as a ranking method or as a defuzzification method, the "value" we associate to the fuzzy number must correspond to a point x where $\mu_{\tilde{A}}(x) \neq 0$, because any fuzzy number $\tilde{A}$ has a non zero reliability degree only within its support.

In order to obtain an evaluation on $\mathcal{F}$, we define at first an evaluation on the intervals in R and then extend it to fuzzy numbers, considered as a collection of their α-cuts $A^\alpha = [a_L(\alpha), a_R(\alpha)]$. We proceed as follows:

Definition 2.1 . Let I be the set of all closed bounded intervals of R, i.e. $\mathrm{I} = [x_1, x_2], x_1, x_2 \in R, x_1 \leq x_2$. We call evaluation of I any function $\phi : I \to R$.

In general, it is not possible to request a priori any property on $\phi(.)$, but it seems reasonable to consider functions which are increasing in x_1, x_2 and have some regularity properties (i.e. $\phi \in C^{(1)}$).

For instance, we can consider the family $\{\phi_\lambda\}_{\lambda \in (0,1)}$ of linear functions

$$\phi_\lambda(\mathrm{I}) = \lambda x_2 + (1-\lambda)\ x_1\ , \lambda \in [0,1]\ . \tag{1}$$

In a decisional context, the decision maker may choose the parameter λ , according to his point of view be optimistic or pessimistic ([7], [8]).

Let us consider a non-normal fuzzy number $\tilde{A} \in \mathcal{FN}$, $A^\alpha = [a_L(\alpha), a_R(\alpha)] = [a_L^\alpha, a_R^\alpha]$ be its α -cuts , $max_{x\in R}\ \mu(x) = h$, $h \leq 1$ and $f : [0,1] \to R$ be a non negative continuous function, usually called *weighting function* . The normalization of this function can be interpreted as a density function [12].

Definition 2.2. We define evaluation of $\tilde{A}$, with respect to the *weighting function* f and the parameter $\lambda \in (0,1)$, the real number

$$V(f, \tilde{A}) = \frac{\int_0^h\ \phi_\lambda(a^\alpha)\ f(\alpha)\ d\alpha}{\int_0^h\ f(\alpha)\ d\alpha} \tag{2}$$

where ϕ_λ is defined by (1).

Remark that if $\tilde{A}$ is the crisp number a, we have $V(f, \tilde{A}) = a$.

When there is no possibility of misunderstanding, we shortly denote $V(f, \tilde{A})$ by $V(\tilde{A})$.

Note that the definition we stated above satisfies the Axiom , that is

Property 2.1.

$V(\tilde{A})$ belongs to the support of $\tilde{A}$.

If we consider the space $\mathcal{H}$ of the fuzzy numbers with the same height h the same properties we listed in [8] hold.

Let us now examine the dependence of $V(\tilde{A})$ on h : just for sake of simplicity, we consider the case $\tilde{A} = (a_1, a_2, a_3, a_4)$ is a trapezoidal f.n. . In this case,

$$\phi_\lambda(a^\alpha) = \lambda a_R(\alpha) + (1-\lambda) a_L(\alpha) = \lambda a_3 + (1-\lambda) a_2 + \frac{c_\lambda}{h}(h-\alpha)$$

where $c_\lambda = \lambda(a_4 - a_3) - (1-\lambda)(a_2 - a_1)$ and the corresponding evaluation is

$$V(f, \tilde{A}) = \lambda a_3 + (1-\lambda) a_2 + \frac{c_\lambda}{h} \cdot \left(h - \frac{\int_0^h\ \alpha\ f(\alpha)\, d\alpha}{\int_0^h\ f(\alpha)\ d\alpha} \right)$$

The quantity $E_f = \left(\int_0^h\ \alpha\ f(\alpha)\, d\alpha\right)\left(\int_0^h\ f(\alpha)\ d\alpha\right)^{-1}$ is the preference index value of the weighting function f introduced by Liu [12] in the case where $h =$

1 and $\int_0^1 f(\alpha)\,d\alpha = 1$. Using the Integral Mean Value Theorem, we know that the preference index coincides with a particular value $\bar{\alpha} \in [0, h]$.
Then we obtain

$$V(\tilde{A}) = \lambda a_3 + (1-\lambda)a_2 + c_\lambda K(f,h) \text{ where } 0 \le K(f,h) = \frac{h - E_f}{h} \le 1.$$

In the trapezoidal case we are dealing with, the function $K(f,h)$ is non decreasing w.r.to h , hence $V(\tilde{A})$ is equally non-decreasing w.r.to h.

3. Fuzzy quantities defined as union of fuzzy sets

We wish to generalize the previous definition to the case of fuzzy quantities, namely to the union of two or more fuzzy numbers, which is not in general a fuzzy number; the interest for this topic arises from the study of fuzzy expert systems (see Section 4).
Let $\tilde{A}$ and $\tilde{B}$ be in $\mathcal{F}$, with membership functions $\mu_{\tilde{A}}$ and $\mu_{\tilde{B}}$; we can define both their union and their intersection by means of several t-norms and t-conorms, well-known in literature. We choose here the most usual ones, that is we define

$$\tilde{D} = \tilde{A} \cap \tilde{B} = \{(x, \mu_{\tilde{D}}(x)) \text{ s.t. } \mu_{\tilde{D}}(x) = min\{\mu_{\tilde{A}}(x), \mu_{\tilde{B}}(x)\}\}$$

$$\tilde{C} = \tilde{A} \cup \tilde{B} = \{(x, \mu_{\tilde{C}}(x)) \text{ s.t. } \mu_{\tilde{C}}(x) = max\{\mu_{\tilde{A}}(x), \mu_{\tilde{B}}(x)\}\}.$$

$\tilde{D}$ is always a fuzzy number, with height h_D ; obviously, $\mu_{\tilde{D}}(x)$ might be everywhere zero, but this is not the case occurring in most of the outputs of a fuzzy expert system. Therefore we'll consider in the following $supp\,\tilde{A} \cap supp\,\tilde{B} \neq \emptyset$.

Let us consider $\tilde{A} = (a_1, a_2, a_3)_{LR}$ and $\tilde{B} = (b_1, b_2, b_3)_{LR}$, $a_1 < b_3$, be Left-Right fuzzy numbers whose heights are respectively h_A and h_B , both less or equal to 1 and $supp\,\tilde{A} \cap supp\,\tilde{B} \neq \emptyset$.
If f is the weighting function defined in Section 2, we introduce the functions $g_i : [0,1]^3 \to R_0^+$, $i = 1, 2, 3$

$$g_i(h_1, h_2, h_3) = \frac{\int_0^{h_i} f(\alpha)\,d\alpha}{\int_0^{h_1} f(\alpha)\,d\alpha + \int_0^{h_2} f(\alpha)\,d\alpha - \int_0^{h_3} f(\alpha)\,d\alpha} \tag{3}$$

where

$$\int_0^{h_1} f(\alpha)\,d\alpha + \int_0^{h_2} f(\alpha)\,d\alpha - \int_0^{h_3} f(\alpha)\,d\alpha \neq 0.$$

Following [8] and using the same notations we used in Definition 2.2, we can now state the following

Definition 3.1 For each pair of fuzzy numbers $\tilde{A}$ and $\tilde{B}$ we call evaluation $\mathcal{V}$ of the fuzzy quantity $\tilde{A} \cup \tilde{B}$ the real number

$$\mathcal{V}(\tilde{A} \cup \tilde{B}) = \gamma_1 V(\tilde{A}) + \gamma_2 V(\tilde{B}) - \gamma_3 V(\tilde{A} \cap \tilde{B}) \tag{4}$$

where $\gamma_i = g_i(h_A, h_B, h_{A \cap B}), i = 1,2,3$ and g_i is defined by (3).
Note that $\gamma_i, i = 1,2,3$ are non negative real numbers such that $\gamma_1 + \gamma_2 - \gamma_3 = 1$.
In the sequel, sometimes we'll use for brevity the notation $\tilde{D} = \tilde{A} \cap \tilde{B}$.
Two different cases may occur:
i) $\tilde{C} = \tilde{A} \cup \tilde{B}$ has convex α-cuts, hence it is a fuzzy number
ii) $\tilde{C}$ has non-convex α-cuts, hence it is a fuzzy quantity.
If we deal with the first case, we could directly define the evaluation of $\tilde{C}$ by means of Definition 2.2 as well and the two definitions produce the same result (it is a consequence of Property 3.2 below).
In the case ii), a geometrical argument developped in [8] leads to the following result: There exists a decomposition of the support of $\tilde{C}$ in such a way that on each subinterval the α-cuts of $\tilde{C}$ be convex, that is we can write $\tilde{C} = \tilde{C}_1 \cup \tilde{C}_2$, where $\tilde{C}_1$ and $\tilde{C}_2$ are fuzzy numbers such that *supp* $\tilde{C}_1 = (c_1, \bar{x}]$ and C_1 has convex $\alpha -$ cuts ; *supp* $\tilde{C}_2 = [\bar{x}, c_3)$ and C_2 has convex $\alpha -$ cuts . The heights are respectively $h_{C_1} = h_A$ and $h_{C_2} = h_B$ if $a_2 < b_2$ or $h_{C_1} = h_B$ and $h_{C_2} = h_A$ if $b_2 < a_2$.
Remark that if we consider the hypographs of the membership functions μ_{C_1} and μ_{C_2} and we call them C_1 and C_2 , they are not disjoint : in fact their intersection is the vertical segment T between $P_1 = (\bar{x}, 0)$ and $P_2 = (\bar{x}, \bar{\alpha})$. Segment T may be considered as the hypograph of the membership function of the non-normal fuzzy number $\tilde{T}$, defined by $\mu_{\tilde{T}}(x) = \bar{\alpha}$ if $x = \bar{x}$ and $\mu_{\tilde{T}}(x) = 0$ elsewhere; its evaluation, by Definition 3.1, is $V(\tilde{T}) = \bar{x}$.
Therefore, we obtain $\tilde{C} = \tilde{C}_1 \cup \tilde{C}_2$ and $\tilde{C}_1 \cap \tilde{C}_2 = \tilde{T}$.
Using Definition 3.1 with the decomposition of $\tilde{C}$ by means of the fuzzy numbers $\tilde{C}_1$ and $\tilde{C}_2$, we obtain :

$$\mathcal{V}(\tilde{C}) = \mathcal{V}(\tilde{C}_1 \cup \tilde{C}_2) = \beta_1 V(\tilde{C}_1) + \beta_2 V(\tilde{C}_2) - \beta_3 V(\tilde{T}) \tag{5}$$

where $\beta_i = g_i(h_{C_1}, h_{C_2}, h_T), i = 1,2,3$ and g_i is defined by (3).
Following the same argument we used in [8] it can be proved that

$$\mathcal{V}(\tilde{C}_1 \cup \tilde{C}_2) = \mathcal{V}(\tilde{A} \cup \tilde{B})$$

This means that, in order to calculate the evaluation of the fuzzy quantity given by Definition 3.1, we can equivalently proceed by decomposing $\tilde{A} \cup \tilde{B}$ in the two fuzzy numbers $\tilde{C}_1$ and $\tilde{C}_2$ we specified above, that is $\mathcal{V}(\tilde{C}) = \mathcal{V}(\tilde{A} \cup \tilde{B}) = \mathcal{V}(\tilde{C}_1 \cup \tilde{C}_2)$.
The evaluation $\mathcal{V}$ satisfies the following properties

Property 3.1.
$\mathcal{V}(\tilde{A} \cup \tilde{B})$ belongs to the closure of the support of $(\tilde{A} \cup \tilde{B})$.

Property 3.2
For any fuzzy numbers $\tilde{A}$, $\tilde{B}$, $\tilde{E}$ and $\tilde{F}$ such that $\tilde{A} \cup \tilde{B} = \tilde{E} \cup \tilde{F} = \tilde{C}$, it results $\mathcal{V}(\tilde{A} \cup \tilde{B}) = \mathcal{V}(\tilde{E} \cup \tilde{F}) = \mathcal{V}(\tilde{C})$.
Moreover, from Property 3.2 we can infer that if $\tilde{A} \cup \tilde{B} = \tilde{C}$ is a fuzzy number, then $\mathcal{V}(\tilde{A} \cup \tilde{B}) = V(\tilde{C})$. As a particular case, if $\tilde{A} \subset \tilde{B}$, it results $\mathcal{V}(\tilde{A} \cup \tilde{B}) = V(\tilde{B})$.
The proofs of the properties can be handled with the same arguments used in [8].

4. AN EXAMPLE

Let us consider now a simple example of fuzzy inference system, the client financial risk tolerance model, proposed in ([1],p.130).
In this model the output y is the Risk Tolerance level (RT) and it depends on two inputs, the Annual Income (AI) x_1 and the Total Networth (TNW) x_2. The ranges of these quantities are: $x_1 \in X_1 = \{x \times 10^3 : 0 \leq x \leq 100\}$; $x_2 \in X_2 = \{x \times 10^4 : 0 \leq x \leq 100\}$; $y \in Y = \{y : 0 \leq y \leq 100\}$ The quantities we consider can be described by the three linguistic values L (low), M (medium) and H (high), as follows:

$$\text{Annual Income} = A^1 = \{A^1_1, A^1_2, A^1_3\} = \{L_1, M_1, H_1\}$$

$$\text{Total Networth} = A^2 = \{A^2_1, A^2_2, A^2_3\} = \{L_2, M_2, H_2\}$$

$$\text{Risk Tolerance} = B = \{B_1, B_2, B_3\} = \{L_3, M_3, H_3\}$$

Just for the sake of simplicity, suppose the terms of the linguistic values be described by the same membership functions

$$\mu_{L_3}(v) = \mu_{L_1}(v) = \mu_{L_2}(v) = \begin{cases} 1 & 0 \leq v < 20 \\ \dfrac{50-v}{30} & 20 \leq v \leq 50 \\ 0 & \text{elsewhere} \end{cases}$$

$$\mu_{M_3}(v) = \mu_{M_1}(v) = \mu_{M_2}(v) = \begin{cases} \dfrac{v-20}{30} & 20 \leq v \leq 50 \\ \dfrac{80-v}{30} & 50 \leq v \leq 80 \\ 0 & \text{elsewhere} \end{cases}$$

$$\mu_{H_3}(v) = \mu_{H_1}(v) = \mu_{H_2}(v) = \begin{cases} \dfrac{v-50}{30} & 50 \leq v \leq 80 \\ 1 & 80 \leq v \leq 100 \\ 0 & \text{elsewhere} \end{cases}$$

The second step consists in constructing the rules block defining the relationships between the linguistic values of the variables: let us write for instance rule R_s in a general form :

$$R_s: \ \textbf{IF} \ (x_1 \text{ is } A^1) \otimes (x_2 \text{ is } A^2) \qquad \textbf{THEN} \ \ y \text{ is } B_k. \tag{6}$$

The first part of relation (6) is called *precondition* or *antecedent* and the second one is called *conclusion* or *consequent*, hence we can say that we are dealing with the case of *multiple antecedents*: the symbol $\otimes$ represents a not specified aggregation operator. More specifically, relation (6) means that we have to take in account more criteria linked by some logical connective (*and* / *or*) which can be translated by means of several t-norms (or t-conorms): in our example, each connective is *and*. In this case, the most commonly applied t-norms are the minimum T_M , the product T_P and the Lukasiewicz T_L. Using one of these t-norms, we can obtain a single number α_s which represents the result of the antecedents calculus in rule R_s

The rules are defined in following Table

x_1	x_2	y
Low_1	Low_2	Low_3
Low_1	Med_2	Low_3
Low_1	$High_2$	Med_3
Med_1	Low_2	Low_3
Med_1	Med_2	Med_3
Med_1	$High_2$	$High_3$
$High_1$	Low_2	Med_3
$High_1$	Med_2	$High_3$
$High_1$	$High_2$	$High_3$

Assume that $\bar{x}_1 = 40$ (AI) and $\bar{x}_2 = 25$ (TNW) ; then $\mu_{L_1}(40) = \frac{1}{3}$, $\mu_{M_1}(40) = \frac{2}{3}$, $\mu_{M_2}(25) = \frac{5}{6}$, $\mu_{L_2}(25) = \frac{1}{6}$.
Let us examine the acting rules, i.e.
R_1 : If $\bar{x}_1$ is Low_1 *and* $\bar{x}_2$ is Low_2 then y is Low_3
R_2 : If $\bar{x}_1$ is Low_1 *and* $\bar{x}_2$ is Med_2 then y is Low_3
R_3 : If $\bar{x}_1$ is Med_1 *and* $\bar{x}_2$ is Low_2 then y is Low_3
R_4 : If $\bar{x}_1$ is Med_1 *and* $\bar{x}_2$ is Med_2 then y is Med_3
The level of firing of both the antecedents can be computed as follows:
$\alpha_{1,1} = \mu_{L_1}(\bar{x}_1) \wedge \mu_{L_2}(\bar{x}_2)$; $\alpha_{2,1} = \mu_{L_1}(\bar{x}_1) \wedge \mu_{M_2}(\bar{x}_2)$
$\alpha_{3,1} = \mu_{M_1}(\bar{x}_1) \wedge \mu_{L_2}(\bar{x}_2)$; $\alpha_{4,2} = \mu_{M_1}(\bar{x}_1) \wedge \mu_{M_2}(\bar{x}_2)$ (7)
where the first index in $\alpha_{s,j}$ suggests we are dealing with Rule s and the second one means that the corresponding output is B_j ; the symbol $\wedge$ denotes an "*and*" operator corresponding to the t-norm T chosen between the above mentioned ones (the minimum T_M , the product T_P and the Lukasiewicz T-norm T_L). The explicit calculus lead us to the following results:

$$\alpha_{1,1} = \begin{cases} \min(\frac{1}{3}, \frac{5}{6}) = \frac{1}{3} & T = T_M \\ \frac{1}{3} \cdot \frac{5}{6} = \frac{5}{18} & T = T_P \\ \max(\frac{1}{3} + \frac{5}{6} - 1, 0) = \frac{1}{6} & T = T_L \end{cases}$$

$$\alpha_{2,1} = \begin{cases} \min(\frac{1}{3}, \frac{1}{6}) = \frac{1}{6} & T = T_M \\ \frac{1}{3} \cdot \frac{1}{6} = \frac{1}{18} & T = T_P \\ \max(\frac{1}{3} + \frac{1}{6} - 1, 0) = 0 & T = T_L \end{cases}$$

$$\alpha_{3,1} = \begin{cases} \min(\frac{2}{3}, \frac{5}{6}) = \frac{2}{3} & T = T_M \\ \frac{2}{3} \cdot \frac{5}{6} = \frac{5}{9} & T = T_P \\ \max(\frac{2}{3} + \frac{5}{6} - 1, 0) = \frac{1}{2} & T = T_L \end{cases}$$

$$\alpha_{4,2} = \begin{cases} \min(\frac{2}{3}, \frac{1}{6}) = \frac{1}{6} & T = T_M \\ \frac{2}{3} \cdot \frac{1}{6} = \frac{1}{9} & T = T_P \\ \max(\frac{2}{3} + \frac{1}{6} - 1, 0) = 0 & T = T_L \end{cases}$$

We can say that $\alpha_{s,j}$ is the fulfilment degree of the antecedents in Rule s; this number has now to be applied to the consequent membership functions, in order to calculate the control output (CO) of each rule: for this purpose, we'll use once again the operation $\wedge$, but in a slightly different context. Indeed, we have to consider
$CO(R_1) : \alpha_{1,1} \wedge \mu_{L_3}(y)$; $CO(R_2) : \alpha_{2,1} \wedge \mu_{L_3}(y)$
$CO(R_3) : \alpha_{3,1} \wedge \mu_{L_3}(y)$; $CO(R_4) : \alpha_{4,2} \wedge \mu_{M_3}(y)$

Here $\wedge$ is working on a number and the membership function of a fuzzy set, whereas in (7) it is performed on two numbers; more precisely, in this case we can consider each number $\alpha_{s,j}$ as the constant function $\mu_{\alpha_{s,j}}(\cdot) = \alpha_{s,j}$ and define $\alpha_{s,j} \wedge \mu_{B_j}(\cdot) = T\left(\mu_{\alpha_{s,j}}(\cdot); \mu_{B_j}(\cdot)\right) = \mu_{\alpha_{s,j} \wedge \mu_{B_j}}(\cdot)$ where as usual T is one of the above mentioned t-norms.

The next-to-last step consists in *aggregation*, i.e. the process of unification of the outputs of all rules in a single (fuzzy) control output Y : its membership function can in general be defined as follows

$$\mu_Y(y) = (\alpha_{1,1} \wedge \mu_{L_3}(y)) \vee (\alpha_{2,1} \wedge \mu_{L_3}(y) \vee (\alpha_{3,1} \wedge \mu_{L_3}(y)) \vee (\alpha_{4,2} \wedge \mu_{M_3}(y))$$

The operation $\vee$ denotes a T-conorm $\perp$: the most frequently used ones are the Max conorm and the Lukasiewicz conorm. This last one generates the "Bounded Sum Operator" which is a suitable tool in Fuzzy Inference Systems when we request to take into account that the same output B_j appears as a consequent in several rules. Anyway, the choice between the conorms depends on the problem we are treating. In what follows, we denote by $\mu_Y(y)_{XZ}$ the output when the norm is X and the co-norm is Z.

More precisely, if we choose the Max co-norm and $T = T_M$, we obtain

$$\mu_Y(y)_{MM} = \begin{cases} 2/3 & 0 \leq y < 30 \\ \dfrac{50 - y}{30} & 30 \leq y \leq 45 \\ 1/6 & 45 \leq y \leq 75 \\ \dfrac{80 - y}{30} & 75 \leq y \leq 80 \\ 0 & \text{elsewhere} \end{cases}$$

If $\perp = \perp_{Max}$ and $T = T_P$ we have a non-convex output, i.e.

$$\mu_Y(y)_{PM} = \begin{cases} 5/9 & 0 \le y < 20 \\ 5/9 \cdot \dfrac{50-y}{30} & 20 \le y \le 45 \\ 1/9 \cdot \dfrac{y-20}{30} & 45 \le y \le 50 \\ 1/9 \cdot \dfrac{80-y}{30} & 50 \le y \le 80 \\ 0 & \text{elsewhere} \end{cases}$$

If $\perp = \perp_{Max}$ and $T = T_{Luk}$

$$\mu_Y(y)_{LM} = \begin{cases} 1/2 & 0 \le y < 20 \\ \frac{35-y}{30} & 20 \le y \le 35 \\ 0 & \text{elsewhere} \end{cases}$$

If we consider the Lukasiewicz co-norm and $T = T_M$, it results

$$\mu_Y(y)_{ML} = \begin{cases} 1 & 0 \le y < 40 \\ \frac{110-2y}{30} & 40 \le y \le 45 \\ \frac{155-3y}{30} & 45 \le y \le 50 \\ 1/6 & 50 \le y \le 75 \\ \frac{80-y}{30} & 75 \le y \le 80 \\ 0 & \text{elsewhere} \end{cases}$$

If $\perp = \perp_{Luk}$ and $T = T_P$

$$\mu_Y(y)_{PL} = \begin{cases} 8/9 & 0 \le y < 20 \\ 8/9 \cdot \frac{50-y}{30} + & \\ + \frac{y-20}{9 \cdot 30} & 20 \le y \le 50 \\ 1/9 \cdot \frac{80-y}{30} & 50 \le y \le 80 \\ 0 & \text{elsewhere} \end{cases}$$

If $\perp = \perp_{Luk}$ and $T = T_{Luk}$

$$\mu_Y(y)_{LL} = \begin{cases} 2/3 & 0 \le y < 20 \\ \dfrac{60-2y}{30} & 20 \le y \le 25 \\ \dfrac{35-y}{30} & 25 \le y \le 35 \\ 0 & \text{elsewhere} \end{cases}$$

The last step in fuzzy inference is defuzzification, as fuzziness help us to evaluate the rules, but the final output of a fuzzy system has to be a crisp number. Let us denote by C_{MM} the fuzzy set whose membership function is $\mu_Y(y)_{MM}$, by C_{PM} the fuzzy quantity whose membership function is $\mu_Y(y)_{PM}$ and so on. Applying Definition 4.1 when we choose $f(\alpha) = ce^{\alpha}$ we obtain

$\mathcal{V}(C_{MM}) = 24.20$ $\mathcal{V}(C_{LM}) = 22.50$ $\mathcal{V}(C_{PM}) = 19.40$

$\mathcal{V}(C_{ML}) = 34.30$ $\mathcal{V}(C_{LL}) = 20.24$ $\mathcal{V}(C_{PL}) = 17.83$

CONCLUSIONS

The definition of ranking plays a fundamental role in fuzzy optimization problems and similarly the choice of the defuzzifier is a fundamental tool in the last step of fuzzy expert systems: the definition of evaluation we propose here turns to be useful in both processes and satisfies the binding condition to associate to the fuzzy quantity a numeric data inside its support.

Our definition depends on two parameters: the first one is connected to the more or less optimistic attitude of the decision maker, the second one depends on the zone of the support where he prefers the numeric data will drop down. This last choice is obtained using weight functions, which the decision maker can handle according to the prominence he gives to certain α-levels.

Besides stating this general definition, we tested it changing the t-norms and the t-conorms one meets in the construction of an expert system. Our definition proves to be handy and allows a remarkable simplification in final computation, even if we use Lukasiewicz or probabilistic norms.

In the future, we'll investigate the possibility to extend to fuzzy quantities the definition of variance introduced by many authors for fuzzy numbers . In fact, such definitions ([4] , [10]) are essentially based on α-cuts: this approach can not be used when we deal with fuzzy quantities, since they are in general neither convex nor normal. Therefore the idea underlying our definition of evaluation might be useful to go deeper into the study of variance, covariance and correlation between fuzzy quantities.

References

[1] G.Bojadzev,M.Bojadzev, Fuzzy Logic for Business, Finance and Menagement, World Scientific (1999)

[2] L.M.Campos,A.Gonzalez, A subjective approach for ranking fuzzy numbers, Fuzzy Set and Systems 29 (1989) 145-153.

[3] L.M.Campos,A.Gonzalez, Further contributions to the study of the Average Value for ranking Fuzzy Numbers, Int. Journal of Approximate reasoning 10 (1994) 135-153.

[4] C.Carlsson,R.Fuller, On possibilistic mean value and variance of fuzzy numbers , Fuzzy Set and Systems 122 (2001) 315-326.

[5] D.Dubois,H.Prade, The mean value of a fuzzy number, Fuzzy Set and Systems 24 (1987) 279-300

[6] D.Dubois,H.Prade, Fuzzy Sets and Systems: Theory and Application, Academic Press,(1980)

[7] G.Facchinetti, Ranking function induced by Weighted Average of fuzzy numbers, Fuzzy optimization and decision making 1 (2002) 313-327.

[8] G.Facchinetti,N.Pacchiarotti, Evaluations of fuzzy quantities, Fuzzy Sets and Systems,157 (2006) 892-903.

[9] P.Fortemps,M.Roubens, Ranking and defuzzification methods based on area compensation, Fuzzy Set and Systems 82 (1996) 319-330.

[10] R.Fuller,P. Majlender, On weighted possibilistic mean and variance of fuzzy numbers,Fuzzy Sets and Systems 136 (2003) 363-374

[11] A.Gonzalez, A study of the ranking function approach through mean values, Fuzzy Set and Systems 35 (1990) 29-41.

[12] X.Liu, On the maximum entropy parameterized interval approximation of fuzzy numbers, Fuzzy sets and Systems,157 (2006) 869-878.

[13] E.Rowenta, T.Spircu, Averaging procedure in defuzzification processes, Fuzzy Set and Systems 136 (2003) 375-385.

[14] W.Van Leekwijck,E.E. Kerre, Defuzzification: criteria and classification, Fuzzy Set and Systems 108 (1999) 159-178.

[15] X.Wang, E.E.Kerre, Reasonable properties for the ordering of fuzzy quantities (I)and (II), Fuzzy Set and Systems 118 (2001) 375-385;387-405.

New Directions in Neural Networks
B. Apolloni et al. (Eds.)
IOS Press, 2009

doi:10.3233/978-1-58603-984-4-205

Neural Network Sieve Bootstrap Prediction Intervals: Some Real Data Evidence

Francesco Giordano [a], Michele La Rocca [a] and Cira Perna [a]
[a] *Department of Economics and Statistics - University of Salerno*
Via Ponte Don Melillo, 84084, Fisciano (SA) - Italy

Abstract. A sieve bootstrap scheme, the neural network sieve bootstrap, for nonlinear time series is discussed. The approach, which is non parametric in its spirit, does not have the problems of other nonparametric bootstrap techniques. The procedure is used to construct prediction intervals and it takes into account the uncertainty associated with the estimation of the model parameters. An application to real data sets is also presented.

Keywords.
Feedforward Neural Networks, Bootstrap, stationary time series

Introduction

Since the seminal paper by Efron on the bootstrap [7], it was clear that completely new statistical techniques, that involve powerful computer calculations, could greatly extend the statistical analysis of complex problems with complicated statistical models. It was soon realized that it was possible to provide statistical tools that work in complex situations without imposing unrealistic and unverifiable assumptions about the data generating mechanism. By now, statisticians have widely agreed on the theoretical importance of the bootstrap to determine more accurately the reliability of data analysis in a wide choice of subjects ranging from politics to medicine to particle physics. The method, in its classical form, was designed for application to samples of independent data while modifications of the original procedure are needed for dependent data, in order to preserve the structure of the original data in the bootstrap samples [15]. In particular, when dealing with stationary time series, the dependence structure of the series can be modeled explicitly and the bootstrap sample can be drawn from the fitted model.

Alternatively, nonparametric purely model-free bootstrap schemes can be used in order to avoid problems of model misspecification which can lead to bootstrap estimators which are not consistent. These techniques are usually based on resampled overlapping blocks of consecutive observations and they are valid under weak conditions, provided that the block length grows with the sample size at a proper rate [6,3].

However, even if they are robust against misspecified models, the resampled series exhibit spurious features which are caused by randomly joining selected blocks and, therefore, several modifications of the original scheme have been proposed. To avoid the so called "whitening effect", Carlstein [5] proposed the matched moving-block bootstrap, based on a quite complex procedure which resamples the blocks according to a Markov chain whose transitions depend on the data. Moreover, to overcome the problem that the bootstrap sample is not (conditionally) stationary, Politis and Romano [13] suggested to take blocks of random length but, in some cases, the approach can be less efficient than the original one [10].

To overcome some of the problems of the available blockwise schemes we proposed [8] a novel nonparametric bootstrap scheme the neural network sieve bootstrap (NN-Sieve), for nonlinear time series. The approach is in the spirit of the sieve bootstrap proposed by Buhlmann [2] but it uses the class of neural network models to approximate the original nonlinear process. The method is flexible and easy to implement as a standard residual bootstrap techinique and it retains the advantage of being a nonparametric technique. It is model free within a general class of nonlinear processes avoiding the specification of a finite dimensional model for the data generating process.

In this paper, the neural network sieve bootstrap tecnique is discussed with a particular focus on forecasting. The method allows the construction of prediction intervals for nonlinear time series with two main adavantages: (i) it can be used when analytical results are not available and (ii) it takes into account the variability associated with parameter estimation.

The paper is organised as follows. In section 2, the general idea of the sieve bootstrap with a neural network model is introduced. In section 3 the novel approach is used for the construction of nonparametric prediction intervals for nonlinear time series. In section 4 the results of an application to some real data sets reported. Some remarks close the paper.

1. The neural network sieve resampling scheme

Let $\{Y_t, t \in \mathbb{Z}\}$ a real valued stationary stochastic process, modeled as

$$Y_t = g\left(Y_{t-1}, \ldots, Y_{t-d}\right) + \epsilon_t$$

where ϵ_t is a sequence of *iid* random variables with zero mean and finite variance σ^2. We also suppose that ϵ_t is independent of $\{Y_{t-d}, d \geq 1\}$, the distribution function of ϵ_t is absolutely continuous with respect to a Lebesgue measure and its density function is continuous and positive on its support. The function $g(\cdot)$ is a nonlinear, unknown function satisfying some regularity conditions as in [16]. Under these assumptions, the Markov chain associated to the process Y_t is geometrically ergodic and Y_t is β-mixing with geometrically decreasing mixing coefficients [14].

The process $\{Y_t, t \in \mathbb{Z}\}$ can be approximated by a family of parametric models $\{M_r,\ r \in \mathbb{N}\}$, equipped with a model selection rule, such that $\bigcup_{r=1}^{\infty} M_r$ contains in some sense the original process. Hence, a key issue is the selection of a proper model family.

For linear processes Buhlmann [2] proposed to use the class of $AR(p)$ models with finite unknown p, assuming that some consistent estimator is available. Even if the method is easy to implement, due to the simplicity of fitting an AR model, it performs better than other bootstrap techniques only if the data generating process is linear, representable as an $AR(\infty)$ process. If the model is nonlinear, the AR-sieve bootstrap is not consistent and it exhibits a bias which does not decrease with increasing sample size.

In this framework, we proposed [8] to use the class of artificial neural network models which provides a rich and powerful modelling tool with proven and effective applications in many fields. In such a network, units are organised in successive layers with links connecting one layer to the following one. Particularly, we focused on the class of one hidden layer feedforward neural network with d inputs, r hidden units and one output unit (in the following $NN(d,r)$). When dealing with time series data, the model can analytically expressed in the following form:

$$f\left(y_{t-1}\dots,y_{t-d};\eta\right)=\sum_{k=1}^{r}c_k\phi\left(\sum_{j=1}^{d}a_{kj}y_{t-j}+a_{k0}\right)+c_0 \tag{1}$$

where d is the number of input neurons (the order of the autoregression), r is the hidden layer size, a_{kj} is the weight of the connection between the j-th input neuron and the k-th neuron in the hidden level; c_k, $k=1,\dots,r$ is the weight of the link between the k-th neuron in the hidden layer and the output; a_{k0} and c_0 are respectively the bias term of the hidden neurons and of the output; $\phi(\cdot)$ is the activation function of the hidden layer. We define $\eta = (c_0, c_1, \dots, c_r, \mathbf{a}'_1, \mathbf{a}'_2, \dots, \mathbf{a}'_r)$ where $\mathbf{a}'_i = (a_{i0}, a_{i1}, \dots, a_{id})$ and we suppose that $\eta \in \mathbb{R}^{r(d+2)+1}$.

Commonly, the hidden activation function is chosen to be a sigmoidal function such as the logistic or the hyperbolic tangent function. In this case, the hypotheses on the function $g(\cdot)$ and on the process Y_t guarantee that single hidden layer neural networks are "universal approximators" [12], in that they can arbitrarily closely approximate, in an appropriate metric, to the unknown function $g(\cdot)$. Moreover, the stochastic process Y_t defined as

$$Y_t = f\left(Y_{t-1},\dots,Y_{t-d};\eta\right)+\epsilon_t$$

shares the same probabilistic structure as the original process.

Therefore, in the NN-sieve bootstrap scheme, we consider feedforward neural networks with fixed number of neurons in the input layer so that the class of models M_r is defined as $NN(d^*,r)$; we assume that the finite unknown hidden layer size r can be appropriately determined.

Given the time series $\{Y_1,\dots,Y_T\}$, let θ be a finite dimensional parameter of interest and $\hat{\theta}_T = h\left(Y_1,\dots,Y_T\right)$ be a scalar-, vector- or curve-valued estimator, which is a measurable function of the data. Inference on θ can be gained by using the NN-Sieve bootstrap approach which runs as follows.

1. Select the input size d^* and estimate the hidden layer size $\hat{r}$ by using some kind of order selection criteria or some inferential procedures [11].
2. Estimate the neural network model $NN(d^*, \hat{r})$ by minimizing a loss function such as the mean square error.
3. Define the empirical distribution function of the centered residuals $\hat{\varepsilon}_t$

$$\hat{F}(x) = (T - d^*)^{-1} \sum_{t=d^*+1}^{T} I(\hat{\varepsilon}_t \leq x)$$

where $I(\cdot)$ denotes the indicator function.
4. Draw a resample ε_t^* of *iid* observations from $\hat{F}$ and define

$$Y_t^* = f\left(Y_{t-1}^*, \ldots, Y_{t-d}^*; \hat{\eta}\right) + \varepsilon_t^*$$

with the first d observations fixed to the mean value of Y_t and $t = 1, \ldots, T + n$. The first n observations are discarded in order to make negligible the effect of starting values.
5. Compute $\hat{\theta}_T^* = h(Y_1^*, \ldots, Y_T^*)$ on the resampled series $Y_1^*, \ldots, Y_T^*$, where $\hat{\theta}_T^*$ is the bootstrap analogue of $\hat{\theta}_T$.
6. Replicate B times the procedure and obtain B bootstrap replicates of the statistic of interest $\{\hat{\theta}_{T,b}^*, b = 1, \ldots, B\}$. The empirical distribution function

$$\hat{F}^*(x) = B^{-1} \sum_{b=1}^{B} I\left(\hat{\theta}_{T,b}^* \leq x\right)$$

can be used to approximate the unknown sampling distribution of the estimator $\hat{\theta}_T$ (or at least of its standard error).

2. Bootstrap prediction intervals

The bootstrap procedure discussed in the previous section, with minor changes, can be used to construct prediction intervals for nonlinear time series. In this case the methodology is not well developed as in the linear framework where, if the distribution of the error process is known, many analytical results are available. If the error distribution is unknown, recently, Alonso et al., 2002 ([1]) proposed the AR-Sieve bootstrap approach with the interesting property of being model-free within the class of linear processes. The approach does not impose the choice of a particular model and provides consistent estimators of the conditional distribution of the future values given the observed data for linear processes. it is also effective for "weakly" nonlinear processes but, in general, it is not consistent for nonlinear time series.

Let $\{Y_1, \ldots, Y_T\}$ be a time series and let Y_{T+h}, with $h > 0$, some future value to be predicted.

The neural network sieve bootstrap procedure for the construction of prediction intervals can be implemented as follows.

1. Let $\{Y_t^*, i = 1, 2, \ldots, T\}$ the bootstrap time series generated by using the NN-Sieve bootstrap.
2. Compute the future bootstrap observations

$$Y_{T+h}^* = f\left(Y_{T+h-1}^*, \ldots, Y_{T+h-d}^*, \hat{\eta}^*\right) + \varepsilon_{T+h}^*,$$

where ε_{T+h}^* is an observation from the empirical distribution function $\hat{F}(x)$ and $Y_t^* = Y_t$ for $t \leq T$. The latter is to get a conditional distribution of Y_{T+h} given the observed data.
3. The bootstrap distribution $F_{Y_{T+h}}^*$ of Y_{T+h}^* is used to approximate the unknown distribution of Y_{T+h}.

As usual a Monte Carlo estimate of the bootstrap distribution is obtained by repeating B times the steps 1–3. Thus, for each forecast horizon h, we obtain a set of B forecasts $\left\{Y_{T+h}^{*,b}, b = 1, \ldots B\right\}$ and the following empirical distribution function

$$\hat{F}_{Y_{T+h}}^*(x) = \frac{1}{B}\sum_{b=1}^{B} I\left(Y_{T+h}^{*,b} \leq x\right),$$

can be used to get an estimate of $F_{Y_{T+h}}^*$.

The $1-\alpha$ prediction interval for Y_{T+h} is given by

$$\left[\hat{Q}^*(\alpha/2), \hat{Q}^*(1-\alpha/2)\right],$$

where $\hat{Q}^*(\cdot) = \hat{F}_{Y_{T+h}}^{*-1}(\cdot)$ is the quantile function associated to the estimated bootstrap distribution.

This procedure incorporates into the bootstrap intervals the variability due to parameter estimation. Alternatively, by fixing the parameters to $\hat{\eta}$ when generating the bootstrap replicates, the resampling plan shares the same logic as the conditional bootsprap of Cao et al. [4].

3. Real data applications

In this section we report the results of an application of the proposed approach to construct bootstrap prediction intervals for some linear and nonlinear time series. A comparison is made between the AR-Sieve bootstrap, which is known to be optimal in the linear case, and the NN-Sieve bootstrap.

The series consist of financial time series: daily indeces of stock markets in Singapore, Frankfurt, Hong Kong and Amsterdam and hydrological time series: flows of Gota river near Sjotop-Vannersburg (Sweden), Neumunas river at Smalininkai (Lituania), Jokulsa Eysti River (Iceland) and Fisher river, near Dallas (USA). The details are reported in table 1.

The series show a quite different dynamic behaviour as clearly showed by the plots (a) and (b) in figure 1 – 4. Moreover, the series Singapore, Hang Sang, Gota and Neu-

Table 1. Description of the time series data.

Series	Period	Description
Singapore	17/03/1995 – 24/01/1997	Daily stock index in Singapore
DAX	16/06/1989 – 17/08/1990	Daily stock index in Frankfurt
Hang Seng	16/04/1993 – 10/02/1995	Daily stock index in Hong Kong
EOE	20/05/1986 – 04/03/1988	Daily stock index in Amsterdam
Gota	1807 – 1957	Mean annual river flows
Neumunas	1811 – 1943	Mean annual river flows
Jokulsa	1/1/1972 – 25/05/1973	Mean daily river flows
Fisher	1/1/1988 – 22/06/1989	Mean daily river flows

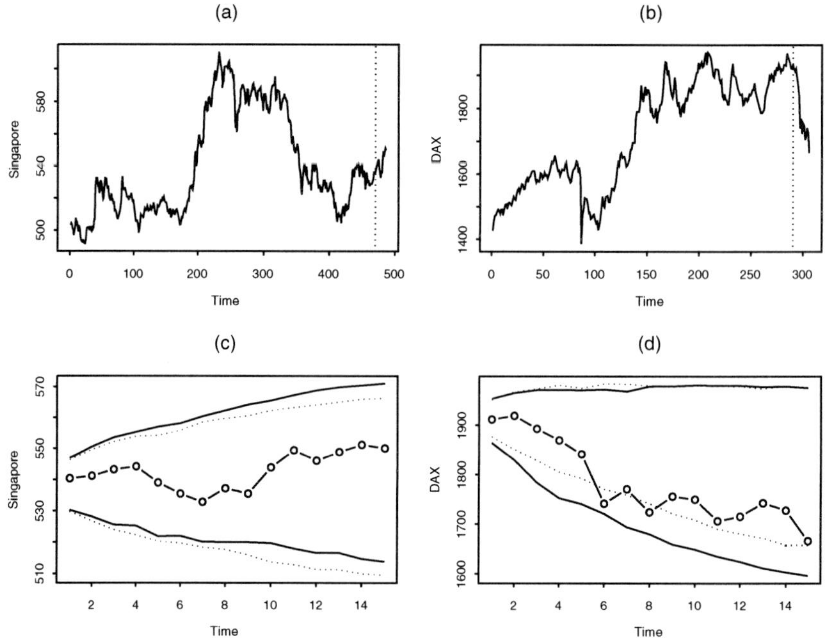

Figure 1. Singapore and DAX financial indeces: data sets, panels (a) and (b); forecast intervals with nominal coverage $1 - \alpha = 0.95$, panels (c) and (d). Pointed line: AR-Sieve bootstrap; solid line: NN-Sieve Bootstrap.

manas can be modeled with a linear structure while the other series show a strong non-linear behaviour as confirmed by the results of the Terasvirta and the White linearity tests reported in table 2.

The result displayed in panels (c) and (d) of figures 1 – 4 were obtained by making prediction of lag h, with h from 1 to 10, for annual data, and from 1 to 15, for daily data. The nominal level is fixed to $1 - \alpha = 0.95$. The number of bootstrap resamplings used to compute the prediction intervals is $B = 999$. For the AR-Sieve bootstrap and for the NN-Sieve bootstrap the determination of, respectively, model order and hidden layer size were based on the Akaike's information criterion with maximum order tried equal to $T/4$.

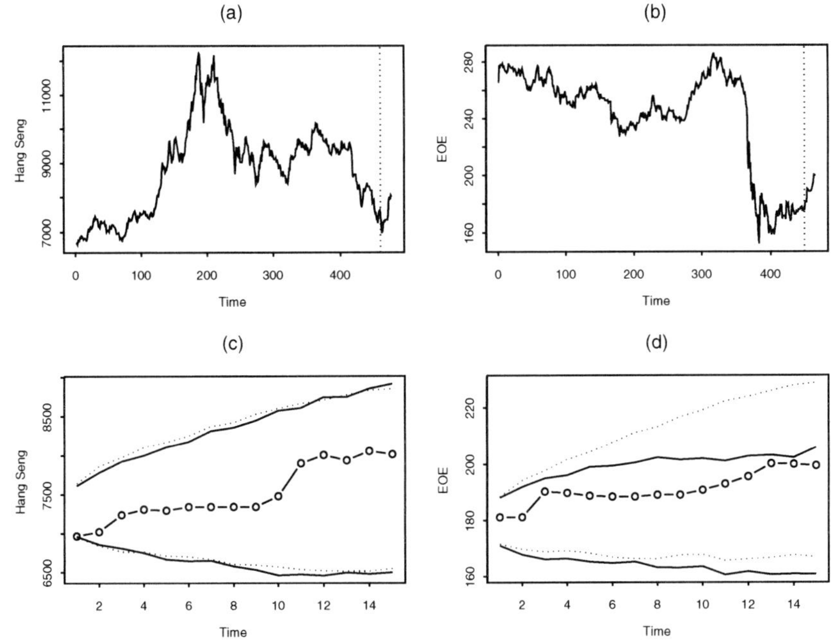

Figure 2. Hang Seng and EOE financial indeces: data sets, panels (a) and (b); forecast intervals with nominal coverage $1 - \alpha = 0.95$, panels (c) and (d). Pointed line: AR-Sieve bootstrap; solid line: NN-Sieve Bootstrap.

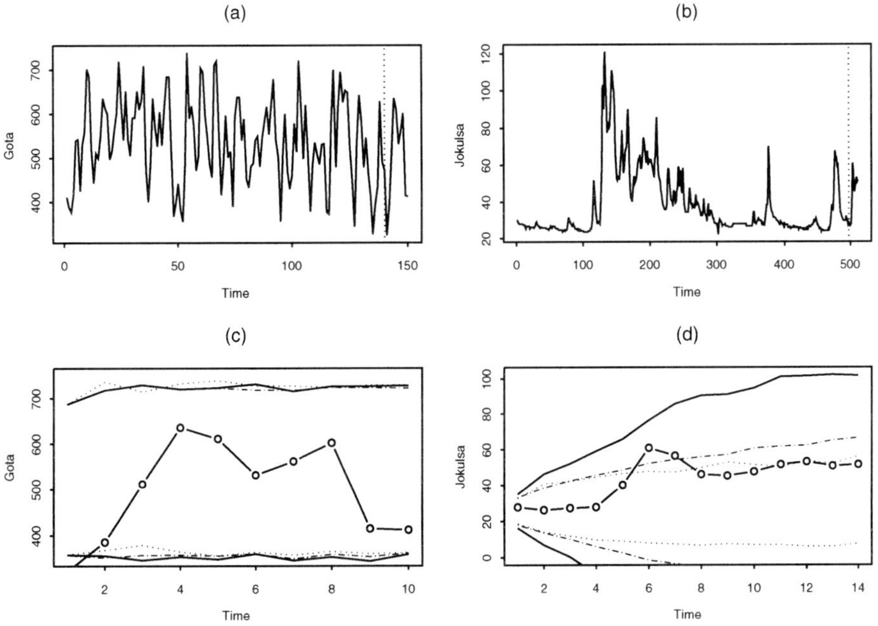

Figure 3. Gota and Jokulsa river flows: data sets, panels (a) and (b); forecast intervals with nominal coverage $1 - \alpha = 0.95$, panels (c) and (d). Pointed line: AR-Sieve bootstrap; solid line: NN-Sieve Bootstrap; dashed line: NN-Sieve with Cao approach.

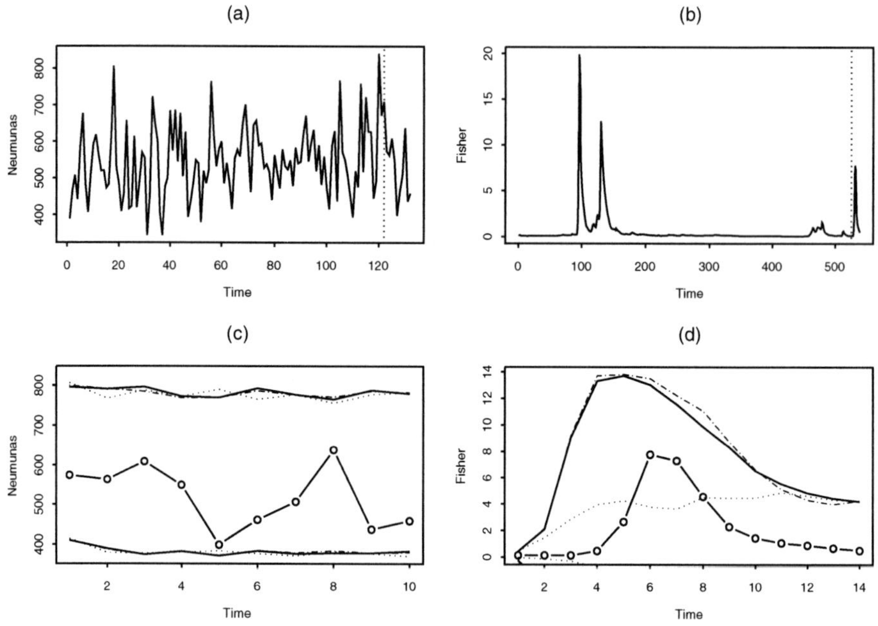

Figure 4. Neumanas and Fisher river flows: data sets, panels (a) and (b); forecast intervals with nominal coverage $1 - \alpha = 0.95$, panels (c) and (d). Pointed line: AR-Sieve bootstrap; solid line: NN-Sieve Bootstrap; dashed line: NN-Sieve with Cao approach.

Table 2. Results of Terasvirta and White linearity tests for the time series data.

	TERASVIRTA TEST		WHITE TEST	
Series	**Test statistic**	**p-value**	**Test statistic**	**p-value**
Singapore	2.7284	0.2530	3.1868	0.2032
DAX	11.0163	0.0040	8.8943	0.0120
Hang Seng	3.1126	0.2109	1.3248	0.5156
EOE	9.2822	0.0096	8.4951	0.0143
Gota	1.1322	0.5677	1.1522	0.5621
Neumunas	2.2079	0.3316	2.2563	0.3236
Jokulsa	7.4524	0.0241	7.6553	0.0218
Fisher	19.9832	0.0001	19.75	0.0001

Clearly, the AR-Sieve bootstrap and the NN-Sieve bootstrap perform similarly when dealing with linear time series data, such as the case of the two financial data sets Singapore and Hang Sang and the two hydrological series Gota and Neumunas rivers (see figures 1 – 4, panel (c)). For nonlinear time series the NN-Sieve outperforms the AR-Sieve since the intervals produced by latter tend to be too short and they often do not have good coverage properties (see figures 1 – 4, panel (d)). The NN-Sieve results obtained when using the Cao approach seem not to be as satisfactory as the standard NN-Sieve bootstrap procedure. This emphasises the importance of incorporating the uncertainty of parameter estimation in the construction of the predictive intervals.

These results confirm on real data the good performances showed by the NN-Sieve procedure in the simulation studies we reported in previous papers [8,9].

4. Concluding remarks

In this paper a nonparametric bootstrap scheme, the neural network sieve bootstrap, is discussed with an application to the construction of prediction intervals for nonlinear data. The good performances of the novel procedure are illustrated on some real data sets where it is compared, in two different implementations, with the AR-Sieve bootstrap. The NN-Sieve bootstrap procedure performs similarly to the AR-Sieve bootstrap for linear processes while it outperforms the AR-Sieve for nonlinear processes in terms both of length and coverage of the intervals.

References

[1] A.M. Alonso, D. Pena, J. Romo, Forecasting time series with sieve bootstrap, *Journal of Statistical Planning and Inference* **100** (2002), 1–11.

[2] P. Bühlmann, Sieve bootstrap for time series, *Bernoulli* **3** (1997), 123–148.

[3] P. Bühlmann and H. R. Künsch, Block Length Selection in the Bootstrap for Time series, *Computational Statistics and Data Analysis* **31** (1999), 295–310.

[4] R. Cao, M. Ferrero-Bande, W. Gonzales-Manteiga, J. M. Prada-Sanchez, and I. Garcia-Jurado, Saving computer time in constructing consistent bootstrap prediction intervals for autoregressive processes, *Communications in Statistics - Simulation Comput.* **26** (1997), 447–456.

[5] E. Carlstein, K. A. Do, P. Hall, T. Hesterberg and H. R. Kunsch, Matched block bootstrap for dependent data *Bernoulli* **4** (1998), 305–328.

[6] A. C. Davison and D. V. Hinkley, *Bootstrap methods and their application*, Cambridge University Press, 1997.

[7] B. Efron, Bootstrap methods: another look at the jackknife, *Annals of Statistics* **7** (1979), 1–26.

[8] F. Giordano, M. La Rocca and C. Perna, Neural Network Sieve Bootstrap for Nonlinear Time Series, *Neural Network World* **4** (2005), 327–334.

[9] F. Giordano, M. La Rocca, and C. Perna, Forecasting Nonlinear Time Series with Neural Network Sieve Bootstrap, *Computational Statistics and Data Analysis* **51** (2007), 3871–3884.

[10] S.N. Lahiri, Theoretical comparisons of block bootstrap methods, *Annals of Statistics* **27** (1999), 386–404.

[11] M. La Rocca and C. Perna, Variable selection in neural network regression models with dependent data: a subsampling approach, *Computational Statistics and Data Analysis* **48** (2005), 415–429

[12] M. Leshno, V. Lin, A. Pinkus, S. Schocken, Multilayer feedforward networks with a nonpolynomial activation function can approximate any function, *Neural Networks* **6** (1993), 861–867.

[13] D.N. Politis and J.P. Romano, The stationary bootstrap, *JASA* **89** (1994), 1303–1313.

[14] M. Rosenblatt, *Markov Processes. Structure and Asymptotic Behavior*, Springer, 1971.

[15] J. Shao and D. Tu, *The Jackknife and the bootstrap*, Springer, 1995.

[16] H. Tong, *Non-linear Time Series A Dynamical System Approach*, Clarendon Press, Oxford, 1990.

New Directions in Neural Networks
B. Apolloni et al. (Eds.)
IOS Press, 2009

doi:10.3233/978-1-58603-984-4-214

Fuzzy Interval Net Present Value

Marco CORAZZA [a,b,1] and Silvio GIOVE [a]

[a] *Department of Applied Mathematics, Ca' Foscari University of Venice, Venice, Italy*
[b] *School for Advanced Studies in Venice Foundation, Venice, Italy*

Abstract. The evaluation of investment projects is an ever-present problem in everyday firm life and in several economic research fields. In this paper we propose a model in which we conjugate the operative usability of the net present value with the capability of the fuzzy and the interval approaches to manage uncertainty. In particular, our fuzzy interval net present value can be interpreted, besides the usual present value of an investment project, as the present value of a contract in which the buyer lets the counterpart the possibility to release goods/services for money amounts that can vary in prefixed intervals, at time instants that can also vary in prefixed intervals. In her/his turn, the buyer can reduce the widths of both these kinds of intervals by paying a proper cost. Given this interpretation, it is "natural" to represent the good/service money amounts and the time instants by means of triangular fuzzy numbers, and the cost of the buyer as a strictly-increasing function of the level $\alpha \in [0, 1]$ associated to the generic cut of the fuzzy interval net present value. Of course, the buyer is characterized by an utility function that, in our case, depends on the features of the net present value of the contract and on the cost. So, the buyer has to determine the optimal value of α which maximizes her/his utility. As far the interest rates regard, noticing that usually the economic operators are ignorant of the future, we assume that they are only able to specify a variability range for each of the considered period interest rate. This is why we represent the interest rates by means of interval numbers. Besides proposing our model, we formulate and solve the nonlinear optimization programming problems which have to be coped with in order to determine the extremals of the generic cut of the fuzzy interval net present value, and we deal with some questions related to the utility function of the buyer.

Keywords. Net present value, fuzzy set theory, interval number theory, α–cut, utility function

Introduction

The correct evaluation of investment projects is an ever-present problem in everyday firm life and in several economic research fields. In order to deal with this problem, many approaches and tools have been developed, from the classical deterministic net present value (NPV)[2] and internal interest rate (IIR) to the refined stochastic real options.

[1]Corresponding Author: Marco CORAZZA, Department of Applied Mathematics, Ca' Foscari University of Venice, Dorsoduro 3825/E, 30123 Venice, Italy; E-mail: corazza@unive.it.

[2]A commonly used formulation of the NPV is $\sum_{j=0}^{n} S_j \Big/ \prod_{k=0}^{j} (1 + i_k)$, where n is the number of (equal length) time periods, S_j is the cash amount at time instant j, and i_k is the interest rate during the time period $(k - 1, k]$.

Of course, a central question concerns the capability of the considered approaches/tools to manage the ignorance of the future. Whereas the classical models simply do not consider this aspect (with conceivable consequences), on the other hand the majority of the stochastic approaches face it in a too much technical way for real-life applications. Because of that, several academic and professional researches presented and present intermediate tools.

In this paper we propose a model of this latter kind, in which we conjugate the operative usability of the NPV with the capability of the fuzzy and the interval approaches to manage uncertainty. It is important to notice that we have chosen to not deal with uncertainty by means of probability and stochastic tools because, coherently with the real life, these tools are usually beyond the knowledge and the computational ability of standard economic operators.

The literature concerning this topic is rich enough. Some of the first models were presented in [2], in which fuzzy cash amounts, a fuzzy interest rate, and a fuzzily defined number of time periods are used. These models are mainly investigated from a theoretical point of view. More operative approaches are proposed in [3] and [4]. In the former, a triangular fuzzy NPV is used for fuzzifying the Myers-Cohn model of property-liability insurance pricing. In the latter, an NPV based on triangular fuzzy cash amounts and triangular fuzzy interest rates is used for specifying dynamic replacement model. In [6], a fuzzy NPV-based procedure is considered as an effective tool for the selection of aviation technologies. In [1], a triangular fuzzy NPV is introduced as intermediate step for the determination of the related fuzzy IRR. In [8], trapezoidal fuzzy cash amounts, crisp interest rates, and probabilistic methods are jointly used for developing a fuzzy-probabilistic NPV algorithm for the evaluation of investment projects.

Of course, this review does not intend to be exhaustive but only exemplificative.

With respect to the cited contributions, and the referred ones therein, our model differs from a technical standpoint, from the economic interpretability, and from its usability.

In short, the NPV we detail in section 1 can be interpreted, besides the usual present value of a generic investment project, as the present value of a contract in which the buyer lets the counterpart the possibility to release goods/services for money amounts that can vary in prefixed intervals, at time instants that can also vary in prefixed intervals. In her/his turn, the buyer can reduce the widths of both these kinds of intervals by paying a proper cost. Given this interpretation of the NPV, also coherently with the cited contributions and with several other fuzzy modelings, it is "natural" enough to represent the good/service money amounts and the time instants by means of triangular fuzzy numbers, and the cost of the buyer as a strictly-increasing function of the level $\alpha \in [0, 1]$ associated to the generic cut of the fuzzy interval NPV.

Of course, the buyer – as any economic operator – is characterized by an utility function that, in our case, depends on the features of the NPV of the contract and negatively depends on the cost. So, recalling that all these quantities depend on α, the buyer has to determine the optimal value of such an α which maximizes her/his utility.

As far the interest rates regard, recalling that the economic operators involved in the investment project/contract are ignorant of the future, we reasonably assume that they are only able to specify a suitable variability range for each of the considered period interest rate. This is why we represent the interest rates by means of interval numbers. Moreover, it is to notice that, to the best of our knowledge, ours is the first model in which the time instants in which one releases the cash amounts/goods/services are fuzzified, and the interest rates are represented in terms of interval numbers.

The remainder of the paper is organized as follows. In the next session we propose our Fuzzy Interval Net Present Value (FINe) model and some of its main features. In section 2 we formulate and solve the nonlinear optimization programming problems which have to be coped with in order to determine the extremals of the generic cut of the FINe. In section 3 we briefly deal with some questions related to the utility function of the buyer. Finally, in section 4 we list some open items.

1. The FINe model

Let we start by specifying the discrete-time frame associated to the considered investment project/contract:

$$t_0, \widetilde{t}_1, \ldots, \widetilde{t}_j, \ldots, \widetilde{t}_n,$$

where

t_0 is the current time instant, which we represent by a crisp number;

$\widetilde{t}_1, \ldots, \widetilde{t}_j, \ldots, \widetilde{t}_n$ are the future time instants in which the cash amounts/goods/services are released, that we represent by triangular fuzzy numbers;[3] as known, the membership functions of this typology of numbers are

$$\mu_{\widetilde{t}_j}(t) = \begin{cases} 0 & \text{if } t < t_{j,1} \\ (t - t_{j,1}) / (t_{j,2} - t_{j,1}) & \text{if } t_{j,1} \leq t < t_{j,2} \\ (t_{j,3} - t) / (t_{j,3} - t_{j,2}) & \text{if } t_{j,2} \leq t < t_{j,3} \\ 0 & \text{if } t \geq t_{j,3} \end{cases}, \text{ with } j = 1, \ldots, n,$$

in which $t_{j,1}, t_{j,2}$ and $t_{j,3}$ are real numbers such that $t_{j,1} \leq t_{j,2} \leq t_{j,3}$ (a commonly used notation for this kind of numbers is $\widetilde{t}_j = (t_{j,1}, t_{j,2}, t_{j,3})$);

n is the number of time periods, which we represent by a crisp number.

In particular, we assume that, as in standard NPV models, the time instants in which the cash amounts/goods/services are released constitute a non decreasing sequence with respect to the deponent, that is we assume that

$$t_0 \leq t_{1,1} \text{ and } t_{j,3} \leq t_{j+1,1}, \text{ with } j = 1, \ldots, n-1. \tag{1}$$

Let we continue by specifying the fuzzy investment project/contract:

$$\widetilde{\mathbf{A}} = \left\{ (-S_0, \widetilde{t}_0), \left(\widetilde{S}_1, \widetilde{t}_1\right), \ldots, \left(\widetilde{S}_j, \widetilde{t}_j\right), \ldots, \left(\widetilde{S}_n, \widetilde{t}_n\right) \right\},$$

where

[3] Throughout the paper, we use the overwriting $\widetilde{\cdot}$ for indicating fuzzy numbers. Moreover, for notational convenience, thereafter we represent the crisp number t_0 in terms of the (degenerate) triangular fuzzy number $\widetilde{t}_0 = (t_0, t_0, t_0)$.

$S_0 > 0$ is the current cash amount/good/service value, which we represent by a crisp number;
$\widetilde{S}_1, \ldots \widetilde{S}_j, \ldots, \widetilde{S}_n$ are the future positive cash amount/good/service values, which we represent by positive triangular fuzzy number.[4]

Finally, let we assume the following time period frame associated to the interest rate structure:

$$(\tau_1, \tau_2], (\tau_2, \tau_3], \ldots, (\tau_{j-1}, \tau_j], \ldots, (\tau_n, \tau_{n+1}], \tag{2}$$

where
$\tau_1 = t_0$, $\tau_2 \in (t_{1,3}, t_{2,1}]$, ..., $\tau_j \in (t_{j-1,3}, t_{j,1}]$,..., $\tau_n \in (t_{n-1,3}, t_{n,1}]$, $\tau_{n+1} > t_{n,3}$ are the crisp time instants in which the interest rates can change.[5]

It is important to notice that, by construction, such time instants constitute a strictly-increasing sequence with respect to the deponent, that is that

$$\tau_1 < \tau_2 < \ldots < \tau_j < \ldots < \tau_n. \tag{3}$$

Of course, it is possible to choose more articulated time period frames than the one specified by (2) and (3). In case of such a choice, one should obtain a model which should be more difficult to algebraically treat than ours, but that at the while should not give significant improvements from the economic meaning standpoint. This is why we opt for the proposed time period frame.

Given this notation, we formulate as follows our FINe model:

$$FINe\left(\widetilde{\mathbf{A}}\right) = -S_0 + \sum_{j=1}^{n} \widetilde{S}_j \left(1 + \widehat{i}_j\right)^{-\left(\widetilde{t}_j - \tau_j\right)} \prod_{k=1}^{j-1} \left(1 + \widehat{i}_k\right)^{-(\tau_{k+1} - \tau_k)}, \tag{4}$$

where
$\widehat{i}_1, \ldots, \widehat{i}_j, \ldots, \widehat{i}_n$ are the current and the future positive interest rates, which we represent by positive interval numbers;[6] as known, the membership functions of this typology of numbers are

$$\mu_{\widehat{i}_j}(i) = \begin{cases} 0 \text{ if } i < i_{j,1} \\ 1 \text{ if } i_{j,1} \leq i \leq i_{j,2} \\ 0 \text{ if } i > i_{j,2} \end{cases}, \text{ with } j = 1, \ldots, n,$$

in which $i_{j,1}$ and $i_{j,2}$ are real numbers such that $i_{j,1} \leq i_{j,2}$ (a commonly used notation for this kind of numbers is $\widehat{i}_j = (i_{j,1}, i_{j,2})$).[7]

[4] A triangular fuzzy number $\widetilde{x} = (x_1, x_2, x_3)$ is defined positive if $x_1 > 0$.

[5] It is to notice that, in general, this (crisp) discrete-time frame differs from the (fuzzy) one associated to the investment project/contract.

[6] Throughout the paper, we use the overwriting $\widehat{\cdot}$ for indicating interval numbers.

[7] An interval number $\widehat{x} = (x_1, x_2)$ is defined positive if $x_1 > 0$.

2. Determination of the α–cuts for the FINe model

Once the NPV of $\widetilde{\mathbf{A}}$ is formulated in terms of fuzzy and interval numbers, we go on to the determination of the shape of this number. In order to carry out that, we have to determine the extremals of the α–cuts, with $\alpha \in [0,1]$, of (4), that is the *minimum* and the *maximum* of the sets:

$$X_{FINe\left(\widetilde{\mathbf{A}}\right),\alpha} = \left\{x : \mu_{FINe\left(\widetilde{\mathbf{A}}\right)}(x) \geq \alpha\right\},$$

that we respectively indicate by $FINe\left(\widetilde{\mathbf{A}}\right)(\alpha)_L$ and $FINe\left(\widetilde{\mathbf{A}}\right)(\alpha)_R$.

In their turn, $FINe\left(\widetilde{\mathbf{A}}\right)(\alpha)_L$ and $FINe\left(\widetilde{\mathbf{A}}\right)(\alpha)_R$ depend on the values the arguments of (4) take in their corresponding α–cuts. Therefore, in order to determine the extremals of $X_{FINe\left(\widetilde{\mathbf{A}}\right),\alpha}$ we have to cope with the following nonlinear optimization programming problems:

$$\begin{array}{ll} \min/\max\limits_{S_1,\ldots,S_n,i_1,\ldots,i_n,t_1,\ldots,t_n} & -S_0 + \sum_{j=1}^{n} S_j\left(1+i_j\right)^{-(t_j-\tau_j)} \prod_{k=1}^{j-1}\left(1+i_k\right)^{-(\tau_{k+1}-\tau_k)} \\ \text{s.t.} & \begin{cases} S_{j,L}(\alpha) \leq S_j \leq S_{j,R}(\alpha), \text{ with } j=1,\ldots,n, \\ i_{j,L}(\alpha) \leq i_j \leq i_{j,R}(\alpha), \text{ with } j=1,\ldots,n, \\ t_{j,L}(\alpha) \leq t_j \leq t_{j,R}(\alpha), \text{ with } j=1,\ldots,n, \end{cases} \end{array} ,(5)$$

where

$S_{j,L} = S_{j,1} + (S_{j,2} - S_{j,1})\,\alpha$ is the *minimum* of the α–cut of the triangular fuzzy number $\widetilde{S}_j$;

$S_{j,R} = S_{j,3} + (S_{j,3} - S_{j,2})\,\alpha$ is the *maximum* of the α–cut of the triangular fuzzy number $\widetilde{S}_j$;

$i_{j,L} = i_{j,1}$ is the *minimum* of the α–cut of the interval number $\widehat{i}_j$;

$i_{j,R} = i_{j,2}$ is the *maximum* of the α–cut of the interval number $\widehat{i}_j$;

$t_{j,L} = t_{j,1} + (t_{j,2} - t_{j,1})\,\alpha$ is the *minimum* of the α–cut of the triangular fuzzy number $\widetilde{t}_j$;

$t_{j,R} = t_{j,3} + (t_{j,3} - t_{j,2})\,\alpha$ is the *maximum* of the α–cut of the triangular fuzzy number $\widetilde{t}_j$.

It is important to notice that the *minimum* programming problem is related to the determination of $FINe\left(\widetilde{\mathbf{A}}\right)(\alpha)_L$, and that the *maximum* programming problem is related to the determination of $FINe\left(\widetilde{\mathbf{A}}\right)(\alpha)_R$.

After some calculations and some arrangements, the following partial derivatives of the target function (TF) of (5) with respect to S_j, i_j, and t_j are obtained:

$$\frac{\partial}{\partial S_j}\mathrm{TF} = \left(1+i_j\right)^{-(t_j-\tau_j)} \prod_{k=1}^{j-1}\left(1+i_k\right)^{-(\tau_{k+1}-\tau_k)}, \text{ with } j=1,\ldots,n;$$

$$\frac{\partial}{\partial i_j}\text{TF} = -\left(t_j - \tau_j\right)\left(1 + i_j\right)^{-(t_j - \tau_j - 1)} S_j \prod_{k=1}^{j-1}\left(1 + i_k\right)^{-(\tau_{k+1} - \tau_k)} -$$
$$-\left(\tau_{j+1} - \tau_j\right)\left(1 + i_j\right)^{-(\tau_{j+1} - \tau_j - 1)} \sum_{k=j+1}^{n} S_k\left(1 + i_k\right)^{-(t_k - \tau_k)} \cdot$$
$$\cdot \prod_{l=1, l\neq j}^{k-1}\left(1 + i_l\right)^{-(\tau_{l+1} - \tau_l)}, \text{ with } j = 1, \ldots, n;$$

$$\frac{\partial}{\partial t_j}\text{TF} = -\left(1 + i_j\right)^{-(t_j - \tau_j)} \ln\left(1 + i_j\right) S_j \prod_{k=1}^{j-1}\left(1 + i_k\right)^{-(\tau_{k+1} - \tau_k)}, \text{ with } j = 1, \ldots, n.$$

Given the positions (1), the results (3), and the positivity of the cash amount/good/service values and of the interest rates, it is easy to verify that $\frac{\partial}{\partial S_j}\text{TF} > 0$ for all j, that $\frac{\partial}{\partial i_j}\text{TF} < 0$ for all j, and that $\frac{\partial}{\partial t_j}\text{TF} < 0$ for all j.

At this point, given the strict monotony of the TF of (5) with respect to S_j, i_j and t_j, and given the latter results, for each $\alpha \in [0, 1]$ we can determine as follows the respective points of *optimum* of the programming problems (5):

Minimum **programming problem**	***Maximum*** **programming problem**
$S_{j,\min}^* = S_{j,L}(\alpha) =$ $= S_{j,1} + (S_{j,2} - S_{j,1})\,\alpha,$ with $j = 1, \ldots, n;$	$S_{j,\max}^* = S_{j,R}(\alpha) =$ $= S_{j,3} + (S_{j,3} - S_{j,2})\,\alpha,$ with $j = 1, \ldots, n;$
$i_{j,\min}^* = i_{j,R}(\alpha) = i_{j,2},$ with $j = 1, \ldots, n;$	$i_{j,\max}^* = i_{j,L}(\alpha) = i_{j,1},$ with $j = 1, \ldots, n;$
$t_{j,\min}^* = t_{j,R}(\alpha) =$ $= t_{j,3} + (t_{j,3} - t_{j,2})\,\alpha,$ with $j = 1, \ldots, n;$	$t_{j,\max}^* = t_{j,L}(\alpha) =$ $= t_{j,1} + (t_{j,2} - t_{j,1})\,\alpha,$ with $j = 1, \ldots, n;$

Of course, exploiting the usual extension principle (for details see [7]):

$$FINe\left(\widetilde{\mathbf{A}}\right)(\alpha)_L = -S_0 + \sum_{j=1}^{n} S_{j,\min}^*\left(1 + i_{j,\min}^*\right)^{-\left(t_{j,\min}^* - \tau_j\right)} \cdot$$
$$\cdot \prod_{k=1}^{j-1}\left(1 + i_{k,\min}^*\right)^{-(\tau_{k+1} - \tau_k)}$$

and

$$FINe\left(\widetilde{\mathbf{A}}\right)(\alpha)_L = -S_0 + \sum_{j=1}^{n} S_{j,\max}^*\left(1 + i_{j,\max}^*\right)^{-\left(t_{j,\max}^* - \tau_j\right)} \cdot$$
$$\cdot \prod_{k=1}^{j-1}\left(1 + i_{k,\max}^*\right)^{-(\tau_{k+1} - \tau_k)}.$$

It is to notice that, if $\alpha = 1$, then $S^*_{j,\min} = S^*_{j,\max} = S_{j,2}$, $i^*_{j,\min} = i_{j,1} < i^*_{j,\max} = i_{j,2}$ and $t^*_{j,\min} = t^*_{j,\max} = t_{j,2}$. So, the width of the 1–cut of $FINe\left(\widetilde{\mathbf{A}}\right)$ depends only on the extremals of the 1–cut of $\widehat{i}_j$.

3. About the buyer's utility function

As premised, in case (4) is the FINe of a contract like the one described in the introduction, the utility function of the buyer depends on the features of this FINe and negatively depends on the cost the buyer has to pay for reducing the widths of the α–cuts related to $\widetilde{S}_j$ and $\widetilde{t}_j$, that is for reducing the width of the α–cut related to $FINe\left(\widetilde{\mathbf{A}}\right)$. Recalling that all these quantities depend on α, in order to determine the optimal value of α itself which maximizes the buyer's utility, at first we have to detail such a function.

Coherently with the rationality of the generic economic operator, for each α we assume that the buyer's utility function positively depends on some return measure of the considered α–cut (that we indicated by $r(\alpha)$), negatively depends on some variability measure of the considered α–cut (that we indicated by $v(\alpha)$), and negatively depends on the cost $c(\alpha)$. In particular, for these quantities we propose the following specifications:

$$r(\alpha) = \frac{FINe\left(\widetilde{\mathbf{A}}\right)(\alpha)_L + FINe\left(\widetilde{\mathbf{A}}\right)(\alpha)_R}{2},$$

$$v(\alpha) = FINe\left(\widetilde{\mathbf{A}}\right)(\alpha)_R - FINe\left(\widetilde{\mathbf{A}}\right)(\alpha)_L$$

and

$$c(\alpha) = b\alpha \in [0, b], \text{ with } b > 0.$$

So, we can indicate the buyer's utility function as $U\left(r(\alpha), v(\alpha), c(\alpha)\right)$.

It is important to notice that $v(\alpha)$ and $c(\alpha)$ are, respectively, a strictly-decreasing function and a strictly-increasing function of the level α, whereas the monotony of $r(\alpha)$ depends of the shape of $FINe\left(\widetilde{\mathbf{A}}\right)$. In fact, it is easy to verify that $r(\alpha)$ is a strictly-decreasing/constant/strictly-increasing function of α according to the occurrence that $FINe\left(\widetilde{\mathbf{A}}\right)$ is a right-skewed/symmetric/left-skewed fuzzy interval number with respect to $r(1)$ (see figure 1).[8]

At this point, in order to determine the optimal value of α which maximizes the buyer's utility we have to deal with the following nonlinear programming problem:

[8] A fuzzy interval number $\widetilde{\widetilde{x}}$ is defined right-skewed/symmetric/left-skewed with respect to $r(1)$ if $r(\alpha) < / = / > r(1)$ for all $\alpha \in [0, 1)$.

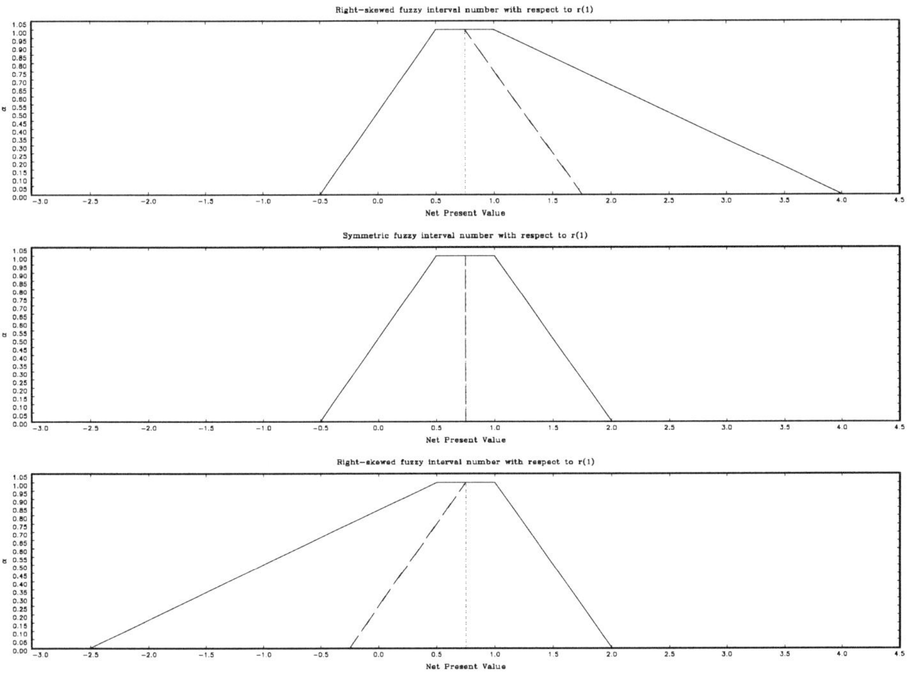

Figure 1. From up to down: a right-skewed/symmetric/left-skewed fuzzy interval number with respect to $r(1)$. In all the figures, the continuous line, the dashed line, and the dotted line represent, respectively, the shape of the considered fuzzy interval number, of its $r(\alpha)$, and of its $r(1)$.

$$\begin{aligned} &\max_{\alpha} U\left(r(\alpha), v(\alpha), c(\alpha)\right) \\ &\text{s.t. } 0 \leq \alpha \leq 1 \end{aligned} . \qquad (6)$$

It is to notice that, simply assuming the continuity of $U\left(r(\alpha), v(\alpha), c(\alpha)\right)$ with respect to α, the existence (but not the uniqueness) of the solution of (6) is ensured.

4. Some open items

Given to its youth, our approach leaves open interesting items that we intend to investigate in future researches. Among the ones we consider the most significant, we list the following:

- specifying some analytical/numerical procedure by which to determine the optimal value of the level α which maximizes the buyer's utility;
- extending our approach in order to be able to apply it, besides to investment projects/contracts, to whatever financial operation;
- given two, or more, fuzzy financial operations/contracts, specifying some methodology by which to order them on the basis of suitable comparisons of their respective FINe.

References

[1] I.E.G. Banholzer, A.L. Sanches, E.O. Pamplona and J.A.B. Montevechi, An interpretation for the internal rate of returns through fuzzy calculation, *Proceedings of the XII Congress of International Association for Fuzzy-Set Management and Economy* (2005), 33–51

[2] J.J. Buckley, The fuzzy mathematics of finance, *Fuzzy Sets and Systems* **21** (1987), 257–273.

[3] J.D. Cummins and R.A. Derrig, Fuzzy financial pricing of property-liability insurance [and Discussions and Authors' reply], *North American Actuarial Journal* **4** (1997) 21–44.

[4] A.O. Esogbue and W.E. II Hearnes, On replacement models via a fuzzy set theoretic framework, *IEEE Transaction on Systems, Man, and Cybernetics – Part C: Applications and Reviews* **28** (1998) 549–560.

[5] S. Giove, Funzioni ed equazioni a coefficienti fuzzy: un'applicazione al tasso interno di rendimento, *Rendiconti del Comitato per gli Studi Economici* **XXX/XXXI** (1993) 227–239 [into Italian].

[6] O. Houseman, A. Tiwari and R. Roy, A methodology for the selection of new technologies in the aviation industry, *Decision Engineering Report Series of the Cranfield University* (2004) i–iii and 1–36.

[7] A. Kaufmann, *Introduction to the Theory of Fuzzy Subsets. Volume I*, Academic Press, New York, NY, 1975.

[8] C.-T. Tsao, Assessing the probabilistic fuzzy net present value for a capital investment choice using fuzzy arithmetic, *Journal of the Chinese Institute of Industrial Engineers* **22** (2005) 106–118.

New Directions in Neural Networks
B. Apolloni et al. (Eds.)
IOS Press, 2009

doi:10.3233/978-1-58603-984-4-223

Interactive Visualization Tools for Meta-Clustering

Ida BIFULCO [a], Francesco IORIO [a,b], Francesco NAPOLITANO [a], Giancarlo RAICONI [a] and Roberto TAGLIAFERRI [a]

[a] *NeuRoNe Lab, DMI, University of Salerno, via Ponte don Melillo, 84084 Fisciano (SA), Italy*

[b] *Telethon Institute of Genetics and Medicine, Via P. Castellino, 111 80131, Naples, Italy*

Abstract. In this work we propose a scientific data exploration methodology and software environment that permits to obtain both data meta-clustering and interactive visualizations. Our approach is based on an elaboration pipeline, including data reading, multiple clustering solution generation, meta clustering and consensus clustering. Each stage is supported by dedicated visualization and interaction tools. Involved techniques include a Price based global optimization algorithm able to build a set of solutions that are local minima of the K-means objective function; different consensus methods aimed to reduce the set of solutions; tools for the interactive hierarchical agglomeration of clusterings and for the exploration and visualization of the space of clustering solutions.

Keywords. Clusters analysis, meta-clustering, interactive visualizations, clustering consensus, clustering maps

Introduction

In the last years the research areas of Knowledge Discovery in Databases (KDD) and of Clustering were becoming of great importance for several fields of applied research from Astronomy to Bioinformatics, from text mining to image classification and many others.

Two main problems arise when dealing with clustering of multidimensional data: the former regards multiple different solutions, the latter concerns the visualization of the results, in terms of different ways of grouping high-D data.

The most used clustering algorithms start from a random or arbitrary initial configuration and then evolve to a local minimum of the objective function. In complex problems (in many real cases) there are several minima and more than one can explain in a convincing manner the data distribution. In this case, we need, at least, to run many times the algorithms to choose the more reasonable solutions. This is due to the intrinsic ill-posedness of clustering where the existence of a global solution cannot be assured and small perturbations of data due to the noise can lead to very different solutions. Some discussions about this point can be found in [15,1,17].

In such context, clustering becomes a Global Optimization (GO) problem. A GO algorithm aims at finding a global minimizer or its close approximation of a function $f : S \subset R^n \rightarrow R$. A point x^* is said to be a global minimizer of f if $f^* = f(x^*) \leq f(x); \forall x \in S$. However, in many applications the function of interest is multi-modal and possibly not differentiable and it is with this view in mind that the Controlled Random Search (CRS) algorithm [23] was initially developed. CRS is a Śdirect searchŠ technique and purely heuristic. It is a kind of contraction process where an initial sample of N points is iteratively contracted by replacing the worst point with a better point. The replacement point is either determined by a global or a local technique. The global technique is an iterative process in which a trial point, the ŚnewŠ point, is defined in terms of $n + 1$ points selected from the whole current sample of N points until a replacement point is found. Some CRS algorithms also apply genetic algorithms or a local technique where the replacement point is searched for near a subset of best points in the current sample [10,11]. We applied such technique to cluster analysis. We used a Price based GO algorithm to explore local minima of the K-means objective function, but, instead of sticking to the best found solution, we collected all the solutions corresponding to local minima.

At this point, the problem of analyzing many different solutions arises. One possible approach to this problem is to merge more solutions to obtain a new clustering: that is called Consensus Clustering [14,22,24,25,20]. Another approach consists in the process of clustering such solutions, namely Meta Clustering [12]. The problem is that both the approaches alone are not adequate to give the required information to the domain expert, because the consensus algorithm gives a unique solution which is "the most similar" to all the clusterings, while the meta clustering gives only subsets of solutions.

The idea developed here is to put the two approaches together in a visual interactive environment. In this work we present the architecture of the tool called Modular Interactive Dendrogram Analyzer (MIDA): in section 1 we introduce some simple definitions about meta clustering. In section 2 we illustrate the two consensus algorithms we integrate in our tools. In section 3 we show the visualization and interaction tools which support the exploration and visualization of the spaces of cluster patterns and clustering solutions. Finally, in sections 4 and 5 we show an application of the tool to real data and the conclusions, respectively.

1. Meta Clustering

When clustering complex datasets, the existence of a unique optimal solution is usually questionable. In such cases, the problem of extrapolating a small number of good different solutions becomes crucial. The first step towards this aim can be the generation of a number of solutions, that must be successively analyzed. Analysis of such solutions mainly consists in grouping together the similar ones, that is in turn a clustering problem. This process is called Meta Clustering [12]. The subset of clusterings can be evaluated by the domain expert or by quality indices. Following in part the approach of [12], we divide the meta clustering process into 4 steps:

1. Generate many good different base-level clusterings (in our case local minima of the objective function generated by global optimization techniques)[8].
2. Measure the similarity between each couple of base clusterings.

3. Exploit the computed similarities to build a dendrogram (in our case with complete linkage method) and an MDS Euclidean embedding of the clustering solutions.
4. Use consensus algorithms to obtain a single solution from each meta-cluster.

Quality measures for the aggregations are used to decide the threshold of mergeability of the clusterings.

The use of interactive tools derived from our previous work ([21,13]) permits to give the user the information he needs to make decisions on the best meta clustering solutions.

2. Consensus Clustering

Consensus clustering, also known in literature as clustering ensembles and clustering aggregation, is the process of extrapolating a single clustering solution from a collection, in such a way to maximize a measure of agreement. This problem is NP complete [3]. In [14] some methods are introduced for consensus proving a 3-approximation algorithm. On the other hand, in [5] is suggested that the complexity of approximation algorithms can be unjustified, given the comparable performances of heuristic approaches. The authors also indicate the combined use of unsampling techniques and approximation algorithms as the best compromise. In [22] three EM-like methods are illustrated showing comparable performance with other 11 algorithms. EM approach is also exploited in [24], but combining weak clusterings. In [25] consensus clustering was improved by adaptive weighted subsampling of data. A different approach is shown in [20], based on non-negative matrix factorization. In the following we shall consider two kinds of approach: the consensus method of [14], and a novel method that obtains a subpartition of data using the intersection between corresponding clusters belonging to all solutions that are included in a metacluster.

The first algorithm we use in this paper is the consensus "Balls Algorithm" proposed in [14] for the correlation clustering problem. It first computes the matrix of pairwise distances between patterns. Then, it builds a graph whose vertices are the tuples of the dataset, and the edges are weighted by the distances. Aim of the algorithm is to find a set of vertices that are close to each other and far from other vertices. Given such a set, it can be considered a cluster and removed from the graph. The algorithm proceeds with the rest of the vertices. The algorithm is defined with an input parameter α that guarantees a constant approximation ratio [7].

The second algorithm we propose [7] builds a consensus clustering from a set of candidate solutions (a clustering ensemble [8]) by 'intersection': the final solution keeps only the common points between related clusters of different clusterings. To achieve this target we must sort clustering ensemble using the same similarity measure and than sort each cluster of the new ordered clustering set. Finally, we can build a chain of the most similar clusters whose intersection gives the final solution.

3. Visualization tools

Different techniques can be exploited to produce low-dimensional approximations of high-dimensional data, like Multi Dimensional Scaling (MDS) or Principal Component

Analysis (PCA). MDS is an iterative technique that approximates pairwise dissimilarities between N-dimensional datasets into an M-dimensional space, with $M < N$. Any dissimilarity function can be exploited, including metric and non-metric. PCA can be exploited to project the N-dimensional data onto the first M eigenvectors of the corresponding correlation matrix. In both techniques, when $M < 4$, a visual approximation of the original data can be produced by using ordinary plotting tools.

3.1. MDS Visualization for clusterings

With the aim of further investigating the space of clusterings for a given dataset, we produce a meaningful visualization for it. Well known similarity functions between clusterings are found in literature, like Minkowski Index, Jaccard Coefficient, correlation and matching coefficients (all found in [4]). In our studies we used a measure based on the entropy of the confusion matrix between clustering solutions [9]. Given such a measure, the MDS technique can be exploited to represent each clustering as a point in the plane, with the distance between points representing the distance between the corresponding clusterings. Finally, adding the distortion value as the third coordinate for each point, we obtain a *clustering map* as that in Fig. 4.
Clustering maps allow to intuitively represent the spaces of clustering solutions for a given dataset, independently from the algorithm producing the clusterings. When a clustering map shows more than one region of good distortion value, we can think that there are more than one reasonable way of clusterings the data. Also other information is encoded in the clustering maps, like the distribution of the clusterings with respect to the distortion function, the stability of the clustering algorithm with respect to the data, and the ability of different algorithms to explore different regions of the space of clustering solutions.

3.2. Interactive dendrogram

Since the number of clusterings is variable, we adopt an interactive agglomerative technique, performed on the meta clusters obtained in the global optimization step. The result is a dendrogram in which each leaf is associated to a clustering. The related tool supports the similarity distance mentioned above, which can be computed directly between the clusterings. The dendrogram plotted by our tool allows an interactive analysis (see Fig. 1). In fact, a dashed line, representing the current threshold, is shown on it and the corresponding partitioning is made evident by the use of different colors for the leaves of the dendrogram belonging to different clusterings (see Fig. 2). The threshold can be directly dragged on the dendrogram while the colors corresponding to the new partitioning are updated in real time. Each subtree of the dendrogram is related to a meta cluster and to the corresponding consensus clustering obtained with one of the methods above illustrated. Also, all currently open visualizations are updated accordingly. Here we stress that our tool does this in real time, giving immediate feedback to the user about the clusterings he is taking into account. This technique can be applied to projected datasets in 2D or 3D. All the visualizations can be shown contemporarily together with the dendrogram and updated in real time while acting on its threshold. Our tool also allows to select sub-trees of the dendrogram and to trace back the involved data points simultaneously both on the other visualizations and in an exported file. Finally, in another window, some indicators of the consensus clustering are summarized, such as distortion value, number of clusters, number of points per cluster, number of points eliminated by the intersection method, the mean distance between the solution and the leaves of the subtree, and other information about the current solution, as in Fig. 2.

3.3. Visualization of prior knowledge

It often happens that some or all the objects of a dataset are known to belong to some classes. This information can be used in at least two ways, to validate a clustering result and to infer new knowledge. The validation of a clustering can be obtained comparing the prior knowledge and the knowledge obtained from the clustering itself. We note that this can give a confidence degree about the use of the same partitioning with data on which no prior knowledge is available. The prior knowledge can also be used to produce new knowledge inferred by the presence or absence of objects of a certain class in a certain cluster. Different hypotheses can be made depending on the relations between the prior knowledge and the features used to cluster the objects. Prior knowledge can be visually shown using different forms of points in the dataset belonging to different classes. This permits to visualize, in all the described visualization methods, distance and cluster information together with the prior knowledge. Our tool allows the use of different sets of prior knowledge information and it permits to easily switch from one set to another one.

4. Experimental results

In order to test the proposed procedures we applied them to the "wine dataset" from the UCI repository[1]. We started by running the optimization algorithm to find local minima obtaining 23 different solutions with $k = 4$. We built the hierarchical tree on the 23 solutions as shown in Fig.2, left, where leaves are labeled by numerals in ascending order of distortion value. The tree is built using the complete linkage method based on the similarity matrix as defined in [13]. We used different interconnected visualizations showing the hierarchical tree, where the user can select any subtree; the MDS Clustering Map visualization, that puts into evidence the solutions currently selected on the tree; the visualization of the consensus performed on the leaves of the selected subtree; finally, in another window, some indicators of the consensus clustering are summarized, such as distortion value, number of clusters, number of points per cluster, number of points eliminated by the intersection method, the mean distance between the leaves of the subtree, and other information about the current solution (Fig.1). Through interactive analysis, we found that the best 3-clusters solution that can be obtained with Global Optimization correctly classifies 172 patterns out of 178. Using 4 as the number of clusters, the accuracy of the base solutions reaches 173 out of 178 patterns. Such accuracy can be even improved by aggregating the right subtree of the dendrogram: in this case only 4 patterns are assigned to the wrong clusters, but 15 patterns are assigned to singleton clusters and must be rejected. In this way, we can choose between solutions with different accuracy and rejection values.

[1]see http://archive.ics.uci.edu/ml/

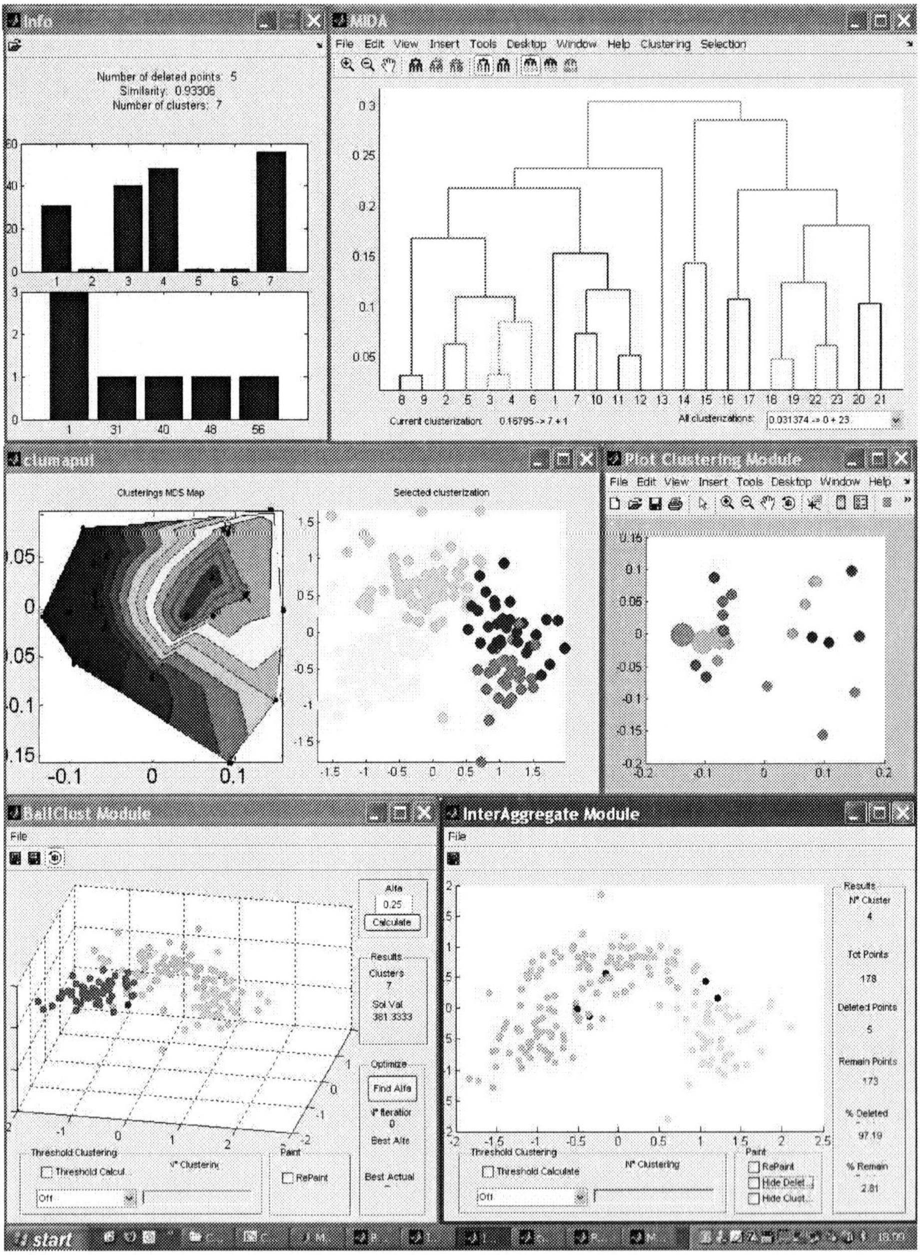

Figure 1. The Wine Data set as analyzed in MIDA. From left to right, top to bottom: Info Module (see Fig. 2, right); MIDA core, displaying the interactive dendrogram (see Fig. 2, left); Clustering Map module, showing the Clustering Map on the left part and currently selected clustering on the right part (see Fig. 4); Clustering Module, showing the current meta clusters as points with the same color; Ballclust and Interaggregate modules, showing the current consensus solutions with the Ballclust algorithm and the intersection method, respectively (see Fig. 3).

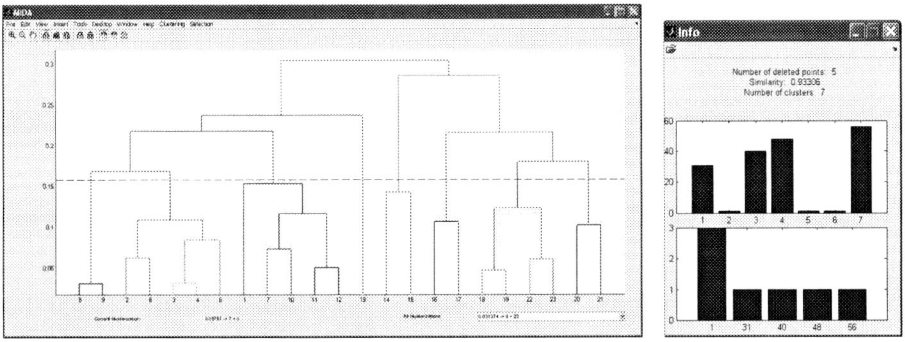

Figure 2. MIDA core and Info module. The MIDA core displays the interactive dendrogram, which is responsible of sending computation requests to the modules according to the current threshold and the selected subtree. Info Module shows quantitative information related to the current selected subtree, including fitness values, number of clusters derived from consensus, histograms of cluster size distribution.

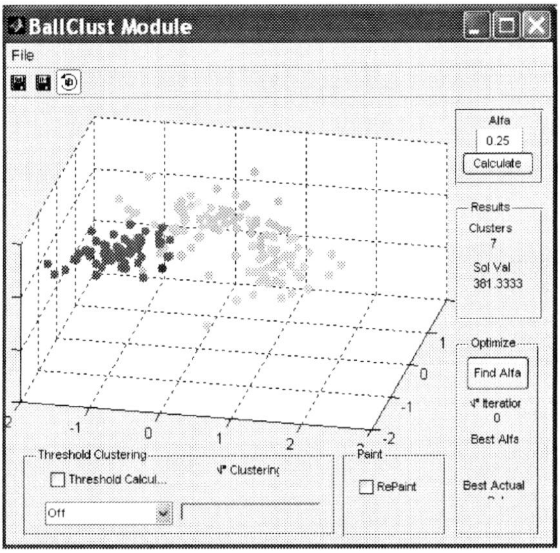

Figure 3. The Ballclust consensus module (that is visually equivalent to the intersection consensus module). The points displayed are a 3D MDS projection of the Wine dataset. Colors reflect the consensus solution obtained by applying Ballclust to the clusterings corresponding to the currently selected subtree on the dendrogram. The modules allow to perform a batch consensus on all the subtrees produced by the current dendrogram threshold, trying different parameter values for the consensus algorithm and interacting with points to highlight single clusters.

5. Conclusions

In this paper we showed how Meta Clustering can be exploited to extract groups of solutions (metaclusters) representing different ways to group data together; moreover, we can obtain a single solution from any metacluster using a consensus algorithm. We used two different approaches to consensus clustering: the first method, known in literature, builds a new clustering by minimizing a disagreement function, while the second one, introduced in this paper, produces a subpartition by cluster intersection. All our tools are

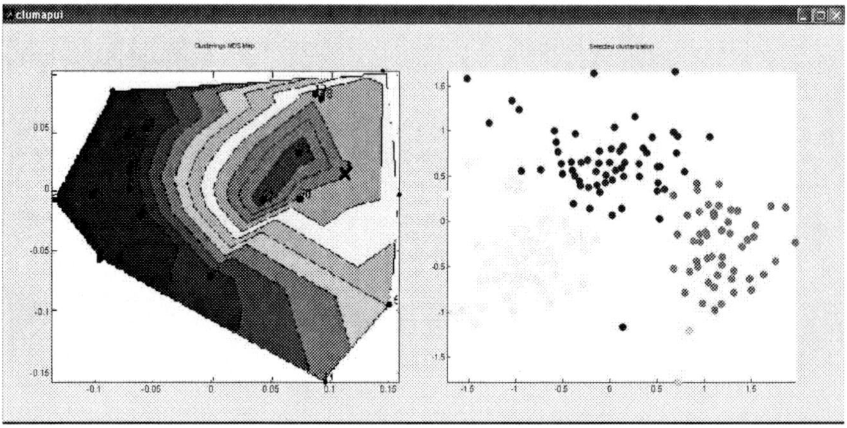

Figure 4. The MDS Clustering Map module, summarizing the 23 clustering solutions found for the Wine dataset. On the left, the solutions are represented as points on the plane, while the colors reflect the fitness value for each solution. The right figure displays the solution currently selected and shown as a cross on the map.

implemented in an interactive environment that simplifies the analysis of the results. Our future plans are to include the application of the most cited consensus algorithms and the quality criteria evaluation in our interactive visualization tool.

References

[1] Agarwal, P.K., and Mustafa, N.H.: k-means projective clustering. Proceedings of the Twenty-Third ACM SIGMOD-SIGACT-SIGART Symposium on Principles of Database Systems (2004) ACM Press, New York, NY, 155-165

[2] Amato, R., Ciaramella, A., Deniskina, N. et al.: A Multi-Step Approach to Time Series Analysis and Gene Expression Clustering. Bioinformatics. **22** (1995) 5 589-596

[3] Barthélemy, J.P., Leclerc, B.: The median procedure for partitions. In: I.J. Cox, P. Hansen, B. Julesz (Eds.), Partitioning Data Sets, American Mathematical Society, Providence, RI, 1995, 3-34

[4] Ben-Hur, A., Elisseeff, A., Guyon, I.: A stability based method for discovering structure in clustered data. Pacific Symposium on Biocomputing **7** (2002) 6-17

[5] Bertolacci, M., Wirth, A.: Are approximation algorithms for consensus clustering worthwhile? 7th SIAM International Conference on Data Mining (2007) 437Ű42

[6] Bertoni, A., Valentini, G.: Random projections for assessing gene expression cluster stability. Proceedings IEEE International Joint Conference on Neural Networks **1** (2005) 149-154

[7] Bifulco, I., Fedullo, C., Napolitano, F., Raiconi, G., and Tagliaferri, R.: Robust Clustering by Aggregation and Intersection Methods. Sub. to KES (2008)

[8] Bifulco, I., Murino, L., Napolitano, F., Raiconi, G., Tagliaferri, R.: Using Global Optimization to Explore Multiple Solutions of Clustering Problems. Sub. to KES (2008)

[9] Bishehsari, F., Mahdavinia, M., Malekzadeh, R., Mariani-Costantini, R., Miele, G., Napolitano, F., Raiconi, G., Tagliaferri, R., Verginelli, F.: PCA based feature selection applied to the analysis of the international variation in diet. Lecture Notes in Artificial Intelligence. **4578** (2007) 551-556.

[10] Brachetti, P., De Felice Ciccoli, M.,Di Pillo, G., Lucidi, S.:A new version of the Price's algorithm for global optimization. Journal of Global Optimization. **10** (1997) 165-184

[11] Bresco, M., Raiconi, G., Barone, F., De Rosa, R., Milano, L.: Genetic approach helps to speed classical Price algorithm for global optimization. Soft Computing Journal. **9** (2005) 525-535

[12] Caruana, R., Elhawary, M., Nguyen, N. and Smith, C.: Meta Clustering. ICDM 2006 (2006) 107-118

[13] Ciaramella, A., Cocozza, S., Iorio, F., Miele, G., Napolitano, F., Pinelli, M., Raiconi, G., Tagliaferri, R.: Interactive data analysis and clustering of genomic data. Neural Networks **21** (2007) 368-378

[14] Gionis, A., Mannila, H., and Tsaparas, P.: Clustering aggregation. ACM Trans. Knowl. Discov. Data. **1** (2007) 1 article 4
[15] Hu, Y., and Hu, Y.P.: Global optimization in clustering using hyperbolic cross points. Pattern Recognition. **40** (2007) 6 1722-1733
[16] Jiang, D., Tang, C., and Zhang, A.: Cluster Analysis for Gene Expression Data: A Survey. IEEE Transactions on Knowledge and Data Engineering **16** (2004) 11 1370-1386
[17] Kaukoranta, T., Franti, P. and Nevalainen, O.: Reallocation of GLA codevectors for evading local minima. Electronics Letters. **32** (1996) 17 1563-1564
[18] Kerr, M.K., and Churchill, G.A.: Bootstrapping cluster analysis: Assessing the reliability of conclusions from microarray experiments. PNAS **98** (2001) 8961-8965
[19] Kuncheva, L.I., Vetrov, D.P.: Evaluation of Stability of k-Means Cluster Ensembles with Respect to Random Initialization. PAMI **28** (2006) 11 1798-1808
[20] Li, T., Ding, C., Jordan,M.I.: Solving Consensus and Semi-supervised Clustering Problems Using Nonnegative Matrix Factorization. ICDM 2007 (2007) 577-582
[21] Napolitano, F., Raiconi, G., Tagliaferri, R., Ciaramella, A., Staiano, A., Miele, A.: Clustering and visualization approaches for human cell cycle gene expression data analysis. International Journal Of Approximate Reasoning. **47** (2008) 1 70-84
[22] Nguyen, N., and Caruana, R.: Consensus Clustering. ICDM 2007 (2007) 607-612
[23] Price, W. L.: Global optimization by controlled random search.Journal of Optimization Theory and Applications **55** (1983) 333-348
[24] Topchy, A., Jain, A.K., Punch, W.: Clustering ensembles: models of consensus and weak partitions. IEEE Transactions on Pattern Analysis and Machine Intelligence **27** (2005) 12 1866- 1881
[25] Topchy,A., Minaei-Bidgoli, B., Jain, A.K., Punch, W.F.: Adaptive clustering ensembles. Pattern Recognition. Proceedings of the 17th International Conference on **1** (2004) 272-275
[26] Valentini, G., Ruffino, F.: Characterization Of Lung Tumor Subtypes Through Gene Expression Cluster Validity Assessment. RAIRO-Inf. Theor. Appl. **40** (2006) 163-176
[27] Xui, R., Wunsch, D.: Survey of clustering algorithms. IEEE Transactions on Neural Networks **16** (2005) 3 645-678

Chapter 4

Remote Sensing Images Processing

New Directions in Neural Networks
B. Apolloni et al. (Eds.)
IOS Press, 2009

doi:10.3233/978-1-58603-984-4-235

Remote Sensing Imagery for Soil Characterization: a Wavelet Neural Data Fusion Approach

Matteo CACCIOLA [a,1], Francesco Carlo MORABITO [a] and Vincenzo BARRILE [a]
[a] *University "Mediterranea" of Reggio Calabria, DIMET*
Via Graziella Feo di Vito, 89100 Reggio Calabria, Italy

Abstract. Technological advances in remote sensing imagery allows to obtain high resolution images, helpful in soil characterizing, monitoring and predicting natural hazards. On the other hand, the different kind of in-service sensors allows inferences on a large frequency band. In spite of this, due to the increasing requirements of industrial and civil entities, the academic research is actually involved in improving the quality of imageries. The aim is to implement automatic tools able to work in real-time applications, above all in order to solve pattern identification problem in remote sensing. Within this framework, our work proposes a data fusion methodology, based on the Multiscale Kalman Filter, in order to improve soil characterization in Ikonos surveys.

Keywords. Image fusion, Multiscale Kalman Filtering, Soil characterization, Remote Sensing

Introduction

Nowadays, an automatic system able to identify the ground composition could be very useful for civil defence authorities as well as for economic and industrial aims, for instance in such frameworks as urban growth of developing countries: here, suburbs are usually composed by unauthorized buildings often constructed without considering the real characteristics of the territory. Moreover, a correct soil classification could improve the agricultural activities. A valid help can be brought by remote sensing, since images captured by airborne or satellite can be very descriptive of a relatively large geographical area or, on the contrary, can provide useful information of a restricted zone with very good resolutions, according to the exploited sensors. In this context, the cheapest information can be provided by images obtained from satellites operating into the visual or infrared spectra, but they do not allow to make such inferences above described. This kind of problem, in fact, can be considered as an inverse problem of pattern recognition, which has a definite place in remote sensing, particularly because of its effectiveness in geospatial analysis (see [1] and references within). Moreover, it can be definitely defined as an ill-posed problem, since different kinds of soils/areas can response in the same way

[1]Corresponding Author: Matteo Cacciola, University Mediterranea of Reggio Calabria, DIMET - Via Graziella Feo di Vito, 89100 Reggio Calabria, Italy; Email: matteo.cacciola@unirc.it.

within the visual frequency range of the electromagnetic spectrum. Usually, traditional pixel or object based classification techniques have more difficulties to deal with classes automatically extracted from very high resolution images. On the contrary, a solution can be approached by a joint use of RGB and infrared images in a sort of data fusion methodology, and exploiting Soft Computing techniques such as Neural Networks to well-pose the problem of land characterization. The new advances in Soft Computing, in fact, make these techniques very reliable for such applications, with the advantage of implementing a real-time classifier able to detect peculiar characteristics of a particular area (please, see [2,3] and references within). Our proposed approach started from IKONOS images and is divided in two steps. The first one is based on a data fusion approach, exploiting the Multiscale Kalman Filter (MKF) on the red, green, blue and near-infrared IKONOS images, in order to obtain an image with a higher resolution than the starting images. The latter step is the proper classification procedure, starting from the data fusion's useful output. In this case, features for discriminating the various kinds of soil have been extracted from the obtained quality-increased image by means of the Wavelet Transform (WT) [4,5]. Finally, a Multi-Layer Perceptron Artificial Neural Network (MLPANN) [6,7,8] has been suitably trained and tested in order to automatically detect each kind of area. During the whole procedure, great care has been paid to reduce as much as possible the number of selected features used as MLPANN inputs, in order to overcome the classical problem of "curse of dimensionality", i.e. the increase of system complexity without remarkable advantages in terms of classification performances, due to an excessive number of training inputs. In this way, a fast and robust system can be implemented for a real-time help to the authorities in land monitoring.

1. Image Quality Enhancing by Fusion Approaches

Data fusion [9] can be defined as the synergistic use of knowledge from different sources to assist in the overall understanding of a phenomenon: data fusion algorithms can be broadly classified as either phenomenological or non-phenomenological. Phenomenological algorithms utilize a knowledge of the underlying physical processes as a basis for deriving the procedure for fusing data. Non-phenomenological approaches, in contrast, tend to ignore the physical process and attempt to fuse information using the statistics associated with individual segments of data. Research on the subject of data fusion aims to obtain more comprehensive information about the system analyzed by using the strategy of combining information from multiple sensors. Particularly for the image sensor, the recent advances in this field make possible to combine information across the electromagnetic spectrum by the fusion of multi-modal images, i.e. by the so called image fusion. The general procedure for image fusion is depicted in Fig. 1 [12]. A lot of different algorithms exploiting well known image fusion techniques are available in scientific literature (see [9,10,11,12] and references within). The most known image fusion algorithms are based on Optimal Filtering (OF), Multi-Resolution Analysis (MRA), Bayesian inference, Dempster-Shafer Theory (DST), or even heuristic methods such as Artificial Neural Networks (ANN). Here, we introduce an innovative data fusion algorithms, i.e. the exploited MKF.

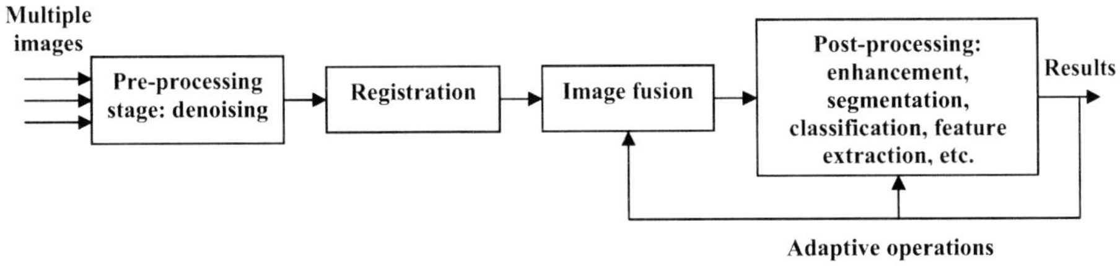

Figure 1. Block schema of the general image fusion procedure.

1.1. The MKF: merging multiple images at different scales

The MKF technique belongs to the realm of multiresolution stochastic processes [13, 14], where one-dimensional time series or multidimensional images have a time-like variable, commonly referred to as scale. Therefore, the MKF algorithm merges data at different resolution scales. Loosely speaking, an image (2D signal) can be decomposed from the coarse to the fine resolution. At the coarsest resolution, the signal will consist of a single value. At the next resolution, there are $q = 4$ values, and, in general, at the m-th resolution, we obtain q^m values. The values of the multiscale representation can be described on the index set (m, i, j), where m represents the resolution and (i, j) the location index. In order to describe the model [15], an abstract index λ is used to specify the nodes on the tree; $\gamma\lambda$ specifies the parent node of λ. The aim of Kalman filtering [16] is to estimate a state vector $x(t)$ of a dynamic process, when measurements $y(t)$ about the process evolution are available. In the case of the MKF, the independent variable is not the time t, but the scale λ; when signals are represented by images (i.e. 2D signals), the aim is to estimate a state vector $\mathbf{X}(\lambda)$, on the basis of observations $\mathbf{Y}(\lambda)$ of the process at different resolutions. This scheme proceeds in two steps: downward and upward. The multiple scale downward (coarse-to-fine resolution) model is given by:

$$\begin{aligned}\mathbf{X}(\lambda) &= \mathbf{A}(\lambda) \cdot \mathbf{X}(\gamma\lambda) + \mathbf{B}(\lambda) \cdot \mathbf{W}(\lambda) \\ \mathbf{Y}(\lambda) &= \mathbf{C}(\lambda) \cdot \mathbf{X}(\lambda) + \mathbf{V}(\lambda)\,.\end{aligned} \tag{1}$$

Since $\mathbf{X}(\gamma\lambda)$ represents the state at a resolution coarser than $\mathbf{X}(\lambda)$, $\mathbf{A}(\lambda) \cdot \mathbf{X}(\gamma\lambda)$ can be considered as a prediction term for the finer level; $\mathbf{B}(\lambda) \cdot \mathbf{W}(\lambda)$ is the new knowledge that we add from one scale to the next. $\mathbf{A}(\lambda)$ contains the cross-information coming from the input images at the different resolution, i.e. the different scales; $\mathbf{B}(\lambda)$ and $\mathbf{C}(\lambda)$ are initially set to eye matrices, and $\mathbf{V}(\lambda)$ is the set of the available images. The noisy measurements $\mathbf{Y}(\lambda)$ of the state $\mathbf{X}(\lambda)$, combined with the same $\mathbf{X}(\lambda)$, form the state estimation problem. The covariance matrices of the state and of the measurements are computed by the following equations:

$$\mathbf{P}_{\mathbf{X}}(\lambda) \equiv E\left[\mathbf{X}(\lambda) \cdot \mathbf{X}^T(\lambda)\right] \tag{2}$$

$$\mathbf{R}(\lambda) \equiv E\left[\mathbf{V}(\lambda) \cdot \mathbf{V}^T(\lambda)\right] = \left[\begin{pmatrix} \sigma_1^2 & 0 & \dots & 0 \\ 0 & \sigma_2^2 & \dots & 0 \\ \dots & \dots & \dots & \dots \\ 0 & \dots & 0 & \sigma_n^2 \end{pmatrix}\right] \tag{3}$$

where σ_1^2, $i = 1, 2, ..., n$ are the variances of the n available measurements, i.e. pixels, for the image at the scale λ. It can be proved that the state covariance can be computed by:

$$\mathbf{P_X}(\lambda) = \mathbf{A}(\lambda) \cdot \mathbf{P_X}(\gamma\lambda)\mathbf{A}^T(\lambda) + \mathbf{B}(\lambda) \cdot \mathbf{B}^T(\lambda) . \tag{4}$$

Equation (3) indicates that the measurements are independent and have different variances. Corresponding to the above downward model, the upward (fine-to-coarse resolution) model is [13]:

$$\begin{aligned} \mathbf{X}(\gamma\lambda) &= \mathbf{F}(\lambda) \cdot \mathbf{X}(\lambda) + \overline{\mathbf{W}}(\lambda) \\ \mathbf{F}(\lambda) &= \mathbf{P_X}(\gamma\lambda) \cdot \mathbf{A}^T(\lambda) \cdot \mathbf{P_X}^{-1}(\lambda) . \end{aligned} \tag{5}$$

$\overline{\mathbf{W}}(\lambda)$ is an uncorrelated sequence with variance:

$$\mathbf{Q}(\lambda) \equiv E\left[\overline{\mathbf{W}}(\lambda) \cdot \overline{\mathbf{W}}^T(\lambda)\right] = \mathbf{P_X}(\gamma\lambda) \cdot \left[\mathbf{I} - \mathbf{A}^T(\lambda) \cdot \mathbf{P_X}^{-1}(\lambda) \cdot \mathbf{A}(\lambda) \cdot \mathbf{P_X}(\gamma\lambda)\right] . \tag{6}$$

We assume that each node has q children. We denote by $\alpha_i\lambda$, the i-th child node of λ for $i = 1, ..., q$. Also define: $\hat{\mathbf{X}}(\lambda|\alpha_i\lambda)$ as the predicted value of $\mathbf{X}(\lambda)$ using the estimation of child node α_i ($i = 1, ..., q$) of λ; $\hat{\mathbf{X}}(\lambda|\lambda-)$ as the predicted value of $\mathbf{X}(\lambda)$ after merging the predictions of the q child nodes of λ; $\hat{\mathbf{X}}(\lambda|\lambda+)$ as the updated value of $\mathbf{X}(\lambda)$ using $\hat{\mathbf{X}}(\lambda|\lambda-)$ and the measurement $\mathbf{Y}(\lambda)$; $\hat{\mathbf{X}}(\lambda)$ as the estimated value of $\mathbf{X}(\lambda)$ after smoothing during the downward step. The error co-variance matrices $\hat{\mathbf{P}}(\lambda|\alpha_i\lambda)$, $\hat{\mathbf{P}}(\lambda|\lambda-)$, $\hat{\mathbf{P}}(\lambda|\lambda+)$ and $\hat{\mathbf{P}}(\lambda)$ are similarly defined. Thus, the estimation by the MKF proceeds along the following steps:

1. Initialization: assign the following prior values at λ corresponding to the finest scale node

$$\hat{\mathbf{X}}(\lambda|\lambda-) = 0; \; \hat{\mathbf{P}}(\lambda|\lambda-) = \mathbf{P_X}(\lambda) \tag{7}$$

where $\mathbf{P_X}(\lambda)$ is the prior error variance, i.e., solution of (4), at the node λ.

2. Upward step: to estimate the state and the error co-variance matrices, we can combine the available measurements and the predicted values $\hat{\mathbf{X}}(\lambda|\lambda-)$, by the following equations:

$$\hat{\mathbf{X}}(\lambda|\lambda+) = \hat{\mathbf{X}}(\lambda|\lambda-) + \mathbf{K}(\lambda) \cdot \left[\mathbf{Y}(\lambda) - \mathbf{C}(\lambda) \cdot \hat{\mathbf{X}}(\lambda|\lambda-)\right] \tag{8}$$

$$\hat{\mathbf{P}}(\lambda|\lambda+) = [\mathbf{I} - \mathbf{K}(\lambda) \cdot \mathbf{C}(\lambda)] \cdot \hat{\mathbf{P}}(\lambda|\lambda-) \tag{9}$$

where the Kalman gain matrix $\mathbf{K}(\lambda)$ is given by $\mathbf{K}(\lambda) = \hat{\mathbf{P}}(\lambda|\lambda-) \cdot \mathbf{C}^T(\lambda) \cdot \left[\mathbf{C}(\lambda) \cdot \hat{\mathbf{P}}(\lambda|\lambda-) \cdot \mathbf{C}^T(\lambda) + \mathbf{R}(\lambda)\right]^{-1}$. Moving up to the parent node, we apply the Kalman filter prediction to get predictions from each child node by using:

$$\hat{\mathbf{X}}(\lambda|\alpha_i\lambda) = \mathbf{F}(\alpha_i\lambda) \cdot \hat{\mathbf{X}}(\alpha_i\lambda|\alpha_i\lambda+) , \tag{10}$$

where $\hat{\mathbf{X}}(\alpha_i\lambda|\alpha_i\lambda+)$ has been computed at the previous step. $\mathbf{F}(\alpha_i\lambda)$ is provided by the fine-to-coarse Equation (5). We are supposing to know $\mathbf{P_X}(\lambda)$ at each resolution by the Equation (4).

$$\hat{\mathbf{P}}(\lambda|\alpha_i\lambda) = \mathbf{F}(\alpha_i\lambda) \cdot \hat{\mathbf{P}}(\alpha_i\lambda|\alpha_i\lambda+) \cdot \mathbf{F}^T(\alpha_i\lambda) + \hat{\mathbf{Q}}(\alpha_i\lambda) \tag{11}$$

Table 1. Characteristics of IKONOS survey.

Channel	Bits/Pixel	Datum	Projection	Resolution	Dimensions
Pancromatic	11	WGS84	UTM 33 N	1 m	7964x7916 pixel
Red, Green, Blue and Near-Infrared	11	WGS84	UTM 33 N	4 m	1991x1979 pixel

where $\hat{\mathbf{P}}(\alpha_i\lambda|\alpha_i\lambda+)$ is related to the previous step, and $\hat{\mathbf{Q}}(\alpha_i\lambda) = \mathbf{A}^{-1}(\alpha_i\lambda) \cdot \mathbf{B}(\alpha_i\lambda) \cdot \mathbf{Q}(\alpha_i\lambda) \cdot \mathbf{B}^T(\alpha_i\lambda) \cdot \mathbf{A}^T(\alpha_i\lambda)$. For each node we obtain q predictions from each of the q child nodes. They are merged to obtain a single prediction using:

$$\hat{\mathbf{X}}(\lambda|\lambda-) = \hat{\mathbf{P}}(\lambda|\lambda-) \cdot \sum_{i=1}^{q} \hat{\mathbf{P}}^{-1}(\lambda|\alpha_i\lambda) \cdot \hat{\mathbf{X}}(\lambda|\alpha_i\lambda) \tag{12}$$

$$\hat{\mathbf{P}}(\lambda|\lambda-) = \left[(1-q) \cdot \hat{\mathbf{P}}_{\mathbf{X}}^{-1}(\lambda) + \sum_{i=1}^{q} \hat{\mathbf{P}}^{-1}(\lambda|\alpha_i\lambda)\right]^{-1} \tag{13}$$

The upward step terminates when the recursion reaches the root node and we obtain the estimation $\hat{\mathbf{X}}(0) = \hat{\mathbf{X}}(0|0+)$.

3. Downward step: the information is propagated downward after the upward step is completed. The estimators are:

$$\hat{\mathbf{X}}(\lambda) = \hat{\mathbf{X}}(\lambda|\lambda+) + \mathbf{J}(\lambda) \cdot \left[\hat{\mathbf{X}}(\gamma\lambda) - \hat{\mathbf{X}}(\gamma\lambda|\lambda+)\right] \tag{14}$$

$$\hat{\mathbf{P}}(\lambda) = \hat{\mathbf{P}}(\lambda|\lambda+) + \mathbf{J}(\lambda) \cdot \left[\hat{\mathbf{P}}(\gamma\lambda) - \hat{\mathbf{P}}(\gamma\lambda|\lambda+)\right] \cdot \mathbf{J}^T(\lambda) \tag{15}$$

where $\mathbf{J}(\lambda) = \mathbf{P}(\lambda|\lambda+) \cdot \mathbf{F}^T(\lambda)\hat{\mathbf{P}}^{-1}(\gamma\lambda|\lambda+)$.

2. Experimentations

Our experimentation has been based on IKONOS images taken on Bagnara Calabra (Calabria region, province of Reggio Calabria, into the South Italy, LON 15° 49' 0" E, LAT 38° 17' 0" N). The considered channels for the MKF are the red, green, blue and near-infrared channels. Characteristics of surveys are resumed into Table 1. Original images have a resolution of 1991x1979 pixels; they have been cut considering the area (508,5)x(1991,1206): in this way, the considered images have a resolution of 1483x1201 pixels. Fig. 2 draws the sources at the different bands. First of all, let us remark that the selected geographical area is highly affected by property speculation and unauthorized buildings. Thence, for instance, urban areas can be detected even among cultivations. In this way, the ill-posedness of the problem is highly increased, as well as the difficulty of classification procedure. Therefore, traditional pattern recognition models are not advised to be used in such kind of applications. Complementarily, a suitable and highly reliable data fusion technique could be very useful in order to enhance the characteristics of the different areas (i.e. classes) and reduce such kind of noise as speckle noise. These data are now considered as the input to the fusion algorithm [15]: the MKF merges data at different resolution scales. The model of the MKF has been applied by using a self-implemented Matlab® function, and results of the image fusion process are described

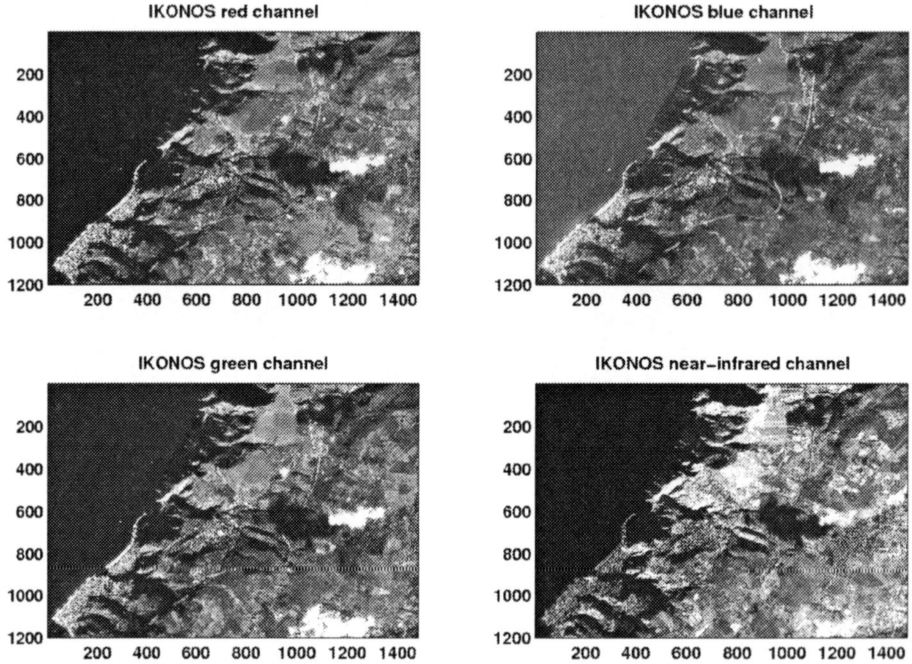

Figure 2. The IKONOS sources, i.e. the survey on the selected geographic site (Bagnara Calabra), split into the four working-channels: red (top-left), blue (top-right), green (bottom-left) and near-infrared (bottom-right).

Table 2. Pixel coordinates of the samples selected within the MKF's merged as well as the RGB superimposed images, and subsequently used for feature extraction procedure.

	Sample #1	Sample #2	Sample #3
Urban area	(831:894,284:347)	(922:985,192:255)	(1037:1100,76:139)
Mountain area	(825:888,976:1039)	(129:182,1191:1254)	(891:954,1286:1349)
Sea area	(135:198,868:951)	(339:402,805:868)	(664:727,1389:1452)
Cultivation area	(27:90,22:85)	(150:213,291:354)	(449:512,130:193)

by Fig. 3. Subsequently we use the full resolution image, i.e. the fused image at $m = 4$ resolution level for our experimentations. In this image we can distinguish four different areas: urban, mountain, sea and cultivation areas. A comparison between the fused data and the result of the superimposition of red, green and blue channels of the IKONOS survey can be carried out by computing the standard deviations of different samples related to these areas. Three samples for each areas have been considered: they are resumed by Table 2. The values of the standard deviation (STD) and the Squared Mahalanobis Distance (SMD) [17,18] for the grey scaled version of the superimposed RGB image and for the fused image at resolution $m = 4$, have been indicated in Tables 3-4. We can note that each sample in the fused image has a standard deviation lower than the corresponding sample of the input image. Therefore, in the fused image at full resolution, neighbourhood pixels corresponding to the same area, have an intensity level more similar; it means that the fusion process has been able to reduce the negative effects of the speckle noise. On the other hand, SMDs have been calculated as the distance between the four clusters representing the four classes (i.e. areas) and composed by the three correspond-

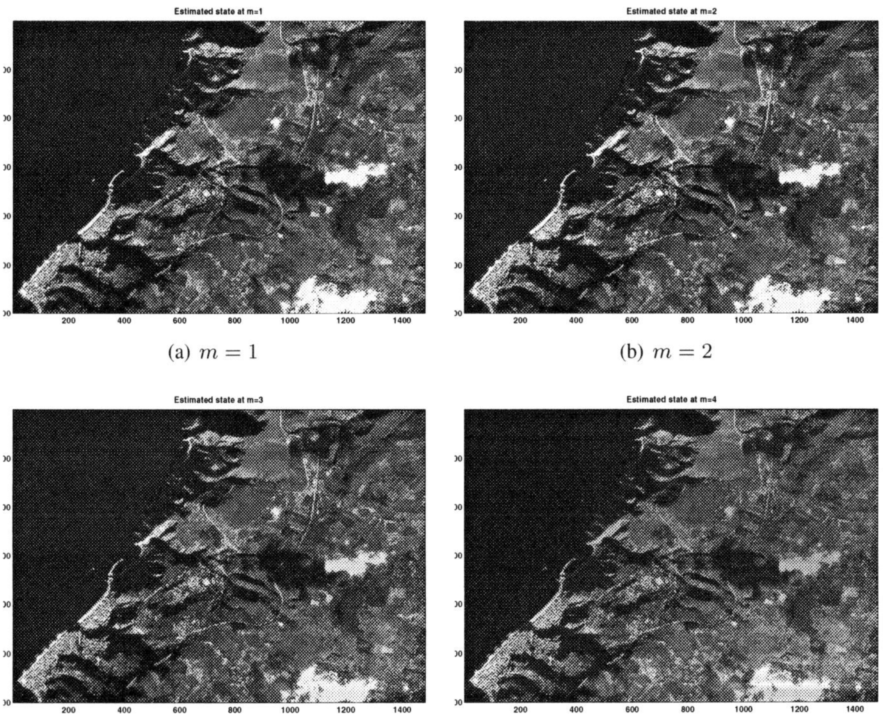

(a) $m = 1$ (b) $m = 2$

(c) $m = 3$ (d) $m = 4$

Figure 3. MKF's estimated state at the different merging resolution.

ing selected samples (i.e. boxplots). In this way, it is possible to give an information about the quality of the data fusion procedure: the bigger the distance between clusters, the easier the subsequent procedure of classification. Generally, the distances between clusters have been increased by using the MKF based data fusion approach, but in three cases, i.e. $SMD_{ua,ma}$, $SMD_{ua,ca}$ and $SMD_{ma,ca}$, they are still too small. It means a possible misclassification by using classical pattern recognition techniques. Therefore, it is strictly important to implement an expert system, able to identify as good as possible the different classes, starting from measurements enhanced by the data fusion approach.

2.1. Classification of similar areas by WT and MLPANN

Subsequently, we implemented the database useful for training the MLPANN. For each above described sample (boxplot), we apply the following procedure: (1) within the i-th boxplot we considered a 8x8 sliding window; (2) within the selected window, we apply the Daubechies 1 bidimensional WT, with a third-level multiresolution analysis; (3) we collected the wavelet approximation coefficients at level 1, 2 and 3 as features; (4) finally we moved the sliding window of 4 pixel in horizontal as well as in vertical sense inner the same boxplot. In this way, we collected 21 features and 2700 patterns useful to train a suitable MLPANN. The training procedure has been carried out by using the Levenberg-Marquardt regularization [19], and considering a neural network with two hidden layer, having 10 and 6 neurons respectively (only the log-sigmoid was used as

Table 3. Comparison of the STDs for samples taken by merged and superimposed images.

		Image merged by MKF at $m = 4$	**Gray scaled RGB superimposed image**
Urban area	sample #1	66.76	84.26
	sample #2	60.61	76.51
	sample #3	65.53	75.88
Mountain area	sample #1	27.02	27.32
	sample #2	23.46	24.85
	sample #3	16.89	19.28
Sea area	sample #1	2.49	4.10
	sample #2	2.57	4.27
	sample #3	2.44	3.60
Cultivation area	sample #1	10.90	18.14
	sample #2	6.36	9.24
	sample #3	26.91	35.02

Table 4. Comparison of the MDs for samples taken by merged and superimposed images.

		Image merged by MKF at $m = 4$	**Gray scaled RGB superimposed image**
$SMD_{ua,ma}$ (urban vs. mountain areas)	0.9	0.28	
$SMD_{ua,sa}$ (urban vs. sea areas)	6.04	4.13	
$SMD_{ua,ca}$ (urban vs. cultivation areas)	0.67	0.34	
$SMD_{ma,sa}$ (mountain vs. sea areas)	10.22	5.05	
$SMD_{ma,ca}$ (mountain vs. cultivation areas)	0.52	0.15	
$SMD_{sa,ca}$ (sea vs. cultivation areas)	23.83	14.56	

activation function). Subsequently, the highest-resolution image obtained by MKF data fusion as well as the grey scaled RGB superimposed image have been classified by the implemented MLPANN, by colouring areas according to their classification, with the following coding: white colour if the area is classified as sea; black colour if the area is classified as mountain; dark-grey colour if the area is classified as urban; light-grey colour if the area is classified as cultivation. Fig. 4 shows results of classifications.

3. Discussion about Results and Conclusions

Obtained quantitative results are resumed by the Table 5. The overall accuracy has been increased of, more or less, 23%, whereas the calculation elapsed time has been increased of, more or less, 10%. Let us remark how it is an interesting results, since the geographical area selected for the application of the proposed method is highly affected by property speculation and unauthorized buildings. The classification carried out by MLPANN by exploiting the wavelet approximation coefficients works better in the case of MKF's merged image than for the grey scaled RGB superimposed image. Moreover, the usage of the MKF allows to have neighbourhood pixels, corresponding to the same area, with

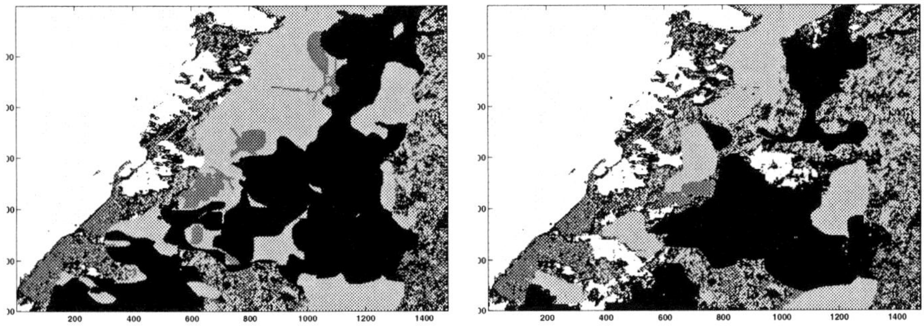

(a) MKF's merged image at resolution $m = 4$

(b) Gray scaled version of the RGB superimposed image

Figure 4. Results of pattern classification.

Table 5. Quantitative evaluation of obtained results: cross-comparison of overall accuracy and computational times for both MKF's merged and RGB superimposed images.

	Image merged by MKF at $m = 4$	**Gray scaled RGB superimposed image**
Overall accuracy	88.45%	72.67%
Computational time	42 s	38.2 s

an intensity level more similar, i.e. a significant reduction of the negative effects of the speckle noise. The usage of WT for feature extraction, on the other hand, gives us useful informative content of the inspected image by means of a restricted number of elements (i.e. wavelet approximation coefficient, containing the most percentage of information), so reducing the problem of "curse of dimensionality" in training the MLPANN. Let us denote how our proposed algorithm suffers of some mistakes next to areas in which such objects as clouds or cloud-shadows are present, or when the different classes are very mixed each other.

References

[1] G.F. Hepner, T. Cova, R. Forster, H. Miller, Use of remote sensing and geospatial analysis for transportation hazard assessment: an integrated university, government and private sector consortium, Proceedings of IEEE/ISPRS Joint Workshop on Remote Sensing and Data Fusion over Urban Areas, IEEE Press, New York, 2001, pp. 241–244.

[2] V. Barrile, M. Cacciola, M. Versaci, Fuzzy Classification with Minimal Entropy Models to Solve Pattern Recognition Problems: a Compared Evaluation in SAR Imagery, *WSEAS Transactions on Information Science and Applications* **3**(4) (2006), 860–867.

[3] G. Angiulli, V. Barrile, M. Cacciola, SAR Imagery Classification Using Multi-Class Support Vector Machines, *Journal of Electromagnetic Waves and Applications* **19**(14) (2005), 1865–1872.

[4] C.K. Chui, *An Introduction to Wavelets*, Academic Press, San Diego, 1992.

[5] A. Graps, An Introduction to Wavelets, *IEEE Comp. Science and Engineering* **2**(2) (1995), 50–61.

[6] S. Grossberg, *Studies of Mind and Brain*, Reidel Press, Dordrecht, The Netherlands, 1982.

[7] M. Caudill,*Neural Networks Primer*, Miller Freeman Publications, San Francisco, 1989.

[8] M. Caudill, C. Butler, *Understanding Neural Networks: Computer Explorations vols. 1 and 2*, MIT Press, Cambridge, MA, 1992.

[9] X.E. Gros, *NDT Data Fusion*, Arnold, New York, 1997.

[10] X.E. Gros, *Applications of NDT Data Fusion*, Kluwer Academic Publishers, Dordrecht, The Netherlands, 2000.

[11] R.S. Blum, Z. Liu, *Multi-Sensor Image Fusion and Its Applications*, In: R.S. Blum and Z. Liu (Eds.), Signal Processing and Communications, CRC Press, New York, 2005.

[12] Z. Liu, D.S. Forsyth, P. Ramuhalli, A. Fhar, *A Data Fusion Framework for Multiple Nondestructive Inspection Images*, In: C.H. Chen (Eds.), Ultrasonic and Advanced Methods for Nondestructive Testing and Material Characterization, World Scientific Publishing, New York, 2007.

[13] K.C. Chou, A.S. Willsky, A. Benveniste, Multiscale Recursive Estimation, Data Fusion, and Regularization, *IEEE Trans. On Automatic Control* **39**(3) (1994), 464–477.

[14] M. Basseville, A. Benveniste, K.C. Chou, S.A. Golden, R. Nikoukhah, A.S. Willsky, Modeling and Estimation of Multiresolution Stochastic Processes, *IEEE Trans. On Information Theory* **38**(2) (1992), 766–784.

[15] G. Simone, A. Farina, F.C. Morabito, S.B. Serpico, L. Bruzzone, Image fusion techniques for remote sensing applications, *Information Fusion* **3** (2002), 3–15.

[16] A. Farina, F.A. Studer, *Radar Data Processing*, Research Studies Press LTD, John Wiley & Sons, New York, 1984.

[17] P.C. Mahalanobis, On the generalised distance in statistics, Proceedings of the National Institute of Science of India, Calcutta, India, 1936, vol. 12, pp. 49–55.

[18] G.V.S Raju, W. Husheng, Sensor data fusion using Mahalanobis distance and single linkage algorithm, Proceedings of the IEEE International Conference on Humans, Information and Technology, IEEE Press, San Antonio, Texas, USA, 1994, vol. 3, pp. 2605–2610.

[19] M.T. Hagan, M. Menhaj, Training feed-forward networks with the Marquardt algorithm, *IEEE Transactions on Neural Networks* **5**(6) (1994), 989–993.

New Directions in Neural Networks
B. Apolloni et al. (Eds.)
IOS Press, 2009

doi:10.3233/978-1-58603-984-4-245

Application of Self Organizing Maps to multi-resolution and multi-spectral remote sensed images

Ferdinando GIACCO [a,1], Silvia SCARPETTA [a,b], Luca PUGLIESE [c], Maria MARINARO [a,b] and Christian THIEL [d]

[a] *Department of Physics, University of Salerno, Italy*
[b] *INFN and INFM CNISM, Salerno, Italy*
[c] *Institute for Advanced Scientific Studies, Vietri sul Mare, Italy*
[d] *Institute of Neural Information Processing, University of Ulm, Germany*

Abstract. In this paper we investigate the performance of the Kohonen's self organizing map (SOM) as a strategy for the analysis of multi-spectral and multi-resolution remote sensed images.

The paper faces the problem of data fusion, by extracting and combining multi-spectral and textural features. Moreover we address the problem of low-quantity and low-quality of labelled pixels in the training set, investigating a two-step strategy: in the first step (unsupervised training) we use a large unlabelled data set to train a SOM, in the second step a limited number of labelled data is used to assign each SOM node to one informative class. Self Organized Maps are shown to be effective way to discover the intrinsic structure of data.

When the SOM is used as a classifier, as here, a majority voting technique is usually used to associate nodes with informative classes. This procedure allows to obtain a SOM output grid which contains labelled and unlabelled nodes. Particularly in the framework of remote sensing, the unlabelled nodes may be important, since they are associated with new classes present in the image, or with the so-called mixed pixels, which represent an area on the ground composed of more then one land-cover class. Comparing the results of the proposed SOM-based strategy and the results of a supervised network such as SVM we show that the unlabelled nodes of the SOM are associated with high percentage to mixed pixels.

Keywords. Remote sensed images, Land-cover maps, Self-organizing maps, Support vector machines, Mixed pixels

Introduction

The dimensionality, the amount, and the heterogeneity of the remotely sensed data available today requires advanced and innovative techniques to extract information and thematic maps useful for environmental monitoring. In the last years innovative methods, not strictly statistical, have been proposed, and among them neural network strategies are

[1]Corresponding Author: Ferdinando Giacco, Department of Physics, University of Salerno, Via S. Allende, 84081 Baronissi (SA), Italy; E-mail: giacco@sa.infn.it.

very promising [1, 2, 3]. They are especially useful for multisource data, since the whole multiple source data set is usually very difficult to model by statistical methods. Neural Network based classification methods allow to include as input both spectral and spatial (texture and context) features. Textural information was found to improve noticeably the classification ability in many problems, when the spatial scale of the texture is proper [4].

This study focuses on cluster detection, visualization, and land-cover classification of multi-spectral multi-source remote sensed images with two different spatial resolution: an high resolution image registered by IKONOS sensor (4 meters/pixel) and low-medium resolution image registered by ASTER sensor (15 meters/pixel). For the image taken from ASTER we also have a manually generated label map (ground truth dataset) for comparison. The labels indicate different land cover types, as detailed in Chap. 1.

To exploit the high-resolution image, we extracted from the high-spatial resolution images some textural features, using the Gray-Level Co-occurrence Matrix [5] [6], and merged them with spectral information of the middle-spatial resolution image. As we will see below, the combination of spectral and spatial information is especially valuable for land-cover classification systems in the areas with complex landscapes.

To discover and visualize the intrinsic cluster structure of the data, and to see how the extracted features can be related to the land cover classes present in the image, we first apply the Kohonen's Self-Organizing Maps (SOM) with a bi-dimensional lattice, and then using a small number of labelled samples, we merge SOM output nodes into meaningful classes. The SOM play a fundamental role, giving the possibility to detect relationships within large amounts of input patterns and to preserve as well as possible the topology of the original space in a lower dimensional output space. Moreover, the SOM algorithm and other neural approaches are suitable for the incorporation of both spectral and non-spectral data into the classification procedure.

This semi-supervised classification strategy, has some advantages over supervised strategies, when, as in the case under consideration, the available labelled samples have low accuracy or may be non-exhaustive.

Indeed, sensing applications the number of available labelled training samples is not large, since gathering reliable prior information is often too expensive both in terms of economic costs and time.

Besides, concerning the quality of training data, there are many problems in remote sensing applications, from the problem of mixed pixels, to the problem of the correlation among training patterns taken from the same area, to the exhaustive definition of the classes. Non exhaustive definition of the classes present in the image may happen when there is not enough a priori information on the territory composition, and in such a case an unsupervised strategy such as SOM, which does not use any a priori information, may be useful to detect the new classes. Mixed pixels, which are often abundant, are pixels that comprised more then a single class. As a pixel is an arbitrary spatial unit, it may represent an area on the ground which comprises more than one discrete land cover class, for example water and pine wood. Alternatively, it may happen that the classes overlap gradually with many areas of mixed class compositions, particularly near imprecise boundaries.

In this paper we address these problems investigating a two-step semisupervised strategy, which makes use of unlabelled data to train a Self Organized Map, and uses a limited number of labelled data to associate the nodes to informative classes. When the SOM is used as a classifier, a majority voting technique is usually used to associate its nodes with informative classes. This technique, however, cannot guarantee that every node in the output layer will be labelled, and thus will produce unclassified pixels in the final map.

We focus on these unlabelled nodes, that is nodes of the SOM map with which none of the labelled pixels is associated to.

These unlabelled nodes come from the presence of mixed pixels or non-exhaustive class definition. Our approach associate pixels with a high degree of mixing with unlabelled SOM nodes. Pure pixels fall into other nodes. The distinction between pure and mixed pixels is carried out both visually and with the help of a SVM strategy.

The reminder of the paper is organized as follows: in Sect. 1 we describe the multi-resolution and multi-spectral images and the feature extraction process. From the high-resolution image, textural features are extracted and fused with spectral features provided by the lower-resolution image. In section 2 the SOM is applied, nodes are labelled with a majority vote criterion, and results are discussed. In sec 3 the relations between SOM unlabelled nodes and the rejected pixels of a SVM with rejection threshold is studied. In sec 4 conclusions are drown.

1. Dataset and Pre-Processing

Satellite multi-spectral data from ASTER (Advanced Spaceborne Thermal Emission and Reflection Radiometer) and Ikonos 2 are used for the experiments. We considered the first nine bands of the Aster data set (from November 2004), spanning from the visible (bands 1-3) to the short wave infrared spectral region (bands 6-9). All the bands were georeferenced for this study and resized to a resolution of 15 m/pixel.

To determine the spatial information we realized some textural measures (detailed in Chap. 1.1) working on Ikonos 2 images from January 2004. The spatial resolution of the data is 4 meters for the visible bands (blue, green, red, near-infrared) and 1 meter for the panchromatic band (grey-level image). In our work we resized also the visible band at 1 meter/pixel resolution.

Both Aster and Ikonos images acquired have been radiometrically and geometrically corrected, cross-calibrated and co-registered to allow multi-scale analysis.

The interested area is located in the southern part of the alluvial plain of Salerno gulf, in the southern part of Italy. The area is primarily an agricultural land (no mountains are situated in the region) with major crops including corn, soybeans, grain, tobacco and canning vegetables. The coastal zone is mostly occupied by pine wood and urbanization consist of urban fabric and other human artefacts, especially for farming practice.

For the Aster image we have a manually generated label map (labelled dataset) for comparison purposes. The labels indicate different land cover types. Seven classes are considered: vegetated agricultural fields, buildings, pine forest, urban green, sea-shore, not vegetated agricultural fields, and water. Among the total number of 236985 pixels, each with a spatial resolution of 15 m, 1657 are labelled. The SOM will be trained on the whole dataset, composed of 236985 vectors, each with 11 dimensions (9 Aster spectral bands and 2 textural features coming from IKONOS). In the second step, the SOM nodes are labelled with majority vote, using about $2/3$ of the labelled dataset. Specifically, we divide the labelled data set into a classification-set (1029 pixels), used to label the SOM

Table 1. The available set of labelled samples. The land cover classes are: Vegetated land (1), Built up area (2), Pine wood (3), Urban green (4), Greenhouse (5), Not vegetated land (6) and Water (7). Training set is used to label the nodes of the SOM with a majority vote strategy (see Section 3), while the test set is used to evaluate the percentage of correct classification and the confusion matrix (Figures. 1 and 2)

Class number	1	2	3	4	5	6	7	TOT
Labelled set	249	188	226	251	273	233	238	1657
Training set	145	90	162	159	166	144	163	1029
Test set	104	98	64	92	106	89	75	628

nodes, and a test-set (628 pixels) used to evaluate the percentage of correct classification of our strategy. The composition of the labelled set is shown in Table 1 table.

1.1. Feature Extraction

In order to exploit the information that are available in two kinds of images we extract textural features from Ikonos, and add it to spectral features obtained from Aster.

Different textural features extracted from Ikonos images were introduced, in addition to the Aster spectral data, to take account for spatial information. The textural features were computed on two different Ikonos data: the panchromatic band (a grey-level imagery of 1 meter per pixel resolution, sensitive to all visible radiation) and the band ratio between near-infrared and red (4 meters per pixel resolution, resized at 1 meter per pixel), widely used in remote sensing to eliminate various albedo effects.

The spectral features were obtained from the well known Grey-Level Co-occurrence Matrix (GLCM), widely used in land-cover mapping [7]. The Gray Level Co-occurrence Matrix is a standard technique for extracting texture characteristics: distance as well as directional relationships among grey levels are summarized in a GLCM, obtaining a measure of the probability of occurrence of two grey levels separated by a given distance in a given direction. GLCM has been used successfully in a variety of applications, including land-cover mapping, crop discrimination and forest studies [4].

A moving window of 15 x 15 Ikonos pixels has been used in the computation of GLCM matrix and variance, in order to add textural information on a window having the same dimension as one Aster pixel [8]. In the computation of the GLCM, data are typically scaled to some fairly modest range of integers, (for example 0-7 in this work, such that the GLCM is a 8 x 8 matrix). After the GLCM is generated for each direction (horizontal, vertical, left diagonal, and right diagonal), the statistical measures are extracted and then the four directions are averaged to remove directional effects; this last choice is due to the absence of preferred direction in the geometry of investigated land-cover classes. We extracted from the GLCM four different statistical measures: Energy, Contrast, Homogeneity and Correlation [9].

2. Application of Self-Organizing Maps

The Kohonen's Self-Organizing Maps (SOM, [10]) used in this work is trained iteratively with a sequential algorithm, the distance measure chosen is the Euclidean one, the lattice is bi-dimensional with a local hexagonal structure, the weight vectors are updated with a

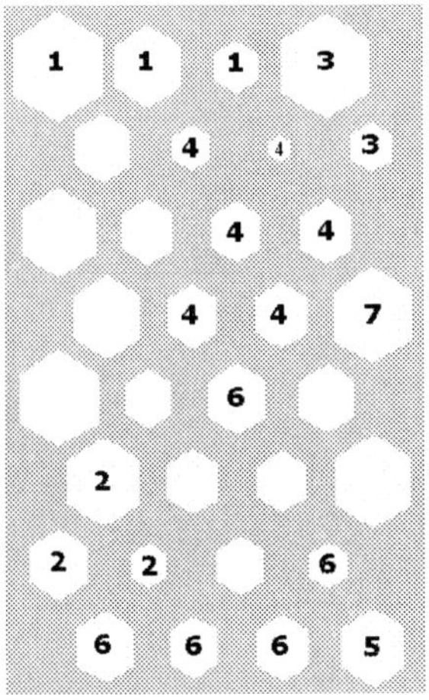

Network Confusion Matrix (Accuracy 78.5 %)

True (rows) / Predicted (columns)

100	0	3	1	0	0	0	0
0	21	0	7	9	45	0	16
0	0	64	0	0	0	0	0
1	0	22	68	0	7	0	4
0	0	0	0	106	0	0	0
0	6	0	0	7	69	0	7
0	0	0	0	0	0	75	0

Figure 1. On the left: SOM with only spectral features (9 Aster bands), without Ikonos information. Labelling of the SOM output nodes is based on a majority vote criterium looking at the training samples. On the right: confusion matrix resulting from labelled SOM. Columns, from left to right, corresponds to classes from 1 to 7, while the 8th column refers to pixels belonging to unlabelled nodes. As shown here, 4% of the test set, that is 27 pixels, are unclassified, since they belong unlabelled nodes.

gaussian neighborhood kernel, and the number of nodes is 32. All the setting parameters are empirically determined, we particularly have not found any critical dependence of the clustering procedure on the number of nodes, as well as on the lattice local structure.

The SOM algorithm achieves two important goals: (a) a clustering of the input data into nodes; and (b) a local spatial ordering of the map in the sense that the prototypes are ordered on the lattice such that similar inputs belong to topographically close nodes. Such an ordering of the data facilitates the understanding of data structures.

The first stage of the experiment was conducted with only the 9 Aster spectral bands as input for the SOM network. After the learning phase, an arrangement of the data on a 32-nodes output lattice is obtained. Looking a the distribution of the labelled classification subset into the SOM nodes, we found that pixels of different land-cover classes mostly falls in different nodes, and that some nodes are not associated to any of the labelled pixels of the classification subset. It means that the complete unlabelled dataset used to train the SOM contains also vectors whose characteristics are different from the ones of the seven land-cover classes. Such vectors are not present into the labelled dataset that we have used for the classification stage.

In the classification stage, we associate a label with those SOM nodes into which at least C labelled pixels fall. Association is accomplished using a majority vote technique. Setting threshold C equal to 3, there are 11 nodes of the lattice which cannot be associated with any label. To evaluate the classification performance, we compute the confusion matrix, on the test set, as shown in Figure 1. The confusion matrix is computed using 8 classes, the 7 land cover classes and the unlabelled-nodes class.

The percentage of correct classification achieved in this way is low, mainly because in this first experiment we used only the ASTER spectral bands, without exploiting the textural information extracted from Ikonos. The overall percentage of correct classification is 78.5% and the confusion matrix shows that main errors occurs for class 2 (built-up area) and class 4 (urban green).

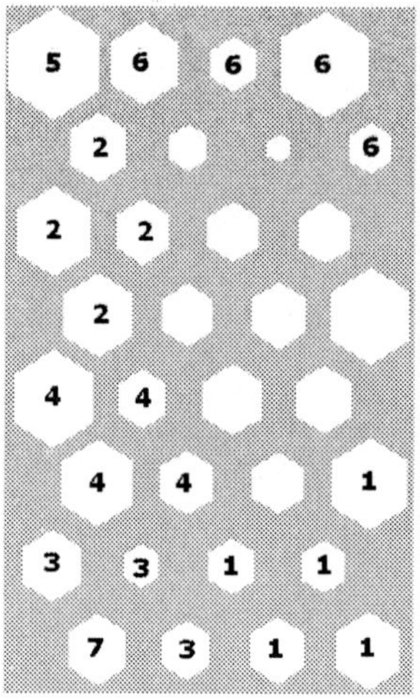

Network Confusion Matrix (Accuracy 92.04 %)

True / Predicted

102	0	0	0	0	0	0	2
0	72	0	8	11	5	0	2
0	0	64	0	0	0	0	0
3	1	6	75	0	0	0	7
0	0	0	0	105	1	0	0
0	1	0	0	2	86	0	0
0	0	1	0	0	0	74	0

Figure 2. On the left: SOM trained with textural information, extracted from the Ikonos bands,in addition to the spectral ones (9 Aster bands). On the right: confusion matrix resulting from the labelled SOM.

When the two-stage strategy described above is applied while adding textural information to the spectral one, and in addition merging information at different spatial scales, significant improvements are achieved.

Among all the possible textural features, we selected the ones who better discriminate among the classes with major overlap in the spectral SOM map [11]. Therefore, we looked for texture measures which were more able to discriminate class 2 (built-up area) and 4 (urban green) from the remaining classes.

Introducing these two new inputs, in addition to the 9 Aster spectral bands, the resulting SOM map is shown in Figure 2. As described in the previous section, we project the labelled training subset on the SOM lattice, and label the SOM nodes with a majority vote criterium (with C=3) as before. We see that the confusion matrix, computed on the test subset, is considerably improved (compare Figure 1), with an overall accuracy percentage of 92.04% on the test set. Among the 32 nodes, 10 are unlabelled, 6 of them are totally empty of labelled data and 4 of them contain less then C labelled pixels. The meaning of the unlabelled nodes is investigated in the next section.

3. SOM Unlabelled Nodes and Mixed Pixels

In this section we compare the two-stage strategy based on the SOM presented above, with the results of a SVM used as a reference. The goal is to better understand the SOM results and particularly to characterize the unlabelled nodes.

The baseline classification of the pixels was accomplished using Support Vector Machines (SVMs, introduced in [12]) with a linear kernel, and a weighting factor C for the slack variables of 0.1. Other than in previous ways [13] we employed the 1vs1-architecture, where a separate SVM is trained for each pair of classes. The distance-valued outputs of each of those machines were then converted into probabilities using a Fermi function, whose multiplicative variable was set to 2 uniformly for all machines. Finally, those pairwise probabilities were subjected to the iterative procedure of pairwise

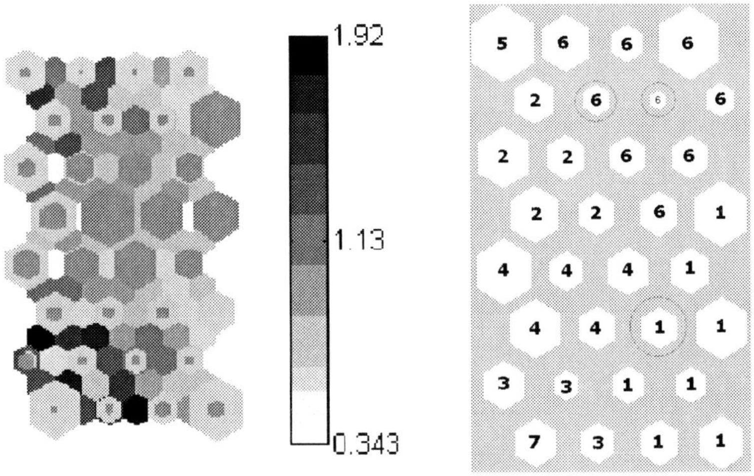

Figure 3. On the left: Distribution of pixels rejected by the SVM classifier, on the SOM lattice. The hexagons depicting the (red/green) SOM nodes are colour-coded (with grey levels, as given below) to represent the distance between the node centres. The size of the central (red) hexagons is directly related to the number of rejected pixels. On the right: SOM labelled lattice, where each SOM node is associated with one of the 7 land cover class, taking into account the SVM hard answers on the whole dataset (236985 pixels). The circles emphasize the unlabelled nodes of Figure 2 that, owing to the SVM analysis, could be assigned to one of the 7 pure land cover classes.

coupling according to the Bradley-Terry model [14], as suggested in [15]. This results in mixed answers for each pixel where the probabilities for each class are more distinguishable than with the initial estimation.

In the following we analyze the projection of the data onto the SOM lattice, using the output of the SVM as a fuzzy-label for pixels, where y_k^n represent the membership of pixel x^n to class k.

First of all, associating each pixel x^n with the class k which has the highest value of y_k^n, k = 1 ...l, we get a "hard" labelling. Evaluating the performance of the hard SVM classification, using the confusion matrix on the set set, we find that it provides a very high performance, with an overall accuracy of 95.4%.

However, not all pixels have a high value of membership towards a specific class as output of the SVM. Usually one can introduce a threshold T, such that each pixel x^n is assigned to the class k if the SVM output vector $y_k^n > T$ and $y_k^n > y_j^n$ holds for all j $\neq$ k. Indeed if we put such a rejection threshold on the SVM output, we see that, for example when T=0.3, a total of 0.14% of the pixels is rejected. Indeed in our images many pixels are mixed pixels, especially when a part of an artificial surface (or built-up area) is mixed with crops, and these mixed pixels than have low memberships in the 7 pure land cover classes. Figure 3 (left side) shows the distribution of rejected pixels on the SOM output grid, where the dimension of the central (red) hexagons is directly related to the total number of rejected pixels. By looking at the position of the big red hexagons in comparison to the white unlabelled nodes in Figure 2, we find a large correspondence: at least six of the unlabelled nodes (in the middle of the grid) have large quantity of SVM-rejected pixels (red hexagons).

Also shown in Figure 3 (right side) is the SOM lattice, where each SOM node is associated (using a majority vote criterion) to one of the 7 land cover classes, exploiting

Table 2. Results of the classification procedure on the whole dataset for the seven investigated classes described in the text. Each column represents the answers provided by the SOM labelled nodes plus the unlabelled ones (see Figure 2, while each row represents the SVM output for the same information classes plus the rejected pixels.

Class number	1	2	3	4	5	6	7	Unlabelled
1	36109	8	31	841	0	2195	0	15024
2	0	32211	0	4219	2140	35	0	2431
3	9	0	8105	181	0	0	504	0
4	2087	117	1583	26199	0	2310	6	11017
5	64	872	10	42	5128	1277	0	242
6	0	3810	4	35	1869	27635	0	22054
7	0	0	59	0	0	0	15294	0
Rejected	117	417	209	662	0	892	2	6422

the hard SVM labels on the whole dataset. One can see then, when forced to have an hard classification on each pixel, pixels with same SVM-class form compact clusters on the SOM lattice.

Considering the pixels belonging to the unlabelled nodes of Figure 2 (left) as unclassified pixels (class 8), we evaluate their distribution with respect to the pixels rejected by the SVM-classifier. Table 2 shows the confusion matrix between the answer provided by the SOM and the one provided by the SVM, evaluated on the whole unlabelled dataset. Columns, from left to right, corresponding to SOM information classes from 1 to 7, while the 8th column refers to the unlabelled nodes. Matrix of table 2 shows an agreement of 86% on the 7x7 information classes, and the 8th row shows that the 74% of the pixels rejected by the SVM (i.e. 6422 pixels) falls into the unlabelled nodes of the SOM.

However, in the 8th column there are high percentages of pixels of SVM-class 1, 4 and 6 assigned to the unlabelled nodes.

To understand this result one has to consider that the number of labelled pixels used in the classification of the SOM nodes is very small (see Table 1), thus some of the unlabelled nodes remain unlabelled due to the absence of sufficient labelled data of the corresponding cover class. This is confirmed by comparing the grid of Figure 3 with the one in Figure 2. It is evident that at least 3 nodes, circled in Figure 3, are unlabelled due to the lack of labelled training data.

4. Conclusions

This work focuses on the classification of satellite multi-spectral images starting from a limited number of labelled data through a two step semisupervised strategy based on the Self Organized Map algorithm. The unsupervised clustering provided by the SOM shows good capability to separate the 7 investigated land-cover classes on a two-dimensional output grid, where each node of the grid is labelled according to a majority vote technique. The resulting land cover map shows an overall accuracy of 92.05% with respect to a labelled test set.

Moreover, we investigate the meaning of the unlabelled nodes on the SOM grid exploiting the results of a Support Vector Machines with a rejection threshold.

According to our results, while some unlabelled nodes are related to the lack of sufficient number of labelled samples, the large part of the unlabelled nodes represent mixed pixels, that is pixels that have characteristic features of several land-cover classes.

References

[1] P. M. Mather. *Computer Processing of Remotely-Sensed Images*, Jonh Wiley and Sons, Chichester, 1999.

[2] T. Villmann , E. Merenyi and B. Hammer, Neural maps in remote sensing image analysis, *Neural Networks*, 16: 389-403, 2003.

[3] G. M. Foody, Status of land cover classification accuracy assessment, *Remote Sensing of Environment*, 80: 185-201, 2002.

[4] M. A. Shaban and O. Dikshit, Improvement of classification in urban areas by the use of textural features: the case study of Lucknow city, Uttar Pradesh, *International Journal of Remote Sensing*, 22: 565-593, 2001.

[5] S. E. Franklin and D.R. Peddle, Classification of SPOT HRV imagery and texture features, *International Journal of Remote Sensing*, 11: 551-556, 1990.

[6] P. Gong, D. J. Marceau and P. J. Horwarth, A comparison of spatial feature extraction algorithms for land-use classification with SPOT HRV data, *Remote Sensing of Environment*, 40: 137-151, 1992.

[7] R. M. Haralick, K. Shaunmugam and I. Dinstein, Textural features for image classification, *IEEE Transactions on Systems, Man and Cybernetics*, Vol 3, pages 610-621, 1973.

[8] D. J. Marceau, P. J. Howarth, J. M. Dubois and D.J. Gratton, Evaluation of the grey-level co-occurrence method for landcover classification using SPOT imagery, *IEEE Transactions on Geoscience and Remote Sensing*, Vol 28, pages 513-519, July, 1990.

[9] R. M. Haralick and L. G. Shapiro. *Computer and Robot Vision: Vol. 1*, Addison-Wesley, 1992.

[10] T. Kohonen. *Self-Organizing Maps. Series in Information Sciences*, Springer Verlag, 1997.

[11] F. Giacco, L. Pugliese, S. Scarpetta, and M. Marinaro: Application of Neural Unsupervised Methods to Environmental Factor Analysis of Multi-spectral Images with spatial information, *Proceedings of Signal Processing, Pattern Recognition, and Applications*, SPPRA, ACTA press, Zurich (2008)

[12] V. N. Vapnik, *The Nature of Statistical Learning Theory*, Springer, 1995.

[13] C. Thiel, S. Scherer and F. Schwenker, Fuzzy-Input Fuzzy-Output One-Against-All Support Vector Machines, *Proceedings of the 11th International Conference on Knowledge-Based and Intelligent Information Engineering Systems KES 2007*, 2007.

[14] A. R. Bradley and M. E. Terry, Rank Analysis of Incomplete Block Designs: The Method of Paired Comparisons, *Biometrika*, Vol 39, pages 324-345, 1952.

[15] T. Hastie and R. Tibshirani, Classification by Pairwise Coupling, *The Annals of Statistics*, Vol 26, Number 2, pages 451-471, 1998.

New Directions in Neural Networks
B. Apolloni et al. (Eds.)
IOS Press, 2009

doi:10.3233/978-1-58603-984-4-254

Comparison of Neural Classification Algorithms Applied to Land Cover Mapping

Christian Thiel [a,1], Ferdinando Giacco [b], Friedhelm Schwenker [a], and Günther Palm [a]

[a] *Institute of Neural Information Processing, University of Ulm, Germany*
[b] *Department of Physics, University of Salerno, Italy*

Abstract We compared the performance of several supervised classification algorithms on multi-source remotely sensed images. Apart from the Multi-Layer Perceptron, K-Nearest-Neighbour and Radial Basis Function network approaches, we looked more in detail at the Support Vector Machine classifier, which recently showed promising results in our setting. In particular, it is able to provide meaningful answers for the analysis of mixed pixels. They correspond to areas on the ground that comprise more than one distinct class, representing a major challenge for the interpretability of the final land-cover maps. To assess their impact, we performed a rejection-based analysis, allowing classifiers to refuse answers on pixels they can not associate mainly with one class.

The experimental results lead to the conclusion that the 1vs1 SVM approach with a linear kernel (using Bradley-Terry coupling) has to be preferred over all other classification algorithms examined, both in terms of accuracy as well as ease of visual interpretation.

Keywords. satellite, land cover mapping, classification, neural, support vector machine, svm, mixed pixels, rejection

1. Introduction

Recently, a new kind of algorithms to produce land cover mappings has caught the eye of the remote sensing community: Support Vector Machines [1,2]. These SVMs calculate distances between samples in a higher-dimensional so-called kernel space, and therefore have an advanced ability to discriminate between classes. Also, they are especially known to work with a limited number of training data, which is especially important in our context, since the labelling of ground pixels is expensive. To evaluate the usefullness of SVMs in land cover mapping, we compared their performance to a number of well-known supervised classification algorithms: Radial Basis Function Networks, Multi-Layer Perceptrons, and K-

[1]Corresponding Author: Christian Thiel, Institute of Neural Information Processing, University of Ulm, 89069 Ulm, Germany; E-mail: email@christianthiel.com

Nearest-Neighbour. Semisupervised [2,3] or unsupervised [4] approaches have not been taken into consideration.

A special focus of this work is to explore the behaviour of the approaches when presented with so-called mixed pixels. Those are areas on the ground which can not be subdivided into smaller parts due to main sensor resolution, but which comprise several different land cover classes. They are abundant in remote sensing applications and present a challenge because assigning them to one class in the map leads to misinterpretations [5]. Moreover, few classifiers are capable of producing correct mixed answers. Because an encompassing analysis of the nature of the mixed answers is not feasible, we performed a rejection-based study. That is, the algorithms were allowed to reject an increasing number of test pixels, related to the degree of mixing in the answer to each pixel. Looking at the resulting accuracy on the not-rejected test set, and the distribution of rejected pixels, we were able to draw conclusions on the suitability of the different classification algorithms. The most important result is the superiority of the 1vs1 linear SVM approach, when Bradley-Terry coupling is used instead of the usual simple voting.

2. Satellite Data

The area of interest is a coastal plain in the southern part of Italy, located in the alluvial plain of the Salerno Gulf. The area is densely inhabited for the fertility of the land since Greek-Roman times. Land use is primarily agricultural, but during the last sixty years an urbanisation phenomenon occurred, giving rise to a very indented and complex landscape. Consequently, the principal types of land covers are agricultural fields (both fallow fields and crop covered ones), rural fabrics (greenhouses), sea water, a coniferous wood strip along the coastline, and small urban areas made up of discontinuous fabric mixed with vegetation[2].

For this study, we take into account two types of multi-spectral satellite imagery [4]: one captured by the Advanced Spaceborne Thermal Emission and Reflection Radiometer (ASTER) on NASA's Terra satellite, and the other captured by IKONOS 2, a commercial earth observation satellite which offers high resolution imagery.

From the Aster data, we used an image taken in winter 2004. One scalar value was extracted for each of the nine bands chosen: going from the visible (bands 1-3, 15 m/pixel resolution) to the short wave infrared region (bands 6-9, 30 m/pixel resolution) of the electromagnetic spectrum. All data was resized to a resolution of 15 m/pixel.

Secondly, textural features extracted from Ikonos images were introduced. This was done in order to add intra-pixel spatial information to the Aster spectral data. Our textural characteristics are based on the well known Grey-Level Cooccurrence Matrix (GLCM), widely used in land-cover mapping [6]. The GLCMs were computed on two different Ikonos data sets: the panchromatic band (a black and white imagery of 1 m/pixel resolution, sensitive to all visible radiation) and the band ratio between near-infrared and red (4 m/pixel resolution, resized to

[2]For our study, we hence defined the following $l = 7$ classes: vegetated agricultural fields, buildings, pine forest, urban green, sea shore, not vegetated agricultural fields, and water.

1 m/pixel), which in remote sensing literature is considered as a reasonable way to avoid shadows. A moving window of 15x15 Ikonos pixels is used in the computation of the GLCM, since a window of such dimensions covers the same spatial area as one Aster pixel. Among the several statistical measures which can be extracted from the GLCM to describe specific textural characteristics of the image [7], we chose the following two: the Correlation function computed on the Ikonos panchromatic band and the Energy function computed on the Ikonos band ratio (see above). These particular choices for the statistical measures provide the best classification performances for our dataset.

Out of all the 236985 pixels, expert photointerpreters labelled two spatially separate sets of pixels with their correct land cover class, the training set containing 1029 pixels, the test set 629.

Summing up, our data vectors are made up of 11 components, the first 9 standing for the spectral information (taken from Aster bands) and the last 2 representing textural measures extracted from Ikonos images.

3. Rejection of Pixels

The supervised classifiers we consider take a training set T, consisting of pairs of training samples z in the feature space $\mathbb{R}^N$ with associated training labels y that detail to which of the l classes the sample belongs:

$$T = \{(z_\mu, y_\mu)|\ \mu = 1, \ldots, M,\ y_\mu \in \{1, \ldots, l\}\ \}$$

Being trained on the data set T, a classifier can now be presented with an hitherto unseen sample, and will output an answer $o \in [0,1]^l$, $\sum_{d=1}^{l} o_d = 1$, that reflects to what degree the classifier thinks the sample belongs to each class. This answer can be interpreted as a probability.

In a rejection setting, a classifier is allowed to reject a test sample presented to him, that is to refuse to take a decision about the class of the sample. In classical machine learning settings, this is done to increase the classification accuracy on the not-rejected samples. An answer which the classifier says he is not sure about, where this can be deducted from the structure of the answer [8], or where different classifiers disagree[9], is rejected. In a remote sensing context, there is a problem with so-called mixed pixels. For those, the classifier's output o is not predominantly in favour of one class, but gives probabilities to multiple ones. These pixels can not be marked as clearly belonging to a certain class. An example might be an area containing both buildings and vegetation. The goal is to detect and flag mixed pixels.

The rejection method we decided to use is based on the maximum probability entry of the answer o to a sample:

$$\texttt{reject if } (\max_d o_d < \mathit{threshold})$$

4. Classifiers

The goal of this article is to compare the performance of several supervised classification algorithms on satellite images. In the following, the classifiers we used will be presented briefly. For an in-depth introduction to each of the architectures, as well as their relations, please refer to [10].

The Multi Layer Perceptron (**MLP**, [11]) is a network of perceptrons, in our case with an input layer, a hidden layer, and an output layer which yields the mixed answer for each pixel, the probabilities. In the hidden layer with a total of 70 neurons the hyperbolic tangent sigmoid transfer function is applied, in the output layer a linear transfer function is used. Optimisation was accomplished using backpropagation [12] with a maximum of 20 epochs.

When presented with a test sample x the weighted K-Nearest-Neighbour algorithm (**KNN**, [13]) employed looks for the $K = 200$ nearest samples n_i in the training data, and answers with a weighted mean of their labels. The weighting function w is a Gaussian:

$$w_i(x) = exp\left(-\frac{\|x - n_i\|^2}{\sigma}\right)$$

The spread $\sigma > 0$ was set for each sample in relation to the median of all its K neighbour distances.

We also used the very powerful Radial Basis Function Network classifier (**RBF**, [14]), a network reconstructing the decision surfaces using Gaussian nodes. The number of kernels in the RBF network was set to 69 using a simple heuristic formula, their position determined by running a fuzzy c-means algorithm on the training data [15,16]. The individual variance of the kernels was set based on an an experimental observation of Breiman [17], which allows to have only one parameter to optimise for the whole net.

Support Vector Machines (**SVMs**) have become a popular method in pattern classification and were originally developed for the discrimination of two-class problems [18]. They work by projecting the data into a higher dimensional feature space using kernel functions, then finding the hyperplane that separates the two classes while providing the widest margin in which no sample points lie (see [19] or [10] for an introduction). The kernels we used are of linear nature, or again Radial Basis Functions. Being in a multi-class setting, we had to pay special attention to the possibilities of extending the originally binary SVMs. There has been quite some research activity in this field recently [20], and architectures like 1vs1 or 1vsAll are widely used nowadays (see [21] for a comparison). In a recent work of ours [22], we dealt with the issue of accepting, and more importantly producing, soft labels. Below, we will briefly present the solutions we decided to explore in the current application, and elaborate a bit on the 1vs1 case where no ready procedure existed.

In the current case, we have samples of $l = 7$ different classes in the data. The 1vsAll approach (also called One vs Rest) now builds l different SVMs, each of which is able to separate one specific class from all the others. Presented with a new sample x, each SVM_i will answer with the distance $d_i(x)$, $i = 1 \ldots l$, that this sample has to its hyperplane. To transfer this distances to soft output answers o_i

that can be interpreted as probabilities, we make use of a sigmoid function (*Fermi* like), as recommended in [23]:

$$o_i(\ d_i(x)\ ) = 1/(1 + \exp(-A_i^T d_i(x) + B_i)), \quad i = 1, \ldots, l$$

The parameters $A_i \in \mathbb{R}^N$ and $B_i \in \mathbb{R}$ are estimated for each SVM_i to minimise the mean squared error on the training data between the original label and the sigmoid output, using a batch gradient descent technique. Details can be found in our article [22] mentioned above.

The solution is not so straightforward in the 1vs1 approach. Here, a SVM_i is built for every pair of classifiers (resulting in $\binom{l}{2} = 21$ machines in our case). To get the desired l-dimensional soft output, the technique employed in most cases today, for example in [1], is as follows: using an indicator function, transform each of the answers d_i into a vote for one of the two classes distinguished by the current machine i. Then sum those votes per class, and normalise[3] the resulting soft label. This method does not have a bad performance, but some limitations (detailed in Section 5) as it does deliberately not take into account the distance information provided by the values d_i. To heal this issue, one can proceed similarly to the 1vsAll case and use a sigmoid, preferably with the same parameter for all pairs, to transfer the distances to soft answers, which can then be summed up and normalised.

But even then, the class-pair information provided by the SVM_i is not used. This can be addressed by the technique of pairwise coupling, based on the statistical Bradley-Terry model [24]. It uses initial estimations for the pairwise probabilities (derived via sigmoid from the distances d_i), and in an iterative process produces soft labels that take into account the coupled distance information. In our experiment, this results in answers with a much lower entropy than without coupling. An introduction to and many interesting theoretical conclusions on pairwise coupling in classification can be found in [25].

A short note on choosing the (universal) scaling parameter for the sigmoid transfer function in the 1vs1 SVMs: unfortunately, there is no perfect choice valid for all data sets. To really get those 2-3 percent points in accuracy increase, and ensure an appropriate hillyness of the coupled answers, the parameter has to be determined experimentally. In our case, 2 turned out to be the best choice. On the other hand, when looking at the rejection versus accuracy curves, the plots for different choices of this parameter were very similar.

5. Results

One aspect in the comparison of the different algorithms is to look at their accuracy on the spatially separate test set. That is, in the following we will concentrate on what portion of the pixels in the test data is correctly classified, allowing for first conclusions. The initial accuracies (that is, when no test sample points are rejected) of the different classifiers are shown in Table 1, and here the SVM based architectures clearly are to be preferred. As mentioned above, the

[3]With normalise we mean to make the values of each label to sum up to one.

Table 1. Accuracy of the different supervised learning algorithms studied, when no samples were allowed to be rejected.

Classifier	Initial Accuracy
RBF	0.88
MLP	0.90
KNN	0.92
SVM, 1vsAll, RBF	0.92
SVM, 1vsAll, Linear	0.93
SMV, 1vs1, coupled Fermis, RBF	0.91
SMV, 1vs1, coupled Fermis, Linear	0.95
SVM, 1vs1, coupled votes, RBF	0.93
SVM, 1vs1, coupled votes, Linear	0.95

goal of our experiments was to assess the behaviour of the classifiers once they were allowed to reject an (increasing) portion of the test samples. This is plotted in Figure 1 for all the classifiers. As the rejection rate is not a direct parameter of the algorithms, we simply raised the rejection threshold from 0 to 1 in steps of 0.01, and noted the respective rates. Looking at the upper graph, the SVM steadily provides the highest accuracy on the test set. The RBF has the worst initial performance, and also the slowest increase of accuracy. Interestingly, the relatively simple KNN algorithm has a good initial accuracy, and raises very fast, so that at a level of rejection of 15% it reaches the performance of the champion SVM. Hence, being much easier to implement, the KNN solution might be to preferred in some applications. Not shown in the graph, the first algorithm to reach a perfect accuracy of 1 is the MLP, at the price of rejecting 43% of the samples. The accuracies of the different SVM architectures and kernels, also plotted against a rising rejection rate, can be found in the lower part of Figure 1. The results do allow only a few conclusions: the 1vs1 architecture with coupled Fermis is the clear winner, always yielding the highest accuracy. And the approaches based on RBFs exhibit a similar behaviour for both the 1vs1 and 1vsAll architecture.

It must be stressed again that the performance of SVMs is highly dependent on selecting the appropriate kernel and its parameters for each data set. Without empirical proof, based solely on experience gained in a range of applications, it seems to us that when properly tuned, the 1vs1 architecture (with coupled Fermis) will always provide a higher accuracy then the 1vsAll scheme.

In 1vs1 SVMs, the single most common method is to use only the votes of the individual classifiers for coupling, but not the transformed distances. And as our results, and experiments in [25] show, the performance in terms of accuracy is nearly identical to the one achieved using coupled sigmoids. Yet, in the sample-rejection scenario, even using Bradley-Tery coupling, we observed a strange behaviour in the machines with coupled votes: the rejection rate would go from nearly 0 to around 80% at a certain threshold, which makes this architecture useless in this context. Examining the answers to the 628 test samples closer, we found that there are only 79 different variants of the vote matrix, leading to 77 different coupled answers, with only 13 different maxima. As ten of those

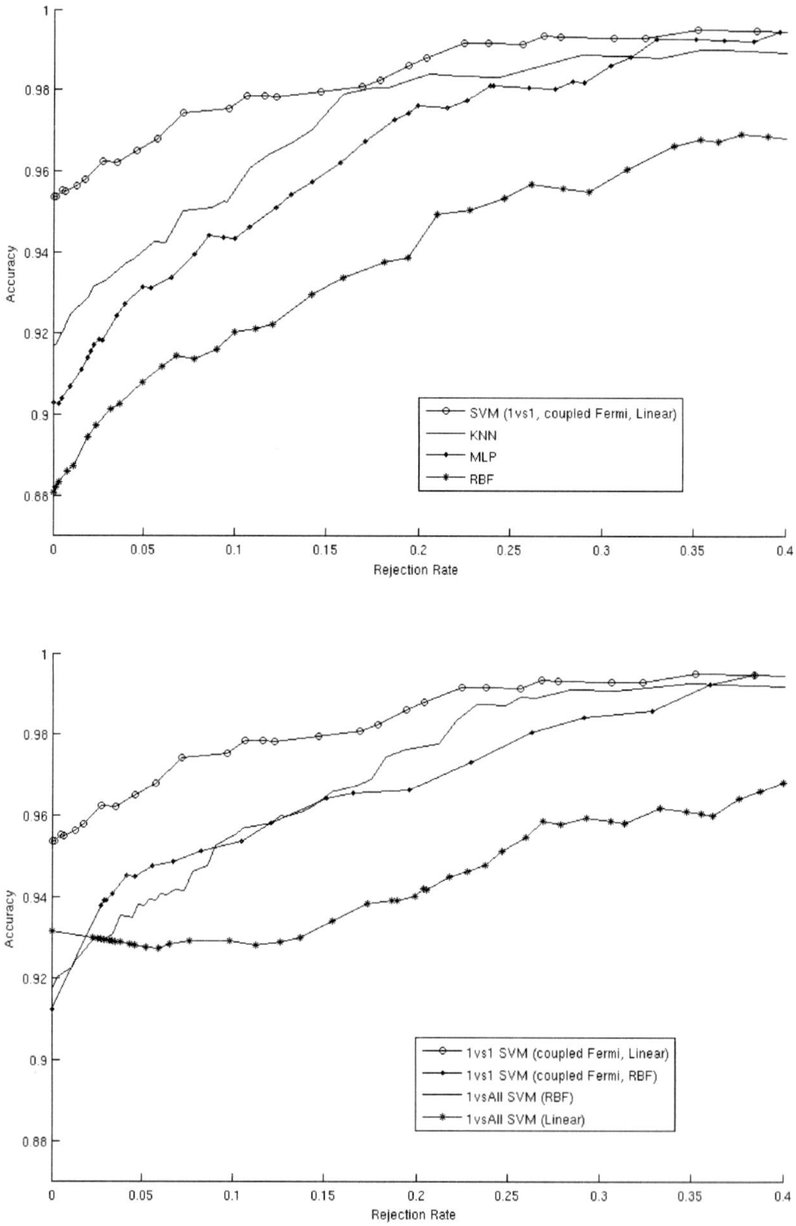

Figure 1. Accuracy of various supervised classifiers, at certain rates of rejection of test samples. The upper plot shows performances across several different architectures (including the best SVM), the lower one across different SVM approaches.

maxima even lie in the narrow range of [0.74 0.76], it is immediately clear that a smooth scaling of the tradeoff accuracy versus rejection rate is not possible. Whereas coupled transformed distances lead to completely individual answers, forcing the SVMs to answer in hard votes in the experiment limited the variance in the answers to a tiny fraction of the possible answer space. Hence, 1vs1 SVMs based on coupled votes should not be used for this purpose.

A visual analysis of the answers on the whole dataset essentially confirms the effectiveness of the 1vs1 SVM approach. The distribution of the rejected pixels is very sparse and indented for the RBF, MLP, KNN, and 1vsAll SVMs. Whereas with the 1vs1 SVMs, both using a linear and a RBF kernel, the rejected pixels are gathered in more compact regions. Using the RBF kernel, however, the 1vs1 SVMs, like the non-SVM classifiers, exhibit a clear overestimation of the urban green class.

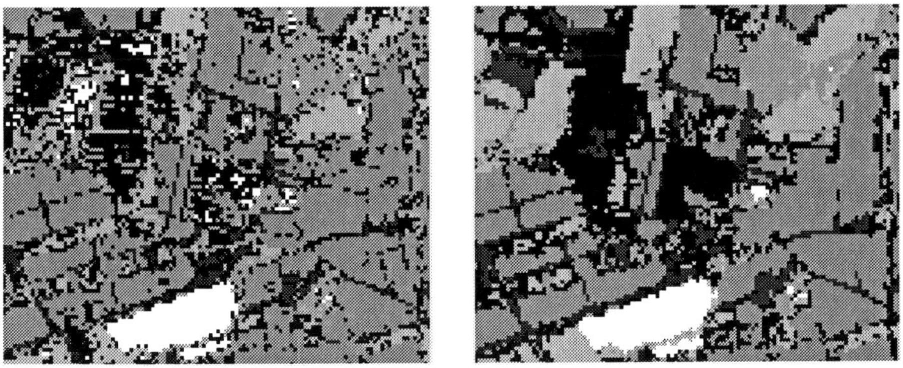

Figure 2. The figure shows a portion of the final map provided by the 1vsAll SVM (RBF kernel, left map), and the 1vs1 SVM (Linear kernel, right map). Black pixels are spread in a compact way with the 1vs1 architecture, enabling an easier interpretation in successive analysis. Note that this figure appears in colour in the electronic version of this article.

To allow the reader a visual comparison, the land cover mappings produced by a 1vs1 SVM and a 1vsAll SVM are depicted in Figure 2. The differences in the distribution of rejected (black) pixels mentioned above is clearly visible. Also, in the 1vsAll case, one can observe an overestimation of the greenhouses (white pixels on the map) to the detriment of not vegetated lands (brown pixels on the map), an error which we found, despite good overall accuracies on the test set, common to all the classifiers except for the 1vs1 SVM architecture.

6. Conclusions

In this work, we compared the capabilites of different supervised classification algorithms to produce meaningful land-cover mappings. Of special interest was the performance of the as yet little explored Support Vector Machine approach, as well as the behaviour of all classifiers when being presented with mixed pixels that contain several land-cover classes on the ground.

The results yielded insights into the comparative performance of different SVM architectures, leading us to the conclusion that the 1vs1 SVMs are to be preferred for best classification accuracies, but are also sensitive to the choice of kernel. The performance of SVM approaches using a RBF kernel is rather stable.

Overall, the best results are provided by the 1vs SVM with a linear kernel: it yields the highest accuracy on the test set, as well as a distribution of rejected pixels on the output map that is much more clear and interpretable than with all other approaches. Looking at the rejection behaviour, it is clear that the fuzzy answers in the 1vs1 architecture have to be produced using a sigmoid transfer function and Bradley-Terry coupling, instead of the usual votes.

For the non-SVM approaches, the relatively simple K-Nearest-Neighbour has the highest classification accuracy.

Our future research in this area will entail incorporating spectral and textural information from higher-resolution images to further improve the meaningfulness of mixed SVM answers, allowing for a richer presentation of the land-cover map.

References

[1] Gidudu, A., Hulley, G., Marwala, T.: Image classification using svms: One-against-one vs one-against-all. In: Proccedings of the 28th Asian Conference on Remote Sensing. (2007)

[2] Bruzzone, L., Marconcini, M.: An Advanced Semisupervised SVM Classifier for the Analysis of Hyperspectral Remote Sensing Data. In: Proceedings of the 12th SPIE International Symposium on Remote Sensing / Image and Signal Processing for Remote Sensing XII. Volume 6365., International Society for Optical Engineering (2006) 63650Y–1–6350Y–12

[3] Baraldi, A., Bruzzone, L., Blonda, P.: A multiscale expectation-maximization semisupervised classifier suitable for badly posed image classification. IEEE transactions on image processing **15**(8) (2006) 2208–2225

[4] Giacco, F., Pugliese, L., Scarpetta, S., Marinaro, M.: Application of Neural Unsupervised Methods to Environmental Factor Analysis of Multi-spectral Images with spatial information. In Sablatnig, R., Scherzer, O., eds.: Proceedings of Signal Processing, Pattern Recognition, and Applications, SPPRA, ACTA press, Zürich (2008)

[5] Xua, M., Watanachaturaporna, P., Varshneya, P.K., Arorab, M.K.: Decision tree regression for soft classification of remote sensing data. Remote Sensing of Environment **97**(13) (2005) 322–336

[6] Haralick, R.M., Shanmugam, K., Dinstein, I.: Textural Features for Image Classification. IEEE Transactions on Systems, Man, and Cybernetics **SMC-3**(6) (1973) 610–621

[7] Mather, P.M.: Computer Processing of Remotely-Sensed Images. Wiley (1999)

[8] Schürmann, J.: Pattern Classification, a unified view of statistical and neural approaches. John Wiley & Sons (1996)

[9] Thiel, C.: Using Dempster-Shafer Theory in MCF Systems to Reject Samples. In Oza, N.C., Polikar, R., Kittler, J., Roli, F., eds.: Proceedings of the 6th International Workshop on Multiple Classifier Systems, MCS 2005. Volume 3541 of Springer LNCS. (2005) 118–127

[10] Webb, A.R.: Statistical Pattern Recognition. second edn. John Wiley & Sons (2002)

[11] Hornik, K., Stinchcombe, M.B., White, H.: Multilayer feedforward networks are universal approximators. Neural Networks **2**(5) (1989) 359–366

[12] Rumelhart, D.E., Hinton, G.E., Williams, R.J.: Learning internal representations by error propagation. In Rumelhart, D., McClelland, J., eds.: Parallel distributed processing: explorations in the microstructure of cognition, vol. 1: foundations. Volume 1. MIT Press (1986) 318–362

[13] Therrien, C.W.: Decision estimation and classification: an introduction to pattern recognition and related topics. John Wiley & Sons (1989)

[14] Powell, M.J.D.: Radial basis functions for multivariate interpolation: A review. In Mason, J.C., Cox, M.G., eds.: Algorithms for Approximation. Clarendon Press, Oxford (1987) 143–168

[15] Schwenker, F., Kestler, H.A., Palm, G.: Three learning phases for radial-basis-function networks. Neural Networks **14** (2001) 439–458

[16] Moody, J., Darken, C.J.: Fast learning in networks of locally-tuned processing units. Neural Computation **1** (1989) 184–294

[17] Breiman, L., Meisel, W., Purcell, E.: Variable Kernel Estimates of Multivariate Densities. Technometrics **19**(2) (May 1977) 135–144

[18] Vapnik, V.N.: The Nature of Statistical Learning Theory. Springer (1995)

[19] Schölkopf, B., Smola, A.J.: Learning with Kernels: Support Vector Machines, Regularization, Optimization, and Beyond. MIT Press (2002)

[20] Angulo, C., Ruiz, F.J., González, L., Ortega, J.A.: Multi-Classification by using Tri-Class SVM. Neural Processing Letters **23** (February 2006) 89–101

[21] Kahsay, L., Schwenker, F., Palm, G.: Comparison of multiclass SVM decomposition schemes for visual object recognition. In: DAGM 2005. Volume 3663 of LNCS., Springer (2005) 334–341

[22] Thiel, C., Scherer, S., Schwenker, F.: Fuzzy-Input Fuzzy-Output One-Against-All Support Vector Machines. Proceedings of the 11th International Conference on Knowledge-Based and Intelligent Information & Engineering Systems KES 2007 **3** (2007) 156–165

[23] Platt, J.C.: Probabilistic Outputs for Support Vector Machines and Comparisons to Regularized Likelihood Methods. In: Advances in Large Margin Classifiers, NIPS 1998, MIT Press (1999) 61–74

[24] Bradley, A.R., Terry, M.E.: Rank Analysis of Incomplete Block Designs: I. The Method of Paired Comparisons. Biometrika **39**(3/4) (1952) 324–345

[25] Hastie, T., Tibshirani, R.: Classification by Pairwise Coupling. The Annals of Statistics **26**(2) (1998) 451–471

New Directions in Neural Networks
B. Apolloni et al. (Eds.)
IOS Press, 2009

Author Index

Apolloni, B.	v, 138
Arca, S.	148
Azzerboni, A.	50
Barrile, V.	235
Bassis, S.	v, 76, 138
Bertoni, A.	60, 148
Bifulco, I.	223
Borghese, N.A.	22
Cacciola, M.	40, 235
Ciaramella, A.	99
Conti, V.	67
Coppola, M.	165
Corazza, M.	214
D'Amato, V.	165
Di Lorenzo, E.	165
Facchinetti, G.	194
Fedrizzi, M.	185
Filippone, M.	118
Folgieri, R.	60
Frattale Mascioli, F.M.	12
Giacco, F.	245, 254
Giordano, F.	205
Giove, S.	185, 214
Gori, M.	127
Graudenzi, A.	109
Inuso, G.	50
Iorio, F.	223
La Foresta, F.	30, 40, 50
La Rocca, M.	205
Lipori, G.	148
Malchiodi, D.	76
Mammone, N.	30, 50
Marinaro, M.	v, 245
Masulli, F.	118
Militello, C.	67
Morabito, F.C.	30, 40, 50, 235
Napolitano, F.	223
Pacchiarotti, N.	194
Palm, G.	254
Palmieri, F.	154
Parisi, R.	89
Perna, C.	205
Petrosino, A.	3
Pugliese, L.	245
Raiconi, G.	223
Resta, M.	176
Rovetta, S.	118
Scarpetta, S.	245
Scarpiniti, M.	89
Schwenker, F.	254
Serra, R.	109
Sibillo, M.	165
Sorbello, F.	67
Staiano, A.	3
Tagliaferri, R.	223
Thiel, C.	245, 254
Uncini, A.	89
Valentini, G.	60
Valerio, L.	76
Versaci, M.	30, 40
Vigliano, D.	89
Villani, M.	109
Vitabile, S.	67
Voci, F.	12